Internet Theory, Technology and Applications

nova
science publishers
www.novapublishers.com

Internet Theory, Technology and Applications

The Robotic Platform Control with Atmega328 and NuttyFi Based on the Internet of Things
Anita Gehlot (Editor)
Rajesh Singh (Editor)
Gaurav Sethi (Editor)
Bhupendra Singh (Editor)
2020. ISBN: 978-1-53617-472-4 (Hardcover)
2020. ISBN: 978-1-53617-473-1 (eBook)

Big Data and Cloud: Trust, Security and Privacy
Abdulrahman Yarali, PhD (Editor)
Michael Lee Ramage, PhD (Editor)
2020. ISBN: 978-1-53616-287-5 (Hardcover)
2021. ISBN: 978-1-53616-288-2 (eBook)

Broadband: Deployment, Access and the Digital Divide
Orlando Harrison (Editor)
2019. ISBN: 978-1-53616-409-1 (Hardcover)
2019. ISBN: 978-1-53616-410-7 (eBook)

Big Data: An Exploration of Opportunities, Values, and Privacy Issues
Cody Agnellutti (Editor)
2014. ISBN: 978-1-63321-397-5 (Hardcover)
2014. ISBN: 978-1-63321-398-2 (eBook)

More information about this series can be found at
https://novapublishers.com/product-category/series/internet-theory-technology-and-applications/

Sandeep Gupta
and Tarun Varshney
Editors

The Future of IoT with Automation in Engineering and Modern Technology

nova
science publishers
www.novapublishers.com

DOI: https://doi.org/10.52305/KLWR1731

NOTICE TO THE READER

Library of Congress Cataloging-in-Publication Data

ISBN: 979-8-89113-655-7 (hardcover)
ISBN: 979-8-89113-704-2 (e-book)

Published by Nova Science Publishers, Inc. † New York

Dedicated to:

- My Grandmother.
- My parents.

Contents

Preface

The purpose of this book is to serve as a forum in which academics and researchers from all over the globe may come together to communicate, promote, and debate numerous new challenges and advancements in many fields related to engineering applications and the internet of things (IoT). One of the key benefits of automation offered by IoT is a large reduction in operational expenditures. It is one of the most significant advantages in terms of productivity and efficiency. Information is shared between different types of hardware in order to make it possible to automate processes and eliminate the need for human interaction. Industrial automation needs to be able to self-organize, self-configure, and expand to vast scales, all while consuming very little power, being inexpensive, and being based on a worldwide standard. This book presents the Internet of Things for fleet management, which helps in geolocation, performance analysis, telemetry control, fuel savings, pollution reduction, and vehicle driving. This book is a collection of ideas that looks at how things are connected to the Internet and how it might help people stay connected.

Chapter 1 - The Internet of Things (IoT) refers to a framework where physical objects are equipped with sensors, actuators, and microcontrollers to enable communication and accomplish specific purposes. This section aims to cultivate a user's understanding of the IoT system by exploring their beliefs and the key factors associated with it. Additionally, it categorizes IoT applications based on services across personal, business, and public domains, delving into the perception model of IoT within various sectors. The document also presents an overview of the scientific, societal, business, and human confrontations related to IoT and explores the issues in the IoT system. Furthermore, it briefly covers the fundamental operational principles of the IoT and its ecosystem.

Chapter 2 - This chapter examines the role of Artificial Intelligence (AI) in the context of the Internet of Things (IoT) and automation. It explores the intersection of AI and IoT, highlighting how AI enhances the capabilities of

IoT devices and presents real-world examples of AI-powered IoT applications. The chapter delves into various AI techniques, including machine learning algorithms, deep learning models, and natural language processing, and their specific applications in the realm of IoT and automation. Furthermore, the chapter explores the impact of AI-enabled automation in industrial IoT, discussing key areas such as robotics, predictive maintenance, quality control, and supply chain management. It also investigates the role of AI in smart cities, addressing infrastructure management, public services, and resource optimization. While discussing the advancements and benefits brought about by AI in IoT and automation, the chapter also addresses challenges and ethical considerations associated with this convergence. Topics such as data privacy, bias in AI algorithms, and transparency in decision-making processes are explored. Finally, the chapter presents future trends in the convergence of AI and IoT, highlighting the need for collaboration among stakeholders and the importance of implementing appropriate regulations to ensure responsible and ethical use of AI in IoT and automation. Overall, this chapter provides a comprehensive exploration of the role of AI in IoT and automation, examining its applications, challenges, and prospects.

Chapter 3 - The Internet of Things (IoT) and smart cities are topics covered in this chapter. In the first section, the idea of the Internet of Things (IoT) is introduced, along with how it has the potential to alter urban environments by supplying real-time data that can be utilized to enhance services and optimize resource utilization. The next section of the chapter explores the essential elements of a smart city, such as intelligent infrastructure, efficient transportation, and high-quality public services, as well as how IoT technology may be used in each of these areas. Additionally, the chapter discusses some of the difficulties that must be overcome when deploying IoT in smart cities, including data security and privacy, interoperability, and scalability. The authors go over some of the approaches that may be taken to deal with these issues and make sure that IoT technology is introduced in a secure and effective way. The chapter concludes by highlighting the potential advantages of utilizing IoT in smart cities, including enhanced quality of life, decreased resource use, and improved service efficiency. To guarantee that IoT is deployed in a way that benefits everyone, the authors stress the significance of cooperation amongst many stakeholders, including governments, enterprises, and individuals. The concept of smart cities has been transformed by the introduction of the Internet of Things (IoT), which has made it possible to integrate a variety of technologies and services to improve urban living. The goal of this analysis of the literature is to examine the wide spectrum of IoT applications in smart cities. It gives a summary of the main IoT technologies, talks about the advantages and difficulties of using IoT in smart cities, and emphasizes the substantial contributions of the existing research in this area.

Chapter 4 - This chapter focuses on the need, design trends, and future directions of IoT-based photovoltaic (PV) system monitoring. The output of PV systems varies with changes in environmental conditions. The main environmental parameters impacting PV module performance are atmospheric temperature, humidity, dust, and luminosity. Monitoring individual solar panels can help maximize energy production by reducing energy loss and identifying areas where the system is not operating efficiently. By monitoring the performance of the solar energy system over time, PV monitoring can help in the prediction of maintenance needs. IoT-based PV monitoring is a good option for real-time monitoring, reducing the need for manual data collection and saving time and resources. IoT monitoring can be used for monitoring the hazardous environmental conditions for PV and helping the user take appropriate actions before any failure occurs.

Chapter 5 - The Internet of Things (IoT), offering previously unimaginable potential for innovation and connectivity, has completely changed the way we interact with our environment. Given the explosive rise of IoT devices and applications, a detailed understanding of the technologies behind this revolutionary area is urgently required. The Internet of Things (IoT) and its significance for enabling seamless connectivity between devices, sensors, and the cloud are briefly described in this chapter. The various communication standards and protocols used to encourage data flow and interoperability are examined, including MQTT, CoAP, and Zigbee. The article also addresses the unique features, range limitations, and trade-offs of Wi-Fi, Bluetooth, and cellular networks. The chapter also looks at the vital role that sensor technologies play in data gathering and transmission, including sophisticated environmental and biometric sensors, as well as temperature and humidity sensors. It examines the rapidly increasing issue of edge computing, describing how edge devices enable real-time data analysis, reduce latency, and increase overall system performance. In addition, the chapter discusses newly discovered technologies that have the potential to totally disrupt the IoT landscape. This includes blockchain technology, which enables decentralized data management and increased trust, as well as artificial intelligence (AI) and machine learning (ML) techniques that enable predictive analytics and autonomous decision-making, and other related technologies. Throughout the chapter, real-world examples, case studies, and relevant considerations explain how these technologies may be applied in several IoT situations, including smart cities, industrial automation, healthcare, and agriculture. In a nutshell, this chapter gives a complete analysis of the technologies involved in IoT development, providing readers with the knowledge and expertise required to successfully navigate the ever-changing world of linked systems.

Chapter 6 - A health monitoring system is a type of technology designed to help individuals track and monitor their health in real-time. This system collects and analyses data on various health parameters, like body temperature and pulse rate. The data is then stored and processed using an IoT (Internet of Things) platform, i.e., Things Speak, which can be accessed by individuals or healthcare professionals. The key advantages of the health monitoring system include its convenience, accuracy, and reliability. It provides users with precise data on their health status, which can help them make informed decisions about their well-being. The monitoring and control of health may be revolutionized by the introduction of a system that monitors health and could play a crucial role in improving health outcomes for individuals around the world. In this work, a detailed system for tracking and monitoring real-time health based on the IoT is discussed. A detailed working design is presented and validated with the experimental prototype.

Chapter 7 - Sports is one of the important areas where the IoT supports plenty of solutions utilising technological advancements. Using IoT, we can train, evaluate player strength and efficiency, guarantee safety in the surroundings, improve fan engagement, and also organise various operational activities in sports activities. This chapter aims to debate sports coaching and performance monitoring utilising IoT. Specifically, in terms of wearable gadgets in performance checking and harm avoidance, tracking the physiological and biomechanical specifications of athletes in real time, smart equipment, sensor-planted clothing, connected stadium infrastructure, tracking and positioning methods by way of GPS, video analytics and sensors, environmental monitoring, real-time observation, data analytics and insight generation, broadcast enhancement, sports analytics, dream sports, etc., Wearable science is one of the trending and progressing sciences, namely helpful to the athlete and coaches in observing the various dossiers in coaching and performance tracking, including Spo2, heart rate tracking, etc., by selecting a specific sports mode particularly applicable within the wearable instruments. Wearable instruments can work more with machine learning, artificial intelligence, and other technologies so that injury avoidance can be further attained. Biomechanical analysis utilising IoT expanded in sports equipment or fabricated to combine athletes' physiques is used to capture dossiers. Sensors in tennis rackets and javelins can measure speed, angle, distance, and impacted forces, which provides insights to improve the players' performance by developing the perfect angle to attain speed, distance, and added forces and also prevents harm. GPS-empowered IoT devices help accompany sports coaching. The IoT-based devices play an outstanding role in gathering facts regarding environmental factors like climate, AQI (Air Quality Index), and weather prediction to optimise hydration and accommodate various climatic conditions. IoT tools also provide instant real-time feedback during instruction and coaching sessions and allow players to make necessary adaptations and improve their abilities. The data generated utilising IoT may be resolved using advanced machine learning algorithms to form conclusions based on the dossier. Through this interpretation, performance can be evaluated and patterns found. Monitoring individual physiological specifications and detecting early warning signs will help prevent injury and muscle fatigue. With this, coaches and medical crews can adjust loads and implement precautionary measures to reduce the risk of injury for athletes. These devices help identify more opportunities to execute future research in the sports industry along with IoT applications.

Chapter 8 - Investigating the use of IoT for smart waste management is a significant step towards building sustainable and efficient waste management systems. The Internet of Things (IoT) technology allows for the interconnectivity of various devices and sensors, enabling real-time data collection and analysis. When applied to waste management, IoT can revolutionize the way waste is handled, monitored, and optimized. By deploying IoT sensors in waste bins, containers, and recycling centers, it becomes possible to track the fill level, temperature, and even detect hazardous materials or leaks. This data can be transmitted to a centralized platform, providing waste management authorities with valuable insights to streamline collection routes, optimize resource allocation, and reduce environmental impact. The implications of this study could have the potential to create cleaner and healthier environments, reduce waste generation, and contribute to the overall sustainability goals of cities and communities.

Chapter 9 - Modern day living requires having access to energy. How well a country is doing has some correlation with energy availability. Therefore, using renewable energy is the only way to satisfy public demand. Solar energy is the most famous, sustainable, and environmentally friendly type of energy. It is readily gathered with the aid of solar photovoltaic (PV) panels. Most solar panels, however, are positioned at predetermined angles. The implementation of a solar tracking system using IoT can lead to several positive outcomes and results. Solar tracking systems optimize the alignment of solar panels with the sun's position, resulting in increased energy generation. By utilizing IOT technology, the solar tracking system can continuously monitor environmental conditions, such as sunlight intensity and cloud cover, and adjust the panels' orientation in real-time. This ensures that maximum solar energy is captured throughout the day, leading to higher energy production compared to fixed solar panels.

Chapter 10 - A three-tier home entrance security system using IoT, and image processing is presented in this chapter. In the authors' proposed system, the authors develop a method for face detection using the haar cascade frontal face feature detection and recognition using the KNN algorithm. The authors obtained some simulation results using PyCharm. In this research work, the authors can achieve Tier 1. To accomplish Tier 2, the authors also designed a remotely accessible door lock system using IoT, which can be controlled using the Blynk app, and a surveillance device using a PIR sensor for intruder detection, which is Tier 3 of this project. The authors' proposed system consists of a Raspberry Pi 4 B+, a Raspberry Pi camera, a node MCU, a solenoid lock, and a PIR sensor. The Node MCU is a microcontroller used to control the relay remotely, the relay switches for the solenoid lock, and the PIR sensor. The PIR senses any human activity that occurs inside the house. In cases of connectivity issues, a tactile switch is also used inside the house to open the door lock manually. If the person wants to exit the house, they can press the switch to unlock the door. The Node MCU is also connected to the Blynk cloud platform to control the door lock and PIR sensor remotely.

Chapter 11 - The exponential progress of the Internet of Things (IoT) has presented novel opportunities for transforming electricity distribution systems. Smart grids have become a crucial solution due to the rising integration of renewable energy sources, the increasing demand for electric vehicles, and the necessity for effective energy management. Nevertheless, the traditional centralized structure of smart grids encounters certain obstacles in relation to scalability, latency, and privacy. This study investigates the potential of edge and fog computing based on the Internet of Things (IoT) in revolutionizing smart grids by effectively tackling the aforementioned difficulties. Edge computing involves localization of computational capabilities close to edge devices, but fog computing expands upon this concept by extending the computational capabilities to intermediate fog nodes. The integration of edge and fog computing facilitates decentralized processing, instantaneous data analysis, and localized decision-making within the framework of intelligent power grids. The work provides a comprehensive overview of smart grids and their key components, highlighting the limitations of the centralized architecture. It then delves into the fundamentals of IoT, edge computing, and fog computing, emphasizing their relevance and benefits in the context of smart grids. The work is also given state-of-the-art in the case of IoT based edge and fog computing by identifying gaps and research opportunities. The proposed methodology involves developing a conceptual framework for integrating IoT, edge computing, and fog computing into smart grids. Machine learning and data analytics techniques will be employed to enable real-time monitoring, predictive maintenance, load balancing, and demand response in the smart grid system. Performance metrics such as latency, scalability, energy efficiency, and privacy will be assessed to quantify the benefits of the proposed IoT-based edge and fog computing approach. Comparative analysis will be conducted against traditional centralized smart grid architectures to highlight the advantages and improvements achieved.

Chapter 12 - The generation, transmission, and consumption of electricity have been completely transformed by the incorporation of Internet of Things (IoT) technologies into smart grids. An overview of the main components of performance improvement made possible by IoT implementation in smart grid systems is given in this chapter. This starts by outlining the difficulties that traditional power networks encounter, including poor visibility, ineffective load balancing, and susceptibility to failure. The idea of IoT-enabled smart grids is then introduced. These grids use real-time data collection, sophisticated analytics, and intelligent decision-making algorithms to enhance the performance and dependability of the grid. This research work lists five crucial areas where IoT improves the efficiency of the smart grid. The first topic covered is better monitoring and control capabilities made possible by IoT devices. These capabilities allow for precise assessment of energy production, consumption, and distribution. Utilities can see inefficiencies, find errors, and optimize resource allocation in real-time because of this improved visibility. Secondly, the abstract highlights how IoT helps smart grids implement demand response and load management. To actively control energy demand during peak hours and lessen the load on the grid and the need for expensive infrastructure upgrades, utilities can communicate and work with consumers by exploiting IoT devices installed in homes, companies, and industrial sites. In addition, the chapter illustrates how IoT might improve grid resilience and fault management. IoT-enabled sensors and monitoring tools can locate faults quickly and perform preventative maintenance by detecting and communicating interruptions. This feature decreases downtime, accelerates the time it takes to fix faults, and increases grid reliability overall. This chapter also discusses the advantages of data-driven analytics for enhancing smart grid performance. Numerous data points are produced by IoT devices, which can be analyzed to learn more about patterns in energy usage, anticipate changes in demand, and improve energy production and distribution methods. Utility companies can make wise decisions, increase grid efficiency, and save operating costs thanks to these data-driven insights. Finally, this chapter highlights the importance of IoT-enabled smart grids in addressing the changing energy requirements of the future while encouraging sustainability and dependability.

Chapter 1

Internet of Things Perception and Basic Workings

Rajiv Dey[1,*], PhD
Anand Bhalla[2], MTech
and Dheeraj Nagar[2], MTech
[1]Department of Electronics and Computer Engineering,
BML Munjal University School of Engineering and Technology,
Gurugram, Haryana, India
[2]Department of Electronics and Communication, Eklavya University, Damoh,
Madhya Pradesh, India

Abstract

The Internet of Things (IoT) refers to a framework where physical objects are equipped with sensors, actuators, and microcontrollers to enable communication and accomplish specific purposes. This section aims to cultivate a user's understanding of the IoT system by exploring their beliefs and the key factors associated with it. Additionally, it categorizes IoT applications based on services across personal, business, and public domains, delving into the perception model of IoT within various sectors. The document also presents an overview of the scientific, societal, business, and human confrontations related to IoT and explores the issues in the IoT system. Furthermore, it briefly covers the fundamental operational principles of the IoT and its ecosystem.

Keywords: five-layer model, internet of things, interoperability, scaling, user perceptions

---

* Corresponding Author's Email: rajiv.dey@bmu.edu.in.

In: The Future of IoT with Automation in Engineering and Modern Technology
Editors: Sandeep Gupta and Tarun Varshney
ISBN: 979-8-89113-655-7

Introduction

The Internet has infused virtually every corner of the world today, exerting an immeasurable influence on people's lives. However, this journey is far from complete. As we transition into an era of increasingly pervasive connectivity, a vast array of appliances is poised to join the online realm. This emerging technological era, known as the Internet of Things (IoT), represents the intersection between the physical and digital worlds (Friess et al., 2009). According to Friess et al. (2009), IoT can be obviously defined as the interaction between the physical and digital realms. It involves the utilization of various sensors and actuators to facilitate communication between these two worlds. Another description in Pena (2005) characterizes IoT as a hypothesis in which computation and networking abilities are integrated into virtually any imaginable device. These embedded abilities allow for monitoring and, when feasible, altering the state of objects. In essence, the term Internet of Things refers to an environment in which nearly all the appliances and objects we utilize are interconnected, enabling them to collaboratively tackle complex tasks requiring high intelligence. IoT devices are characterized by their intelligence and connectivity, incorporating embedded CPUs.

It is important to note that IoT is not a singular technology but rather a collection of interconnected technologies that work in tandem. Sensors and actuators are instrumental in facilitating interaction with the physical world. To derive relevant insights, the sensor data must be intelligently stored and analyzed. It is worth mentioning that the term sensor is broadly defined, encompassing devices such as cell phones or microwaves that transmit information about their internal state and the environment. Actuators, on the other hand, are devices that modify the environment, such as temperature controllers in air conditioners. Data processing and storage can occur either at the edge of the network or on remote servers. Moreover, data pre-processing is often done at the sensor endpoint or another neighboring device before transmitting the processed data to a distant server. The resources available for IoT devices, including size, energy, power, and computational capability, are often constrained, thereby limiting their storage and processing capacities. Consequently, a key challenge in research in the domain of IoT is ensuring the acquisition of appropriate data at an acceptable level of precision. In addition to data collection and handling challenges, communication poses significant obstacles. Due to the geographical dispersion of IoT devices, wireless communication serves as the primary mode of interaction between them.

However, wireless channels are prone to instability and high distortion rates, necessitating reliable data transmission with minimal retransmissions. Communication technologies play a crucial role in addressing this issue in IoT research.

Once data has been processed, appropriate actions need to be taken based on the derived conclusions. These actions can manifest in various forms, including direct alterations of the physical world through actuators or virtual interactions with other sensible devices. The procedure of prompting change in the physical world often relies on contextual awareness, which considers the current state of the environment. For instance, an application may react differently in different contexts, such as a person not wanting to receive office communications while on vacation. The essential foundation of an IoT construction comprises sensors, actuators, computation servers, and communication networks. However, there are several software-related issues to consider as well. Middleware is necessary to connect and manage the diverse components within the IoT ecosystem, and standardization efforts are required to establish interoperability across a wide range of devices.

In summary, the Internet of Things (IoT) has emerged as a transformative technology that has revolutionized how we interact with our surroundings. By connecting everyday objects and devices to the internet, IoT enables communication and data collection, with the capability to impact not only business but also society and daily life (Sethi et al., 2017).

IoT Architecture

The internet of things (IoT), data science, analytics, and artificial intelligence are just a handful of the new concepts that have already taken over the IT industry. What do these terms signify, though, in reality? The term IoT refers to the prevalent connectivity between people and several gadgets, which includes wearables, health monitoring device, home automation, watches, tablets, cell phones, connected vehicles, remote controls, sensors, household equipment's, etc. The system uses a variety of specialized sensors to gather data, which is transferred to the remote servers and information centers for additional analysis, steering mechanization, and actions. However, there is still a sizable and typically invisible architectural structure that is dependent on several constituent parts and interconnections for your command and the efficient performance of your activities.

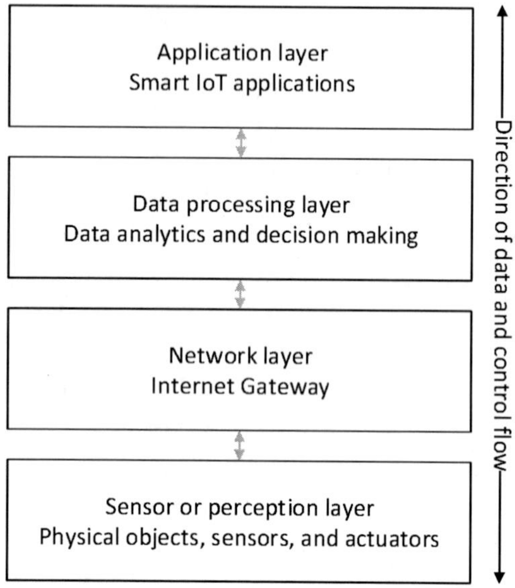

Figure 1. Representation of the layer of IoT.

The architecture of the Internet of Things as shown in Figure 1 describes the precise configuration of the IoT protocols, layers, cloud services, sensors, and actuators that make up the entire IoT architecture. Connected network infrastructures (Leonardo et al., 2023). It usually breaks down into layers to enable administrators to assess, keep an eye on, and maintain the integrity of the system. Data is transmitted from connected devices to sensors, then across a network, and finally to the cloud for analysis, processing, and archiving using the Internet of Things (IoT) framework. The Internet of Things is anticipated to expand dramatically over time, offering customers new and improved experiences.

It is crucial that you understand the meanings of many terminologies used in the IT sector nowadays, for instance, data science and data analytics, artificial intelligence, and the IoT. The Internet of Things can be considered the broad network of connections that exists between consumers and various gadgets, for example, wearables, audio devices like Google Home, Alexa, smart watches, tablets, remote controls, sensors, household equipment, and more. This system gathers data from various devices and sends it to servers and data centers for further analysis, promoting automation and action. However, a sizeable and frequently invisible architectural framework exists that depends on several elements, linkages across orders, and the completion of tasks. IoT architecture refers to the complicated arrangement of components found in IoT networking systems, such as sensors, actuators, cloud services, protocols, and layers. Typically, it is separated into layers so that administrators can evaluate, keep an eye on, and preserve the veracity of the system. The IoT design entails a four-step procedure for information movements, with sensors, linked devices, a network of devices, and lastly, the cloud enabling analysis, processing, and storage. The Internet of Things is anticipated to expand over time, offering users innovative and developed experiences.

Layers of IoT

IoT technology has acquired a reputation recently and has an extensive range of applications. Based on how IoT applications work and the range of their domains, there isn't a global standard architecture that is strictly followed. In accordance with company demands, multiple architecture layers and levels of complexity are used (e.g., three and five layers). The most common and standard architecture has three layers, with the first layer being further divided into two layers, such as the perception layer and the network layer. Figure 1 shows a generalized four-layer architecture, which is made up of the perception layer, the network layer, the processing layer, and the application layer (Said et al., 2013).

Perception or Sensing Layer

The things/physical devices, or end nodes, serve as a connection linking the physical and virtual worlds together, making up the initial level in an IoT system. The devices directly integrated into the actuators and sensors in this layer, often referred to as the perception layer, serve to collect, accept, and process information through a network. The connectivity can be wireless or wired and is used to connect actuators and sensors. The location or accessibility of the components does not impose restrictions on the architecture.

Network Layer

The network layer provides a broad in scope picture of data flow. Internet/Network Gateways and Information Acquiring Systems (GIAS) are included. GIAS carries out activities, including gathering and aggregating sensor data. Between devices, servers, smart devices, and network components, interactions and connections are made possible by this layer. It controls how each device's information is transmitted.

Processing Layer

The ecosystem's main brain comprises the processing layer. Before being sent to the data center, information is often analyzed, processed, and stored in this layer. Software programmes ingest data from this layer, process it, and set up further operations. This layer includes edge IT and edge analytics.

Application Layer

User interaction and application-specific services are offered at the application layer. Examples include a dashboard that shows system device health or an intelligent home app that allows users to manage equipment remotely. Numerous industrial applications, such as intelligent/smart homes, intelligent/smart cities, and intelligent/smart health, use the Internet of Things. The three-layer layout captures the core notion of the Internet of Things. However, studies on IoT frequently concentrate on its more complicated components; therefore, they are inadequate. Because of this, research has suggested a lot more layered structures. One is the five-layer architecture, which consists of the business and processing levels as shown in Figure 2.

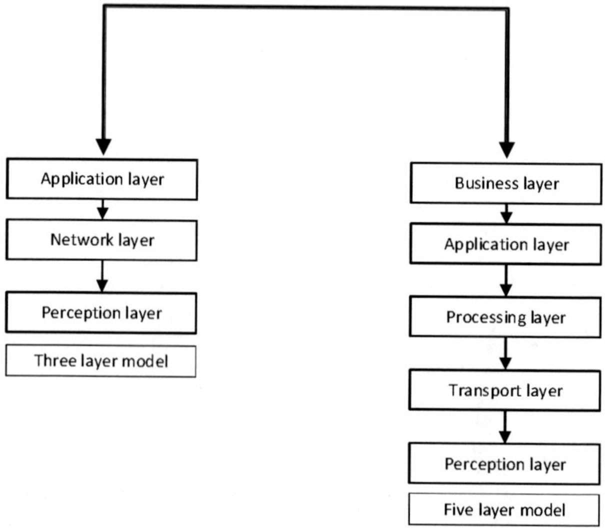

Figure 2. Three and five-layer model of IoT.

Business Layer

The business layer controls the entire Internet of Things (IoT) system, which includes all applications, sources of income, and user privacy. The business layer isn't addressed in this essay.

Working Principle of Internet of Things (IoT)

IoT is a vast network of interconnected devices, as shown in Figure 3, many of which are equipped with sensors. The devices can gather information about their surroundings thanks to these sensors. The collected data is stored in various types of storage systems. Mobile phones, coffee machines, microwaves, geysers, fire alarms, air conditioners, cars, and other appliances are examples of these gadgets. These gadgets' sensors send information about their functioning and surroundings in real-time. IoT serves as a platform for collecting and managing the data generated by these devices. The platform utilizes large databases and cloud servers to store and process the data. It analyzes and integrates the collected data to derive relevant information. Based on this information, the platform provides instructions for future actions, aiming to improve performance. The aggregated data is also shared with other devices to enhance their functionality and user experience. The future of the IoT appears promising. According to a Business Insider article, it was estimated that by 2020, around 24 billion IoT devices would be deployed. Additionally, the International Trade Commission (ITC) projects that IoT sales will surpass $300 billion in the coming years. This growth in the IoT industry creates numerous job opportunities in the technology sector and various other industries.

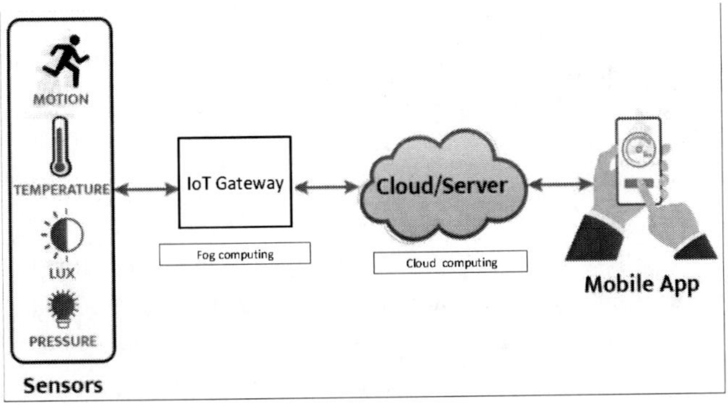

Figure 3. Working principle of IoT.

IoT Solution Architecture Phases

Organizations can leverage the various layers of IoT to increase its value and maximize its benefits. While devices and protocols are part of the IoT ecosystem, the data generated by these devices is often fragmented and isolated, residing in silos. To develop a comprehensive IoT strategy that justifies the investment, enterprises need to enable devices and systems to interact freely and maximize synergies. To ensure compatibility with the IoT architecture, organizations should follow the implementation phases outlined in Figure 4.

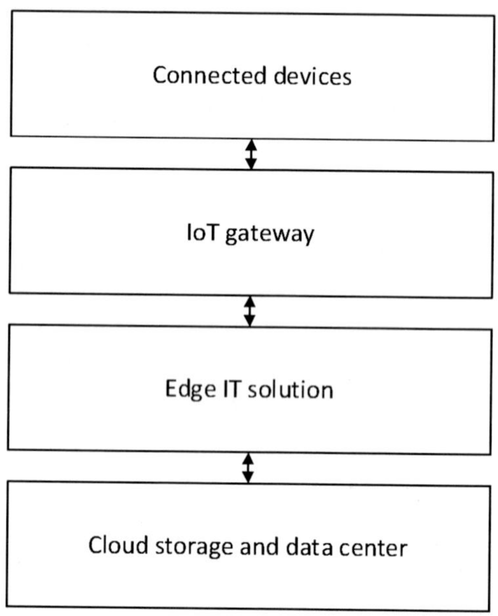

Figure 4. Phases of IoT solution architecture.

Connected Devices

The initial step in IoT architecture implementation is to establish the physical layer by incorporating smart and connected objects. These objects typically include wireless sensors or actuators deployed in the perception layer. Sensors gather environmental data, and actuators measure and respond to changes. Wired or wireless connections, such as personal area networks (PANs) and local area networks (LANs), are used to facilitate sensing and actuation.

IoT Gateway

Once the first step is completed, the next phase involves setting up an internet gateway. The gateway converts the analogue data collected by sensors and actuators into digital data for processing. At this point, the cloud receives unprocessed raw data via devices that have been pre-processed. The analogue information is transformed into digital representation using data capture systems. The gateway sets up connections with sensors and actuators, aggregates the data, and facilitates its transmission across the network. Additional features, like analytics and security, can be incorporated to enhance performance and effectiveness.

Edge IT Solutions

The 3rd level of IoT architecture comprises advanced data analytics and pre-processing at the edge. Edge IT infrastructures are vital for offloading the primary network infrastructure because of the enormous quantity of data that Internet of Things (IoT) devices collect and the corresponding bandwidth needs. These systems use machine learning and visualization strategies to extract insightful information from the gathered data. The speed and network bandwidth of the system might be enhanced by processing and analyzing information at the edge. To reduce storage needs and handle only vital information important to the organization, it is advised to convert data from analogue to digital format.

Cloud Storage and Data Centers

The information is delivered to information/data centers and cloud servers. Analytics, device management, and security controls are used to handle the data in data centers and cloud services. Data transfer to end-user applications is made easier by cloud platforms across a variety of industries, including healthcare, retail, environment, emergency services, energy, and others. While the cloud platform can help reduce hardware expenses, data security remains a concern. Physical servers and data centers offer enhanced security but come at a higher cost.

Applications of IoT

The Internet of Things (IoT) has a wide variety of applications across different sectors which include personal, business, and public domains shown in Figure

5. These examples are discussed in detail in (Sousa et al., 2015; Lee et al., 2015).

Personal applications

In this domain, we consider IoT application areas that could enhance personal life quality. The subsequent sectors are part of the Private domain: Smart Home, Intelligent Education, and Intelligent Healthcare and Wellness.

Intelligent Healthcare

IoT systems can monitor individuals' health using wearable devices and provide real-time insights. They can aid in diagnostics, notify appropriate agencies in case of emergencies, and make recommendations for personalized care. IoT is also useful in hospital settings to monitor medical equipment's, tools, and pharmaceuticals (Domingo, 2012; Mandler et al., 2016).

Intelligent Education

Wearable devices and IoT systems can monitor the physical and mental well-being of students and notify relevant authorities in case of emergencies. These systems can assist in improving learning outcomes and providing personalized educational experiences.

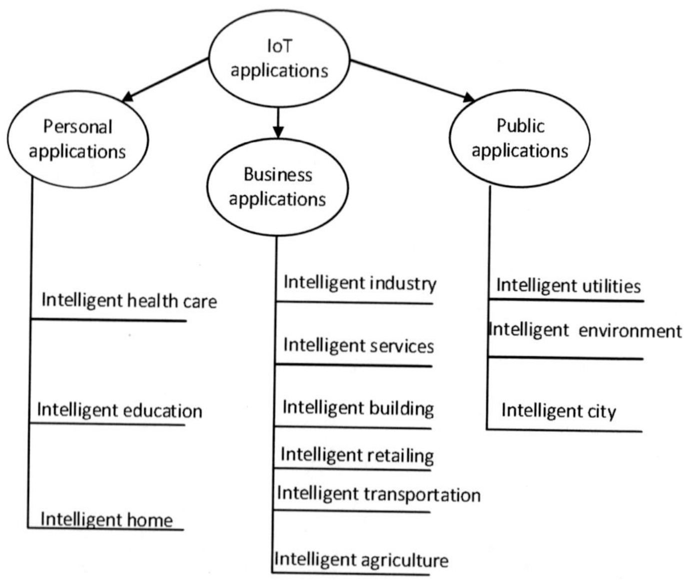

Figure 5. Sagrregation of IoT applications.

Intelligent Home

IoT systems can monitor and manage various aspects of a home, including security, environment, appliances, energy consumption, and safety. Users can control and manage household equipment and systems remotely, enhancing convenience and efficiency (Economides, 2009a; 2009c).

Business Applications

IoT offers numerous applications to businesses across different sectors. These include smart buildings, smart factories, smart services, smart retailing, and smart transportation. IoT can optimize processes, improve productivity, enhance customer experiences, and enable data-driven decision-making.

Intelligent Industry

Intelligent industries can be defined as the industries that utilizes the latest emerging technologies and database to take smart decisions for example industries like manufacturing, mining, and construction would use connected machinery and robots to improve their output (e.g., customized, real time, and on-request production) (Jeschke et al., 2017).

Intelligent Services

The service sectors such as financial, banking, and healthcare e.g., healthcare, house, car, etc. utilize IoT systems to track people, information, and assets to improve the services they provide (Gil et al., 2016). For instance, IoT devices might track travelers and suggest vacation spots, activities, tours, lodging, driving routes, and hiking trails based on their interests.

Intelligent Buildings

The building's entrance, lighting, heating/cooling, equipment, and resource use, among other things, would be monitored and managed by IoT systems (Pan. et al., 2015). This might employ Internet of Things (IoT) technology for smart/intelligent metering to manage power consumption to lower costs. Additionally, IoT systems applications can be seen in the field of security and monitoring, alarms in the event of emergencies (like fire or intruders), or initiating necessary steps (e.g., enhancing air quality or shutting off lights for the case if no one is present).

Intelligent Retailing

IoT devices will be used to track products, monitor commodities, and keep an eye on facilities to optimize supply and reserve stages, prevent theft, and safeguard the quality of products. When goods are not maintained in accordance with regulations, when the item's expiration date is approaching, or when unauthorized penetration occurs, an Internet of Things (IoT) system will screen the state of the goods during storage and throughout transportation, offer recommendations, and issue notifications (Balaji and Roy, 2017).

Intelligent Transportation

IoT systems will be used to track passenger data (such as mobile device tickets), luggage, vehicle data (such as cars, buses, planes, ships), container data, and facility data like roads, airports, railways, harbors, bridges, tunnels, and tolls to optimize conveyance by terrestrial, air, or water as well as to plan preventive repairs. As a case study, sensors might control tunnel lighting and monitor traffic (Protogeros et al., 2007).

Smart cars and connected automobiles would work together to reduce traffic jams, power consumption, pollution, and wasted time while preventing accidents, improving infotainment, and all the above. Smart fleet management would cut back on costs, delivery times, unused track space, etc. (Protogeros et al., 2007). The transportation of dangerous goods like corrosives, flammables, toxic matters, and explosives would also get better.

Intelligent Agriculture

IoT devices would monitor a farmhouse, harvest, vineyard, greenhouse, cattle, animals, agricultural equipment's, and infrastructure, such as agricultural machinery, fertilizer delivery, and they could offer advice or carry out necessary tasks, such as irrigation and feeding, to increase both the quantity and quality of produce (Karapistoli et al., 2014).

Public applications

These are the IoT application areas that assist the major community sector in using IoT to deliver superior services to citizens. The following industries are part of the public domain, for example intelligent communities and cities, smart utilities, and smart environmental practices.

Intelligent/Smart Cities

IoT equipment can enhance safety by monitoring the streets and alerting authorities in case of crimes or violent acts. It can also observe the town's environment and notify residents and responsible authorities in the event of emergencies such as fires, chemical leaks, air pollution, accidents, protests, or overcrowding. IoT systems are responsible for managing traffic signals, parking spots, public transit (including autos, buses, and metro), smart ticketing, and bike sharing. Additionally, IoT systems can control waste removal, recycling, park irrigation for water conservation, streetlights for energy savings, and provide information about nearby activities like concerts, celebrations, festivals, creative happenings, and open education lectures (Chourabi et al., 2012).

Intelligent Utilities

IoT systems play a significant role in Intelligent utilities by handling tasks such as smart metering, maintenance (e.g., leak monitoring), and utility billing for electricity, water, and gas. The smart grid makes it possible to improve the production, delivery, storage, exchange, and pricing of electricity.

Intelligent Environment

IoT devices are used to track environmental conditions and alert citizens about pollution, radiation, bad weather, natural disasters, forest fires, tsunamis, volcano outbursts, earthquakes, and avalanches. These technologies also assist rescuers in saving individuals in danger. Furthermore, IoT technologies are employed for border surveillance, territorial monitoring, and dropping sensors from aircraft or helicopters to detect marine oil slicks, forest fires, and snow avalanches (Laplante, 2016).

Model of IoT User Perceptions

Users' acceptance of intent to use, and actual use of an IoT system depend on a number of variables. These factors can be divided into those that concern the consumer, the IoT system itself, the manufacturer of the Internet of Things (IoT) system, and the setting in which stakeholders work shown in Figure 6. Age, gender, education level, familiarity with technology (including cellphones and computers), personality, emotions, preferences, interests, skills, and competences are all examples of user qualities. Usability, functionality, performance, dependability, security, and interoperability are all properties of IoT systems. The IoT system's producer-related characteristics also have an impact. Further, users of IoT systems, manufacturers, sociological and economic situations, market dynamics, competitiveness, governmental regulations, and ethics are all components of the environment (Economides, 2009b).

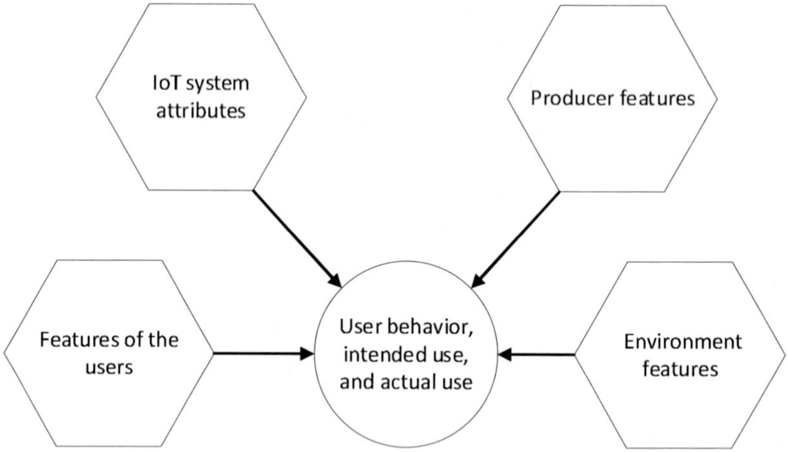

Figure 6. Factors affecting a user's outlook about using the IoT system.

Users' characteristics interact with those of the Internet of Things system, the company that made it, and the surroundings. The Internet of Things (IoT) system's features act together with each other analogous to how the user, IoT system, as environmental features connect with one another and with the features of the IoT system manufacturer. Although it might be desirable, it is not always straightforward or practical to quantify and precisely analyze these features. Thoughts regarding the customer, the IoT system, its manufacturer, and the surroundings must be considered. Consequently, Real Context and Perceived Context are separate ideas.

IoT from the Perspective of India

India's government places a high priority on fostering a welcoming environment, raising living conditions, and encouraging the adoption of smart gadgets to broaden the market. According to a 2015 COMSNETS report, the government is thinking about spending $7,060 million to build 100 smart cities using the Internet of Things (IoT). Due to the unique needs of Indians, IoT-based smart gadgets are essential into many industries. Therefore, numerous companies are investing in fields including smart supply chains, smart farming, smart disposal of waste, smart water management, and smart environment. However, it is said that it's difficult to find competent individuals in this occupation in India. The country faces ecological and infrastructure challenges such as the electrical grid, severe air pollution, high temperatures, and dust.

The Digital India Programme is a government initiative aimed at strengthening digital integration and making India a digitally advanced nation. It is expected that the knowledge economy will drive the extension of IoT manufacture in the country. While the IoT has gained significance, the sheer volume of information makes gathering, communicating, controlling, and raising awareness more challenging. However, the growth of IoT will continue to accelerate. As the Internet of Things becomes integrated, inclusive, and omnipresent in the future, the establishment of standards becomes crucial. To ensure the continuity of IoT as a strategic approach, collaboration, awareness, competence, resilience, privacy, trust, confidentiality, and security are crucial. The Internet of Things (IoT) is now a commonly anticipated information development that will improve people's quality of lives.

This chapter examines some of the major problems and difficulties relating to the Internet of Things from an Indian viewpoint, including active initiatives and areas that need more focus. Potential enhancements include the deployment of integrated, effortless, and globally internet access management, optimization, and cooperation. In IoT studies, security, confidentiality, and security are also crucial variables to consider. The prospects for engagement with business, industry, and education will be made easier by addressing these difficulties.

Operation of an IoT System

1. Perceived efficiency: Users' perception of their ability to attain a particular degree of performance and results using an IoT system whilst reducing resources such as energy, time, effort, cost, storage, processing, and bandwidth
2. Perceived functionality: Users' belief in an IoT system's ability to provide the necessary capabilities to achieve their goals.

3. Performance: Users' perception of an IoT system's pace, reaction times, job completion times, and throughput rates meeting their expectations.
4. Availability: Users' belief in the uninterrupted use of an IoT system, both during internal and external failures or disruptions.
5. Perceived energy efficiency: Users' perception of an IoT system's ability to operate efficiently for the specified amount of time while implementing energy-saving techniques
6. Perceived security: Users' sense of security against unauthorized system resources or private information use, availability, modification, devastation, or disclosure throughout data processing, storage, and transmission.
7. Perceived safety: Users' perception of being shielded from potential dangers, risks, losses, and undesirable outcomes associated with the use of an IoT system.
8. Perceived endurance: Users' belief that an IoT system will be usable for a long time without becoming obsolete.
9. Perceived flexibility: Users' perception of an IoT system's ability to be used effectively in different environments, modified easily, or repurposed for various goals beyond the initial requirements.

Issues in IoT

Nothing big comes without difficulties, similarly IoT opportunities are not without their share of difficulties. Technological, societal, business, and human difficulties are the four categories we use to categorize these issues (Mashal et al., 2015) and are discussed below.

Technical Issues

Even though a lot of work has been put into developing technology, it is never enough to support consumers and applications that are demanding. There is an everlasting need to develop advanced technologies on the following areas: Platforms, Data Management and Analytics, Decision Making Systems, Applications and Services, Devices (Sensors, Actuators, etc.), Networking and Communications, Computing and Storage, Platforms, etc. The following are additional multidisciplinary issues: Security and Privacy, Interoperability and Standards, Seamless Integration, Scalability, Energy efficiency, among other (Anastasios et al., 2017; Daniele et al., 2012).

Societal Issues

Technology advancement raises several questions that society must address. We categorize social issues according to the following categories:

1. How can experts and the public be educated on IoT?
2. How may IoT be used to improve education?
3. Democratization and involvement: how democratization and public involvement will be affected by IoT?
4. How can the Internet of Things (IoT) improve civic engagement and democracy?
5. What kind of laws are required for the Internet of Things era? How may IoT be used to improve rules and regulations?
6. Economics: How will the state of the world economy impact IoT?
7. How to use IoT to enhance the economy?

Safety and confidentiality

1. How will IoT influence security and privacy? How can IoT be used to improve security and privacy?
2. How will the Internet of Things (IoT) affect things like free access, inclusion, and non-discrimination, etc.?
3. How might IoT be used to improve non-discrimination, inclusion, and universal access?

Economy

1. How will the current state of the world economy impact IoT?
2. How can IoT be used to grow the economy?

Business Issues

Businesses should adapt to these new developments and changes, whether they are businesses that develop and market IoT systems or enterprises that purchase and use IoT systems. They should alter not only their working methods but also their perspectives and boundaries. For instance, businesses should cooperate and work together with other private as well as public organizations, even with rival businesses, to adapt to these extreme and quick changes. They should modify their approaches, alliances, partnerships, business models, marketing campaigns, products, and services considering changing technology as well as other factors including the global economy, competition, laws, and regulations.

Human Issues

The acceptance of the proposed IoT systems by users is necessary for this new revolution to take place. So, it is essential to comprehend what consumers require, desire, and anticipate? Why do they choose to purchase and use the available IoT systems? What keeps them from utilizing the IoT systems that are available? How much money are they ready to spend? etc.

Conclusion

This chapter tried to explain the basic concepts of IoT perception from the human point of view. It also explored the three- and five-layer design model of IoT and highlighted its characteristics, possibilities, and potential. Additionally, the impact of IoT on India, noting the discovery of various industrial and residential applications, is discussed. The chapter discussed in detail the applications of IoT in the basics of three categories: personal, business, and public. The chapter also acknowledged the importance of IoT applications for solving a variety of human-centric problems. Finally, the chapter acknowledged the significant issues of IoT that still need to be addressed.

References

Anastasios A. Economides, *User perception of internet of things*. Springer international publishing (2017).

Balaji, MS, Roy SK. Value co-creation with Internet of things technology in the retail industry. *Journal of Marketing Management* (2017) 33: 7–31.

Chourabi H, Nam T, Walker S, Gil Garcia JR, Mellouli S, Nahon K., Pardo TA, Scholl HJ. Understanding smart cities: An integrative framework. *Proceedings of the Annual Hawaii International Conference on System Sciences* (2012): 289–2297.

Daniele M, Sabrina S, Franscesco DP, Imrich C. Internet of things: Vision, applications and research challenges, *Elsevier Ad Hoc Networks* (2012) 10(7): 1497-1516.

Domingo MC. An overview of the Internet of Things for people with disabilities. *In Journal of Network and Computer Applications* (2012) 35(2): 584–596.

Economides AA. Adaptive context-aware pervasive and ubiquitous learning. *International Journal of Technology Enhanced Learning* (2009a) 1(3): 169–192.

Economides AA. Conative feedback in computer-based assessment. *Computers in the Schools* (2009c) 26(3): 207–223.

Friess P, Guillemin P, Gusmeroli S, Di Milano P, Sundmaeker H. Internet of Things Strategic Research Roadmap, *IMPReSS-Intelligent System Development Platform for Intelligent and Sustainable Society* (2009).

Gil D, Ferrández A, Mora Mora H, Peral J. Internet of things: A review of surveys based on context aware intelligent services. *Sensors* (2016) 16(7): 1069.

Jeschke S, Brecher C, Meisen T, Özdemir D, Eschert T. *Industrial Internet of Things and Cyber Manufacturing Systems.* Springer International Publishing (2017): 3–19.

Karapistoli E, Mampentzidou I, Economides A A. Environmental monitoring based on wireless sensor networking technology: A survey of real-world applications. International *Journal of Agricultural and Environmental Information Systems* (2014) 5(4): 1–39.

Laplante PA, Standards for the Internet of Things: A Case Study in Disaster Response, *IEEE computer society* (2016) 49(5): 87-90.

Lee In and Kyoochun L. The Internet of Things (IoT): Applications, investments, and challenges for enterprises. *Elsevier Business Horizons* (2015) 58(4).

Leonardo B Furstenau, Yan PRR, Michele KS, Michael SD, José R R, Manuel JC, Nicola LB. Internet of things: Conceptual network structure, main challenges and future directions, *Digital Communications and Networks* (2023) 9(3): 667-687.

Mandler B, Marquez Barja J, Mitre Campista ME, Cagáňová D, Chaouchi H, Zeadally S, Badra M, Giordano S, Fazio M, Somov A, Vieriu R L. *Internet of Things IoT Infrastructures*. Springer International Publishing (2016).

Mashal I, Alsaryrah O, Chung TY, Yang CZ, Kuo WH, Agrawal DP. Choices for interaction with things on Internet and underlying issues. *Elsevier Ad Hoc Networks* (2015) 28: 68–90.

Pan J, Jain R, Paul S, Vu T, Saifullah A, Sha M. An Internet of Things Framework for Smart Energy in Buildings: Designs, Prototype, and Experiments. *IEEE Internet of Things Journal* (2015) 2(6): 527–537.

Pena Lopez I. *Itu Internet Report 2005: The Internet of Things*. (2005).

Protogeros N, Economides AA, Papagiannis GK, Syleos C. Developing a Near-optimal Lowest-consumption Tunnel Lighting System Using Software Agents through Power Line Communications. *Journal of Computing and Information Technology-CIT* (2007) 15: 1–8.

Sethi P, Sarangi SR. Internet of Things: Architectures, Protocols, and Applications. *Journal of Electrical and Computer Engineering* (2017).

Said O, Masud M. Towards Internet of Things: Survey and Future Vision, *International Journal of Computer Networks (IJCN)* (2013) 5(1): 1-17.

Sousa Nunes DS, Zhang P, Sa Silva J. A Survey on human-in-The-loop applications towards an internet of all. *IEEE Communications Surveys and Tutorials* (2015) 17(2): 944-965.

Chapter 2

The Role of AI in IoT with Automation

Ramsagar Yadav[1,*], MSc
Seema Ukidve[1], PhD
Jasleen Randhawa[2], Med
and Doopinder Kaur[3], MA
[1]Department of Mathematics and Computing, L. S. Raheja College, University of Mumbai, Maharashtra, India
[2]Department of Education, Panjab University, Chandigarh, India
[3]Department of English, Government Mohindra College Patiala, India

Abstract

This chapter examines the role of Artificial Intelligence (AI) in the context of the Internet of Things (IoT) and automation. It explores the intersection of AI and IoT, highlighting how AI enhances the capabilities of IoT devices and presents real-world examples of AI-powered IoT applications. The chapter delves into various AI techniques, including machine learning algorithms, deep learning models, and natural language processing, and their specific applications in the realm of IoT and automation. Furthermore, the chapter explores the impact of AI-enabled automation in industrial IoT, discussing key areas such as robotics, predictive maintenance, quality control, and supply chain management. It also investigates the role of AI in smart cities, addressing infrastructure management, public services, and resource optimization. While discussing the advancements and benefits brought about by AI in IoT and automation, the chapter also addresses challenges and ethical considerations associated with this convergence. Topics such as data

* Corresponding Author's Email: ramsagar.yadav@lsraheja.org.

In: The Future of IoT with Automation in Engineering and Modern Technology
Editors: Sandeep Gupta and Tarun Varshney
ISBN: 979-8-89113-655-7

privacy, bias in AI algorithms, and transparency in decision-making processes are explored. Finally, the chapter presents future trends in the convergence of AI and IoT, highlighting the need for collaboration among stakeholders and the importance of implementing appropriate regulations to ensure responsible and ethical use of AI in IoT and automation. Overall, this chapter provides a comprehensive exploration of the role of AI in IoT and automation, examining its applications, challenges, and prospects.

Keywords: Artificial Intelligence, Internet of Things, automation, machine learning, deep learning, natural language processing, AI techniques, industrial IoT, smart cities

Introduction

The concept of the Internet of Things (IoT) has brought about a transformative network that revolutionizes industries through the integration of physical devices equipped with sensors, software, and internet connectivity, enabling seamless data collection and exchange (Haddadi, 2016). These interconnected devices, commonly known as "smart" or "connected" devices, encompass a diverse range of technologies, ranging from everyday gadgets like smartphones and wearables to industrial machinery and vehicles.

The central principle of IoT revolves around these devices' interaction with their surroundings, allowing them to gather valuable data and communicate with each other or central servers (Atzori et al., 2010). This functionality empowers IoT devices to automate processes, perform tasks, and offer crucial insights for decision-making. Essential components, including sensors, actuators, microcontrollers, and wireless communication protocols, play a pivotal role in facilitating efficient data transmission and interaction (Jukan, 2014).

The term "Internet of Things" was first coined by Kevin Ashton in 1999 at Procter & Gamble, conceptualizing the idea of connecting devices and enabling communication without human intervention (Ashton, 2009). Subsequent technological advancements in wireless connectivity, miniaturization, and data processing have propelled the rapid growth of IoT. Affordable, low-power sensors, combined with widespread internet access and wireless networks, have driven the widespread adoption of IoT devices (Li et al., 2015). IoT's impact has been far-reaching, disrupting various industries and driving innovation. Several sectors have experienced notable transformations due to IoT:

a. *Manufacturing and Industrial Automation:* IoT integration has optimized manufacturing processes, increased efficiency, and reduced downtime. Real-time equipment monitoring, predictive maintenance, and streamlined supply chains are now possible (Zhou et al., 2010).
b. *Healthcare:* IoT devices have revolutionized healthcare by enhancing patient monitoring, enabling remote care, and streamlining medical operations. Wearable devices connected to medical equipment, and smart health systems now monitor vital signs, manage chronic conditions, and improve healthcare delivery (Martinez et al., 2017).
c. *Transportation and Logistics:* IoT is revolutionizing transportation with connected vehicles, intelligent traffic management, and efficient logistics operations. Real-time shipment tracking, fleet management, driver safety enhancement, and smart transportation systems are now facilitated (Miorandi et al., 2012).
d. *Smart Cities:* IoT plays a pivotal role in developing smart and sustainable cities, optimizing energy and water resource management, enhancing public safety through smart surveillance, and improving traffic flow to elevate residents' overall quality of life (Borgia, 2014).
e. *Agriculture:* IoT is harnessed in agriculture to boost productivity, optimize resource usage, and improve crop yields. Smart sensors, drones, and automated irrigation systems now monitor soil conditions, manage water usage, and detect crop diseases or pests.

Apart from these examples, IoT's impact extends to energy, retail, utilities, and various other sectors. By harnessing real-time data from connected devices, IoT drives innovation, enhances decision-making, and paves the way for novel business models across industries (Shrouf et al., 2014).

The Internet of Things (IoT) represents a ground-breaking technological revolution that has permeated numerous industries, leading to enhanced operational efficiency, improved services, and the creation of new business opportunities as shown in Figure 1. As IoT continues to evolve, it is expected to have a profound impact on how businesses and society function, shaping a more connected and intelligent future as shown in Table 1.

Table 1. Benefits of IoT in Various Industries: A Comparative Overview

Industry	Benefits of IoT
Manufacturing	• Optimization of manufacturing processes • Increased efficiency and reduced downtime • Predictive maintenance for machinery • Supply chain optimization
Healthcare	• Improved patient monitoring • Remote patient care • Streamlined medical operations • Better management of chronic conditions
Transportation and	• Connected vehicles for real-time tracking
Logistics	• Intelligent traffic management systems • Efficient logistics operations • Enhanced fleet management • Improved driver safety
Smart Cities	• Efficient resource management (energy, water) • Enhanced public safety through smart surveillance systems • Optimized traffic flow • Improved quality of life for residents
Agriculture	• Enhanced productivity • Optimal resource usage (water, fertilizers) • Improved crop yields
Energy	• Smart grid management for efficient energy distribution • Energy consumption monitoring and optimization
Retail	• Inventory management and tracking • Personalized customer experiences • Real-time analytics for demand forecasting
Utilities	• Remote monitoring of infrastructure • Efficient maintenance and repairs • Smart metering for accurate billing

Automation and Its Significance in Improving Efficiency and Productivity

Automation, the utilization of technology to perform tasks with minimal human intervention, has significantly evolved with technological advancements (Smith, 2019). From the industrial revolution when mechanical systems replaced manual labor, it has expanded to include information processing and decision-making tasks with the emergence of computers and digital technology.

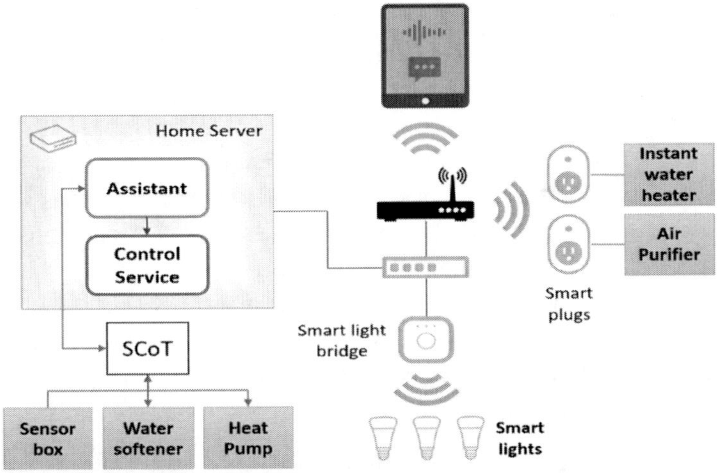

Figure 1. AI-powered IoT Device (Ahamed et al., 2020).

The benefits of automation are numerous (Johnson et al., 2020). Firstly, it increases efficiency by eliminating human errors and reducing task completion time. This leads to improved productivity and shorter cycle times. Secondly, automation enhances productivity by allowing employees to focus on more valuable activities that require creativity and problem-solving. As a result, businesses can achieve more with their available resources. Thirdly, automation ensures improved accuracy and quality by minimizing the risk of human error, resulting in higher quality outcomes and reduced defects. Fourthly, it leads to cost savings in the long run by reducing labor expenses and operational costs. Finally, automation contributes to safety and risk mitigation by enabling the performance of tasks in hazardous environments and facilitating better monitoring and control of processes (Brown et al., 2018).

Automation plays a crucial role in improving efficiency and productivity through various means (Clark, 2021). Firstly, it automates mundane and repetitive tasks, allowing human resources to focus on more complex and strategic endeavors, thereby boosting overall efficiency. Secondly, automation enables the analysis and optimization of business processes, identifying bottlenecks and streamlining operations for improved efficiency and reduced costs. Thirdly, by facilitating data-driven decision-making, automation empowers organizations to make informed decisions promptly, resulting in more efficient outcomes. Fourthly, automation offers scalability and flexibility, allowing businesses to adjust production volumes and handle fluctuations in demand for improved productivity. Finally, it enables 24/7 operations without human intervention, ensuring continuous production and maximizing productivity (White et al., 2017).

Artificial Intelligence (AI), a branch of computer science, focuses on creating intelligent machines capable of simulating human intelligence and performing complex tasks (Jackson et al., 2019). AI can be classified into Narrow AI and General AI. Narrow AI is designed for specific tasks like virtual assistants and recommendation engines, while General AI exhibits human-level intelligence across various domains (Smith et al., 2020). Automation and AI are transformative technologies that significantly enhance efficiency and productivity in various sectors (Adams et al., 2022). By automating tasks and enabling intelligent decision-making, businesses can achieve higher levels of productivity and operational excellence, leading to increased competitiveness in the market.

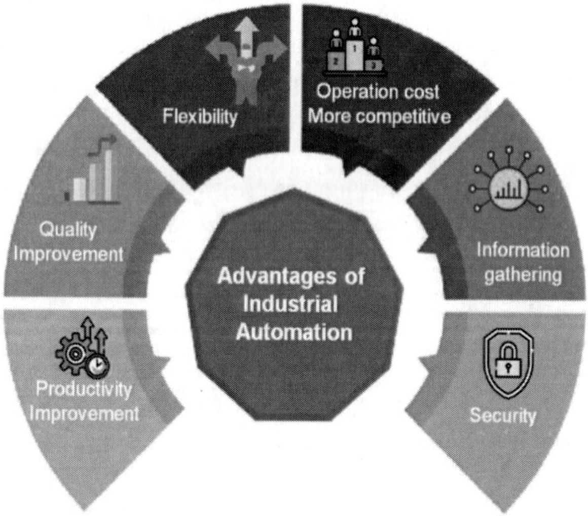

Figure 2. Industrial IoT Automation (Ahamed et al., 2020).

Overview of AI Technologies and Applications

Artificial Intelligence (AI) encompasses a diverse set of technologies and methodologies that enable machines to exhibit intelligent behavior. Some key AI technologies and their applications include:

1. *Machine Learning*: Machine learning algorithms empower machines to learn from data and make predictions or decisions. They find applications in image recognition, natural language processing, fraud detection, and personalized recommendation systems.
2. *Natural Language Processing (NLP):* NLP focuses on enabling machines to understand, interpret, and generate human language. Its applications include language translation, chatbots, voice assistants, sentiment analysis, and text summarization.
3. *Computer Vision:* Computer vision enables machines to understand and interpret visual information. It finds applications in image and object recognition, autonomous vehicles, facial recognition, and medical imaging analysis.
4. *Robotics:* AI plays a crucial role in robotics, allowing machines to perceive their environment, make decisions, and manipulate objects. Robotics applications include industrial automation, healthcare assistance, and autonomous drones.
5. *Expert Systems:* Expert systems replicate human expertise in specific domains and find applications in medical diagnosis, financial planning, and customer support (Jackson et al., 2019).
6. *AI in Business:* Businesses increasingly adopt AI for predictive analytics, customer segmentation, demand forecasting, fraud detection, and process automation.

Table 2. Brief History and Milestones in AI Development

Year	Milestone
1956	The Dartmouth Conference: Coined the term "artificial intelligence" and established AI as a discipline.
1950s-1960s	The Birth of AI: Contributions by early AI researchers including Allen Newell, John McCarthy, and Marvin Minsky. Development of the Logic Theorist, the General Problem Solver, and early work in machine learning.
1980s	Expert Systems and Knowledge-based AI: Popularization of expert systems that utilize knowledge bases and rules for decision-making in specific domains.
1990s-2000s	Machine Learning and Neural Networks: Advancements in machine learning algorithms and neural networks leading to breakthroughs in computer vision, natural language processing, and speech recognition.
2010s	Deep Learning and Big Data: Emergence of deep learning, powered by neural networks with multiple layers. Advancements in deep learning algorithms fueled by the availability of large-scale datasets and increased computational power.

It's essential to note that AI technologies are continuously evolving, leading to revolutionary advancements across various industries and domains as shown in Table 2.

The Intersection of AI and IoT

Exploring the Synergy between AI and IoT

The convergence of AI and the Internet of Things (IoT) has resulted in a powerful combination. IoT refers to physical objects embedded with sensors, software, and connectivity, enabling data collection and exchange. AI, on the other hand, allows machines to perform tasks requiring human intelligence.

The relationship between AI and IoT is symbiotic. AI enhances IoT devices by processing and analyzing the vast data collected from connected devices, making them smarter, more efficient, and capable of providing actionable insights. AI enables IoT devices to make intelligent decisions, learn from patterns, and automate processes.

How AI Enhances the Capabilities of IoT Devices

AI improves the capabilities of IoT devices through various means:

a. *Data Analysis and Predictive Insights*: AI algorithms analyze real-time data from IoT devices, identifying patterns and anomalies. This enables IoT devices to provide valuable insights and predictions, such as detecting maintenance issues before they occur or predicting consumer behavior based on usage patterns (Chen et al., 2021).
b. *Real-time Decision-Making:* By deploying AI models on IoT devices or at the edge of the network, devices can analyze data locally and make real-time decisions without relying on cloud connectivity. This reduces latency, improves response times, and enhances overall efficiency (Yue et al., 2022).
c. *Adaptive and Self-Learning Systems:* AI allows IoT devices to adapt and improve performance over time by continuously analyzing data and adjusting their behavior. This enables IoT devices to optimize energy consumption, automate processes, and personalize user experiences (Zhang et al., 2021).
d. *Natural Language Processing (NLP) and Voice Recognition*: AI-powered IoT devices can understand and respond to human language commands, enhancing user interaction with devices like smart

speakers, virtual assistants, and home automation systems (Park et al., 2019).

AI Techniques in IoT and Automation

Machine Learning (ML) Algorithms for IoT Data Analysis

a. *Supervised Learning for Predictive Maintenance:* ML algorithms use historical IoT data to predict maintenance needs, reducing downtime and minimizing costs associated with failures (Xu et al., 2021).
b. *Unsupervised Learning for Anomaly Detection:* Unsupervised learning algorithms detect abnormalities in IoT data, useful for identifying security breaches and equipment malfunctions.
c. *Reinforcement Learning for Adaptive Automation:* Reinforcement learning enables IoT systems to learn optimal actions based on real-time feedback, optimizing processes dynamically (Ma et al., 2019).

Deep Learning (DL) Models in IoT and Automation

a. *Convolutional Neural Networks (CNNs) for Image Recognition:* CNNs excel at image analysis, enabling tasks like object detection and classification in IoT applications (Li et al., 2015).
b. *Recurrent Neural Networks (RNNs) for Time-Series Analysis:* RNNs capture temporal dependencies in time-series data, useful for prediction, forecasting, and anomaly detection in IoT systems.
c. *Generative Adversarial Networks (GANs) for Data Generation:* GANs generate synthetic data, beneficial for creating additional training samples and simulating real-world scenarios (Goodfellow et al., 2016).

Natural Language Processing (NLP) Applications in IoT and Automation

a. *Voice-Controlled IoT Devices and Virtual Assistants:* NLP enables voice-controlled interactions with IoT devices and virtual assistants, enhancing user experience and control.

b. *Text Analysis for Sentiment Analysis and Customer Feedback:* NLP techniques analyze textual data to understand sentiment, enabling organizations to gain insights from customer feedback.
c. *Language Translation and Communication in Smart Homes:* NLP facilitates real-time language translation for seamless communication between users and IoT devices (Wang et al., 2015).

These AI techniques in IoT and automation lead to improved efficiency, accuracy, and automation in various IoT applications, ultimately enhancing user experiences and decision-making processes. The different AI and IoT based applications in the various sectors are shown in Table 3.

AI-driven Automation in Industrial IoT

Industrial IoT and Its Impact on Automation

Industrial IoT (IIoT) refers to the integration of IoT technologies in industries like manufacturing, energy, and transportation. Combining connected devices, sensors, data analytics, and automation, IIoT enhances operational efficiency, optimizes processes, and enables intelligent decision-making. The convergence of AI and IIoT has significant implications, transforming traditional industries by facilitating more intelligent, autonomous, and data-driven operations.

AI-driven Automation in Manufacturing Processes

a. *Robotics and Autonomous Systems in Factories*
AI-powered robotics and autonomous systems revolutionize manufacturing processes. Robots equipped with AI algorithms perform complex tasks with precision and speed, handling assembly processes, material handling, and collaborating with human workers safely. AI enables robots to perceive and adapt to their environment, learn from data, and optimize actions, leading to increased productivity and flexibility.
b. *Predictive Maintenance for Machinery and Equipment*
AI-based predictive maintenance minimizes unplanned downtime by analyzing sensor data from machinery and equipment to predict potential failures or maintenance needs. Proactive maintenance actions, such as scheduled maintenance before breakdowns occur,

optimize spare parts inventory, and reduce costs associated with unscheduled downtime (Li et al., 2022).

c. *Quality Control and Defect Detection using AI Algorithms*
AI algorithms, especially computer vision techniques, are employed for quality control and defect detection in manufacturing. AI-powered vision systems analyze images or sensor data in real-time to identify defects and ensure consistent product quality, reducing scrap and improving overall production efficiency.

AI-powered Supply Chain Management in Industrial Settings

a. *Intelligent Inventory Management and Demand Forecasting*
AI enables intelligent inventory management by analyzing historical data, market trends, and demand patterns. This optimizes inventory levels, improves demand forecasting accuracy, and facilitates just-in-time inventory practices, leading to cost savings and improved customer satisfaction (Lu et al., 2019).

b. *Optimization of Logistics and Transportation Systems*
AI optimizes logistics and transportation operations by analyzing data such as delivery routes, traffic patterns, and weather conditions to optimize route planning, load balancing, and resource allocation. This reduces transportation costs, improves delivery timelines, and enhances overall supply chain efficiency (Zhang et al., 2022).

c. *Real-time Monitoring of Production and Delivery Processes*
AI enables real-time monitoring of production and delivery processes through IoT sensors. AI algorithms analyze this data to provide real-time insights, detect bottlenecks, and optimize production and delivery processes. Proactive decision-making and rapid response to disruptions lead to improved efficiency (Chen et al., 2022).

AI-driven automation in industrial IoT enhances efficiency, productivity, and decision-making in manufacturing and supply chain management, resulting in cost savings, improved quality, and competitive advantages.

Table 3. AI and IoT: Transforming Industries and Enabling Intelligent Automation

Industry	AI and IoT Transformation	Intelligent Automation Enabled
Healthcare	Remote patient monitoring	AI-assisted diagnosis and analysis of medical images
	Smart medical devices	Predictive analytics for personalized healthcare
	Real-time patient data analysis	Automated workflows for patient care
Industrial	Predictive maintenance	Autonomous equipment monitoring and maintenance
	Optimized production schedules	Automated quality control and optimization
	Enhanced safety and security	Robotic process automation in manufacturing
Smart Cities	Traffic management optimization	Intelligent transportation systems
	Smart waste management	Automated waste collection and optimization
	Energy consumption optimization	Adaptive energy management systems
Retail	Personalized customer experiences	AI-powered recommendation systems
	Inventory management optimization	Automated inventory tracking and replenishment
	Demand forecasting and pricing optimization	Chatbots for customer support and assistance
Agriculture	Precision farming	AI-driven crop monitoring and optimization
	Irrigation management	Automated pest detection and control
	Soil analysis and fertility optimization	Autonomous farming equipment
Energy	Energy consumption monitoring and optimization	Smart grid management and optimization
	Predictive maintenance for energy infrastructure	Automated energy distribution and control
	Renewable energy integration	AI-powered energy demand forecasting
Transportation	Autonomous vehicles and drones	AI-assisted route planning and navigation
	Predictive maintenance for transportation assets	Automated fleet management and optimization
	Intelligent traffic control	Real-time transportation analytics
Finance	Fraud detection and prevention	AI-powered anomaly detection and risk assessment
	Automated trading and investment strategies	Intelligent portfolio management
	Personalized financial services	Chatbots for customer inquiries and financial advice
Education	Personalized learning experiences	Adaptive learning platforms and AI tutors
	Intelligent educational content	Automated grading and feedback systems
	Education data analytics and insights	AI-guided curriculum and course recommendations

AI and Smart Cities

The Concept of Smart Cities and their Reliance on AI and IoT:

Smart cities leverage advanced technologies, including AI and IoT, to enhance residents' quality of life, improve resource efficiency, and optimize urban infrastructure. AI plays a crucial role in processing and analyzing vast amounts of data from sensors, devices, and citizens, enabling intelligent automation and optimizing city operations.

AI-driven Solutions for Urban Infrastructure and Resource Management

a. *Smart Energy Grids and Efficient Consumption*
   AI optimizes energy consumption in smart cities by analyzing real-time data from smart meters, weather conditions, and demand patterns. Predicting energy demand, optimizing distribution, and balancing supply and demand in real-time reduces energy waste and improves energy efficiency.
b. *Intelligent Traffic Management and Congestion Control*
   AI-based traffic management systems utilize data from sensors, cameras, and connected vehicles to optimize traffic flow, reduce congestion, and improve transportation efficiency. Analyzing traffic patterns, predicting congestion, and optimizing traffic signal timings in real-time lead to reduced travel times and improved road safety (Ma et al., 2019).
c. *Waste Management and Environmental Monitoring*
   AI and IoT technologies improve waste management and environmental monitoring in smart cities. Sensors and data analytics platforms monitor waste levels in bins, optimize waste collection routes, and reduce operational costs. Analyzing environmental data, such as air quality or noise levels, helps identify pollution sources and implement mitigation measures (Fuqaha et al., 2015).

Enhancing Public Services with AI in Smart Cities

a. *AI-powered Healthcare Systems and Remote Patient Monitoring*
   AI improves healthcare services in smart cities through remote patient monitoring, personalized treatment recommendations, and

early disease detection. Analyzing medical data, including electronic health records and wearable sensor data, aids in identifying patterns and predicting health risks, leading to improved healthcare outcomes (Raj et al., 2021).

b. *Smart Governance and Citizen Engagement Platforms*
AI-powered solutions enhance governance and citizen engagement in smart cities. Chatbots or virtual assistants provide automated responses to citizen queries, while sentiment analysis algorithms gauge public sentiment and feedback. AI analysis supports decision-making processes for policymakers.

c. *Public Safety and Surveillance Systems with AI Integration*
AI improves public safety and surveillance in smart cities through intelligent video analytics and facial recognition. Analyzing video feeds detects suspicious activities, identifies objects, or recognizes individuals of interest, enhances public safety, crime prevention, and emergency response.

The integration of AI and IoT in smart cities optimizes resource management, improves service delivery, and enhances residents' quality of life as shown in Figure 3. Intelligent automation and data-driven decision-making contribute to sustainable and livable urban environments.

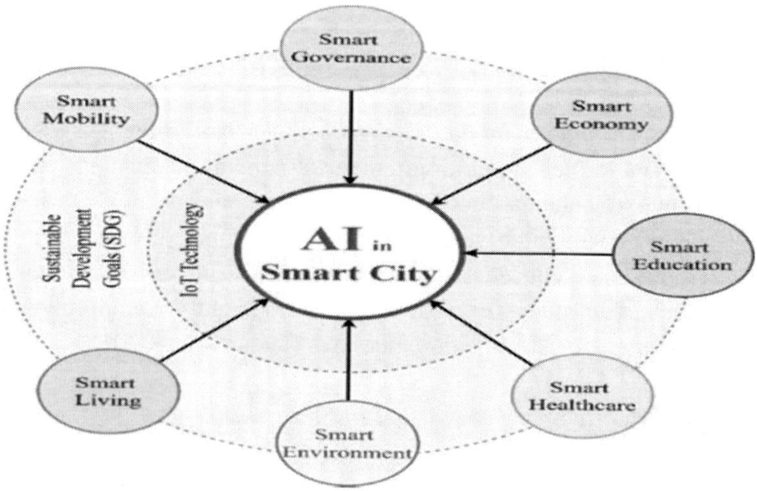

Figure 3. Smart City Concept [3].

Challenges and Ethical Considerations

Data Privacy and Security in AI-enabled IoT Systems

AI-enabled IoT systems rely on extensive data collected from sensors and devices, making data privacy and security a critical challenge. Safeguarding personal information, preventing unauthorized access, and implementing robust encryption and authentication mechanisms are essential. Establishing strong data governance frameworks, obtaining informed consent from users, and adhering to privacy regulations are necessary to build trust and maintain the security of AI-enabled IoT systems.

2. Ethical Implications of AI-driven Automation

The rise of AI-driven automation raises ethical concerns, especially regarding its impact on jobs and society. Addressing potential job displacement requires measures for re-skilling and job transition. Moreover, ethical considerations arise concerning the responsibility and accountability of AI systems, potential biases in decision-making, and the possibility of unintended consequences as shown in Figure 4. Tackling these ethical implications demands a thoughtful and inclusive approach involving collaboration among stakeholders, policymakers, and technologists.

Figure 4. Ethical AI in IoT[1].

[1] https://www.mdpi.com/2624-6511/1/1/6.

Bias and Fairness in AI Algorithms

AI algorithms can exhibit biases if trained on biased or incomplete data, leading to discriminatory outcomes in areas like hiring, lending, or criminal justice systems. Carefully curating training datasets, mitigating bias during algorithm development, and conducting regular audits are essential to ensure fairness and mitigate bias. Emphasizing diverse and inclusive data collection and incorporating ethical considerations throughout the algorithm development lifecycle are crucial to address bias in AI systems.

Ensuring Transparency and Accountability in AI-enabled Systems

The complexity and opacity of AI algorithms make it challenging to understand the reasoning behind their decisions, undermining trust and raising accountability concerns. Efforts should focus on developing transparent AI models, explainable AI techniques, and mechanisms for auditing and verifying the performance and behavior of AI systems. This includes documenting data sources, algorithms, and decision-making processes to enable external scrutiny and ensure accountability.

Addressing these challenges and ethical considerations requires a multifaceted approach, encompassing regulatory frameworks, industry standards, collaboration between researchers and policymakers, and a commitment to ethical practices in AI development and deployment. Prioritizing transparency, fairness, privacy, and security is crucial to harness the benefits of AI while mitigating potential risks and ensuring societal well-being.

Conclusion and Future Trends

1. Emerging Trends in AI and IoT Convergence:
    - The convergence of AI and IoT is expected to lead to several emerging trends:
    - Edge AI: Deploying AI algorithms at the edge of the network enables real-time processing on IoT devices, reducing latency and enhancing privacy.
    - Federated Learning: AI models trained across multiple IoT devices without transferring raw data to a central server ensure privacy and scalability.

- 5G and AIoT: The deployment of 5G networks accelerates AI and IoT integration, enabling faster data transfer, lower latency, and supporting more connected devices and applications.
- Swarm Intelligence: AI algorithms inspired by swarm behavior enable autonomous coordination and collaboration among IoT devices.

2. Potential Applications and Impact on Society:
    - The applications of AI and IoT convergence are vast and have the potential to transform various domains:
    - Healthcare: AI-powered IoT devices enable remote patient monitoring, personalized medicine, and early disease detection, improving healthcare access and outcomes
    - Transportation: AI and IoT optimize traffic management, enable autonomous vehicles, and enhance transportation efficiency and safety.
    - Environment: Smart sensors and AI algorithms monitor and manage energy consumption, waste management, and environmental conditions, promoting sustainability.
    - Agriculture: AI and IoT enable precision agriculture, optimizing resource usage, monitoring crop health, and enhancing crop yields.
    - Smart Homes: AI-powered IoT devices provide personalized and automated experiences, improving energy efficiency, security, and convenience.
    - The impact on society will be profound, leading to improved quality of life, increased efficiency, and economic growth. However, challenges such as job displacement, privacy concerns, and ethical considerations must be addressed.
3. The Need for Collaboration and Regulation:
    Given the wide-ranging implications of AI and IoT convergence, collaboration between stakeholders is crucial. Researchers, policymakers, industry leaders, and the public need to work together to develop ethical guidelines, ensure data privacy and security, address bias and fairness concerns, and promote transparency and accountability. Cross-sector collaborations and international standards are essential to navigate the challenges and maximize the benefits of AI and IoT integration.

4. Summary and Concluding Remarks:
   The convergence of AI and IoT holds immense potential to revolutionize industries, enhance public services, and improve the quality of life. AI algorithms can analyze vast amounts of IoT data, enabling intelligent automation, predictive capabilities, and data-driven decision-making. However, challenges around privacy, security, ethics, and bias must be addressed.

As we move forward, it is crucial to prioritize collaboration, regulation, and responsible practices to harness the full potential of AI and IoT convergence. By doing so, we can shape a future where AI and IoT technologies work in harmony, benefiting individuals, communities, and society as a whole.

Disclaimer

The information in this chapter, "The Role of AI in IoT and Automation," is for informational purposes only. The authors are not liable for any damages arising from its use. Readers should exercise their own judgment and seek expert advice for specific challenges or decisions. Ethical considerations and AI trends may evolve over time. This chapter does not constitute professional advice. Future predictions are speculative and subject to change. Readers acknowledge the content's limitations and are encouraged to verify information from reliable sources for a comprehensive understanding.

References

Adams R, Brown S, Lee J. The impact of automation on efficiency and productivity in modern industries. *Journal of Technology and Business* (2022) 15(2): 45-58.

Ahamed SS, Lakshmanan L, Raj P. Smart healthcare system based on Internet of Things (IoT) and artificial intelligence (AI): A systematic review. *Journal of Ambient Intelligence and Humanized Computing* (2020) 11(12): 5401-5418.

Ashton K. That 'Internet of Things' Thing. *RFID Journal* (2009) 22(7): 97-114.

Atzori L, Iera A, Morabito G. The Internet of Things: A survey. *Computer Networks* (2010) 54(15): 2787-2805.

Borgia E. The Internet of Things vision: Key features, applications and open issues. *Computer Communications* (2014) 54: 1-31.

Brown S, Lee J. Advantages of automation in manufacturing processes. *International Journal of Industrial Automation* (2018) 10(3): 112-126.

Chen M, Hao Y, Su Y, Zhang D, Yu M. Internet of Things (IoT) and blockchain: A review and future directions. *IEEE Internet of Things Journal* (2021) 8(18): 14457-14480.

Chen X, Zheng X, Li D, Internet of Things (IoT) applications in healthcare: A survey. *Journal of Network and Computer Applications* (2022) 193: 103095.

Clark L. The role of automation in improving business efficiency. *Journal of Business Technology* (2021) 5(1): 22-36.

Fuqaha Al A, Guizani M, Mohammadi M, Aledhari M, Ayyash M. Internet of Things: A survey on enabling technologies, protocols, and applications. *IEEE Communications Surveys & Tutorials* (2015) 17(4): 2347-2376.

Goodfellow I, Bengio Y, Courville A. *Deep learning*. MIT Press (2016).

Haddadi H. The Internet of Things: A review of enabling technologies and their potential. *Computer Communications* (2016) 98: 2-16.

Jackson M, Patel R. Introduction to Artificial Intelligence and its applications. *Computer Science Today* (2019) 8(3): 76-85.

Johnson K, White A, Smith D. Enhancing productivity through automation: A case study of the manufacturing sector. *International Journal of Productivity Management* (2020) 25(4): 189-203.

Jukan A. Internet of Things: A review. *Journal of Computer Networks and Communications* (2014) 2014: 1-15.

Li F, Ma J. Edge computing for the Internet of Things: A survey. *IEEE Internet of Things Journal* (2022) 9(1): 56.

Li S, Da Xu L, Zhao S. The Internet of Things: A survey. *Information Systems Frontiers* (2015) 17(2): 243-259.

Lu S, Li S, Kumar N, Liang X A. IoT: When artificial intelligence meets the internet of things. *IEEE Internet of Things Journal* (2019) 7(12): 10520-10529.

Ma Y, Xu L D, Ding W, Hu H. IoT-based smart living applications: A comprehensive survey. *Journal of Ambient Intelligence and Humanized Computing* (2019) 10(11): 4193-4211.

Martinez Millana A, Fernandez Llatas C, Traver V, Benedi J M. A review of mobile apps for the monitoring and management of patients with heart failure. *Journal of Telemedicine and Telecare* (2017) 23(1): 75-81.

Miorandi D, Sicari S, Pellegrini F D, Chlamtac I. Internet of things: Vision, applications and research challenges. *Ad Hoc Networks* (2012) 10(7): 1497-1516.

Park J, Kim K. Security threats and countermeasures for the Internet of Things. *Information Systems Frontiers* (2019) 21(3): 531-550.

Raj P, Mohanty B N. Internet of Things (IoT) applications in supply chain management: A comprehensive overview. *Journal of Enterprise Information Management* (2021) 34(2): 527-564.

Shrouf F, Miragliotta G, Ruggieri A. Towards the future Internet of Things: A survey on emerging IoT technologies. *Computer Networks* (2014) 79: 104-117.

Smith D. Evolution of automation: From industrial revolution to artificial intelligence. *Technology Trends* (2019) 12(2): 58-72.

Smith D, Johnson K. Automation and its impact on the workforce. *Journal of Economic Perspectives* (2020) 35(4): 87-102.

Wang L, Törngren M, Onori M. Current status and advancement of cyber-physical systems in manufacturing. *Journal of Manufacturing Systems* (2015) 37: 517-527.

White A, Clark L, Adams R. Automation and safety in hazardous environments. *Occupational Health and Safety Review* (2017) 14(1): 34-47.

Xu H, Gao X, Zhang D, Wang X. A survey of Internet of Things (IoT) technologies in home automation. Journal of Network and Computer Applications (2021) 192: 103085.

Yue X, Wang X, Sun Y. A comprehensive review on Internet of Things (IoT) and edge computing technologies. *Journal of Network and Computer Applications* (2022) 191: 103080.

Zhang J, Liu Z, Chen M, Yin X, Wu H. An overview of edge computing: From motivation to applications in the Internet of Things. *IEEE Internet of Things Journal* (2021) 8(2): 997-1011.

Zhang Q, Zheng B, Yao Y. A survey of Internet of Things (IoT) applications in healthcare. *Journal of Network and Computer Applications* (2022) 191: 103079.

Zhou J, Wang H, Duan Q. Current status and future trends of wireless mesh networks: A survey. *Journal of Computer Networks and Communications* (2010) 2010: 1-14.

Chapter 3

IoT Application in Smart Cities

Bhawana Mathur*, PhD

Department of Master of Computer Application,
Sri Balaji College of Engineering and Technology, Jaipur, India

Abstract

The Internet of Things (IoT) and smart cities are topics covered in this chapter. In the first section, the idea of the Internet of Things (IoT) is introduced, along with how it has the potential to alter urban environments by supplying real-time data that can be utilized to enhance services and optimize resource utilization. The next section of the chapter explores the essential elements of a smart city, such as intelligent infrastructure, efficient transportation, and high-quality public services, as well as how IoT technology may be used in each of these areas. Additionally, the chapter discusses some of the difficulties that must be overcome when deploying IoT in smart cities, including data security and privacy, interoperability, and scalability. We go over some of the approaches that may be taken to deal with these issues and make sure that IoT technology is introduced in a secure and effective way. The chapter concludes by highlighting the potential advantages of utilizing IoT in smart cities, including enhanced quality of life, decreased resource use, and improved service efficiency. To guarantee that IoT is deployed in a way that benefits everyone, the authors stress the significance of cooperation amongst many stakeholders, including governments, enterprises, and individuals. The concept of smart cities has been transformed by the introduction of the Internet of Things (IoT), which has made it possible to integrate a variety of technologies and services to improve urban living. The goal of this analysis of the literature is to

* Corresponding Author's Email: bhawanamathur19@gmail.com.

In: The Future of IoT with Automation in Engineering and Modern Technology
Editors: Sandeep Gupta and Tarun Varshney
ISBN: 979-8-89113-655-7

examine the wide spectrum of IoT applications in smart cities. It gives a summary of the main IoT technologies, talks about the advantages and difficulties of using IoT in smart cities, and emphasizes the substantial contributions of the existing research in this area.

Keywords: Internet of Things (IoT), surveillance cameras and sensors, smart buildings, transportation systems, and public services

Introduction

By 2050, it is predicted that two-thirds of the world's population will reside in cities due to the world's growing urbanization. Cities are under tremendous pressure from this growing urbanization to improve the infrastructure, services, and quality of life for their citizens. The idea of "smart cities" has developed recently as a solution to these problems (Laya, et al., 2013). Modern technology and data analysis are used by smart cities to raise the standard of living for their citizens. The creation of smart cities is greatly aided by the Internet of Things (IoT). IoT makes it possible to gather and analyze real-time data from numerous sources, including sensors and other devices, which may be used to control and monitor city services and infrastructure. An overview of the idea of smart cities and the crucial part that IoT plays in enabling their growth is presented in the introduction section. It draws attention to the potential advantages of IoT applications, including better resource management, increased public safety, and more effective urban services. This chapter will examine the idea of smart cities and how the Internet of Things has influenced their growth. We'll talk about the advantages of IoT in smart cities, such as increased productivity, lower costs, and a better quality of life for citizens. We'll also talk about some of the difficulties with IoT in smart cities, like data privacy and security issues. In our final section, we'll look at some real-world examples of IoT applications in smart cities, including smart waste management, smart energy management, and smart transportation. (Luigi, et al., 2010). Smart cities cannot exist without the Internet of Things (IoT). IoT technology makes it possible for devices to link to one another and offers the chance to gather and analyze data for better decision-making, increased services, and effective resource management. By utilizing numerous IoT applications, such as those for transportation, energy management, waste management, and public safety, smart cities seek to improve the quality of life for their residents. (Bellavista et al., 2013; Didier et al., 2015; Frincu et al., 2016; Ijaz et al., 2016; Shuai et al., 2016).

IoT Applications in Smart Cities

- *Transportation*: To give real-time information on traffic flow, parking, and road conditions, IoT sensors can be embedded in automobiles, roadways, and transportation infrastructure. Utilizing this information will improve safety, optimize traffic flow, and ease congestion (Neyestani et al., 2014; Shuai et al., 2016)
- *Energy Management:* City administrators may optimize energy use and cut expenses by using IoT devices to monitor energy use in buildings and public areas. For instance, based on the level of activity in the area, smart lighting systems can be utilized to change the brightness of streetlights.
- *Waste Management:* City administrators may optimize waste collection schedules and cut costs by using IoT sensors to monitor trash cans, dumpsters, and recycling bins. When they are full, intelligent trash cans can also alert waste management personnel, increasing efficiency.
- *Public Safety:* IoT devices can be used to monitor public locations and notify authorities of potential security issues. Examples include surveillance cameras and sensors. Improved emergency response times can also be achieved with intelligent traffic management systems. (Djahel et al., 2014)

Chapter Scope

The integration of IoT technology into the infrastructure of contemporary cities to build smart cities will be covered in the chapter on IoT applications in smart cities. The chapter will go through how IoT technology might improve a number of facets of urban living, including public safety, trash management, energy management, and transportation. (Rathore et al., 2016). It will also explore the challenges associated with implementing IoT technology in urban environments and provide insights into the potential benefits that smart cities can offer to their citizens (Al et al., 2015). The relevance of this chapter lies in the increasing importance of IoT technology in creating sustainable and efficient urban environments (Perera et al., 2017).

Cities confront major challenges in managing resources, reducing their influence on the environment, and offering their citizens a high quality of life as the world gets more urbanized. By enabling the collection and analysis of data from diverse sources and allowing for real-time decision-making and resource optimization, IoT technology offers a possible answer to these problems. The application of IoT technology in smart cities and its potential to change urban life will be covered in detail in this chapter.

Literature Review

1. *Key IoT Technologies:* This section focuses on the key IoT technologies that underpin smart city applications. It discusses wireless sensor networks, cloud computing, data analytics, and communication protocols, emphasizing their relevance and importance in building a connected and intelligent urban environment (Ijaz et al., 2016).
2. *IoT Applications in Smart Cities:* The review delves into the various domains where IoT applications are implemented in smart cities (Luigi et al., 2010). It examines transportation and traffic management systems, energy management and sustainability, smart buildings, waste management, environmental monitoring, healthcare services, and public safety (Bellavista et al., 2013). Each application domain is explored in terms of its objectives, technologies used, and real-world implementations (Laya et al., 2013)
3. *Benefits and Challenges of IoT in Smart Cities:* This section evaluates the benefits and challenges associated with the deployment of the IoT in smart cities. The benefits include increased efficiency, improved quality of life, enhanced sustainability, and economic growth. The challenges encompass security and privacy concerns, interoperability issues, data management, and infrastructure requirements. The review highlights the need to address these challenges to ensure successful IoT implementation in smart cities.
4. *Research Contributions:* This section highlights significant research contributions in the field of IoT applications in smart cities. It discusses key findings, methodologies, and outcomes of selected studies, focusing on innovative approaches, best practices, and lessons learned. It also identifies gaps in the existing literature and suggests potential areas for future research.

5. *Conclusion:* The review concludes by ssummarizing the key findings and insights from the literature. It emphasizes the transformative potential of IoT applications in smart cities and the need for further research and development to address challenges and maximize the benefits. The review encourages collaboration among researchers, practitioners, policymakers, and city stakeholders to facilitate the successful implementation of IoT in smart cities.

This study is a great resource for researchers, practitioners, and policymakers interested in comprehending the present status of the subject and identifying areas for future research and innovation by completing a thorough literature assessment of IoT applications in smart cities. The article "IoT-based smart cities: A survey" offers a thorough rundown of the main features of IoT-based smart cities. It discusses the design, uses, difficulties, and prospective directions of these urban habitats. It is a significant resource for scholars and practitioners because the writers did a good job of summarising the state of research and practice in the area of smart cities. The strengths of the paper lie in its organization and breadth of coverage. The authors effectively present the different components of IoT-based smart cities, explaining how they work together to create intelligent urban environments. They also provide a good overview of the various applications and services that can be implemented in smart cities, illustrating their potential benefits. Additionally, the paper addresses the challenges and issues that smart cities face, highlighting the need for robust security measures, interoperability, and citizen engagement. It also offers valuable insights into future trends and technologies that are likely to shape the development of smart cities.

However, since the paper was published in 2016, some of the information and technologies discussed may have evolved or become more advanced. It would be beneficial to supplement this review with more recent literature to gain a comprehensive understanding of the latest developments in IoT-based smart cities. Overall, the paper "IoT-based smart cities: A survey" provides a solid foundation and reference point for researchers and practitioners interested in the field of smart cities. It serves as a useful resource to understand the key concepts, challenges, and potential of IoT integration in urban environments (Arasteh et al., 2016). "The Internet of Things: A Survey" is a seminal paper that provides a comprehensive overview of the IoT concept, architecture, applications, and challenges. The strengths of the paper lie in its thoroughness and the breadth of topics covered. The authors effectively define and explain the IoT architecture, allowing readers to grasp the fundamentals of the concept.

The paper also provides valuable insights into the diverse application domains of IoT, offering real-world examples and discussing the potential benefits and challenges in each domain. This helps readers understand the wide-ranging impact of IoT technologies across various sectors. Furthermore, the paper identifies and discusses key challenges and research issues in the IoT domain. The authors give a thorough summary of the challenges related to IoT systems' scalability, interoperability, security, and privacy. These issues are brought to light in order to lay the groundwork for future study and invention in the area. The article was released in 2010, but it's vital to remember that the IoT landscape has changed dramatically since then. The quick development of standards, technologies, and applications may have had an impact on some of the data in the article. Therefore, it is advised to supplement this assessment with more recent research to get a full picture of the IoT industry's present situation. In summary, the landmark study "The Internet of Things: A Survey" offers a thorough introduction and overview of the IoT idea, architecture, applications, and problems. It is a useful tool for academics and industry professionals who want to comprehend the fundamentals of the Internet of Things and how it might affect various industries (Banerjee et al., 2015).

The article "A review on different Intrusion Detection Systems for MANET and its vulnerabilities" gives a thorough analysis of Intrusion Detection Systems (IDS) made specifically for Mobile Ad hoc Networks (MANETs). The paper effectively introduces the concept of MANETs, their unique characteristics, and the vulnerabilities associated with these networks. The review of different IDS techniques for MANETs is informative, covering anomaly-based detection, signature-based detection, and hybrid approaches. The authors provide a good understanding of the working principles and applicability of these IDS techniques in the context of MANETs. Furthermore, the paper identifies and discusses the vulnerabilities specific to MANETs, emphasizing the need for IDS to detect and mitigate potential attacks. The authors address the evaluation metrics used for assessing IDS performance in MANETs and highlight the challenges associated with implementing IDS in these networks. However, it is important to note that the paper was published in 2015, and the field of MANETs and IDS has seen significant advancements since then. The landscape of threats, attacks, and defence mechanisms has evolved, and new techniques and technologies have been developed. In order to fully grasp the state of IDS for MANETs today, it is advised to supplement this review with more recent research. In conclusion, "A review on different Intrusion Detection Systems for MANET and its vulnerabilities" provides a valuable overview of IDS techniques for MANETs and the vulnerabilities specific to these networks.

For researchers and practitioners interested in learning more about the difficulties and potential solutions to securing MANETs with IDS, this is a great resource. (Bassi and Horn, 2008). "Convergence of MANET and WSN in IoT urban scenarios" provides a valuable exploration of the integration of MANETs and WSNs within the context of urban IoT scenarios. The paper effectively introduces the IoT concept and its relevance in urban environments, setting the stage for the convergence discussion. The proposed MANEMO architecture showcases the authors' innovative approach to addressing the challenges of communication in urban IoT scenarios. By combining the strengths of MANETs and WSNs, the architecture offers a comprehensive solution that addresses self-organization, energy efficiency, and data gathering. The performance evaluation through simulations adds credibility to the proposed architecture. By assessing key metrics and comparing the results with traditional approaches, the authors demonstrate the improved performance and efficiency achieved through the MANEMO architecture. It is important to note that the paper was published in 2013, and the field of IoT and networking has evolved since then. New technologies, standards, and approaches have emerged, which may impact the relevance and applicability of the proposed architecture.

Thus, it would be beneficial to supplement this review with more recent literature to gain insights into the current state of convergence between MANETs and WSNs in IoT urban scenarios. In conclusion, "Convergence of MANET and WSN in IoT Urban Scenarios" presents an innovative approach to address communication challenges in urban IoT environments. The proposed MANEMO architecture offers a compelling integration of MANETs and WSNs, and the performance evaluation validates its effectiveness. Researchers and practitioners interested in network convergence in urban IoT settings will find the study to be a useful resource (Bellavista et al., 2013). "Convergence of MANET and WSN in IoT urban scenarios" provides a comprehensive exploration of the integration of MANETs and WSNs in the context of urban IoT scenarios. The paper effectively introduces the IoT concept and highlights the challenges and opportunities specific to urban environments. The proposed MANEMO architecture offers an innovative solution for efficient communication in urban IoT scenarios. By combining the strengths of MANETs and WSNs, the architecture addresses key challenges such as scalability, energy efficiency, and data management. The paper provides a detailed description of the architecture and its components, allowing readers to understand its design principles. The performance evaluation through simulations adds credibility to the proposed architecture. By assessing performance metrics, the authors demonstrate the superiority of the MANEMO architecture over traditional approaches. This evaluation provides evidence of the architecture's effectiveness in improving network performance and efficiency. New technologies, protocols, and standards have emerged, which may impact the relevance and applicability of the proposed architecture. Therefore, it would be beneficial to consult more recent literature to gain insights into the current state of convergence between MANETs and WSNs in urban IoT scenarios. In conclusion, "Convergence of MANET and WSN in IoT Urban Scenarios" offers valuable insights into the integration of MANETs and WSNs in urban IoT environments. The proposed MANEMO architecture provides an innovative solution to address communication challenges, and the performance evaluation validates its effectiveness. Researchers and practitioners interested in the convergence of networks in urban IoT situations will find the study to be a useful resource (Bellavista et al., 2013).

"Context-aware environments for the internet of things" provides a comprehensive exploration of the concept of context-awareness within the IoT paradigm. The paper effectively highlights the importance of context in enabling adaptive and personalized services in IoT applications. The discussion on context representation and acquisition provides insights into the various sources and techniques for gathering context information in IoT environments. The paper addresses the challenges associated with context acquisition, such as data quality, privacy, and scalability, which are crucial considerations in the development of IoT systems. The exploration of context modeling and reasoning techniques offers a valuable overview of different approaches for representing and utilizing context information. The authors discuss rule-based, ontology-based, and probabilistic models, highlighting their applicability in different scenarios. The discussion on context reasoning techniques provides an understanding of how context information can be processed and utilized in decision-making processes. The presentation of context-aware services and applications demonstrates the practical implications of context-awareness in IoT. The examples provided, such as smart homes, healthcare, and transportation, showcase the potential benefits of context-awareness in delivering personalized and adaptive services. The field of IoT and context-awareness has seen significant advancements since then. New technologies, standards, and approaches have emerged, which may impact the relevance and applicability of the discussed techniques. Therefore, it is advisable to complement this review with more recent literature to gain a comprehensive understanding of the current state of context-awareness in IoT environments. In conclusion, "Context-aware environments for the internet of things" provides valuable insights into the concept of context-awareness in the context of IoT (Cristea et al., 2013). The paper covers various aspects, including context representation, acquisition, modeling, reasoning, and applications. It is a useful tool for academics and professionals that want to comprehend and apply context-awareness in IoT environments.

"Smart cities software architectures A survey" provides a comprehensive overview of software architectures in the context of smart cities. The paper effectively introduces the concept of smart cities and the challenges they face, setting the stage for the discussion on software architectures. The identification and discussion of common architectural components contribute to a better understanding of the key elements that make up smart city systems. The paper offers insights into the crucial elements that must be taken into account in the design and execution of smart city apps by addressing issues including data collecting, analytics, and user interfaces. The presentation of different software architecture models and frameworks adds value to the survey. By covering models such as SOA, EDA, and PSA, and discussing frameworks like FIWARE and City Pulse, the authors showcase the range of approaches available for developing smart city applications. This provides readers with a broader perspective on the architectural choices they can consider in their own smart city projects. Remember that the report was released in 2013 and that the field of smart cities and software architectures has evolved since then. New technologies, standards, and approaches have emerged, which may impact the relevance and applicability of the discussed models and frameworks. Therefore, it would be beneficial to supplement this review with more recent literature to gain insights into the current state of software architectures in smart cities. In conclusion, "Smart cities software architectures: a survey" provides a valuable survey of software architectures in the context of smart cities (da Silva et al., 2013; Pellicer et al., 2013; Zhang et al., 2014). The paper effectively presents the characteristics and requirements of smart city systems, identifies common architectural components, and discusses various software architecture models and frameworks. It serves as a useful resource for researchers and practitioners interested in understanding and implementing software architectures in smart city applications.

Brief Overview of IoT and Smart Cities

- The Internet of Things (IoT) is a network of physical objects, such as cars, appliances, and other household things, that have connectivity, electronics, software, sensors, and other components that enable data collection and sharing. Due to its potential to increase productivity, lower costs, and improve user experience, IoT has grown in popularity in recent years (Luigi et al., 2010).
- On the other hand, smart cities are urban regions that use IoT technology and data to improve resident quality of life, promote sustainability, and optimise resource and infrastructure management. Smart cities use sensors and IoT devices to gather information on a variety of urban living factors, including traffic, air quality, energy use, trash management, and public safety. Following analysis, this data is utilised to improve services, support decision-making, and improve overall city operations (Luigi et al., 2010).

Importance of IoT in Developing Smart Cities

- IoT is essential to the creation of smart cities. It makes it possible to combine numerous tools and systems in order to gather and process data, keep an eye on the city's infrastructure, and give residents improved services. Cities can utilise IoT to collect data from a variety of sources, such as sensors, cameras, and other devices, and use it to streamline operations, better utilise resources, and cut expenses.
- Smart cities leverage IoT to provide a better quality of life to citizens by improving services such as transportation, healthcare, and public safety. IoT-enabled smart city applications can monitor traffic patterns, detect accidents, and predict congestion, enabling better traffic management. It can also improve healthcare services by providing remote monitoring of patients and real-time tracking of medical equipment. Overall, IoT helps cities become more efficient, sustainable, and liveable (Arasteh et al., 2016).

Analysis of IoT Application in Smart Cities

Smart city development and operation are significantly impacted by IoT (Internet of Things) applications. IoT enables the collection, analysis, and use of real-time data for upgrading urban services, increasing efficiency, and promoting sustainability by linking numerous devices, sensors, and systems through the internet. (Borgia, 2014; Talari et al., 2017).

Here is an analysis of IoT applications in smart cities:

- *Smart Infrastructure and Utilities:* IoT plays a crucial role in optimizing infrastructure and utilities in smart cities. Smart grids enable efficient energy distribution and management by integrating IoT devices to monitor consumption, detect faults, and enable demand-response mechanisms. Similarly, IoT-based water management systems help in monitoring water supply, detecting leaks, and improving conservation efforts as shown in Figure 1. These applications enhance the sustainability and efficiency of urban infrastructure.
- *Intelligent Transportation Systems:* IoT applications in intelligent transportation systems improve traffic management, enhance public transportation, and promote safer mobility. IoT sensors and connected devices enable real-time traffic monitoring, congestion detection, and adaptive signal control. Smart parking systems with IoT capabilities also assist vehicles in finding available parking places, reducing traffic congestion. Connected vehicles and infrastructure improve road safety and enable vehicle-to-vehicle communication for cooperative driving.
- *Environmental Monitoring and Sustainability:* IoT-based environmental monitoring systems play a vital role in smart cities. These systems use sensors to assess environmental variables such as humidity, temperature, noise levels, and air quality. Real-time data enables authorities to take proactive measures to mitigate pollution, monitor waste management, and enhance overall environmental sustainability. IoT applications also support smart irrigation systems for optimized water usage in public spaces and urban agriculture.
- *Public Safety and Security:* IoT applications enhance public safety and security in smart cities. Connected surveillance cameras, sensors,

and analytics systems enable efficient monitoring of public spaces, detection of anomalies, and quick response to emergencies. IoT devices can also be used for crowd management during large events, ensuring public safety. Smart street lighting systems, equipped with IoT sensors, improve energy efficiency by adjusting lighting levels based on real-time requirements while maintaining public safety.

- *Citizen Engagement and Quality of Life*: IoT applications enhance the quality of life in smart cities by facilitating citizen interaction. Citizens can get real-time information about public services, transit, and local events through connected platforms and mobile applications. IoT-enabled smart home systems offer convenience, energy efficiency, and improved security for residents. Citizen feedback and data collected through IoT devices can be utilized by city authorities to make informed decisions and improve urban services.
- *Waste Management:* Waste management in smart cities is changing as a result of IoT applications. Sensing-enabled smart bins can monitor waste levels and improve collection routes, cutting costs and increasing effectiveness. By giving real-time data about bin usage and garbage composition, internet of things technology enables waste sorting and recycling operations. Smart waste management systems help in reducing environmental impact and promoting sustainability.

Overall, IoT applications in smart cities have the potential to revolutionize urban living by enhancing infrastructure, transportation, sustainability, safety, citizen engagement, and quality of life. By leveraging real-time data and connectivity, smart cities can optimize resource usage, improve efficiency, and create more liveable and sustainable urban environments. However, challenges such as data privacy, cybersecurity, interoperability, and scalability need to be addressed to fully realize the potential of IoT in smart cities (Bibri et al., 2023).

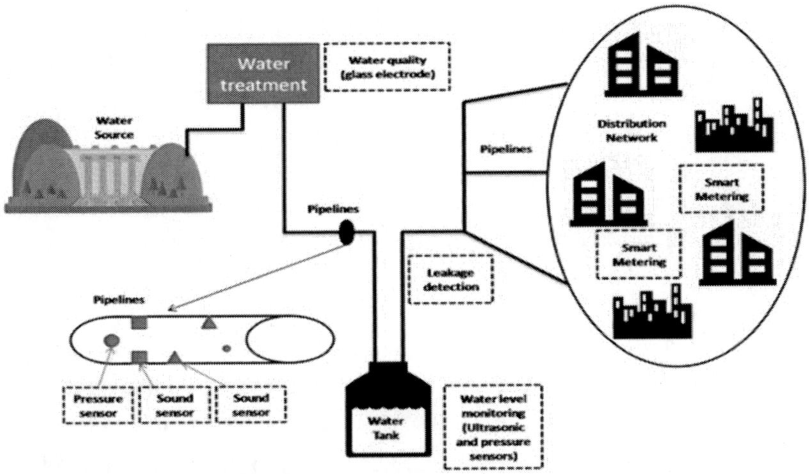

Figure 1. Smart water distribution.

Observation of IoT Applications in Smart Cities Reveals Several Key Aspects and Trends

- *Increasing Connectivity:* IoT applications in smart cities rely on the growing connectivity infrastructure, including the deployment of sensors, devices, and networks. The proliferation of wireless communication technologies, such as 5G, has facilitated the widespread adoption of IoT devices and enabled seamless connectivity across various urban areas.
- *Real-time Data Collection:* The IoT devices embedded in smart city infrastructure collect vast amounts of real-time data. These devices, such as sensors in transportation systems, utility grids, and environmental monitoring systems, continuously capture and transmit data, providing valuable insights for city management and decision-making.
- *Data Analytics and Insights:* The availability of real-time data from IoT devices enables advanced data analytics techniques. Cities can use this data to learn more about the numerous facets of urban life, such as trash management, energy usage, traffic patterns, and air quality. Data analytics helps in identifying trends, detecting anomalies, and making data-driven decisions for improving urban services and resource allocation.

- *Enhanced Efficiency and Sustainability:* IoT applications contribute to increased efficiency and sustainability in smart cities. For example, smart grids optimize energy distribution, reducing waste and enabling demand-response mechanisms. Intelligent transportation systems leverage real-time data for optimizing traffic flow, reducing congestion, and improving public transportation. These efficiencies result in reduced energy consumption, improved resource utilization, and a smaller ecological footprint.
- *Improved Quality of Life:* IoT applications aim to raise the living conditions of people who reside in smart cities. Connected systems and services, such as smart home automation, digital healthcare, and personalized transportation experiences, provide convenience, safety, and personalized experiences. Citizens can access real-time information, participate in decision-making processes, and enjoy more efficient and comfortable urban living.
- *Citizen Engagement and Collaboration:* IoT applications promote citizen engagement and collaboration in smart cities. Through mobile applications, online platforms, and interactive technologies, citizens can actively participate in urban governance, provide feedback, and contribute to community initiatives. This collaboration fosters a sense of ownership and empowers citizens to shape the development and operation of their cities.
- *Challenges and Considerations:* The deployment of IoT applications in smart cities also presents challenges. Data privacy and security concerns must be addressed to protect citizens' sensitive information. Interoperability standards and protocols need to be established to ensure seamless integration and communication among diverse IoT devices and systems. Additionally, cities must address the digital divide to ensure equitable access to IoT-enabled services and technologies.

IoT has the potential to alter urban services, sustainability, citizen involvement, and general quality of life, as evidenced by the observation of its uses in smart cities. Real-time data collection, advanced analytics, and connectivity lay the foundation for efficient resource management and data-driven decision-making. As cities continue to embrace IoT, addressing challenges and considering citizen needs will be crucial to maximize the benefits and create truly smart and inclusive urban environments.

Smart City Infrastructure

- The deployment of IoT solutions is greatly aided by the infrastructure of a smart city. The major components of the smart city infrastructure that enable the integration of IoT devices and sensors will be covered in this chapter's part, including communication networks, cloud computing, data centres, and edge computing (Zanella et al., 2014).
- Firstly, communication networks are essential for connecting IoT devices and sensors to each other and to the internet. The section will discuss the different types of communication networks used in smart cities, including cellular networks, Wi-Fi, and low-power wide-area networks (LPWAN) (Rashid et al., 2016).
- Secondly, a crucial part of the infrastructure for smart cities is cloud computing. It makes it possible to handle and store the enormous amounts of data that IoT devices and sensors produce. Scalability, flexibility, and cost-effectiveness of cloud computing in smart cities will all be covered in this section (Luong et al., 2016).
- Thirdly, for handling and analysing the enormous amounts of data produced by IoT devices and sensors, data centres are crucial. The function of data centres in smart cities, their design and construction, and the significance of data security and privacy will all be covered in this section.
- Lastly, the infrastructure of smart cities is increasingly relying on edge computing. By processing data more quickly and efficiently close to the source, latency and bandwidth usage are reduced. The advantages of edge computing will be covered in this part, including decreased data transmission costs, faster reaction times, and better privacy and security.

Infrastructure for Smart Cities Described

Smart city infrastructure comprises a range of components that work together to enable data collection, analysis, and management as shown in Figure 2. Some of the essential components of smart city infrastructure are:

- *Sensors:* These are devices that can detect changes in the environment, communicate this information to a central system, along with information on air quality, humidity, and temperature.
- *Communication network:* A communication network is required to connect the various devices and sensors in a smart city to a central control system. This can be achieved using wired or wireless networks.
- *Data management system:* large amounts of data are produced by smart cities, and this data need to be managed and analysed. This data must be stored, processed, and analysed using a data management system.
- *Control systems:* Control systems are employed to monitor and control a number of functions in a smart city, including trash disposal, street lighting, and traffic flow.
- *Power supply:* Smart city infrastructure requires a reliable power supply to ensure uninterrupted operation.
- *Security:* Smart city infrastructure must be designed with security in mind to prevent cyber-attacks and ensure the safety and privacy of citizens (Banerjee et al., 2015; Bellavista et al., 2013).

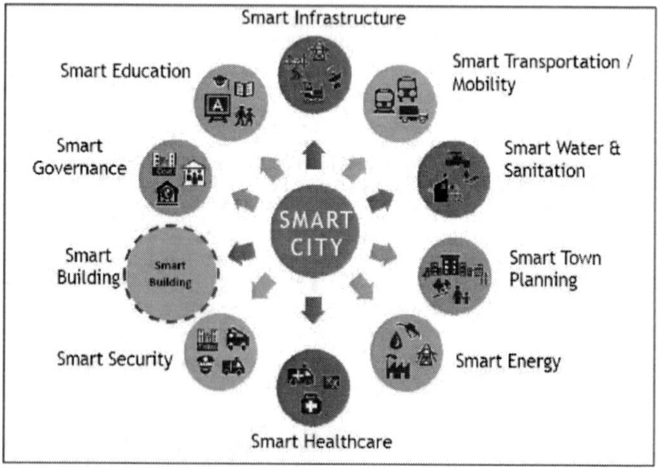

Figure 2. Smart City Components.

Together, these elements make it possible to gather and analyse data that can be used to increase a city's productivity and sustainability (Dwivedi et al, 2015).

IoT's Involvement in Creating the Infrastructure for Smart Cities

- The infrastructure for smart cities is built in large part thanks to the Internet of Things (IoT). IoT devices are integrated into a number of smart city infrastructure components such as traffic management systems, public transportation, energy management systems, and waste management systems. These devices collect data from the environment, process it in real-time, and provide valuable insights that can be used to optimize the functioning of the infrastructure. For example, IoT sensors embedded in traffic management systems can collect real-time data on traffic congestion, pedestrian footfall, and air quality. This data can be used to optimize traffic flow and reduce congestion, which can lead to reduced air pollution and improved public safety (Wang et al., 2015). Similarly, IoT sensors in energy management systems can monitor energy consumption patterns and help optimize energy usage, reducing energy costs and carbon footprint. In summary, the role of IoT in building smart city infrastructure is to provide real-time data, enable predictive analysis, and optimize the functioning of various components of the infrastructure as shown in Figure 3.

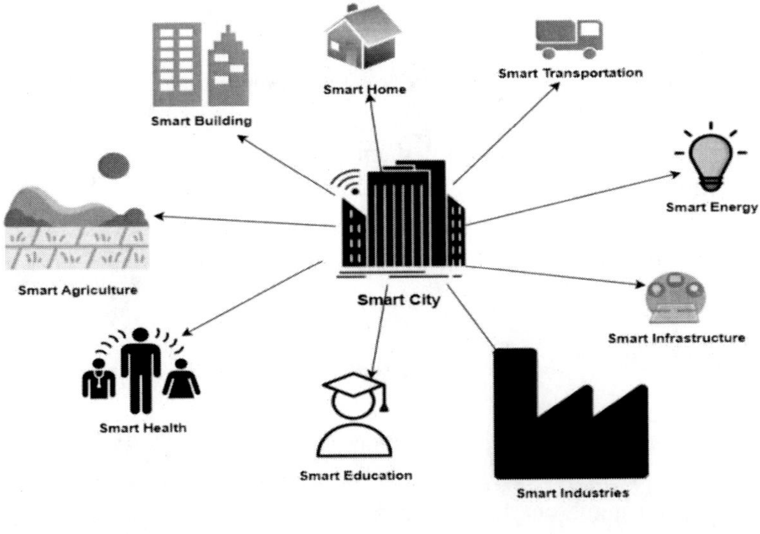

Figure 3. Cloud Based IoT Applications and Role of Smart Cities.

Examples of Smart City Infrastructure Projects

Here are some examples of smart city infrastructure projects that utilize IoT:

1. *Methods for savvy traffic management:* These systems use cameras and IoT sensors to watch traffic, spot accidents, and alter traffic signals for the best possible flow. For instance, Barcelona's implementation of a smart traffic management system resulted in a 21% reduction in traffic congestion.
2. *Smart waste management systems:* These systems optimise waste collection and disposal by using IoT sensors and data analytics, leading to reduced costs and improved environmental sustainability. For example, the city of Amsterdam uses an IoT-based waste management system that saves up to 30% in collection costs.
3. *Smart lighting systems:* These systems use IoT sensors and data analytics to optimize lighting based on occupancy, weather conditions, and time of day. The city of Los Angeles has implemented a smart street lighting system that saves up to $9 million per year and reduces carbon emissions by 60,000 metric tons.
4. *Smart water management systems:* These systems monitor water usage and identify leaks using IoT sensors and data analytics, which improves water conservation and lowers expenses. The city of San Diego, for instance, implemented a smart water management system that resulted in a 20% reduction in water usage.
5. *Smart parking systems:* These systems identify available parking spaces and direct drivers to them using IoT sensors and data analytics, minimising traffic jams and carbon emissions. Madrid has implemented a smart parking system that has decreased CO2 emissions by 9% and traffic congestion by 23%.

IoT Applications for Smart Cities

IoT applications in smart cities are numerous and diverse, providing chances to improve liveability, public services, and resource efficiency. We will give an overview of numerous IoT applications in smart cities in this section and highlight a few particular applications (Murthy, 2015).

1. *Smart transportation systems*
   Smart transport systems are one of the most significant IoT applications in smart cities. These systems aim to reduce traffic congestion, improve public transportation, and enhance road safety. Intelligent traffic management systems, real-time transit information systems, and intelligent parking systems are a few examples of smart transportation systems.
2. *Smart parking systems*
   Smart parking systems are another IoT application that is gaining popularity in smart cities. The goal of these systems is to reduce the amount of time and fuel used for parking search by providing real-time information on available places. By integrating IoT sensors and machine learning algorithms, these systems can efficiently manage parking spaces and reduce traffic congestion (Neyestani et al., 2015).
3. *Smart waste management systems*
   Another IoT application that can assist improve the cleanliness and hygienic conditions of smart cities is smart waste management systems. These devices track the condition of trash cans and provide real-time information on waste levels using Internet of Things sensors. This information can be utilized to streamline waste collection routes, lower collection frequency, and boost waste disposal effectiveness.
4. *Smart energy management systems*
   Systematic smart energy management is another crucial IoT use in smart cities. These technologies seek to increase energy efficiency, lower carbon emissions, and optimise energy use. Smart grid systems, intelligent heating and cooling systems, and smart lighting systems are a few examples of smart energy management systems.
5. *Smart water management systems*
   Another IoT application that can assist enhance the quality and accessibility of water in smart cities is smart water management systems. IoT sensors are used by these systems to track water use, find leaks, and improve water distribution systems. These devices can assist in reducing waste and enhancing the effectiveness of water management by providing real-time information on water usage.

Smart Healthcare Systems

Another IoT application that can help boost the calibre and accessibility of healthcare services in smart cities is smart healthcare systems. These systems track patients' health conditions, offer in-the-moment medical advice, and enable remote consultations via IoT sensors and wearable tech. Intelligent healthcare systems can save costs while enhancing the quality of healthcare services by utilising the potential of IoT and big data analytics and improving patient outcomes (Janani et al., 2021).

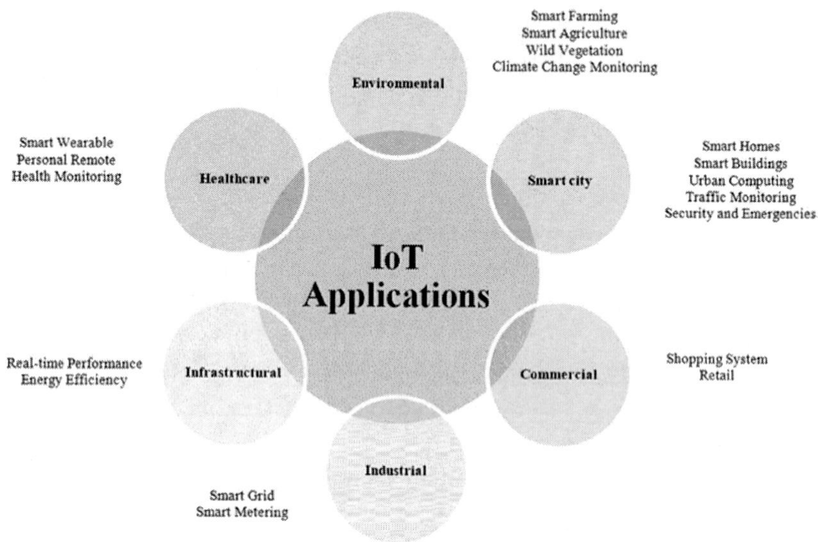

Figure 4. IoT Applications for Smart cities in India.

Smart healthcare systems are among the most promising IoT applications in smart cities. These systems make use of IoT technology to boost the effectiveness and efficiency of healthcare services, eventually raising citizens' quality of life as shown in Figure 4. The following are some of the major IoT uses in modern healthcare systems:

- *Remote patient monitoring:* Vital indicators such as heart rate, blood pressure, and oxygen saturation can be continuously monitored by IoT devices. This makes it possible for medical professionals to remotely monitor individuals and identify potential health problems before they get out of hand.

- *Smart medical devices:* IoT-enabled medical devices, such pacemakers and insulin pumps, can send information about a patient's health straight to medical professionals. This makes it possible for medical professionals to keep track of a patient's status in real time and alter their treatment plan as necessary (Hammi et al., 2018).
- *Predictive analytics:* IoT data can be utilised to create predictive algorithms that pinpoint patients who are most likely to contract specific diseases. This enables medical professionals to take early action and offer preventative care, which can enhance health outcomes and lower medical expenses.
- *Telemedicine*: IoT technologies can be used to deliver healthcare services remotely, such as through video consultations. This enables healthcare providers to deliver care to patients who are unable to travel to a healthcare facility, which can improve access to care in underserved areas (Talari et al., 2017).

IoT technology have the potential to greatly improve the quality and accessibility of healthcare services in smart cities (Gubbi et al., 2013 and Adarsh et al., 2022).

Case Studies of IoT Applications in Smart Cities

Case Study 1: Barcelona Smart City

One of the world's most cutting-edge smart cities is Barcelona, Spain. The city started its Smart City Project in 2011 as a comprehensive initiative to use data and technology to raise the quality of life for its residents. The project is supported by six pillars: smart living, smart mobility, smart environment, smart economy, and smart people (Da Silva et al., 2013). The development of a smart parking system is one of the most effective Internet of Things (IoT) applications in the Barcelona Smart City Project. The system consists of sensors placed on the surface of the road that identify parked cars and transmit the information to a centralized server. The data is then processed and made available to drivers in real-time through a mobile application (Ahlgren et al., 2016; Frincu et al., 2016). The system reduces traffic congestion and air pollution caused by drivers searching for parking spaces, improving the quality of life for citizens.

Another successful IoT application in Barcelona is the smart lighting system. The city has replaced traditional streetlights with LED lights that are connected to a network. The system allows city officials to remotely control the intensity of the lights and detect any malfunctions, improving energy efficiency and reducing maintenance costs. Barcelona has also put in place a smart waste management system that consists of sensors placed in the garbage cans throughout the city. In order to reduce the number of garbage trucks on the road and improve waste collection routes, the sensors monitor the level of the trash cans' fill and transmit the data to a centralised server. This reduces air pollution and traffic congestion and enables city officials to better manage waste collection. In general, the Barcelona Smart City Project shows how IoT applications may enhance inhabitants' quality of life by boosting productivity, lowering traffic, and enhancing environmental sustainability (Fernandez et al, 2016).

Overview of Barcelona Smart City Project

Barcelona Smart City is a flagship project that strives to improve urban sustainability and liability by utilising technology and innovation. The project involves the implementation of a range of smart city solutions that rely heavily on IoT technologies. One of the key components of the project is the development of a comprehensive data platform that enables real-time monitoring of various aspects of city life.

- Role of IoT in Barcelona Smart City project
- Applications of IoT in Barcelona Smart City project
- Benefits and outcomes of Barcelona Smart City project
- Case study 2: Singapore Smart Nation
- Overview of Singapore Smart Nation project
- Role of IoT in Singapore Smart Nation project
- Applications of IoT in Singapore Smart Nation project
- Benefits and outcomes of Singapore Smart Nation project
- Case study 3: Amsterdam Smart City
- Overview of Amsterdam Smart City project
- Role of IoT in Amsterdam Smart City project
- Applications of IoT in Amsterdam Smart City project
- Benefits and outcomes of Amsterdam Smart City project

Case Study 2: Amsterdam's Smart City Project

- *Introduction:* The Netherlands' capital city of Amsterdam has become a model for executing smart city initiatives around the world. The Amsterdam Smart City Project is a comprehensive and collaborative effort to transform the city into a sustainable, connected, and liveable urban environment. This case study explores the key features, initiatives, and impacts of the Amsterdam Smart City Project.
- *Background:* The Amsterdam Smart City Project was initiated in 2009 as a collaborative venture between the municipality of Amsterdam, businesses, knowledge institutions, and citizens. The project intends to address urban difficulties and enhance inhabitants' quality of life by utilising technology and data-driven solutions.

Key Initiatives

a. *Smart Energy Grid:* Amsterdam has implemented a smart energy grid that integrates renewable energy sources, energy storage systems, and smart meters. This allows for efficient energy distribution, load balancing, and real-time monitoring, reducing energy consumption and carbon emissions.
b. *Electric Mobility:* The city promotes electric mobility by establishing a network of electric vehicle charging infrastructure and incentivizing the adoption of electric vehicles. It has also introduced electric shared mobility services, such as electric taxis and public transport options, reducing air pollution and congestion.
c. *Smart Buildings:* Amsterdam encourages the development of energy-efficient and smart buildings. These buildings incorporate advanced technologies for optimized energy use, indoor climate control, and intelligent resource management.
d. *Waste Management:* The city has implemented smart waste management systems, including underground waste containers equipped with sensors that monitor fill levels. This enables efficient waste collection, reducing unnecessary trips and improving overall waste management efficiency.
e. *Citizen Engagement:* The Amsterdam Smart City Project emphasizes citizen participation and engagement. Through digital platforms and initiatives, residents are encouraged to contribute ideas, provide

feedback, and actively participate in shaping the city's smart solutions.

f. *Data and Innovation:* Amsterdam recognizes the value of data and innovation in building a smart city. It promotes open data initiatives, making data accessible to businesses, researchers, and developers to create innovative solutions. The city collaborates with various stakeholders to foster entrepreneurship and supports start-ups working on smart city technologies.

Impact

The Amsterdam Smart City Project has had significant impacts on the city and its residents. Some notable achievements include:

a. Reduction in energy consumption and greenhouse gas emissions.
b. Increased adoption of renewable energy sources.
c. Improved air quality and reduced noise pollution.
d. Enhanced mobility options, including electric vehicles and smart transportation systems.
e. Efficient waste management and reduced waste collection costs.
f. Empowered citizens and improved quality of life through active participation and engagement.

Conclusion

The Amsterdam Smart City Project serves as a model for other cities aspiring to become smarter, more sustainable, and citizen-centric. By leveraging technology, data, and citizen engagement, Amsterdam has successfully implemented various initiatives to address urban challenges and create a more livable and sustainable city. The project's success lies in its collaborative approach, combining the efforts of the government, businesses, knowledge institutions, and residents to drive innovation and positive change.

Case Study 3: Songdo International Business District, South Korea

- *Introduction:* Songdo International Business District (IBD) in South Korea is an innovative and technologically advanced city built from scratch, with a strong focus on integrating IoT (Internet of Things) technologies. This case study explores how Songdo IBD leverages

IoT to create a smart and sustainable urban environment, highlighting key initiatives and the impact on residents and businesses.

- *Background:* Songdo IBD, located near Incheon, was designed as a planned city from the ground up, incorporating cutting-edge infrastructure and IoT technologies. The city aims to be a model for sustainable development and efficient resource management.

IoT Integration

a. Smart Infrastructure: Songdo IBD's infrastructure is embedded with IoT sensors and devices, enabling collecting and analysing data in real-time. This includes smart streetlights, water management systems, and waste management systems. The data collected helps optimize resource usage, improve efficiency, and enhance the overall urban experience.

b. *Intelligent Transportation:* IoT is used extensively in transportation systems, including traffic management, parking guidance, and public transportation. Sensors and cameras monitor traffic flow, provide real-time information to drivers, and enable efficient management of parking spaces. This reduces congestion, improves traffic flow, and enhances the overall transportation experience.

c. *Smart Buildings:* Songdo IBD's buildings are equipped with IoT technologies for energy management, security, and comfort. Sensors and automation systems regulate lighting, heating, and cooling based on occupancy, reducing energy waste. IoT-enabled security systems enhance safety and provide real-time monitoring.

d. *Waste Management:* IoT sensors are integrated into waste management systems, enabling efficient waste collection and recycling. Smart bins equipped with fill-level sensors optimize waste collection routes, minimizing unnecessary pickups and reducing operational costs. This leads to more sustainable waste management practices.

Data Analytics and Decision-Making

Songdo IBD leverages IoT-generated data for advanced analytics and decision-making. By analysing the collected data, city administrators can gain insights into resource usage patterns, traffic patterns, and energy consumption. This data-driven approach helps in making informed decisions to improve city operations, urban planning, and service delivery.

Impact

The integration of IoT technologies in Songdo IBD has resulted in significant impacts:

- Improved energy efficiency through optimized resource management.
- Reduced traffic congestion and enhanced transportation efficiency.
- Enhanced safety and security through real-time monitoring and surveillance.
- Efficient waste management, leading to reduced environmental impact.
- Data-driven decision-making for effective urban planning and resource allocation.

Songdo International Business District serves as a compelling case study for cities looking to embrace IoT technologies to create smart and sustainable urban environments. By integrating IoT into various aspects of city infrastructure, transportation, buildings, and waste management, Songdo IBD has demonstrated the potential of IoT in improving efficiency, sustainability, and quality of life for residents and businesses. The city's success lies in its holistic approach, combining technology, data analytics, and smart governance to create a vibrant and forward-thinking urban environment.

Implementing of IoT Application in Smart Cities in India

In order to address the issues of rapid urbanisation, increase efficiency, and improve the quality of life for its residents, India has been actively deploying IoT applications in smart cities. Several initiatives and projects have been undertaken across the country to leverage IoT technology in smart city development. Here are some key areas where IoT applications are being implemented in Indian smart cities:

1. *Smart Infrastructure and Utilities:* IoT is being utilized to optimize infrastructure and utilities in Indian smart cities. Smart grid solutions are being implemented to improve energy distribution, monitor consumption, and enable demand-response mechanisms. IoT-based water management systems are being deployed to monitor water

supply, detect leaks, and enhance water conservation efforts. These measures increase the infrastructure services' sustainability and efficacy.

2. *Intelligent Transportation Systems:* Indian smart cities are leveraging IoT applications in transportation to alleviate traffic congestion, improve public transportation, and enhance road safety. Real-time traffic monitoring, adaptive signal control, and dynamic route optimisation are all made possible by IoT-based traffic management systems. IoT sensors are used in smart parking solutions to direct drivers to open parking spaces and ease traffic. Connected vehicles and infrastructure enable cooperative driving and enhance transportation efficiency.
3. *Environmental Monitoring and Sustainability:* In India's smart cities, IoT-based environmental monitoring systems are essential. Sensors are deployed to measure air quality, noise levels, temperature, and humidity. Real-time data helps in proactive pollution control, waste management, and urban planning. Smart irrigation systems are being implemented to optimize water usage in parks, gardens, and public spaces. These initiatives contribute to improving environmental sustainability in cities.
4. *Citizen Services and Engagement:* IoT applications in Indian smart cities focus on providing citizen-centric services and enhancing citizen engagement. Real-time information about public services, transportation, and other topics is provided by mobile applications and web platforms, and community events. People can actively participate in decision-making processes, provide feedback, and report issues using IoT-enabled devices and applications. These initiatives empower citizens and promote transparency in urban governance.
5. *Safety and Security:* IoT applications enhance safety and security in Indian smart cities. Connected surveillance cameras, sensors, and analytics systems help in monitoring public spaces, detecting anomalies, and enabling quick response to emergencies. IoT-based street lighting systems improve energy efficiency by adjusting lighting levels based on real-time requirements. These initiatives enhance public safety and promote a secure urban environment.
6. *Waste Management:* Waste management procedures in Indian smart cities are changing as a result of IoT applications. Real-time monitoring of garbage levels is made possible by intelligent waste

containers with sensors, optimizing waste collection routes, and reducing costs. IoT technology is also used for waste sorting and recycling initiatives, promoting sustainable waste management practices.

7. *Data-driven Decision Making:* IoT applications provide enormous volumes of data, which can be used in Indian smart cities for data-driven decision-making. IoT device data collected in real-time enables local officials to analyse patterns, pinpoint areas for improvement, and allocate resources more efficiently. Data analytics and visualization tools enable better urban planning, infrastructure development, and service delivery.

IoT application deployment in Indian smart cities is complicated by issues with interoperability, infrastructure, and data protection. However, the Indian government, along with technology partners and local authorities, is actively working towards overcoming these challenges and scaling up IoT deployments across the country. Overall, the implementation of IoT applications in smart cities in India holds immense potential for improving urban services, sustainability, citizen engagement, and overall quality of life. It is anticipated to have a big impact on how Indian cities develop in the future and help make cities smarter and more habitable.

Key Finding of IoT Application in Smart Cities in India

IoT applications in India's smart cities have generally shown to have a beneficial influence on efficiency, quality of life, environmental sustainability, and citizen engagement. The growth and success of smart cities in India will be aided by ongoing efforts to fix issues and take advantage of IoT's potential.

1. *Enhanced:* Efficiency and Resource Optimization: IoT applications have contributed to improved efficiency and resource optimization in Indian smart cities. Smart grids, intelligent transportation systems, and water management solutions have helped optimize energy consumption, reduce traffic congestion, and enhance water conservation efforts.
2. *Improved Quality of Life:* The quality of living in Indian smart cities has improved because to IoT technologies. Citizen-centric services, such as real-time information on public services and transportation,

mobile applications for citizen engagement, and IoT-enabled safety and security measures, have improved convenience, safety, and overall well-being for residents.

3. *Environmental Sustainability:* IoT applications have played a significant role in promoting environmental sustainability in Indian smart cities. Real-time monitoring of air quality, waste management, and water conservation efforts have led to better pollution control, efficient waste management practices, and optimized resource usage.
4. *Data-driven Decision Making:* IoT applications have generated a wealth of data, enabling data-driven decision-making processes in Indian smart cities. Real-time data collection and analysis have helped city authorities gain insights into various aspects of urban life, leading to informed decision-making, better urban planning, and improved service delivery (Rodrigues et al., 2018).
5. *Citizen Engagement and Participation:* IoT applications have facilitated citizen engagement and participation in Indian smart cities. Mobile applications, online platforms, and IoT-enabled devices have empowered citizens to actively participate in urban governance, provide feedback, and contribute to community initiatives, fostering a sense of ownership and inclusivity.
6. *Challenges and Considerations:* There have been difficulties with IoT application implementation in Indian smart cities such as infrastructure limitations, interoperability issues, and data privacy concerns. Addressing these challenges and ensuring robust security measures are crucial for the successful and widespread adoption of IoT technology in smart cities.

Status of IoT Application in Smart Cities in India in 2023

IoT application deployment in India's smart cities was still ongoing in 2021 as shown in Figure 5. Launched in 2015, the Smart Cities Mission of the Government of India sought to create 100 smart cities across the nation, with a focus on leveraging technology and IoT for sustainable urban development. Here are some key aspects of the status of IoT applications in Indian smart cities:

1. *Pilot Projects and Demonstrations:* Several pilot projects and demonstrations of IoT applications were underway in various smart

cities. Various topics, including intelligent energy management, intelligent transportation systems, waste management, environmental monitoring, and citizen services, were the focus of these projects. These initiatives served as testbeds for evaluating the feasibility and effectiveness of IoT solutions in real-world scenarios.

2. *Deployment of IoT Infrastructure:* The deployment of IoT infrastructure was taking place in many smart cities. This included the installation of IoT sensors, devices, and communication networks to collect and transmit data in real-time. Smart street lighting systems, smart meters for utilities, smart parking solutions, waste bins with sensors, and environmental monitoring stations were being deployed to enable data-driven decision-making and improve city services.

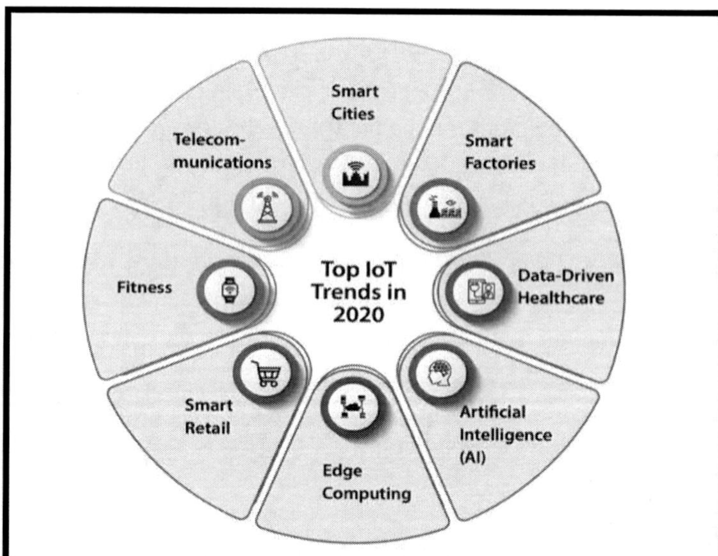

Figure 5. The Top IoT 2020 Trends in India.

3. *Data Analytics and Insights:* IoT-generated data was being processed and analyzed using data analytics platforms. These platforms helped extract valuable insights, patterns, and trends from the collected data. The aim was to derive actionable intelligence for urban planning, resource optimization, and service delivery. Advanced analytics techniques, including machine learning and artificial intelligence, were used to gain deeper insights from the data.

4. *Integration with Existing Systems:* Efforts were being made to integrate IoT applications with existing urban infrastructure and systems. Integration with transportation networks, utility grids, and government service delivery platforms was a focus to ensure seamless operation and efficient data exchange. Interoperability standards and protocols were being developed to enable the integration of various IoT components.
5. *Citizen Engagement and Participation:* IoT applications aimed to enhance citizen engagement and participation in smart cities. Mobile applications, online platforms, and IoT-enabled devices were used to provide citizens with access to real-time information, enable feedback submission, and facilitate participation in decision-making processes. In order to enhance overall quality of life and involve individuals in municipal administration, citizen-centric services were being developed.
6. *Policy and Regulatory Framework:* The government was working on establishing a policy and regulatory framework for IoT applications in smart cities. This included data privacy regulations, cybersecurity guidelines, and standards for IoT deployments. These measures aimed to address concerns related to data security, privacy, and ethical use of IoT technology.
7. *Challenges and Future Directions:* Infrastructure constraints, interoperability concerns, and talent deficiencies made it difficult to develop IoT applications in smart cities. Addressing these challenges and investing in capacity building, research, and innovation were seen as essential to accelerate the adoption and scale-up of IoT applications in smart cities. Continued collaboration between the government, industry, and academia was crucial for fostering innovation and driving the growth of IoT in smart cities in India.

Challenges in Implementing IoT Applications in Smart Cities

1. *Security and Privacy:* Because IoT devices are susceptible to security breaches, they could be the target of cyberattacks. A significant difficulty is ensuring the security and privacy of data that is transmitted and stored by IoT devices.
2. *Scalability:* As smart cities grow and more IoT devices are deployed, managing the scalability of the infrastructure becomes challenging.

To handle the growing number of data and devices, it is important to scale up networks, storage, and processing capacity (Li et al., 2019; Petrolo et al., 2017).

3. *Interoperability:* IoT devices are manufactured by different vendors, using various protocols and standards. Ensuring interoperability and seamless integration among devices and systems from different manufacturers is a complex challenge that needs to be addressed.
4. *Data Management:* Applications for the Internet of Things produce tonnes of data. Gathering, preserving, processing, and analysing this data in real-time is a significant challenge. Efficient data management strategies and infrastructure need to be in place to handle the high data volumes effectively.
5. *Energy Efficiency*: IoT devices require power to operate and stay connected. Energy resources are strained by the extensive deployment of these devices in smart cities. Finding energy-efficient solutions and optimizing power consumption are essential challenges to address.

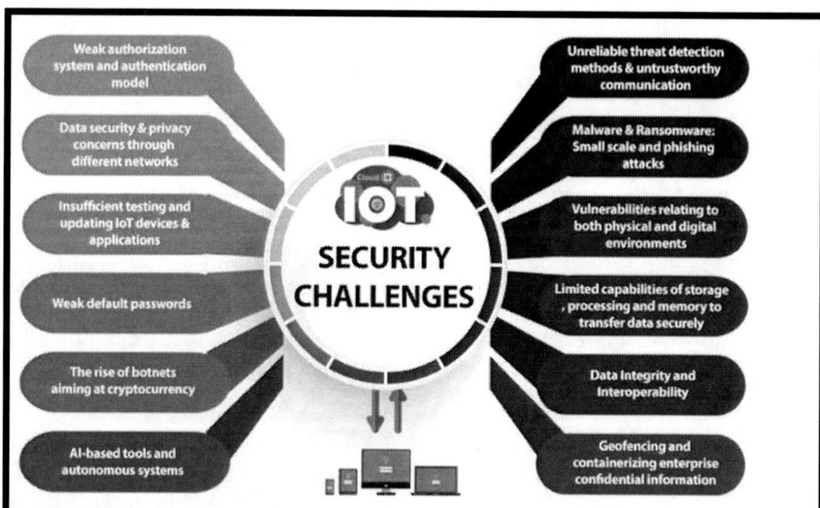

Figure 6. Data Security Council of India (DSCI) identifies issues in securing IoT.

Future Directions for IoT Applications in Smart Cities

1. *Edge Computing:* It is possible to decrease latency, enhance real-time decision-making, and lighten the burden on central cloud infrastructure by moving data processing and analysis closer to the edge devices. When it comes to enabling IoT applications in smart cities, edge computing will be essential.
2. *5G and Beyond:* High-speed, low-latency connectivity will be made available by the rollout of 5G networks, allowing for the seamless integration and communication of a huge number of IoT devices. The possibilities of IoT applications in smart cities will be further enhanced by technologies like 6G, which go beyond 5G.
3. *Artificial Intelligence and Machine Learning:* The enormous amounts of data produced by IoT devices can be analysed by AI and ML algorithms to yield insightful information and allow predictive capabilities. IoT applications with AI and ML integration will open up new opportunities for smart cities.
4. *Blockchain Technology:* Blockchain can enhance security, privacy, and trust in IoT applications. It can provide decentralized and tamper-resistant data storage, authentication, and authorization mechanisms, ensuring the integrity of IoT data in smart cities.
5. *Sustainability and Resilience:* Future IoT applications in smart cities should prioritize sustainability and resilience. Incorporating renewable energy sources, optimizing resource utilization, and designing systems that can withstand disruptions and disasters will be crucial.

Recommendations for Overcoming Challenges and Improving IoT Applications in Smart Cities

1. *Security by Design:* Security should be a fundamental consideration in the design and development of IoT applications as shown in Fig. 6. Employing robust encryption, authentication mechanisms, and secure coding practices will help mitigate security risks.
2. *Standardization and Interoperability:* Encouraging industry-wide standards and protocols for IoT devices will ensure interoperability and seamless integration. Collaborative efforts among stakeholders,

including governments, industries, and standardization bodies, are essential.

3. *Public-Private Partnerships:* Establishing strong partnerships between government entities, private sector organizations, academia, and communities will foster innovation, knowledge sharing, and investment in IoT applications. Initiatives for smart cities can be developed and put into action through public-private partnerships.
4. *Data Governance and Privacy Regulations:* Implementing comprehensive data governance frameworks and privacy regulations is crucial. Governments should establish policies that protect the privacy of citizens' data while enabling the responsible use of IoT-generated data for public benefits.
5. *Citizen Engagement and Education:* Educating citizens about IoT applications, their benefits, and potential risks is essential. Trust, acceptance, and adoption of IoT technology in smart cities will be facilitated by encouraging citizen participation, input, and resolving their concerns.

The Following Suggestions Can Be Taken into Account in Order to Address the Issues and Enhance IoT Applications in Smart Cities

1. *Security by Design:* Implementing security measures in the early stages of IoT application development can help minimize vulnerabilities. This includes using encryption, strong authentication mechanisms, and regular security audits to identify and address potential risks.
2. *Standardization and Interoperability:* Encouraging the adoption of common standards and protocols across IoT devices and systems will promote interoperability. To create and enforce these standards and enable smooth integration and communication across devices from various suppliers, governments and industry organisations should work together.
3. *Public-Private Partnerships:* Foster collaborations between government entities, private sector organizations, academia, and communities. These collaborations can speed the development and implementation of IoT applications in smart cities by leveraging knowledge, assets, and investments.

4. *Data Governance and Privacy Regulations:* Establish robust data governance frameworks and privacy regulations to protect citizen data while enabling the responsible use of IoT-generated data. Governments should define clear guidelines on data collection, storage, usage, and access to maintain transparency and build trust among citizens.
5. *Citizen Engagement and Education:* Participate the public in the creation and implementation of IoT applications. Conduct public awareness campaigns, workshops, and educational programs to educate citizens about the benefits and potential risks of IoT technologies. Encouraging citizen participation and addressing their concerns will build trust and facilitate widespread adoption.
6. *Infrastructure Investment:* To enable the scalability of IoT applications in smart cities, allocate resources for infrastructure development, including networks, storage, and processing capabilities. Investments in technologies like edge computing and high-speed networks such as 5G will enable efficient data processing and real-time decision-making.
7. *Energy Efficiency Solutions:* Encourage the usage of IoT devices that utilise minimal energy and explore renewable energy sources to power these devices. Governments can incentivize manufacturers to develop energy-efficient solutions, and smart energy management systems can optimize power consumption in smart cities.
8. *Continuous Monitoring and Maintenance:* Implement regular monitoring and maintenance procedures to guarantee the efficient running of IoT systems and devices. This includes proactive monitoring of security vulnerabilities, software updates, and regular maintenance checks to identify and fix any issues promptly.

By addressing these challenges and implementing the recommended strategies, IoT applications in smart cities have the potential to become more scalable, secure, and effective, enhancing citizen quality of life and facilitating sustainable urban growth (Cristea et al., 2013; Gluhak et al., 2014).

Discussion

Applications related to the IoT (Internet of Things) have become very popular in this situation of smart cities, revolutionizing the way cities operate, interact, and serve their residents. The discussion of IoT applications in smart cities encompasses several key aspects:

1. *Enhanced Efficiency and Resource Management:* IoT applications enable cities to optimize resource usage increase operational effectiveness. Through collecting and analyzing data in real-time, cities can monitor and manage critical infrastructure systems like energy grids, water networks, and transportation systems more effectively. For example, smart grids enable better energy distribution, reduce waste, and allow for demand response mechanisms. Intelligent transportation systems improve public transportation services by optimizing traffic flow, reducing congestion, and using IoT sensors and data analytics. Such efficiencies result in cost savings, reduced environmental impact, and improved overall resource management.
2. *Improved Public Services and Urban Planning:* IoT apps aid in the improvement of public services in smart cities. Cities can collect real-time data on a variety of topics, including trash management, air quality, and public safety, by using sensors and linked equipment. Predictive maintenance may be implemented, the quality of services can be improved, and well-informed decisions can be made with the help of this data. Urban planning made possible by the Internet of Things (IoT) enables cities to evaluate data on population density, traffic patterns, and environmental elements to create smarter, more liveable cities.
3. *Citizen Engagement and Empowerment:* IoT applications empower citizens to actively participate in urban life and contribute to decision-making processes. Through mobile applications, online platforms, and IoT-enabled devices, citizens can access real-time information, provide feedback, and actively engage in community initiatives. For example, citizens can report issues like potholes or faulty streetlights through mobile apps, enabling authorities to address them promptly. IoT applications foster a sense of ownership and enable citizens to co-create their cities, leading to increased satisfaction, trust, and civic engagement.
4. *Environmental Sustainability and Resilience*: IoT applications play a vital role in promoting environmental sustainability and resilience in smart cities. Real-time monitoring of air quality, noise levels, and waste management enables cities to implement targeted interventions

and improve environmental conditions. IoT-based water management systems help with efficient water usage and conservation. Additionally, IoT devices can assist in early detection and response to natural disasters, improving the overall resilience of cities.

5. *Data Privacy and Security:* The IoT's rapid use in smart cities has led to worries about data security and privacy. As more devices and sensors collect vast amounts of personal and sensitive data, cities must implement robust security measures to protect citizens' information. This includes ensuring secure data transmission, implementing encryption, and implementing access controls to prevent unauthorized access. When developing and implementing IoT applications in smart cities, it is important to take ethical and privacy standards in mind.
6. *Collaborative Ecosystem and Interoperability:* The successful implementation of IoT applications in smart cities requires collaboration among various stakeholders, including city authorities, technology providers, and citizens. Establishing interoperability standards and protocols is crucial to ensuring seamless integration and communication among diverse IoT devices and systems. Open data initiatives and public-private partnerships facilitate the development of a collaborative ecosystem, enabling cities to leverage the expertise and resources of multiple stakeholders.

The discussion of IoT applications in smart cities shows the revolutionary potential of IoT technology in numerous facets of urban life, in light of the foregoing. IoT is a key factor in determining the future of smart cities, with benefits ranging from resource management and public service improvement to increased citizen engagement and environmental sustainability (Bassi and Geir, 2008; Evans, 2011 and Wang and Dennis, 2015). However, challenges such as data privacy, security, interoperability, and citizen inclusivity need to be addressed to maximize the benefits and ensure the long-term success of IoT applications in smart cities.

Conclusion

In conclusion, there are a number of obstacles that need to be resolved in order to adopt IoT applications in smart cities. These issues include security and privacy concerns, scalability problems, interoperability problems, data management challenges, and demands for energy efficiency. However, the importance of IoT applications in developing smart cities cannot be understated. IoT applications enable the collection, analysis, and utilization of real-time data, allowing cities to optimize resource allocation, enhance infrastructure management, improve public services, and promote sustainability. By connecting various devices and systems, IoT applications contribute to the creation of livable, efficient, and sustainable urban environments. Looking towards the future, IoT applications in smart cities hold tremendous potential. Advancements in technologies such as edge computing, 5G, artificial intelligence, machine learning, and blockchain will further enhance the capabilities of IoT applications. Edge computing will reduce latency and enable real-time decision-making, while 5G networks will enable seamless connectivity and the integration of a vast number of IoT devices. The difficulties and potential directions for establishing IoT applications in smart cities were covered in this chapter. The challenges identified included security and privacy concerns, scalability issues, interoperability difficulties, data management complexities, and the need for energy efficiency. These challenges pose obstacles to the successful implementation of IoT applications in smart cities. The future directions highlighted several areas of development. Edge computing was recognized as a crucial technology to reduce latency and improve real-time decision-making. The deployment of 5G and beyond was seen as a significant advancement that would enhance connectivity and integration among IoT devices. IoT applications in smart cities can be improved by the use of blockchain technology, artificial intelligence, and machine learning. Finally, it was emphasised how crucial sustainability and resilience will be for future IoT applications.

IoT applications in smart cities have bright future potential. As technology continues to advance, IoT applications will become more intelligent, interconnected, and integrated. The deployment of technologies such as edge computing, 5G, AI, ML, and blockchain will unlock new possibilities and capabilities. Future IoT applications in smart cities will focus on addressing the challenges discussed earlier, such as security, scalability, interoperability, and data management. These applications will leverage edge computing to process data closer to the devices, ensuring low latency and real-time decision-making. A huge number of IoT devices will be able to connect and integrate with ease once 5G and other technologies are widely used. Furthermore, the integration of AI and ML algorithms will enhance data analysis capabilities, enabling predictive analytics and intelligent automation. Blockchain technology will provide secure and trusted data management and enable decentralized applications. The future prospects also emphasize the importance of sustainability and resilience. IoT applications will incorporate renewable energy sources, optimize resource utilization, and enhance the ability to withstand disruptions and disasters.

References

Adarsh Srivastava, Ankit Yadav, Ashwani Sharma, Sourav Sharma, Mr. Dharmesh Kumar. Smart Cities through IoT. *International Journal for Research in Applied Science & Engineering Technology* (IJRASET, ISSN: 2321-9653) (2022) 10(IV): 2041-2045.

Ahlgren Bengt, Markus Hidell, Edith CH. Ngai. Internet of things for smart cities: Interoperability and open data. *IEEE Internet Computing* (2016) 20(6): 52-56.

Al Fuqaha Ala, Mohsen Guizani, Mehdi Mohammadi, Mohammed Aledhar, Moussa Ayyash. Internet of things: A survey on enabling technologies, protocols, and applications. *IEEE communications surveys & tutorials* (2015) 17(4): 2347-2376.

Arasteh Hamidreza, Hosseinnezhad Vahid, Loia Vincenzo, Tommasetti Aurelio, Troisi Orlando, Shafie khah Miadreza, Siano Pierluigi. IoT-based smart cities: A survey. *In 2016 IEEE 16th International Conference on environment and electrical engineering* (EEEIC) (2016): 1-6.

Banerjee Sayan, Nandi Roshni, Dey Rohan, Nath Saha, Himadri. A review on different Intrusion Detection Systems for MANET and its vulnerabilities. *In 2015 International Conference and Workshop on Computing and Communication* (IEMCON) (2015): 1-7.

Bassi, Alessandro, Geir Horn. Internet of Things in 2020: A Roadmap for the Future. *European Commission: Information Society and Media* (2008) 22: 97-114.

Bellavista Paolo, Giuseppe Cardone, Antonio Corradi, Luca Foschini. Convergence of MANET and WSN in IoT urban scenarios. *IEEE Sensors Journal* (2013) 13(10): 3558-3567.

Bibri Simon Elias, Alahi Alexandre, Ayyoob Sharifi, John Krogstie. Environmentally sustainable smart cities and their converging AI, IoT, and big data technologies and solutions: an integrated approach to an extensive literature review. *Energy Informatics* (2023) 6(1): 9-15.

Borgia Eleonora. The Internet of Things vision: Key features, applications and open issues. *Computer Communications* (2014) 54: 1-31.

Cristea Valentin, Ciprian Dobre, Florin Pop. Context-aware environments for the internet of things. *Internet of Things and inter-cooperative computational technologies for collective intelligence* (2013): 25-49.

Da Silva, Welington M, Alexandre Alvaro, Gustavo HRP Tomas, Ricardo A Afonso, Kelvin L Dias, and Vinicius C Garcia. Smart cities software architectures: a survey. In *Proceedings of the 28th Annual ACM Symposium on Applied Computing* (2013): 1722-1727.

Didier El Baz, Julien Bourgeois. Smart cities in Europe and the alma logistics project. *ZTE Communications* (2015) 13(4): 10-15.

Djahel Soufiene, Ronan Doolan, Gabriel Miro Muntean, John Murphy. A communications-oriented perspective on traffic management systems for smart cities: Challenges and innovative approaches. *IEEE Communications Surveys & Tutorials* (2014) 17(1): 125-151.

Dwivedi Manish, Uniyal, Aniruddha, Mohan Rajiva. New Horizons in Planning Smart Cities using LiDAR Technology. *IJARSGIS* (ISSN-2394-8698) (2015) 2(1): 40-50.

Evans Dave. The internet of things: How the next evolution of the internet is changing everything. *CISCO white paper* (2011) 1: 1-11. http://www.cisco.com/c/dam/en_us/about/ac79/docslinnov/IoT_IBSG_0411FINAL.pdf.

Fernandez Anez, Victoria. Stakeholders approach to smart cities: A survey on smart city definitions. *In Smart Cities: First International Conference* Proceedings, Smart-CT 2016, Málaga, Spain, June 15-17, 2016, Springer International Publishing (2016) 1: 157-167.

Frincu Marc, Draghici Robert. Towards a scalable cloud enabled smart home automation architecture for demand response. In 2016 *IEEE PES Innovative Smart Grid Technologies Conference Europe* (ISGT-Europe) (2016): 1-6.

Gluhak Alexander, Sebastian Lange, Henrich C Pöhls. A survey of middleware for the Internet of Things: Current and future trends. *IEEE Internet of Things Journal* (2014) 1(5): 430-454.

Gubbi Jayavardhana, Rajkumar Buyya, Slaven Marusic, Marimuthu Palaniswami. Internet of Things (IoT): A vision, architectural elements, and future directions. *Future generation computer systems* (2013) 29(7): 1645-1660.

Hammi Badis, Rida Khatoun, Sherali Zeadally, Achraf Fayad, Lyes Khoukhi. IoT technologies for smart cities. *IET networks* (2018) 7(1): 1-13.

Ijaz Sidra, Munam Ali Shah, Abid Khan, Mansoor Ahmed. Smart cities: A survey on security concerns. *International Journal of Advanced Computer Science and Applications* (2016) 7(2): 612-625.

Janani RP, Renuka Aruna, AK, Lakshmi Narayanan. IoT in smart cities: A contemporary survey. *Global Transitions Proceedings* (2021) 2: 187–193.

Laya Andres, Bratu Vlad loan, Markendahl. Who is investing in machine-to-machine communications. *Proc. 24th Eur. Reg. ITS Conf. Technology*, Investment and Uncertainty, Florence, Italy, Publisher: *International Telecommunications Society (ITS)*, 20th-23rd October (2013).

Li Siqi, Kewei Sha, Jianhua Ma, Yuhui Zheng, Zhenghui Jiang. A Survey on Internet of Things: Architecture, Enabling Technologies, Security and Privacy, and Applications. *IEEE Access* (2019) 7: 99447-99465.

Luigi Atzori, Antonio Iera, Giacomo Morabito. The internet of things: A survey. *Computer networks* (2010) 54(19): 2787-2805.

Luong, Nguyen Cong, Dinh Thai Hoang, Ping Wang, Dusit Niyato, Dong In Kim, Zhu Han. Data collection and wireless communication in Internet of Things (IoT) using economic analysis and pricing models: A survey. *IEEE Communications Surveys & Tutorials* (2016) 18(4): 2546-2590.

Murthy C. *Emerging Geospatial Trends in Smart City Development.* In Hyderabad International Convention Centre, Hyderabad, and India geospatial forum (2015).

Neyestani Nilufar, Damavandi Maziar Yazdani, Shafie Khah Miadreza, Contreras Javier, Catalão João PS. Allocation of plug-in vehicles' parking lots in distribution systems considering network-constrained objectives. *IEEE Transactions on Power Systems* (2014) 30(5): 2643-2656.

Neyestani Nilufar, Maziar Yazdani Damavandi, Miadreza Shafie Khah, and João PS Catalão. Modeling the PEV traffic pattern in an urban environment with parking lots and charging stations. In 2015 *IEEE Eindhoven Power Tech* (2015): 1-6.

Pellicer Soledad, Guadalupe Santa, Andres L Bleda, Rafael Maestre, Antonio J Jara, Antonio Gomez Skarmeta. A global perspective of smart cities: A survey. In 2013 Seventh International Conference on *Innovative Mobile and Internet Services in Ubiquitous Computing* (2013): 439-444.

Perera Charith, Yongrui Qin, Julio C Estrella, Stephan Reiff Marganiec, Athanasios V Vasilakos. Fog computing for sustainable smart cities: A survey. *ACM Computing Surveys* (CSUR) (2017) 50(3): 1-43.

Petrolo Riccardo, Valeria Loscri, Nathalie Mitton. Towards a smart city based on cloud of things, a survey on the smart city vision and paradigms. *Transactions on emerging telecommunications technologies* (2017) 28(1): 2931.

Rashid Bushra, Mubashir Husain Rehmani. Applications of wireless sensor networks for urban areas: A survey. *Journal of network and computer applications* (2016) 60: 192-219.

Rathore M Mazhar, Awais Ahmad, Anand Paul, Seungmin Rho. Urban planning and building smart cities based on the internet of things using big data analytics. *Computer Networks* (2016) 101: 63-80.

Rodrigues Joel JPC, Rui J Lopes, Pedro JS Cardoso, Francisco LG Marques, Filipe F Faria. Internet of Things for Smart Cities: Interoperability and Open Data. *IEEE Communications Magazine* (2018) 56 (9): 40-45.

Shuai Wenjing, Patrick Maillé, Alexander Pelov. Charging electric vehicles in the smart city: A survey of economy-driven approaches. *IEEE Transactions on Intelligent Transportation Systems* (2016) 17(8): 2089-2106.

Talari Saber, Miadreza Shafie Khah, Pierluigi Siano, Vincenzo Loia, Aurelio Tommasetti, and João PS Catalão. A review of smart cities based on the internet of things concept. *Energies* (2017) 10(4): 421.

Wang Li and Dennis Sng. Deep learning algorithms with applications to video analytics for a smart city: A survey. *arXiv preprint* arXiv:1512.03131 (2015).

Zanella Andrea, Nicola Bui, Angelo Castellani, Lorenzo Vangelista, Michele Zorzi. Internet of things for smart cities. *IEEE Internet of Things journal* (2014) 1(1): 22-32.

Zhang Daqing, Laurence T Yang. Guest editorial: Internet of things in smart environments. *IEEE Internet of Things Journal* (2014) 1(2): 81-82.

Chapter 4

IoT-based Photovoltaic Monitoring System: Need, Trends, Architecture, and Future Directions

Suman Lata*, PhD
Tarun Varshney, PhD
Soma Deb, PhD
and Burhan U Din Abdullah, MTech
Department of Electrical Electronics and Communication Engineering,
Sharda School of Engineering and Technology, Sharda University, India

Abstract

This chapter focuses on the need, design trends, and future directions of IoT-based photovoltaic (PV) system monitoring. The output of PV systems varies with changes in environmental conditions. The main environmental parameters impacting PV module performance are atmospheric temperature, humidity, dust, and luminosity. Monitoring individual solar panels can help maximize energy production by reducing energy loss and identifying areas where the system is not operating efficiently. By monitoring the performance of the solar energy system over time, PV monitoring can help in the prediction of maintenance needs. IoT-based PV monitoring is a good option for real-time monitoring, reducing the need for manual data collection and saving time and resources. IoT monitoring can be used for monitoring the hazardous environmental conditions for PV and helping the user take appropriate actions before any failure occurs.

* Corresponding Author's Email: Suman.Lata@dr.sharda.ac.in.

In: The Future of IoT with Automation in Engineering and Modern Technology
Editors: Sandeep Gupta and Tarun Varshney
ISBN: 979-8-89113-655-7

Keywords: internet of things, irradiance, monitoring, photovoltaics, renewable

Introduction

Solar energy, harnessed through Photovoltaic (PV) systems, has emerged as a transformative solution to address the growing challenges of climate change, depleting fossil fuels, and energy security. Solar energy offers a long-term and sustainable energy supply as a renewable energy source. Investing in solar energy infrastructure is a step towards securing a reliable and stable energy future. Solar energy is a renewable and sustainable resource that offers numerous benefits, and PV systems play a crucial role in converting sunlight into electricity. Solar energy is derived from the sun's rays, which are abundant and available throughout the day. Unlike fossil fuels, solar energy is clean and does not produce harmful greenhouse gas emissions or air pollutants during operation. This characteristic makes solar power a critical component in reducing carbon emissions and mitigating the impacts of global warming. As a renewable energy source, solar energy offers a long-term and sustainable energy supply. Unlike fossil fuels, which are finite and subject to price fluctuations, solar energy relies on a constant and inexhaustible source, the sun. Investing in solar energy infrastructure is a step towards securing a reliable and stable energy future.

A photovoltaic (PV) system is the primary technology used to capture solar energy and convert it into electricity. PV systems consist of solar panels made of semiconductor materials, typically silicon, which absorb sunlight and release electrons. When sunlight strikes the solar cells, electrons are freed, creating an electric current that can be harnessed as electricity. The generated electricity can be used to power homes, businesses, and industries and even support off-grid applications. Due to technological advancements, declining costs, and supportive government policies, the adoption of PV systems has increased significantly globally. Improvements in PV cell efficiency and manufacturing processes have increased the energy output of solar panels, making them more economically viable and appealing to consumers and businesses (Rasheed et al., 2021). PV systems offer various advantages, making them a sustainable and attractive energy option. One of their key benefits is their modularity and scalability. Solar panels can be installed on rooftops and open spaces and even integrated into building facades, allowing for distributed energy generation. This decentralization reduces the need for long-distance power transmission and improves energy security (Shrihariprasath et al., 2016).

Keeping in mind the simultaneous increase in demand for power and reduction in greenhouse emissions, most of the electrical utilities are inclined towards the use of renewable energy resources over non-renewable sources. Among renewable energy resources, solar energy is considered a vital sustainable resource for electrification. That is why day by day, at the global level, solar energy covers a major portion of the cumulative installed renewable capacity (Phung et al., 2017). To utilize this resource, a photovoltaic (PV) system is needed. PV system transforms directly, sunlight directly into electrical energy. The following subsections discuss the basic PV system, the mathematical modeling of PV systems under various environmental conditions, and the advantages of IoT-based monitoring in detail.

Photovoltaic (PV) System

The basic component of a PV system is a solar cell. It follows the principle of the photovoltaic effect. The electrical properties of a PV cell vary when it is exposed to light. A solar cell is a p-n junction diode. A single-junction silicon solar cell produces an approximate open-circuit voltage of 0.5 V to 0.6 V, which is insufficient to use as a generating source for outside applications. Solar cells are appropriately grouped for the formation of modules. Several modules are connected in various configurations to increase the voltage and current ratings of a solar panel. A considerable amount of renewable energy can be generated only when individual solar cells are combined into a large solar panel. The analogous circuit that represents the PV cell is given below in Figure 1.

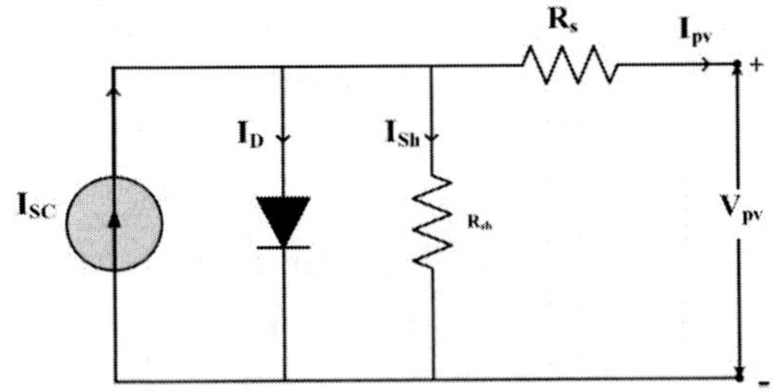

Figure 1. Representation of a PV cell.

Output current, often known as I_{PV}, may be calculated concerning the model's output voltage (V_{PV}). Irradiance (G), and cell temperature (TC), all have an impact on the power, current, and voltage output of the model of a PV cell. Equations 1 and 2 are the current-voltage (I-V) characteristic equations for a photovoltaic (PV) cell, which relate the current output (I_{PV}) to its voltage output (V_{PV}) under different lighting conditions.

$$I_{PV} = I_{SC} \times \left[1 - A_1 \times \left(e^{\left(\frac{V_{PV}}{A_2 \times V_{OC}}\right)} - 1\right)\right] \tag{1}$$

where,

$$A_1 = \left(1 - \frac{I_{MP}}{I_{SC}}\right) \times e^{\left(\frac{-V_{MP}}{A_2 \times V_{OC}}\right)}$$
$$and \qquad A_2 = \frac{\left(\frac{V_{MP}}{V_{OC}} - 1\right)}{\ln\left(1 - \frac{I_{MP}}{I_{SC}}\right)} \tag{2}$$

where,

A_1 is a parameter that depends on a photovoltaic cell's characteristics. It can be observed that A_1 decreases as I_{MP} / I_{SC} increase. Parameter A_2 controls the rate at which A1 decreases as V_{MP} increases. I_{MP} represents the current generated by the PV cell at the maximum power point (MPP) and I_{SC} is the short-circuit current of the PV cell and is defined as the current generated when the voltage across the cell or module is zero. V_{MP} is the voltage at MPP. V_{OC} is the PV cell open-circuit voltage and refers to the voltage generated when the current through the cell or module is zero. Parameter A_2 gives a measure of the curvature of the I-V characteristics of the PV cell and is dependent on the properties of the PV cell. A_2 increases as the ratio of I_{MP}/I_{SC} rises and V_{MP} approaches V_{OC}. Irradiance and temperature are two major factors that influence the values of the parameters V_{MP}, I_{MP}, V_{OC}, and I_{SC} for the PV panel. Equations (3) relate the current-voltage, characteristics of a photovoltaic module as a function of temperature (T ℃) and irradiance (G), among other parameters.

$$I_{SC}(G, T_C) = I_{SCS} \times \frac{G}{G_S} \times \left(1 + \delta \times (T_C - T_S)\right) \tag{3}$$

$$I_{MP}(G, T_C) = I_{MPS} \times \frac{G}{G_S} \times \left(1 + \delta \times (T_C - T_S)\right) \tag{4}$$

I_{SC} (G, T_C) represents the short-circuit current under given irradiance and temperature conditions. The short-circuit current at standard test conditions (STC) is represented by I_{SCS}. The standard test conditions are i) 25°C cell temperature and ii) 1.5 kg air mass. GS is the reference irradiance (1000 W/m2) and δ is the temperature coefficient at short-circuit current, which measures how much the current decreases as temperature rises.

IMP (G, T_C) is the maximum power point (MPP) current that has been generated by the PV cell under given irradiance and temperature conditions. Under STC, I_{MPS} is the current at MPP. Using the above parameters and their dependencies, Equation (3) connects I_{SC} and IMP to G and T_C. The open circuit voltage for a given cell temperature (T_C), $V_{OC}(T_C)$ and maximum power point voltage generated by a PV cell can be represented mathematically as given below in Equations 4.

Where, the open circuit voltage at STC is denoted by V_{OCS}. The ε is the temperature coefficient of the open-circuit voltage and is a measure of the variation of voltage with temperature. VMPS is the voltage at MPP at STC. So, Equation (4) uses the above parameters and their dependencies to relate V_{OC} and V_{MP} to T_C. The mathematical model (T_C) is given by Equation 5 below.

$$T_C = 1.14 \times (T - T_S) + 0.0175 \times (G - 300) \quad (5)$$

The module temperature (T) and irradiance are functions that determine the cell temperature (T_C). The reference temperature, T_S, is 25 °C. Using a simplified model of the thermal behavior of the PV module, the equation connects T_C to T and G. These equations collectively offer a thorough representation of the I-V properties of a PV module under different levels of irradiance and temperature conditions, taking into account the effects of temperature coefficients and other parameters. Figure 2 represents the current I-V and power vs. voltage characteristics of a photovoltaic cell under variable environmental conditions.

From the above discussions, it can be concluded that the output of the PV system is variable, and for the generation of optimized power from it, appropriate environmental conditions are to be maintained, hence the need for monitoring the PV system. A major challenge in studying the performance of a PV system is that it is a dynamic system where changes in input parameters result in a change in output power generated by the PV module. Thus, a real-time remote monitoring system is needed for the assessment of its performance.

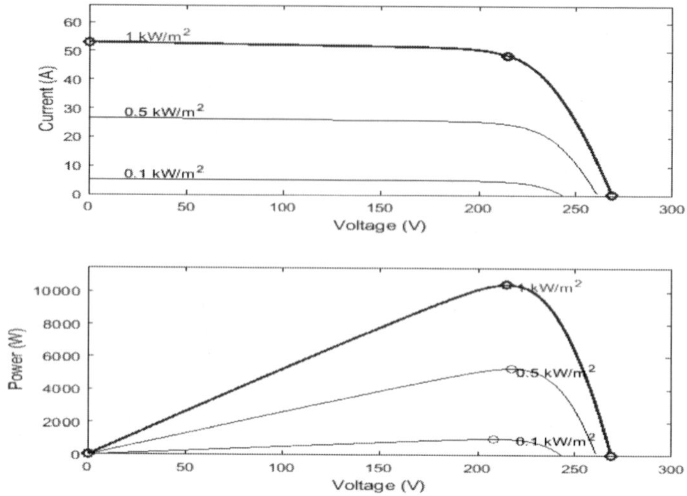

Figure 2. IV and PV characteristics of Photovoltaic cell.

Need for Monitoring of PV System

The capacity of photovoltaic (PV) solar systems to generate electricity is sensitive to changes in a wide range of characteristics, including the temperature of the surrounding air, the amount of solar radiation, and the prevailing weather. According to Shrihariprasath et al., (2016), it is thus very important to monitor the conditions of such installations. Monitoring the performance of a photovoltaic (PV) system is essential to guaranteeing that a solar energy system will operate at its highest level of productivity and efficiency. The following are some of the reasons why monitoring photovoltaic systems is crucial:

a. PV monitoring systems can discover problems with solar panels before they cause a major drop in the amount of energy produced. This benefit is known as "detection." Because of this, it may be possible to avoid costly repairs and downtime.
b. Maximizing Energy Output: PV monitoring may contribute to the identification of areas where improvements can be made to maximize energy output by monitoring the performance of individual solar panels and the system as a whole. This might involve optimizing the

positioning of panels and altering the angle of the panels to catch more sunlight.

c. Efficiency Improvement: PV monitoring systems may detect portions of the system that are not performing effectively, such as when there is a mismatch between the output of the solar panels and the inverter. This allows for improvements to be made to the system's overall efficiency. If you put this information to use, you can improve the efficiency of the system and reduce the amount of energy lost.
d. Preventing the Need for Maintenance by Monitoring System Performance Over Time: PV monitoring may help prevent the need for maintenance by monitoring the performance of the solar energy system over time. This can help determine when panels need to be replaced or cleaned. Therefore, the amount of money spent on maintenance and the number of times it is required could be reduced.

IoT-Based PV Monitoring

A photovoltaic (PV) system is a sustainable and renewable energy solution that has gained significant popularity as the world seeks cleaner alternatives to traditional fossil fuels. Concurrently, the Internet of Things (IoT) has emerged as a transformative technology that connects physical devices and objects, enabling data exchange and intelligent automation. It has found immense applications (Li Da et al., 2014). The integration of PV systems with IoT offers a myriad of advantages that enhance the efficiency, reliability, and management of solar power generation. IoT devices, such as sensors and smart meters, can be incorporated into PV installations to provide real-time monitoring of critical parameters, including solar irradiance, panel temperature, and energy production. The remote monitoring of PV cells can boost the efficiency of maintenance. The emerging paradigm of the Internet of Things (IoT) and the availability of low-cost sensors (wearable, implantable, and environmental) can bring lots of benefits to efficient clean energy production and the monitoring of the state of PV cells (Deriche et al., 2019). This real-time monitoring capability allows for proactive management, as operators can quickly detect any deviations in performance and respond promptly to optimize energy generation.

The integration and stability of the grid are also improved by the combination of photovoltaic (PV) systems and the Internet of Things (IoT). It is possible for smart grids powered by the Internet of Things to connect in both directions with solar panels and other renewable energy sources. This communication makes it possible to manage the supply and demand of energy effectively, which helps to balance the intermittent nature of solar power and maintain grid stability. Using IoT technology for monitoring solar photovoltaic systems can improve the normal operation and maintenance of solar power plants. The use of IoT overcomes the risks associated with wired systems (Shrihariprasath et al., 2016).

IoT solutions are constructed from a range of components, including physical devices such as sensors, actuators, and interactive gadgets, in addition to a network that connects all of these individual components together. These components capture data, collect that data, and do analysis on it before delivering orders to their actuators, which ultimately results in an improved monitoring system. Because there are so many benefits associated with utilizing the Internet of Things (IoT) for monitoring:

a. M*onitoring system* that is based on the IoT might be a suitable choice if you want to keep track of the health of PV panels as well as the amount of solar energy they generate. IoT devices may gather data and communicate it in real time, delivering up-to-the-minute information on a broad variety of factors such as temperature, humidity, and motion. One of the major advantages is real-time monitoring. Real-time monitoring is one of the major benefits.
b. *Increased productivity*: Because Internet of Things monitoring systems can gather data automatically, they may minimize the need for manual data collection, which saves both time and resources.
c. *Predictive maintenance*: IoT sensors can identify when equipment is beginning to exhibit indications of wear and tear, which allows maintenance staff to undertake repairs before any problem occurs.
d. *Cost reductions*: Internet of Things monitoring may help decrease costs by minimizing the need for human labor, decreasing downtime due to faults in equipment, and optimizing the amount of energy used.
e. *Increased safety*: sensors connected to the internet of things may be used to monitor potentially harmful areas, such as factories or mines, helping to keep employees safe by recognizing and reacting to risky circumstances.

The need for an IoT-based photovoltaic (PV) monitoring system stems from the increasing importance of solar energy as a clean and renewable power source. PV systems play a crucial role in generating electricity from sunlight, but to ensure their optimal performance and maximize energy efficiency, real-time monitoring and data-driven insights are essential. IoT-based monitoring systems offer a range of benefits that address these needs, making them an indispensable tool in the solar energy industry. There is a potential to reduce the operating and maintenance (O&M) expenses associated with stand-alone PV systems by using remote monitoring systems that are based on the Internet of Things (IoT). This research investigates the features of the IoT platforms that are most often used, as well as their capabilities and the operational and maintenance cost reductions that are linked to them. A study of the costs of avoided field trips is done using three solar PV plants that are monitored from afar (Renata et al., 2019). This is done by grouping together system problems and ignoring the more serious ones that need to be seen in person.

Real-time monitoring is a fundamental requirement for PV systems to track their performance and health continuously. IoT-enabled sensors integrated into the PV installations collect data on various parameters such as solar irradiance, temperature, and energy production, transmitting it to a central monitoring platform (Badave et al., 2018). This real-time data empowers system operators to promptly detect and address any anomalies, ensuring that the PV system operates at its peak efficiency and minimizing downtime (Li et al., 2017).

One of the most important aspects of improving the efficiency of solar power production is the optimization of energy processes. During times of high solar generation and low energy demand, for example, the Internet of Things system can direct surplus electricity to energy storage systems or feed it back into the grid, thereby optimizing energy self-consumption and minimizing waste. This takes place because IoT devices within the PV system analyze real-time data on patterns of energy consumption and adjust energy use accordingly.

Grid operators can balance the intermittent nature of solar energy with the energy requirements of consumers, ensuring grid stability and reliability. In remote or off-grid areas, where PV systems are often deployed, IoT-based monitoring systems are particularly valuable. With remote access and control capabilities, these systems allow operators to monitor and manage PV systems in distant or inaccessible locations (Gupta et al., 2018). This enhances the feasibility and efficiency of rural electrification projects and microgrid setups. An IoT-based photovoltaic monitoring system is crucial for the efficient and sustainable management of solar energy. Real-time monitoring, predictive maintenance, energy optimization, grid integration, and remote accessibility are among the many advantages that IoT brings to PV systems. The IoT-based system does not require any manual intervention. All the data is stored, but in this way, we can also store the data for future reference.

Designing of IoT-Based PV Monitoring System

Following a typical design of a complete architecture of an IoT-based PV monitoring system, the following section considers current trends in PV monitoring through a literature review.

Recent Trends

In the literature, many solutions for monitoring PV systems are available for achieving various goals. A summary of such solutions is presented hereafter. To achieve better management and repair of PV systems, an intelligent remote monitoring system using GPRS, and gateways has been proposed by the authors (Shrihariprasath et al., 2016).

Various research articles focusing on monitoring PV systems using IoT to manage the flow of power and system instabilities are available in the literature (Phung et al., 2017; Patil et al., 2017; Jana et al., 2016). Integration of IoT, servers, and terminal applications can be done with fewer errors using ZigBee and the 4G module. The authors (Kun Xai et al., 2020) have proposed as well as validated such work using hardware. The authors concluded that preventive maintenance could not only extend the life of PV systems but also lower running costs. The authors (P. Srivastava et al., 2018) implemented an IoT-based monitoring and control strategy for a hybrid power plant. A web-based remote monitoring solution for PV systems has been presented by the authors (Nicoleta et al., 2013). An ARM Cortex-M3 microcontroller has been considered in this solution. An IoT solution for monitoring three grid-connected distributed power plants has been considered by the authors (Renata et al., 2019). A CC3200 microcontroller with ARM Cortex-M4 as the core processor has been considered by authors (Badave et al., 2018) for monitoring the health of the PV system. 30 seconds was the sampling time used in this system.

Monitoring of various meteorological parameters that impact the performance of PV systems has been considered by (Li et al., 2017). The authors proposed a system for monitoring PV consisting of a data acquisition module and a data gateway module. DSP-TMS320F28335 has been used in this work for collecting data from sensors. Through the ZigBee network, the acquired data was transmitted to the data gateway along with the geographic information via the GPS module. The paper (Mondal et al., 2022) implemented a remote PV monitoring system on a 20-watt solar panel. Arduino Uno has been used for the collection of data from sensors and further sending it to BOLT using serial communication. BOLT has been used for graphically displaying the various solar parameters.

An Internet of Things (IoT)-based embedded monitoring system that gives real-time information on photovoltaic (PV) systems was disclosed in the paper (Kekre et al., 2017). The writers of this study published the data on the internet using a GPRS module. Priharti, W., et al., (2019) described a solar PV monitoring system that is Internet of Things-based. The information was seen on a smartphone in this instance. The authors concluded that the transmission time is much longer than it may be in the future. The Internet of Things was used to create a solar power monitoring system, as described by the paper's concept (Gupta, A.K. et al., 2018). Monitoring of the sun-tracking system was the primary focus of attention. An ESP32 board, an MPPT circuit, a shunt resistor lithium battery, an active Wi-Fi network, a temperature sensor, and a voltage divider circuit are the primary components used in the completion of this work. The authors of this paper only considered the influence of a single parameter, namely temperature. The authors (Cheragee et al., 2021) reported on a real-time solar power monitoring system that uses the Internet of Things. The system built has been used to gather environmental data in real time from a PV panel and to continually monitor the amount of electricity that is produced by the panel. Mule et al. (2016) reported on solar panel monitoring systems that use the Internet of Things to predict failure. Pereira et al. (2019) developed an Internet of Things monitoring system with the goal of measuring the temperature of the PV module's center as well as its outside border. During this investigation, a comparative examination of the temperatures at the center and edges was carried out using embedded Internet of Things technologies. An experimental investigation using an advanced virtual RISC (AVR) AT mega microprocessor was published by Abou Saltouh Tarek M.E. and colleagues (2018). This study was conducted to monitor the sun in PV systems. The paper (Basir Khan et al., 2012) described a method for tracking the efficiency of wireless photovoltaic modules in a monitoring system. The authors of this paper set out to determine which PV modules operate under less-than-ideal conditions, which may take place as a result of an increase in the temperature of PV cells, a reduction in the performance of PV modules, or a decrease in the Maximum Power Point Tracker (MPPT) performance. The microcontroller boards, used in the study and created by a number of different manufacturers employing a wide range of microcontrollers, were the ones used. The paper (Kartikh et al., 2019) provided an explanation of a method that could be used to monitor the accumulation of dust on solar panels. This would allow for the collection of the maximum amount of power feasible for application, which would lead to an improvement in the effectiveness of solar panels. Controllers, node microcontroller units (MCUs), and light-dependent resistor (LDR) sensors are the components that come together to form a functional system. An independent building solar photovoltaic (PV) monitoring system as well as a solar photovoltaic (PV) system for the fertigation system were both created by the authors (Abudullah et al., 2020), who reported their results. In their study, Njoka et al. (2022) conducted an investigation of the capabilities of the Internet of Things platforms that are most frequently used, as well as the corresponding savings in the costs of operation and maintenance. An internet framework was explored by Madadi S. et al. (2021) with the intention of maximizing the amount of electricity that solar panels produce. Several metrics relating to the solar panel are shown on the LCD screen thanks to the Internet of Things technology. These characteristics include temperature, current, and voltage. According to the paper (Ranjit et al., 2018), monitoring the health of solar photovoltaic panels serves an important role. The integration of an Internet of Things-based system with four thermocouples of the K-type as temperature sensors was demonstrated by the authors. Each thermocouple was wired up to an amplifier for thermocouples that was manufactured by Adafruit and numbered MAX31855. The Raspberry Pi Zero Wireless, an Adafruit MAX31855 thermocouple amplifier, and an INA219 voltage/current sensor were the other components that were used. Several other writers, including Srinivasan et al., have also taken into consideration the Raspberry Pi and flask frameworks. The paper (Abdullah et al., 2022) developed a remote photovoltaic (PV) monitoring system that was constructed using nodeMCU and Thing Talk cloud servers. In their research, the authors made use of a variety of sensors, including current sensors, voltage sensors, and dual temperature and humidity sensors. The authors have taken into account previous research that is comparable to their own (Samuel et al., 2021; Mangore et al., 2022; Manish Katyrmal et al., 2018; Shailesh Sarswat et al., 2019; Babu et al., 2018; Sutikno et al., 2021; N. M. Kumar et al., 2022). An Internet of Things system was built by the authors Kavidha, V., and Malathi, V., for the purpose of collecting and analyzing solar energy parameter data. The fundamental purpose of the study that has been published is to anticipate PV performance in order to guarantee consistent electricity production. Several alternative graphs have been constructed to illustrate the various parameters.

Design and Implementation

A typical block diagram of the IoT-based monitoring of PV systems is given below in Figure 3. It has both hardware and software parts.

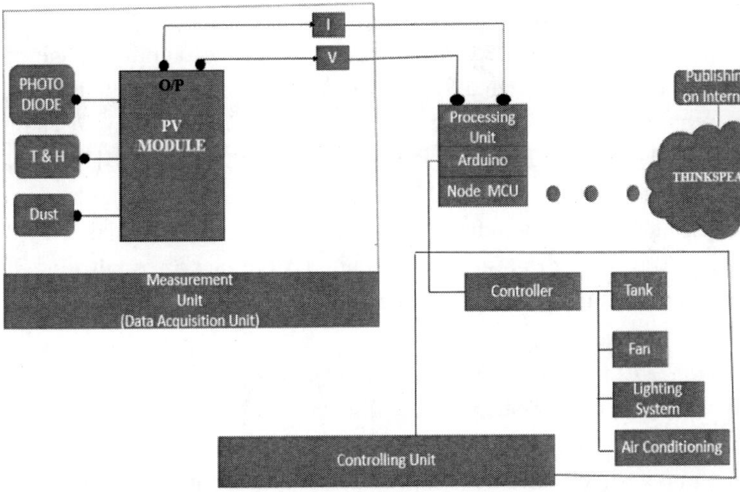

Figure 3. A typical block diagram of an IoT-based PV monitoring system.

Hardware Section

The hardware part of the monitoring module consists of two major units, namely, the measurement (data acquisition) unit and the processing unit. Many miscellaneous components may be added as per the need. The details of these units have been discussed in the following sections:

Measurement Section

The measuring section comprises sensors necessary for detecting the input factors that will affect the output of the PV module. Additionally, the sensors necessary for measuring the output current and output voltage are needed.

Power calculations can be done by using the acquired voltage and current. Sensors form the front end of this monitoring system. The sensors sense real-time physical variables and produce analog or digital electrical signals, depending on the type of sensor selected. Generally, smart sensors with output in standard analog or digital are selected over conventional sensors. In the system, several sensors, including an optical sensor for dust detection (GP2Y1010AU0F), an integrated humidity and temperature sensing module (DHT11), and a photodiode for measuring irradiance level, have been taken into consideration for PV monitoring. It has been determined that DHT11 is preferred over DHT22 as a result of its higher degree of accuracy. In addition to this, an impedance divider sensor is used so that the input voltage from the PV module may be measured independently from the output voltage of the solar panel. The measurement of the current may be carried out using suitable current sensors, such as the model number ACS712, for example. There are three different types of current sensors available, each categorized by the range of current that they are able to detect. These sensors feature an Arduino microcontroller as well as an ESP8266 in their design. After successfully connecting to the Wi-Fi network, the ESP826 communicates with the Thing Speak server to transmit the solar sensing configuration parameters.

Processing Unit

It is used for the collection of data from various sensors and processes the same. It may also control the operation of other components. When and where to send the data is decided by the processing unit after collaborating on the data. Time-sensitive digital signal processing, communication protocols, and application programs are among the other programs that it executes. The data processing device is generally a microcontroller. However, digital signal processors with programming capabilities or field-programmable gate arrays can also be used. Flexibility, speed, energy efficiency, and cost are the main criteria for selecting the type of processing unit. For storing the intermediate results, small-size RAM (4 kB) or flash memory is used. For the storage of program code, either EEPROM or flash memory is used. ESP8266-based NodeMCU controllers have been used in the recent past for PV monitoring. The 32-bit-bit06 has a RISC microprocessor along with a Wi-Fi module. It is the main component of the processing unit and acts as the brain of the proposed system. An open-source firmware with a development kit known as NodeMCU helps in the execution of an IoT-based application framework. The use of NodeMCU makes the programming interface for IO devices easy. The effort in configuring and modifying hardware devices is decreased with the aid of APIs. The advantage of NodeMCU is that it can be programmed using an open-source IDE with a range of languages. Using the Arduino IDE facilitates direct uploading of the code to the NodeMCU device. A small Wi-Fi chip (ESP8266) is integrated with the NodeMCU. When designing a controlling section, the appropriate actuators must carry out the control signal that the processing unit generates.

Miscellaneous Components

Some miscellaneous components may also be required, such as real-time clock (RTC) modules like DS1302. It is used as a time reference data logger as it stores the precise time and date at which data has been acquired. Very small-sized flash memory cards can be used as a data logger for storage.

Controlling Unit

A controlling unit has also been shown in Figure 3. Here, control of the water tank is incorporated to remove the dust from the PV panels. Control of the fan may be incorporated to reduce the PV panel temperature. The control signal will be generated by the microprocessor based on the set values of these parameters. A directive will be given to the pumping mechanism of the tank as soon as the quantity of dust in the air reaches a certain threshold that it has been set to. In a similar manner, the control of the fan will be activated if the temperature reaches a threshold that has been set.

Software Layout

The Internet of Things analytics tool known as Thing Speak allows users to visualize data in real time that has been gathered from a variety of cloud-based sensors. The platform, which includes a location field, a data field, and a status field, is the "brain" of the Thing Speak system. The characteristics of real-time data collection, the location of the data gathered geographically, data processing, and visualization are some of the main aspects of Thing Spaak's functionality.

Implementation

Before hardware connections are done as per Figure 3, the sensors should be calibrated with reference to standard sensors. A flow chart representing the algorithm for IoT-based monitoring of PV systems is given in Figure 4.

Step 1: Select the parameters that are to be monitored.

Step 2: Choose appropriate sensors.

Step 3: Calibrate the sensors with standard sensors.

Step 4: Connect all the components as per the block diagram.

Step 5: Turn on the power supply and detect whether the Wi-Fi module is active or not.

Step 6: Choose the sampling time for data acquisition from sensors. Data from each sensor is read by a microcontroller (NodeMCU) with an RTC for time logging.

Step 7: The integrated Wi-Fi module (ESP8266) of NodeMCU will transfer the collected data to a cloud server.

Step 8: Also, collected data is saved on the SD card module.

Steps 5 to 8 are to be reiterated until the device is turned off.

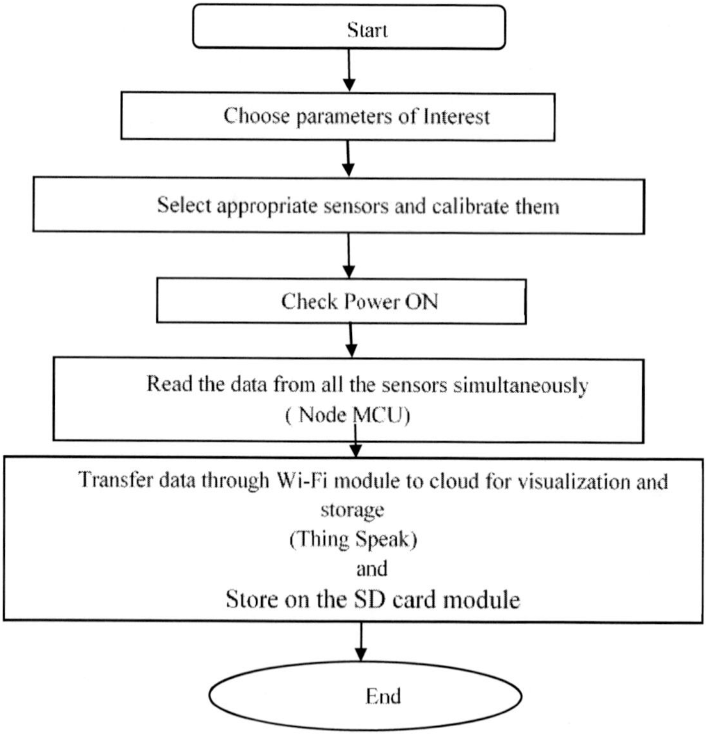

Figure 4. Flowchart for Implementation of IoT-based Solar PV Remote Monitoring System.

Conclusion and Future Trends

Internet of Things (IoT) based monitoring of PV systems reduces the costs incurred due to commercial data loggers, which need proprietary software. Another drawback of commercialized solutions is fixed sensor options and, thus, low expansion flexibility. Also, dependency on the manufacturer for maintenance and complexity in connections due to wired connections. As the IoT-based PV monitoring systems use free software, free usage and communication with a server in the cloud through Wi-Fi are possible. A web page may be developed for continuous monitoring. The objective of PV monitoring may be to detect failures that may result from overheating, partial shadowing, etc. Monitoring of environmental parameters like solar irradiance, ambient temperature, relative humidity, and wind speed can help in the impact analysis of these variables on the PV module's performance. IoT costs may result in reduced maintenance costs as well as operating expenses since they require the least amount of human involvement. This can lead to lower overall costs. Also, human errors will be minimized, resulting in improved accuracy of measurement.

In the future, IoT-based monitoring and control of voltage, current, temperature, and humidity, in addition to defect finding in solar panels, can be extended to hybrid PV systems. Also, collected data may be used for prediction using AI and machine learning. The demand for photovoltaic energy is growing, but the PV panels and cells do not deliver maximum power to the load because of varying ambient conditions. Thus, it becomes essential to force the PV systems to follow maximum power point tracking (MPPT). So, in the future, IoT monitoring can be integrated with a control system to achieve the same. Utilizing the technical advancements in IoT can result in the resolution of challenges faced in complex energy grids and make the management of panels and energy output easier.

Disclaimer

None.

References

Abdullah BUD, Lata S. IoT-Based Solar Monitor System. In 2022 *IEEE International Conference on Computing, Communication, and Intelligent Systems* (ICCCIS) (2022): 997-1002.

Abdullah MN and Sapuan I. Stand-alone Solar Monitoring System using Internet of Things for Fertigation System. *Evolution in Electrical and Electronic Engineering* (2020) 1(1): 106-115.

Abou Saltouh, TM, Nafeha AESA, Fahmya FH and Yousefb HK, Microcontroller based sun tracking system for PV module. *International Journal of Smart Grid and Clean Energy* (2018) 7(4): 286-296.

Babu RL, Rambabu D, Rajesh Naidu A, Prasad RD, Gopi Krishna P. IoT enabled solar power monitoring system. *Int. J. Eng. Technol* (2018) 7(12): 526-530.

Badave Prutha M, Karthikeyan B, Badave SM, Mahajan SB, Sanjeevikumar P, Gurjit Singh Gill. Health monitoring system of solar photovoltaic panel: an internet of things application. In *Advances in Smart Grid and Renewable Energy*: Proceedings of ETAEERE-2016 Springer Singapore (2018) pp. 347-355.

Basir Khan, Reyasudin M, Jidin Razali, Shaaya Sharifah, Daryll Dzesmillson. Wireless PV Module Performance Monitoring System. In *Proceedings National Graduate Conference* (2012): pp. 1-4.

Cheragee SH, Hassan N, Ahammed S, Islam AZMT. A Study of IoT Based Real-Time Solar Power Remote Monitoring System. *Int. J. Amb. Syst. Appl.* (2021) 9(2): 27-36.

Deriche M, Raad MW, Suliman W. An IOT based sensing system for remote monitoring of PV panels. 16th *International Multi-Conference on Systems, Signals & Devices (SSD)*, Istanbul, Turkey (2019): 393-397.

Gupta AK, Chauhan YK, Maity T. Experimental investigations and comparison of various MPPT techniques for photovoltaic systems. *Sădhană*, (2018) 43: 1-15.

Jana J, Adhya S, Saha D, Das A. An IoT Based Smart Solar Photovoltaic Remote Monitoring and Control unit. 2nd International Conference on *Control, Instrumentation, Energy & Communication (CIEC), IEEE,* January (2016).

Karthik S, Mahalakshmi M, Mahitha R, Meena S. IoT based solar panel fault monitoring and control. *International Journal of Information and Computing Science* (2019) 6(3): 238-243.

Kavitha V, Malathi V. A smart solar PV monitoring system using IoT. Comput. *Sci. Inf. Technol* (2019) 9:15.

Kekre A, Gawre SK. Solar photovoltaic remote monitoring system using IOT. In 2017 IEEE International conference on *recent innovations in signal processing and embedded systems* (RISE) (2017): 619-623.

Kumar NM, Atluri K and Palaparthi S. Internet of Things (IoT) in Photovoltaic Systems. *National Power Engineering Conference (NPEC)*, Madurai, India (2018): 1-4.

Li Da Xu, Wu He, Shancang Li. Internet of Things in Industries: A Survey. *IEEE Transactions on Industrial Informatics* (2014) 10(4): 2233-2243.

Li YF, Lin PJ, Zhou HF, Chen ZC, Wu LJ, Cheng SY, Su FP. On-line monitoring system of PV array based on internet of things technology. In IOP Conference Series: *Earth and Environmental Science*, (2017) 93(1): 012078.

Mondal A, Ali MJ, Dutta P. IoT Enabled Smart Solar Panel Monitoring System Based on Boltuino Platform. *IEEE International IOT, Electronics and Mechatronics* Conference (IEMTRONICS), Toronto, Canada (2022): 1-7.

Madadi S. A Study of Solar Power Monitoring System Using Internet of Things (IoT). *International Journal of Innovative Science and Research Technology* (2021) 6(5).

Mangore A, Chougale S, Palekar M, Bhosale K, Kadam S, Kshirsagar K, Bagwan MS. IoT Based Solar Power Monitoring System. *Open Access Repository* (2022) 9(7): 35-46.

Manish Katyarmal, Suyash Walkunde, Arvind Sakhare. Solar power monitoring system using IoT. *International Research Journal of Engineering and Technology* (IRJET) (2018) 5(3).

Mule S, Hardas RS, Kulkarni NR. P&O, IncCon and Fuzzy Logic implemented MPPT scheme for PV systems using PIC18F452. *International Conference on Wireless Communications, Signal Processing and Networking* (WiSPNET) (2016): 320-1325.

Nicoleta Stroia, Daniel Moga, Zsolt Barabas. Web based monitoring of solar power systems. *IFAC Proceeding* (2013) 46(6): 131-136.

Njoka F, Thimo L, Agarwal A. Evaluation of IoT-based remote monitoring systems for stand-alone solar PV installations in Kenya. *Journal of Reliable Intelligent Environments* (2022): 1-13.

Patil S, Vijaya Lakshmi M, Tapaskar R. Solar energy monitoring system using IoT. *Indian Journal of Scientific Research* (2017) 15(2): 149-155.

Pereira RIS, Jucá SCS, Carvalho PCMD, Fernández Ramírez LM. *Comparative analysis of photovoltaic modules center and edge temperature using IoT embedded system.* http://www.repositorio.ufc.br/handle/riufc/64558 (2019).

Phung MD, La Vill efromoy MD, and Ha Q. Management of Solar Energy in Microgrids Using IoT-Based Dependable Control. 20th *IEEE International Conference on Electrical Machines and Systems (ICEMS),* (2017): 1-6.

Prakhar Srivastava, Mohit Bajaj, Ankur Singh Rana. IoT Based Controlling of Hybrid Energy System using ESP8266. *IEEE IEEMA Engineer Infinite Conference* (eTechNxT) (2018).

Priharti Wahmisari, Rosmawati A, Wibawa I. (2019). IoT based photovoltaic monitoring system application. *Journal of Physics: Conference Series.* 1367. 012069.10.1088/1742-6596/1367/1/012069.

Ranjit SSS, Abbod M. *Research and integration of IoT based solar photovoltaic panel health monitoring system.* (2018).

Rasheed A, Al Turjman F. IoT Based Energy Monitoring of PV Plants - An Overview. In: Ever, E., Al-Turjman, F. (eds) Forthcoming Networks and Sustainability in the IoT Era. FoNeS-IoT 2020. *Lecture Notes of the Institute for Computer Sciences, Social Informatics, and Telecommunications Engineering*, (2021) 353.

Renata IS, Pereira Sandro CS, Jucá Paulo CM, Carvalho. IoT embedded systems network and sensors signal conditioning applied to decentralized photovoltaic plants. *Measurement* (2019) 14: 195-12.

Samuel J, Rajagopal B. IoT Based Solar Panel Monitoring and Control. *Nat. Volatiles & Essent Oils* (2021) 8(5):7609-7618.

Shailesh Sarswat, Indresh Yadav, Sanjay Kumar Maurya. Real Time Monitoring of Solar PV Parameter Using IoT. *International Journal of Innovative Technology and Exploring Engineering* (IJITEE) (2019) 9(1S).

Shrihariprasath B, Vimalathithan Rathinasabapathy. A Smart IoT System for Monitoring Solar PV Power Conditioning Unit. *IEEE World Conference on Futuristic Trends in Research and Innovation for Social Welfare* (WCFTR'16) (2016).

Srinivasan KG, Vimala Devi K, Chakravarthi S. Solar energy monitoring system by IoT. Special Issue Published in *Int J Adv Network Appl (IJANA)* (2019).

Sutikno Tole, Purnama Hendril, Pamungkas Anggit, Fadlil Abdul, Alsofyani IM, Jopri MH. Internet of things-based photovoltaics parameter monitoring system using Node MCUESP8266. *International Journal of Electrical and Computer Engineering* (2021) 11: 5578-5587.

Xia K, Ni J, Ye Y, Xu P, Wang Y. A real-time monitoring system based on ZigBee and 4G communications for photovoltaic generation. *CSEE Journal of Power and Energy Systems* (2020) 6(1): 52-63.

Chapter 5

Technologies Involved in IoT Development: Unleashing the Power of Connected Systems

Anand Vardhan Bhalla[1,*], MTech
Dheeraj Nagar[1], MTech,
and Rajiv Dey[2], PhD

[1]Department of Electronics and Communication Engineering, Eklavya University, School of Engineering, Damoh, Madhya Pradesh, India
[2]Department of Electronics and Computer Engineering, BML Munjal University, School of Engineering and Technology, Gurugram, Haryana, India

Abstract

The Internet of Things (IoT), offering previously unimaginable potential for innovation and connectivity, has completely changed the way we interact with our environment. Given the explosive rise of IoT devices and applications, a detailed understanding of the technologies behind this revolutionary area is urgently required. The Internet of Things (IoT) and its significance for enabling seamless connectivity between devices, sensors, and the cloud are briefly described in this chapter. The various communication standards and protocols used to encourage data flow and interoperability are examined, including MQTT, CoAP, and Zigbee. The article also addresses the unique features, range limitations, and trade-offs of Wi-Fi, Bluetooth, and cellular networks. The chapter also looks at the vital role that sensor technologies play in data gathering and transmission, including sophisticated environmental and biometric sensors, as well as temperature and humidity sensors. It examines the rapidly increasing issue of edge computing, describing how edge devices enable real-time data analysis, reduce latency, and increase overall

---

* Corresponding Author's Email: anandvardhanbhalla@gmail.com.

In: The Future of IoT with Automation in Engineering and Modern Technology
Editors: Sandeep Gupta and Tarun Varshney
ISBN: 979-8-89113-655-7

system performance. In addition, the chapter discusses newly discovered technologies that have the potential to totally disrupt the IoT landscape. This includes blockchain technology, which enables decentralized data management and increased trust, as well as artificial intelligence (AI) and machine learning (ML) techniques that enable predictive analytics and autonomous decision-making, and other related technologies. Throughout the chapter, real-world examples, case studies, and relevant considerations explain how these technologies may be applied in several IoT situations, including smart cities, industrial automation, healthcare, and agriculture. In a nutshell, this chapter gives a complete analysis of the technologies involved in IoT development, providing readers with the knowledge and expertise required to successfully navigate the ever-changing world of linked systems.

Keywords: Internet of Things (IoT), blockchain technology, Artificial Intelligence (AI), Machine Learning (ML), edge intelligence, fog computing

Introduction

This chapter examines the continued expansion of the Internet of Things (IoT) and the advent of new technologies that help it progress. It lays the groundwork for a chapter that delves into these fascinating advances in the IoT.

The Internet of Things (IoT) is a network of interconnected physical devices, sensors, and software that communicate, collect, and exchange data. New developments continue to improve the capabilities of the IoT ecosystem as technology advances (Gleiston G. et al., 2023; Bharadwaj et. al., 2023). The chapter emphasizes how quickly these improvements are occurring, demonstrating the dynamic nature of the IoT landscape. The purpose of this chapter is to look into these developing technologies and their implications for IoT development. The technologies listed in Figure 1 will be investigated.

Blockchain Technology

Blockchain technology has the potential to improve the security, trust, and dependability of IoT networks because it is decentralized and transparent. It can provide safe and temper-proof data exchanges, making it suited for applications requiring data integrity and privacy.

Artificial Intelligence (AI)

The simulation of human intelligence in machines is referred to as Artificial Intelligence (AI). AI can enable IoT devices and systems to analyze and interpret massive volumes of data, make intelligent decisions, and automate activities (Stephan et al., 2023). It allows Internet of Things devices to learn from patterns and adapt to changing situations.

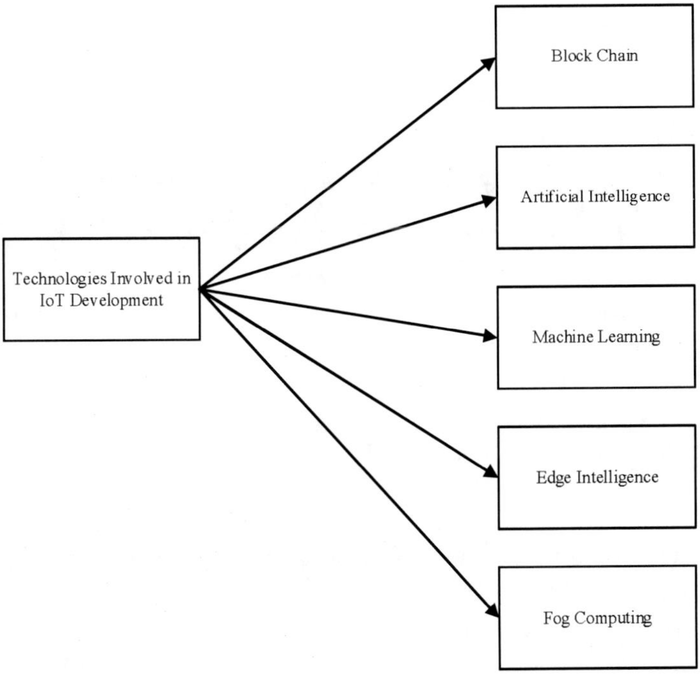

Figure 1. Technologies Involved in IoT development.

Machine Learning (ML)

ML is a variation of AI that focuses on algorithms and statistical models that allow systems to gain insight and improve from experience without being explicitly programmed (Kamalrulnizam et. al., 2023). ML algorithms can be used to extract important insights from IoT-generated data, enabling predictive analytics and anomaly detection.

Edge Intelligence

Edge intelligence involves processing and analyzing data at the edge of the network, closer to the source of data generation. This approach reduces latency, optimizes bandwidth usage, and enhances real-time decision-making capabilities in IoT systems.

Fog Computing

Fog computing is a distributed computing paradigm that extends cloud computing capabilities to the networks edge (Motaharul et al., 2023). Fog computing accelerates data analysis, decreases latency, and improves scalability in IoT contexts by decentralizing data processing and storage.

More importantly, this chapter reinforces the significance of security and privacy in the IoT context. As more devices become connected, protecting sensitive data and protecting user privacy become key considerations (Kamalrulnizam et al., 2023).

This chapter will give real-world examples and case studies to provide practical insights. These case studies will demonstrate how emerging technologies are revolutionizing diverse IoT areas such as smart cities, industrial automation, healthcare, and agriculture. This chapter tries to highlight the concrete influence of these technologies in transforming the way IoT systems operate and adding value to various sectors by illustrating these applications. Overall, this chapter shows the latest developments in IoT technology, blockchain, AI, ML, edge intelligence, fog computing. Security considerations are also revolutionizing the IoT landscape across multiple industries.

Blockchain Technology in IoT

At its foundation, blockchain technology is a distributed ledger that is decentralized and records transactions across a number of computers, or nodes. Because it functions under the tenets of immutability, transparency, and consensus, it is the perfect technology for the Internet of Things (IoT) ecosystem. The term "Internet of Things" (IoT) describes how numerous devices and items are linked together and equipped with sensors, software, and network connectivity so they can trade and collect data (Konstantinos et al., 2022).

Building trust between devices and preserving the integrity and security of the data they produce is one of the major issues in the IoT area (Priyanka et al., 2022). Single points of failure, data manipulation, and hacking are all possibilities with traditional centralized systems. Here, blockchain technology is useful (Laxmi et. al., 2023). This is where blockchain comes into play. By leveraging its unique features, blockchain technology offers several advantages for IoT applications (Thomas et al., 2019):

Decentralization

A blockchain-based IoT network lacks a central authority or point of control as shown in Figure 2. Instead, the network is made up of numerous nodes that take part in transaction validation and verification. Due to the lack of a central authority that may compromise or manipulate the data, this decentralized structure improves the security and dependability of the system (Zakir et al., 2022).

Data Integrity

Blockchain ensures the integrity of IoT data by providing a tamper-resistant and immutable ledger (Arun et al., 2022). Each transaction or data entry is encrypted, timestamped, and linked to the previous transaction, creating a chain of blocks. Once a block is added to the chain, it cannot be altered without consensus from the majority of network participants. This feature ensures that the data stored in the blockchain is reliable and trustworthy.

Secure Transaction

Blockchain utilizes advanced cryptographic techniques to secure transactions and communications between IoT devices (Deyang et al., 2023; Ted, 2022). Public key cryptography and digital signatures are employed to verify the authenticity of the devices, ensuring that only authorized devices can participate in the network (Mahdi et al., 2018). Additionally, blockchain's consensus mechanisms, such as Proof-of-Work (PoW) or Proof-of-Stake (PoS), provide a robust layer of security against malicious attacks.

Identity Management

Managing identities and permissions of IoT devices is crucial for secure interactions. Blockchain enables the creation of decentralized identity management systems, where each device has a unique cryptographic identity stored on the blockchain. This identity can be used to authenticate and authorize devices, enabling secure communication and data exchange between them.

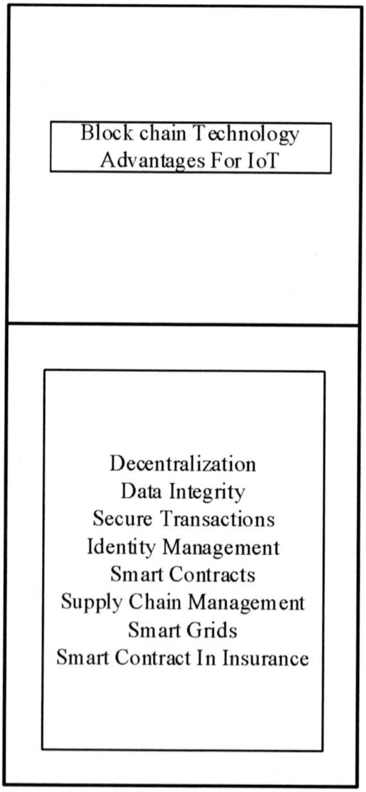

Figure 2. Blockchain Technology advantages for IoT applications.

Smart Contracts

Smart contracts are self-executing contracts with the terms and conditions directly written in the code. Blockchain platforms, such as Ethereum, allow the execution of smart contracts in a decentralized manner. In the context of IoT, smart contracts enable automated and trustless interactions between devices, triggering actions based on predefined conditions. For example, in a supply chain management scenario, smart contracts can automatically verify the authenticity of goods, track their movement, and trigger payments when specific conditions are met.

Real-world use cases demonstrate the potential of blockchain technology in the IoT domain:

Supply Chain Management

Blockchain can enhance transparency and traceability in supply chains by recording the movement of goods from their origin to the end consumer. Each step of the supply chain, including manufacturing, transportation, and storage, can be securely documented on the blockchain, preventing fraud, counterfeiting, and ensuring product quality.

Energy Grid

Blockchain-enabled microgrids can enable peer-to-peer energy transactions between IoT devices, such as solar panels, batteries, and electric vehicles. This decentralized energy trading can optimize energy usage, reduce reliance on centralized energy providers, and enable efficient management of renewable energy resources.

Smart Contracts in Insurance

Blockchain-based smart contracts can automate insurance processes, eliminating the need for intermediaries and reducing paperwork. For example, in the case of parametric insurance for crops, IoT sensors can collect data on weather conditions, and smart contracts can automatically trigger payouts based on predefined conditions, such as drought or frost.

Case Studies

Blockchain Technology in Supply Chain Management

Blockchain technology is utilized to improve transparency, security, and efficiency in supply chain management, enabling enhanced traceability and trust among stakeholders (Rahul et. al, 2019).

The supply chain industry faces challenges related to transparency, trust, and accountability. Traditional supply chain systems often lack a unified and transparent record of transactions, making it difficult to trace the origin, authenticity, and movement of goods. Additionally, the involvement of multiple parties and intermediaries can lead to inefficiencies, delays, and increased costs.

By integrating Blockchain technology with IoT devices, a decentralized and immutable ledger can be established, providing a transparent and tamper-proof record of transactions and events throughout the supply chain. IoT devices, such as sensors and RFID tags, can collect and transmit data about the movement, temperature, and condition of goods at different stages. This data is securely recorded on the blockchain, creating an auditable and traceable history of the product's journey from its origin to the end consumer. Smart contracts can be used to automate and enforce contractual agreements, ensuring transparency and trust among all parties involved.

With the implementation of Blockchain technology in supply chain management, several benefits are realized. Firstly, the transparency provided by the blockchain enables stakeholders to have real-time visibility into the movement, condition, and authenticity of goods. This reduces the risk of fraud, counterfeiting, and unauthorized alterations. Secondly, the decentralized nature of the blockchain eliminates the need for intermediaries and streamlines the verification and validation processes, reducing costs and improving operational efficiency. Finally, the automated execution of smart contracts ensures that contractual obligations are met, reducing disputes and enhancing trust among supply chain participants.

By leveraging Blockchain technology in IoT-enabled supply chain management, companies can establish a trusted and efficient ecosystem, enabling seamless tracking, authentication, and verification of goods throughout the supply chain. This approach not only improves the overall transparency and security of the supply chain but also enhances customer trust and satisfaction.

Blockchain-Based Energy Grid Management

Blockchain technology is used to enable peer-to-peer energy transactions and improve the management of decentralized energy grids (Fernando et al., 2022).

Traditional energy grids are centralized and heavily dependent on intermediaries for energy distribution and billing. This can lead to inefficiencies, high transaction costs, and limited options for renewable energy integration (Nuzhat et al., 2022).

By combining Blockchain technology with IoT devices, a decentralized energy grid management system can be established. IoT devices such as smart meters can collect real-time energy consumption data from households or businesses. This data is securely stored and verified on the blockchain, enabling transparent and automated energy transactions between energy producers and consumers. Smart contracts can be used to execute and enforce energy agreements, ensuring accurate billing and efficient energy distribution. Additionally, blockchain-based platforms can incentivize energy producers to generate renewable energy and allow consumers to choose their energy sources.

The integration of blockchain technology in energy grid management offers several benefits (Nuzhat et al., 2022). It enables peer-to-peer energy transactions, reducing reliance on intermediaries and lowering transaction costs. It also facilitates the integration of renewable energy sources into the grid, promoting sustainability and reducing carbon emissions. By providing transparency and accountability, blockchain-based energy grid management systems enhance trust among participants and empower consumers to make informed energy choices.

Blockchain-Enabled Supply Chain for Food Safety

Blockchain technology is utilized to improve food safety by enhancing traceability and ensuring the authenticity and quality of food products (Liang et al., 2018).

The food supply chain often faces challenges related to food safety, such as contamination, adulteration, and fraud. Traditional systems struggle to quickly and accurately trace the origin of food products, making it difficult to identify and address safety issues.

By leveraging blockchain technology in the IoT-enabled supply chain, a transparent and traceable record of food products can be established. IoT devices, such as temperature sensors and RFID tags, collect and transmit data about the temperature, storage conditions, and handling of food products. This data is securely recorded on the blockchain, creating an immutable and auditable history of the product's journey from farm to fork. Additionally, smart contracts can be used to automate quality checks, certifications, and compliance requirements, ensuring that food safety standards are met at each stage of the supply chain.

The integration of blockchain technology in the food supply chain brings significant advantages. It enables faster and more accurate traceability of food products, facilitating rapid recalls in case of safety issues. The transparency provided by the blockchain enhances consumer trust and confidence in the authenticity and quality of food products. Additionally, the automation of compliance processes reduces administrative burden and improves operational efficiency for food producers and regulators.

These case studies highlight the diverse applications of Blockchain technology in the IoT domain, addressing challenges and bringing improvements in various industries. By leveraging the transparency, security, and decentralization provided by Blockchain, organizations can enhance trust, efficiency, and accountability in their operations.

Artificial Intelligence and Machine Learning in IoT

The combination of artificial intelligence (AI) and machine learning (ML) is having a profound impact on the Internet of Things (IoT) landscape (Pradeepkumar et al., 2023). These technologies empower IoT systems with intelligent decision-making capabilities and predictive analytics. In this section, we will delve into the wide-ranging applications of AI and ML algorithms in IoT, highlighting their ability to extract valuable insights from the vast volumes of data generated by IoT devices. By doing so, AI and ML facilitate optimized processes, improved efficiency, and enhanced user experiences. To illustrate the transformative potential of AI and ML in IoT, we will explore real-world examples in healthcare monitoring, predictive maintenance, and anomaly detection.

AI and ML algorithms play a pivotal role in unlocking the value of IoT-generated data. The sheer volume and complexity of data produced by IoT devices can be overwhelming for traditional data processing techniques (Arun et al., 2022). However, AI and ML provide the means to effectively analyze and interpret this data, extracting meaningful patterns and trends. By leveraging advanced algorithms, IoT systems can gain valuable insights into user behavior, environmental conditions, and system performance.

In the realm of healthcare monitoring, AI and ML algorithms can process real-time data from wearable devices, sensors, and medical equipment (Kwok et al., 2008). These algorithms can analyze vital signs, detect anomalies, and predict health conditions. For instance, ML models can learn from historical patient data to identify early signs of diseases or complications, allowing healthcare providers to intervene proactively. Such predictive capabilities enable personalized healthcare, early intervention, and improved patient outcomes.

Predictive maintenance is another area where AI and ML bring significant benefits to IoT systems. By continuously monitoring the performance and behavior of connected devices, AI-powered algorithms can identify patterns that indicate potential failures or malfunctions (Castano et al., 2009). This proactive approach helps optimize maintenance schedules, prevent costly breakdowns, and minimize downtime. For example, in manufacturing plants, ML algorithms can analyze sensor data from machinery to predict equipment failure, allowing for timely repairs or replacements before the failure occurs.

Anomaly detection is a crucial aspect of IoT security, and AI and ML algorithms excel in this area. These algorithms can learn normal patterns and behaviors within an IoT system and quickly identify any deviations that may indicate a security breach or malicious activity. By continuously monitoring network traffic, device behavior, and data flows, AI-powered anomaly detection systems can rapidly respond to potential threats and mitigate risks. This capability is particularly important in sectors such as smart cities and critical infrastructure, where the consequences of security breaches can be severe.

Real-world examples further showcase the potential of AI and ML in IoT. For instance, in agriculture, AI-powered systems can analyze sensor data, weather patterns, and crop characteristics to optimize irrigation, pest control, and crop yield. This leads to more sustainable farming practices and increased productivity. In transportation, AI and ML algorithms can process data from connected vehicles, traffic sensors, and navigation systems to improve traffic management, optimize routes, and enhance overall transportation efficiency (Darcy et al., 2013).

In conclusion, AI and ML are playing a transformative role in the IoT landscape. These technologies enable intelligent decision-making, predictive analytics, and valuable insights from massive volumes of IoT-generated data. By leveraging AI and ML algorithms, IoT systems can achieve optimized processes, improved efficiency, and enhanced user experiences. Real-world applications in healthcare monitoring, predictive maintenance, and anomaly detection demonstrate the significant potential of AI and ML in revolutionizing the IoT domain. As AI and ML continue to advance, they will further empower IoT systems and contribute to a more connected, intelligent, and efficient world.

Case Studies

Predictive Maintenance in Industrial IoT

Manufacturing Company aimed to improve equipment maintenance and reduce downtime by implementing AI and machine learning in their IoT infrastructure (Ko et al., 2017)

To achieve their objective, the manufacturing company installed sensors and IoT devices on their machines to collect real-time data on temperature, pressure, vibration, and energy consumption. This data is then integrated with an AI-enabled platform that combines IoT and machine learning capabilities.

Machine learning algorithms are trained using historical data to identify patterns and correlations between sensor readings and equipment failures. The algorithms employed techniques like regression, clustering, and anomaly detection to predict potential equipment failures. Real-time alerts and notifications are generated by the AI system whenever anomalies or potential equipment failures are detected, allowing maintenance technicians to take proactive actions.

The implementation of predictive maintenance using AI and machine learning yielded significant results for Manufacturing Company. They experienced a notable reduction in unplanned downtime, as potential issues are identified and addressed before complete breakdowns occurred. The company also achieved cost savings by minimizing emergency repairs and avoiding production delays. Moreover, maintenance schedules are optimized, leading to improved overall maintenance efficiency. Ultimately, the implementation of AI and machine learning in their IoT infrastructure enhanced the equipment lifespan by ensuring timely servicing and early detection of potential issues.

Smart Home Automation with AI and Machine Learning

Smart Homes aimed to enhance the home automation experience for their customers by leveraging AI and machine learning in their IoT devices.

To accomplish this objective, Smart Homes deployed a range of IoT devices, including smart thermostats, cameras, motion sensors, and smart plugs, to gather data on user behavior, environmental conditions, and energy consumption. This data is sent to a cloud-based AI platform that utilizes machine learning algorithms for analysis.

The AI system learned individual users' preferences by analyzing the data and created personalized automation profiles. For example, it learned preferred temperature settings, lighting preferences, and security requirements for each user. Additionally, the system continuously adapted to changing user behavior and environmental conditions. It learned from user feedback and adjusted automation profiles, accordingly, optimizing comfort, security, and energy efficiency.

The implementation of AI and machine learning in their IoT ecosystem resulted in an enhanced home automation experience for Smart Homes' customers. The system provided a personalized and adaptive automation experience, tailored to each user's preferences. It optimized energy consumption by learning user patterns and automatically adjusting devices like lighting and climate control to minimize energy waste. The AI system also improved home security by detecting anomalies in activity and triggering alerts and automated security responses. Furthermore, the solution demonstrated scalability, accommodating additional devices and continuously learning from a growing dataset.

These case studies illustrate the power of AI and machine learning in IoT applications. By implementing predictive maintenance in an industrial setting and leveraging AI for smart home automation, these companies achieved significant improvements in efficiency, cost savings, user experience, and overall system performance.

Edge Intelligence and Fog Computing

Edge intelligence refers to the concept of performing data processing, analytics, and decision-making at the edge of a network, closer to the data source or the IoT devices generating the data. Traditional cloud computing models involve transmitting all data to a centralized cloud server for processing, which can result in increased latency, bandwidth consumption, and potential privacy and security concerns (R. M. et al., 2018). Edge intelligence addresses these challenges by pushing computational tasks and intelligence to the edge devices themselves.

By deploying intelligent capabilities directly on edge devices, such as sensors, gateways, and routers, organizations can achieve real-time data analysis and localized decision-making. Edge devices can perform data filtering, aggregation, preprocessing, and even complex analytics, enabling faster response times and reducing the need for continuous data transmission to the cloud (R. M. et al., 2016). This approach is particularly beneficial in scenarios where low latency and real-time responsiveness are critical, such as industrial automation, autonomous vehicles, and smart cities. The advantages of edge intelligence are shown in Figure 3.

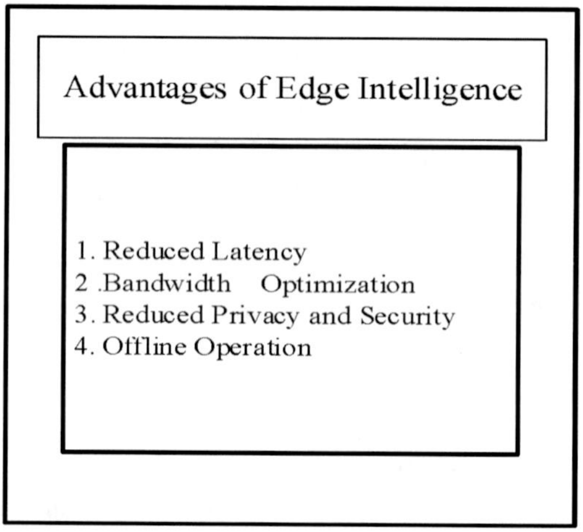

Figure 3. Advantages of Edge Intelligence.

Reduced Latency

By processing data locally at the edge, latency is significantly reduced as there is no need to transmit data to a remote server for processing. This is crucial for applications that require real-time decision-making, such as autonomous vehicles or monitoring systems.

Bandwidth Optimization

Edge intelligence helps optimize network bandwidth by performing data filtering and aggregation at the edge devices. Only relevant data or summarized information is transmitted to the cloud, reducing the volume of data transferred and the associated costs.

Enhanced Privacy and Security

With edge intelligence, sensitive data can remain within the local network, minimizing the exposure to external threats and potential privacy breaches. This is particularly important for applications dealing with personal or confidential data.

Offline Operation

Edge devices equipped with intelligence can continue to function even when the connection to the cloud is lost. This ensures uninterrupted operations and allows critical tasks to be performed locally.

Fog computing complements edge intelligence by extending the concept to a more distributed computing infrastructure. While edge computing focuses on processing tasks at the edge devices themselves, fog computing introduces intermediate computing nodes called "fog nodes" or "fog servers." These fog nodes are placed closer to the edge devices, forming a distributed fog network. Fog computing aims to address the limitations of edge devices, such as limited processing power, storage capacity, and energy constraints. By offloading some of the computational tasks to the fog nodes, the overall system performance can be improved. Fog nodes can have more resources, including higher computational power, storage, and connectivity, enabling them to handle more complex tasks and support a larger number of edge devices.

The benefits of fog computing include (S. Yi et al., 2015):

Scalability

Fog computing enables the scalability of edge intelligence by distributing computational tasks across multiple fog nodes. This allows for efficient resource utilization and the ability to handle a growing number of IoT devices and data volumes.

Higher Processing Power

Fog nodes can have more powerful processors and storage capabilities than individual edge devices. This enables the execution of resource-intensive applications and complex analytics closer to the edge, without overburdening the limited resources of the edge devices.

Redundancy and Fault Tolerance

Fog computing provides redundancy and fault tolerance by distributing computational tasks across multiple fog nodes. If one fog node fails, the workload can be seamlessly transferred to another node, ensuring continuous operation and minimizing downtime.

Contextual Awareness

Fog nodes can collect and process data from multiple edge devices, enabling them to gain a broader contextual understanding of the environment. This facilitates more comprehensive analysis and decision-making based on aggregated data from multiple sources.

Case Studies

Edge intelligence and fog computing have found practical applications in various domains. Here are a few examples:

Healthcare

In the healthcare industry, edge intelligence and fog computing can enhance patient monitoring, diagnostics, and emergency response. For instance, wearable devices equipped with edge computing capabilities can collect vital signs data in real-time and analyze it locally. This enables continuous monitoring of patients' health, early detection of abnormalities, and immediate alerts to medical staff in case of emergencies, improving patient outcomes and reducing response times.

Industrial Automation

Edge intelligence and fog computing play a vital role in industrial automation systems. By deploying edge devices and fog nodes in factories and manufacturing plants, real-time data processing and analysis can be performed locally. This enables predictive maintenance, quality control, and optimization of production processes. For example, sensors embedded in machinery can collect data on temperature, vibration, and performance, allowing for proactive maintenance and reducing downtime.

Agriculture

Edge intelligence and fog computing have the potential to transform the agricultural sector. By deploying edge devices and fog nodes in farms, farmers can collect and analyze data on soil moisture, temperature, humidity, and crop health in real-time. This information can be used to optimize irrigation, monitor plant health, and detect diseases or pests at an early stage. With localized decision-making and automated systems, farmers can improve crop yield, reduce water usage, and minimize the need for manual intervention.

Retail

In the retail industry, edge intelligence and fog computing can be used to enhance customer experiences and optimize operations. For example, smart shelves equipped with edge devices can monitor inventory levels, detect product placement, and gather data on customer interactions. This enables real-time inventory management, personalized advertising, and efficient restocking. Additionally, edge-based facial recognition systems can provide personalized recommendations and enable seamless checkout experiences.

Environmental Monitoring

Edge intelligence and fog computing are valuable for environmental monitoring applications. By deploying edge devices and fog nodes in remote locations such as forests or oceans, real-time data collection and analysis can be performed locally. This enables early detection of natural disasters, wildlife tracking, and monitoring of pollution levels. Localized decision-making and reduced reliance on centralized servers improve the speed and efficiency of environmental monitoring efforts.

Smart Transportation

In intelligent transportation systems, edge devices installed in vehicles, traffic lights, and road infrastructure can collect and process data in real-time. This enables traffic monitoring, congestion detection, and adaptive traffic signal control, improving overall traffic management and reducing commute times.

Video Surveillance
Deploying edge devices with embedded intelligence in video surveillance cameras allows for real-time video analysis. Edge devices can perform object detection, facial recognition, and anomaly detection locally, reducing the need for transmitting massive amounts of video data to a central server. This approach enhances security and enables rapid response to potential threats.

Smart Grids
Edge devices and fog nodes in smart grid infrastructure can monitor energy consumption, analyze power quality, and detect anomalies. By performing these tasks locally, energy providers can optimize energy distribution, identify faults, and ensure efficient utilization of resources (Laxmi et al., 2023).

In summary, edge intelligence and fog computing bring computational capabilities closer to IoT devices, enabling real-time data analysis, localized decision-making, reduced latency, and improved scalability. These technologies have the potential to revolutionize various industries and pave the way for more efficient and intelligent IoT deployments.

Security and Privacy in IoT

Security and privacy in IoT have become critical concerns as the number of connected devices and the amount of sensitive data being transmitted continue to grow. The unique characteristics of IoT deployments, such as resource-constrained devices, diverse communication protocols, and distributed nature, pose significant challenges to ensuring robust security and protecting user privacy. Let's delve into the key aspects and measures related to security and privacy in IoT.

Access Control and Authentication

Access control mechanisms are crucial for preventing unauthorized access to IoT devices and networks. This involves implementing strong authentication protocols to verify the identity of devices and users before granting access.

Common authentication methods include passwords, digital certificates, and two-factor authentication. Additionally, techniques like role-based access control (RBAC) can be used to manage and enforce access privileges based on user roles and device capabilities.

Data Encryption

Encryption plays a vital role in protecting the confidentiality and integrity of data transmitted and stored within IoT systems. End-to-end encryption ensures that data is securely transmitted between devices and gateways, preventing eavesdropping and data tampering. Robust encryption algorithms, such as AES (Advanced Encryption Standard), are employed to encrypt data at various levels, including transport layer security (TLS) for communication protocols and storage encryption for data at rest.

Secure Device Provisioning

Ensuring the security of IoT devices from the initial setup is crucial. Secure device provisioning involves securely onboarding and configuring devices onto the network, establishing trust relationships, and securely managing cryptographic keys. Techniques like secure boot, secure firmware updates, and device attestation can help prevent unauthorized modifications to device firmware and ensure the authenticity of the software running on IoT devices.

Network Segmentation

Segmenting IoT networks into logical zones or subnetworks helps contain potential security breaches and limit the impact of compromised devices. By implementing firewalls, virtual LANs (VLANs), and network access control (NAC) mechanisms, organizations can control the flow of traffic and enforce security policies between different segments of the IoT infrastructure.

Intrusion Detection and Prevention Systems

Deploying intrusion detection and prevention systems (IDPS) within IoT environments can help identify and mitigate potential security threats. IDPS solutions monitor network traffic, analyze device behavior, and detect anomalies or malicious activities. These systems can generate alerts, block suspicious traffic, or even initiate automated responses to mitigate security incidents.

Blockchain-Based Security

Blockchain technology is gaining attention for its potential to enhance security in IoT deployments. Blockchain provides a decentralized and tamper-resistant ledger that can be leveraged to establish trust, enable secure peer-to-peer communication, and ensure data integrity. It can be used for secure device identity management, secure data sharing, and auditability of IoT transactions.

Privacy by Design

Privacy considerations should be integrated into IoT system design from the outset. Privacy by Design principles advocate for minimizing data collection, ensuring data anonymization and pseudonymization, obtaining user consent, and providing transparent data handling practices. Implementing privacy-enhancing technologies like differential privacy can further protect user privacy by anonymizing and aggregating data while preserving its utility for analysis.

Real-world examples have demonstrated the consequences of inadequate security measures in IoT. Instances of unauthorized access to critical infrastructure, data breaches exposing personal information, and IoT botnets harnessing compromised devices for large-scale attacks highlight the urgency of implementing comprehensive security practices in IoT development.

In conclusion, addressing security and privacy challenges in IoT requires a multi-layered approach, encompassing access control, authentication, encryption, secure device provisioning, network segmentation, intrusion detection, and privacy by design principles. As the IoT landscape continues to evolve, it is crucial for organizations, developers, and policymakers to prioritize and invest in robust security measures to ensure the trust, reliability, and privacy of IoT ecosystems.

Integrating Emerging Technologies: Synergistic Possibilities

The integration of emerging technologies such as blockchain, AI, machine learning, edge computing, and fog computing in IoT systems offers immense potential to create more secure, intelligent, and efficient environments. Let's explore the synergistic possibilities of combining these technologies and examine case studies in different domains.

Blockchain and IoT

Integrating blockchain with IoT can enhance security, trust, and data integrity. Blockchain provides a decentralized and tamper-resistant ledger that can be used to establish trust among IoT devices and ensure the integrity of data exchanged between them. By leveraging blockchain, IoT systems can enable secure and transparent transactions, device identity management, and data sharing. For example, in supply chain management, blockchain can be used to track and verify the authenticity and provenance of goods, ensuring transparency and mitigating counterfeiting.

AI and Machine Learning in IoT

The combination of AI and machine learning with IoT enables intelligent data analysis, predictive modeling, and automation. AI algorithms can process and analyze vast amounts of IoT data, uncover hidden patterns, and generate valuable insights. Machine learning models can be trained on IoT data to make accurate predictions, detect anomalies, and optimize system performance. In smart cities, AI and machine learning can analyze sensor data to optimize traffic flow, predict energy consumption, and improve waste management.

Edge Computing and IoT

Edge computing brings computation and intelligence closer to the edge devices, reducing latency, optimizing bandwidth, and enabling real-time decision-making. When integrated with IoT, edge computing enables local data processing, analytics, and control, minimizing the need for continuous data transmission to the cloud. Edge devices can perform tasks such as data filtering, preprocessing, and localized decision-making, enhancing responsiveness and reducing dependency on cloud resources. In precision agriculture, edge computing can analyze sensor data from farms in real-time, enabling timely irrigation, pest management, and crop monitoring.

Fog Computing and IoT

Fog computing complements edge computing by providing intermediate computing nodes (fog nodes) between edge devices and the cloud. Fog nodes have more resources and processing power than individual edge devices, enabling the execution of more complex tasks and supporting a larger number of devices. Fog computing enhances scalability, fault tolerance, and contextual awareness in IoT deployments. In industrial automation, fog computing can enable real-time monitoring, control, and optimization of manufacturing processes by collecting and analyzing data from multiple edge devices.

Case Studies

Smart Cities

In smart city deployments, the integration of blockchain, AI, edge computing, and IoT can create a secure and intelligent ecosystem. Blockchain can provide secure and transparent transactions for services like electric vehicle charging, parking, and waste management. AI and machine learning can analyze data from various IoT sensors to optimize traffic flow, predict energy demand, and enhance public safety. Edge computing can enable real-time decision-making and reduce latency in applications like smart traffic management and surveillance systems.

Precision Agriculture

The combination of AI, machine learning, edge computing, and IoT in precision agriculture can revolutionize farming practices. IoT sensors can collect data on soil moisture, temperature, and crop health. Edge devices equipped with AI and machine learning capabilities can analyze this data locally to optimize irrigation, detect diseases, and predict crop yields. Blockchain can provide traceability and transparency in the supply chain, ensuring the authenticity and quality of agricultural products.

Industrial Automation

In industrial automation, fog computing, AI, and IoT integration can enhance operational efficiency and safety. IoT devices can collect data from sensors, machines, and production lines, while fog nodes perform real-time analytics and control. AI algorithms can optimize production processes, detect anomalies, and predict equipment failures. Blockchain can secure supply chain transactions, track product quality, and ensure compliance with regulations.

In summary, the integration of blockchain, AI, machine learning, edge computing, and fog computing in IoT systems offers synergistic possibilities. By combining these technologies, organizations can create secure, intelligent, and efficient IoT environments in various domains, including smart cities, precision agriculture, and industrial automation. These integrated technologies have the potential to transform industries, optimize resource utilization, and improve decision-making in the IoT landscape.

Discussion

The integration of emerging technologies such as blockchain, AI, machine learning, edge intelligence, and fog computing in IoT systems presents exciting opportunities for the development and deployment of innovative solutions. These technologies, when combined, offer a range of benefits, including improved security, enhanced data analysis capabilities, real-time decision-making, reduced latency, and increased efficiency.

One key aspect discussed in this chapter is the integration of blockchain technology with IoT. Blockchain's decentralized and tamper-resistant nature provides a secure framework for IoT devices to interact and exchange data in a trustless manner. The use of blockchain in supply chain management, for example, ensures transparency, traceability, and authenticity throughout the supply chain, combating issues such as counterfeiting and improving consumer confidence. The integration of blockchain in other domains can also provide similar benefits, reinforcing the importance of secure and transparent transactions.

Another significant aspect discussed is the integration of AI and machine learning with IoT. The ability to process and analyze vast amounts of data generated by IoT devices empowers organizations to derive meaningful insights and make data-driven decisions. AI algorithms and machine learning models can identify patterns, detect anomalies, and predict future trends, leading to more efficient resource allocation, improved operational processes, and enhanced user experiences. This integration has particular relevance in domains such as smart cities, where optimizing traffic flow, predicting energy consumption, and improving waste management can have a substantial impact on sustainability and quality of life.

The chapter also highlights the importance of edge intelligence and fog computing in IoT environments. By moving computational tasks closer to the data source, these technologies enable real-time data analysis, localized decision-making, and reduced latency. Edge devices equipped with intelligence can perform data filtering, preprocessing, and analytics, reducing the need for continuous data transmission to the cloud. Fog computing, with its intermediate computing nodes, further enhances scalability and fault tolerance, allowing for more complex processing and increased device capacity. The advantages of edge intelligence and fog computing are exemplified in case studies such as precision agriculture and industrial automation, where timely decision-making and efficient resource management are crucial.

Addressing security and privacy concerns is a paramount consideration in IoT deployments, as highlighted in this chapter. The exponential growth of interconnected devices increases the attack surface and potential vulnerabilities. Implementing robust security measures, such as access control mechanisms, authentication protocols, data encryption, and intrusion detection systems, is vital to protect IoT ecosystems from unauthorized access and data breaches. Additionally, privacy considerations, including minimizing data collection, implementing privacy-enhancing technologies, and ensuring transparent data handling practices, are essential to respect user privacy rights and comply with regulations.

Overall, the integration of these emerging technologies in IoT systems opens up exciting possibilities for various industries. By leveraging the capabilities of blockchain, AI, machine learning, edge intelligence, and fog computing, organizations can develop secure, intelligent, and efficient IoT solutions. Real-world examples and case studies demonstrate the transformative potential of these integrated technologies in domains such as smart cities, precision agriculture, and industrial automation. However, it is important to note that challenges still exist, including interoperability, standardization, and scalability issues. Continued research, development, and collaboration among stakeholders are necessary to fully realize the benefits and address the challenges in integrating these technologies effectively into IoT ecosystems.

Conclusion

This chapter has demonstrated the transformative potential of integrating these technologies in diverse industries. The integration of blockchain technology with IoT systems offers enhanced security, trust, and data integrity. Blockchain's decentralized and tamper-resistant nature enables secure transactions, device identity management, and transparent data sharing. In domains like supply chain management, blockchain can ensure authenticity, provenance, and transparency, mitigating issues such as counterfeiting and improving traceability.

The convergence of AI and machine learning with the IoT enables intelligent data analysis, predictive modeling, and automation. By leveraging AI algorithms and machine learning models, IoT systems can process and analyze vast amounts of data, uncover valuable insights, and make accurate predictions. This integration finds practical applications in optimizing traffic flow, predicting energy consumption, and improving resource management in smart city environments.

Edge intelligence and fog computing bring computational capabilities closer to the edge devices, facilitating real-time data analysis, localized decision-making, and reduced latency. These technologies address the limitations of traditional cloud-centric approaches by enabling edge devices to perform data filtering, preprocessing, and even complex analytics. The advantages include reduced latency, optimized bandwidth utilization, enhanced privacy and security, and uninterrupted operation even in the absence of cloud connectivity. Use cases in precision agriculture and industrial automation exemplify the benefits of edge intelligence and fog computing in optimizing processes and improving efficiency.

The emphasis on the significance of security and privacy in IoT has been underscored. With the increasing connectivity and data exchange in IoT ecosystems, robust security measures are essential to protect against unauthorized access, data breaches, and potential vulnerabilities. Access control mechanisms, authentication protocols, data encryption, secure device provisioning, and intrusion detection systems are among the key measures employed to safeguard IoT environments.

The presented case studies have showcased the practical implications of these integrated technologies in domains such as smart cities, precision agriculture, and industrial automation. From optimizing traffic management and resource allocation in smart cities to enhancing crop monitoring and supply chain transparency in precision agriculture, the integration of blockchain, AI, machine learning, edge computing, and fog computing demonstrates the potential to revolutionize industries, improve operational efficiency, and drive innovation in the IoT landscape.

References

Arun Narayanan, Mohamed Selim Korium, Dick Carrillo Melgarejo, Hafiz Majid Hussain, Arthur Sousa De Sena, Pedro E. Gória Silva, Daniel Gutierrez-Rojas, Mehar Ullah, Ali Esmaeel Nezhad, Mehdi Rasti, Evangelos Pournaras, Pedro H. J. Nardelli. Collective Intelligence Using 5G: Concepts, Applications, and Challenges in Sociotechnical Environments. *IEEE Access* (2022) 10: 70394-70417.

Bharadwaj Cheruvu, S. Bhargavi Latha, Mada Nikhil, Hitesh Mahajan, Kongari Prashanth. Smart Farming System using NPK Sensor. *9th International Conference on Advanced Computing and Communication Systems (ICACCS)* (2023) 1: 957-963.

Castano B, R Moreno M D. *An Integrated AI and RFID System for People Detection and Orientation*. (2009).

Darcy P, Tucker S, and Stantic B. Integrating RFID Technology with Intelligent Classifiers for Meaningful Prediction Knowledge. *Adv. Internet Things* (2013) 3(2): 27–33.

Deyang Chen, Zhiwang Guo, Jinbei Fang, Chenyang Zhao, Jingwen Jiang, Keji Zhou, Haidong Tian, Xiankui Xiong, Xiaoyong Xue, Xiaoyang Zeng. A 1T2R1C ReRAM CIM Accelerator with Energy-Efficient Voltage Division and Capacitive Coupling for CNN Acceleration in AI Edge Applications. *IEEE Transactions on Circuits and Systems II: Express Briefs* (2023) 70(1): 276-280.

Fernando Lopes, Victor D. N. Santos, Marina S. Perdigão, Jorge García. Design and Implementation of a Signal Processing Course to Integrate Master Studies in Sustainable Transportation and Electrical Power Systems. *31st Annual Conference of the European Association for Education in Electrical and Information Engineering (EAEEIE)* (2022) 1-6.

Gleiston Guerrero Ulloa, Carlos Rodríguez Domínguez, Miguel J Hornos. Agile Methodologies Applied to the Development of Internet of Things (IoT)-Based Systems: A Review. *Sensors* (2023) 23(2): 790.

Kamalrulnizam Bin Abu Bakar, Fatima TulZuhra, BabangidaIsyaku, Sapiah Binti Sulaiman. A Review of the Immediate Advancement of the Internet of Things in Wireless Telecommunications. *IEEE Access* (2023) 11: 21020-21048.

Kiş M, Kalayci TE. RFID infrastructures and AI approachs for security. *1st IEEE Annual RFID Eurasia* (2007): 1-6.

Ko CH. *RFID, Web-based, and Artificial Intelligence integration in facilities management* (2017).

Konstantinos Ntafloukas, Daniel P Mc Crum, Liliana Pasquale. A Cyber-Physical Risk Assessment Approach for Internet of Things Enabled Transportation Infrastructure. *Applied Sciences* (2022) 12(18): 9241.

Kwok SK, Albert HC Tsang, Jacky SL Ting, Wing Bun Lee, Benny CF Cheung. An intelligent RFID-based electronic anti-counterfeit system (InRECS) for the manufacturing industry. *IFAC Proceedings Volumes* (2008) 41(2): 5482-5487.

Laxmi Goswami, Neeraj Sharma. Latest Developments in Smart Grid and Wireless Security Technologies Serve to Protect the Environment for Better Upcoming Generations. *2023 International Conference on Artificial Intelligence and Smart Communication (AISC)* (2023): 390-393.

Liang Liu, Budong Xu. Research on Information Security Technology Based on Blockchain. *IEEE International Conference on Cloud Computing and Big Data Analysis* (2018): 5386-4301.

Mahmud R, Kotagiri R, Buyya R. Fog computing: a taxonomy, survey and future directions. *Internet of Everything: Algorithms, Methodologies, Technologies and Perspectives, Springer Singapore, Singapore* (2018): 103–130.

Mahdi H. Miraz, Maaruf Ali. Applications of Blockchain Technology beyond Cryptocurrency. *Annals of Emerging Technologies in Computing (AETiC)* (2018) 2(1).

Motaharul Islam Md, Zaheed Ahmed Bhuiyan. An Integrated Scalable Framework for Cloud and IoT Based Green Healthcare System. *IEEE Access* (2023) 11: 22266-22282.

Nuzhat Yamin, Ganapati Bhat. Near-Optimal Energy Management for Energy Harvesting IoT Devices Using Imitation Learning. *IEEE Transactions on Computer-Aided Design of Integrated Circuits and Systems* (2022) 41(11): 4551-4562.

Pradeep kumar G, Ramraj B, Manimuthu Ayyannan, Rohith Bhat C, Kalavathi Devi T, Neelam Sanjeev Kumar. Internet of Things (IoT) Feedback System using Raspberry Pi. *7th International Conference on Computing Methodologies and Communication (ICCMC)* (2023): 1399-1404.

Priyanka Arora, Ritu Makani. Blockchain Technology, and Its Applications: A Systematic Review of Literature. *International Conference on Computational and Intelligent Data Science* (2022): SSRN 4121824.

Resul Das, Muhammad Muhammad Inuwa. A review on fog computing: Issues, characteristics, challenges, and potential applications. *Telematics and Informatics Reports* (2023) 10.

Stephanie Baker, Wei Xiang. Artificial Intelligence of Things for Smarter Healthcare: A Survey of Advancements, Challenges, and Opportunities. *IEEE Communications Surveys & Tutorials* (2023) 25(2):1261-1293.

Stojmenovic I, Wen S, Huang X, Luan H. An overview of fog computing and its security issues. *Concurr. Comput,* 2016, 28(10): 2991–3005.

Ted H Szymanski. The Cyber Security via Determinism Paradigm for a Quantum Safe Zero Trust Deterministic Internet of Things (IoT). *IEEE Access* (2022) 10: 45893-45930.

Thomas Kitsantas, Athanasios Vazakidis, Evangelos Chytis. A review of blockchain technology and its applications in the business environment. *In International Conference on Enterprise, Systems, Accounting, Logistics & Management* (2019).

Vokerla RR, Shanmugam B, Azam S, Karim A, De Boer F, Jonkman M, Faisal F. An overview of blockchain applications and attacks. *IEEE International conference on vision towards emerging trends in communication and networking (ViTECoN)* (2019): 1-6.

Yi S, Li C, Li Q. A survey of fog computing: concepts, applications, and issues. *Proceedings of the 2015 Workshop on Mobile Big Data, ACM, Hangzhou China* (2015): 37–42.

Zakir Ahmad Sheikh, Yashwant Singh, Pradeep Kumar Singh, Kayhan Zrar Ghafoor. Intelligent and secure framework for critical infrastructure (CPS): Current trends, challenges, and future scope. *Computer Communications* (2022) 193: 302.

Chapter 6

System for Health Monitoring Built on IoT Using ESP8266-01 and Arduino

Lenience Saha, BTech
Shneha Prasad, BTech
Himangshu Chetia, BTech
Sanjay Chural, BTech
and Anish Ahmad*, PhD
Department of Electrical Engineering, Tezpur University, Napaam, Tezpur, India

Abstract

A health monitoring system is a type of technology designed to help individuals track and monitor their health in real-time. This system collects and analyses data on various health parameters, like body temperature and pulse rate. The data is then stored and processed using an IoT (Internet of Things) platform, i.e., Things Speak, which can be accessed by individuals or healthcare professionals. The key advantages of the health monitoring system include its convenience, accuracy, and reliability. It provides users with precise data on their health status, which can help them make informed decisions about their well-being. The monitoring and control of health may be revolutionized by the introduction of a system that monitors health and could play a crucial role in improving health outcomes for individuals around the world. In this work, a detailed system for tracking and monitoring real-time health based on the IoT is discussed. A detailed working design is presented and validated with the experimental prototype.

* Corresponding Author's Email: anishahmad.ee@gmail.com.

In: The Future of IoT with Automation in Engineering and Modern Technology
Editors: Sandeep Gupta and Tarun Varshney
ISBN: 979-8-89113-655-7

Keywords: health monitoring, health parameters, IoT, Things Speak, Arduino

Introduction

Internet of Things (IoT) is quickly revolutionizing the healthcare sector because of the abundance of innovative healthcare technology start-ups. The system for monitoring health is a cutting-edge piece of technology designed to help individuals track and monitor their health in real-time (Khan et al., 2017). Using Arduino and ESP8266, a system that monitors health built on the Internet of Things are discussed in this chapter. The Internet of Things platform is identified as Thing Speak. Thing Speak is an open-source IoT application and API that saves and retrieves data from devices using the HTTP protocol over the Internet or a Local Area Network. This monitoring system is equipped to collect and analyze data on various health parameters, including temperature and pulse rate (Teaw et al., 2005; Stone et al., 2021; Padmanaban et al., 2022). It continually updates an IoT platform with the temperature and pulse rate readings (Ru et al., 2021). The Arduino Sketch running on the system, includes receiving the sensor's data, converting it to strings, transmitting it to the Internet of Things platform, and outputting measured recorded heart rate and body temperature on an LCD (Thing Speak. (n.d) Internet of Things (IoT) Analytics Platform) are used in this book chapter.

As the world becomes more health-conscious, people are looking for convenient and non-intrusive ways to monitor their health and wellness. Traditional health monitoring systems/devices, such as fitness trackers and smart watches, are often bulky and uncomfortable to wear and may not provide accurate data. Furthermore, these systems/devices are not always suitable for continuous monitoring and may not offer insights into specific health conditions.

There is a need for a system that is compact, comfortable, and capable of providing accurate and seamless health monitoring. By measuring various biometric data, including pulse rate, systolic pressure, and levels of oxygen saturation, all from the comfort of a compact machine, the health monitoring system could provide a solution. One of the key advantages of this health monitoring system is its convenience. The system is also designed to be highly accurate and reliable, providing users with precise data on their health status. This information can be used to help individuals make informed decisions about their health and well-being, such as adjusting their diet and exercise routines or seeking medical attention if necessary (UNO R3 Arduino Documentation).

Overall, the health monitoring system could revolutionize the way people track and manage their health, enabling them to take proactive steps towards achieving their wellness goals and improving health outcomes for individuals around the world. One of the key advantages of this health monitoring system is its convenience. The system is also designed to be highly accurate and reliable, providing users with precise data on their health status. This information can be used to help individuals make informed decisions about their health and well-being, such as adjusting their diet and exercise routines or seeking medical attention if necessary (Ru et al., 2021).

IoT-Based Health Monitoring System

A system needs to be created so it can accurately and conveniently monitor the wearer's health metrics in real-time (Islam et al., 2020; Xu et al., 2017). Outlined below are several solutions a health monitoring system could implement:

Identify Key Health Metrics to Monitor

The first step in creating a health monitoring system is to identify the key health metrics that the system will monitor. These could include metrics such as heart rate and body temperature.

Determine the Technology Required

Once the key health metrics have been identified, the next step is to determine the technology required to monitor them, which could include sensors to track heart rate, blood pressure, body temperature, and activity levels.

Develop the Hardware

Once technology requirements have been determined, the next step is to develop the hardware for monitoring the system's health. This could involve designing a sleek and comfortable system that incorporates the necessary sensors and other technology (UNO R3 Arduino Documentation).

Create the Software

The software for the system is just as important as the hardware. The software should be able to accurately collect and analyze the data from sensors and provide meaningful insights to the wearer.

Test and Refine

Once hardware and software have been developed, the next step is to test the system and refine it as needed. This could involve working with a group of beta testers to gather feedback and make improvements to the system.

By using the techniques listed above, it is feasible to develop a health monitoring system that properly tracks the user's health indicators in real-time, offers insightful information, and aids in promoting overall wellbeing and good health.

The health monitoring system focuses on two major goals:

Continuous Health Monitoring

Heart rate, blood pressure, and body temperature should be continually monitored by the system.

Early Detection of Health Issues

Any unusual changes in the user's health metrics should be detected by the system, and a real-time notice should be sent to them. Early detection can help prevent serious health issues and allow for timely medical intervention.

Overall, the objective of a health monitoring system is to empower users to take control of their health by providing them with real-time insights and alerts and seamless access to healthcare providers with a user-friendly design that is comfortable to wear and easy to use.

Brief of Components

The basic components that are used are discussed one by one as follows:

Hardware Parts

The list of hardware parts is shown in Table 1. The details of the components are discussed in sub-sections.

Table 1. List of Hardware Parts

Part Name	Quantity	Description
Arduino Uno Board	1	Microcontroller board used in building and prototyping electronic projects and devices.
ESP8266-01 Wi-Fi Module	1	Microcontroller to correlate the entire process and connect to the cloud.
16 x 2 LCD	1	Display
Pulse sensor	1	To measure the pulse
Potentiometer 10K	1	Adjustable variable resistor
LM35	1	Temperature-measuring sensor
2K and 1K Resistors	1	Regulate the flow of electrical current.
LED 5 mm	1	Indication of action
Connecting wires	As required	Used for connection
Breadboard	1	Connection base

Arduino

Arduino, an open-source software and hardware initiative, creates and produces single-board microcontrollers for constructing digital devices. The software is freely available, enabling anyone to make Arduino boards and share the program under the GPL and GNU licenses and the hardware under the CC BY-SA license. Authorized distributors and the official website offer commercially available Arduino boards.

Arduino boards include expansion boards known as "shields," breadboards, and additional circuits that are connected to the digital and analog (I/O) pins on the boards. They also feature communication interfaces (serial), some of which allow for program loading via USB. To program the microcontrollers, the Arduino boards support the programming languages C and C++ and provide the Arduino Programming Language.

Arduino boards typically consist of an Atmel 8-bit AVR microcontroller at their core, which possesses varying features, flash memory, and pin counts. In 2012, the Arduino Due was introduced, incorporating a 32-bit Atmel SAM3X8E microcontroller. To facilitate programming and circuit integration, the boards utilize female headers or single- or double-row pins, enabling connections with auxiliary modules in a shield-style arrangement. Multiple shields are interconnected, allowing for layered functionality. However, certain designs, like the LilyPad, due to their unique form-factor limitations, do not include an in-built voltage regulator.

The boot loader that comes pre-installed on Arduino microcontrollers makes it easier to upload programs to the built-in flash memory. Instead of using the Arduino IDE, conventional microcontroller tools employ regular AVR in-system programming (ISP) when working with these boards.

The Arduino board provides access to a majority of i/o pins, allowing them to be utilized by other circuits. Models like Diecimila offer 14 I/O pins (digital), of which 6 generate PWM signals. Additionally, 6 inputs (analog) are used as I/O pins (digital). Moreover, there are several application shields on the market that can be plugged into the Arduino board.

Arduino Uno

Arduino Uno is a popular open-source microcontroller board that serves as an excellent platform for beginners and professionals alike to explore the world of electronics and programming. Developed by the Arduino team, it provides a user-friendly interface for creating interactive projects and prototypes. The Arduino Uno board is based on the ATmega328P microcontroller, which contains all the necessary components to run programs and interact with various electronic components. It features digital input/output pins, analog inputs, PWM (Pulse Width Modulation) outputs, and serial communication interfaces, making it versatile and capable of handling a wide range of tasks.

The decision was made to use the Italian word "uno," meaning "one," to represent a significant upgrade to the Arduino platform's hardware and software. In the 9th iteration of the USB-based Arduino board line, the Uno board replaced the Duemilanove release. As subsequent iterations were introduced, the Arduino Integrated Development Environment for the board progressed beyond its initial version 1.0. The built-in bootloader on the ATmega328 chip equipped on the board enables the upload of new code without using a third-party hardware programmer.

The board sets itself apart from its predecessors by not relying on the USB-to-UART serial chip. The board's hardware utilizes 14 digital input/output pins to establish connections with LEDs, buttons, and various components. Programming can be done using the pin Mode (), digital Write (), and digital Read () methods. For interfacing with external devices, UART TTL (5V) serial connections are accessible through pin 0 and pin 1 for receiving data and transmitting data, respectively. The conversion of voltage levels from temperature or pressure sensors into legible digital temperature or pressure values can be done using one of the six analog inputs. This allows computers to process and store data quickly. A built-in LED is located next to the GND (Ground) 0 pins and is managed via pin 13. When the value is high, pin 13 will be activated, and it will be deactivated when the value is low. Standard USB COM drivers are installed on a USB connector (5V) using 16U2 firmware. Through this USB-to-Serial chip and USB connection, Arduino may send or receive data from other devices like PCs and other microcontrollers. The TX and RX LEDs underneath pin 13 LED will flash when data is transferred.

The Arduino software enables users to personalize the software of the Arduino Uno. The setup section for initialization and the loop section for function realization make up the program's structure. And there are several libraries accessible in the software to help programmers. Particularly, a Software Serial library with functions like Serial. write () and Serial. read () is made for serial communication.

Technical Specifications

The technical specifications of the microcontroller are elaborated in the sub-sections.

Microcontroller

The ATMEGA328 microcontroller in the diagram is given in Figure 1.

IC: The ATmega328P is a microcontroller with an 8-bit RISC processor core, belonging to the mega AVR family. Initially created by Atmel and later acquired by Microchip Technology in 2016, this microcontroller utilizes a customized Harvard architecture and is intended to function as a comprehensive single-chip solution.

Clock Speed: 16 MHz on the Uno board; 20 MHz is the maximum IC at 5 volts.

Flash Memory: 32KB, of which the Bootloader uses 0.5 KB.

SRAM: 2KB

EEPROM: 1KB

USART peripherals: 1 (Arduino software defaults to configuring USART as an 8N1 UART).

USB port. The USB bus specification mandates a voltage range of 4.75 to 5.25 volts, which is applicable to USB ports. While third-party boards may include a mini-USB, micro-USB, or USB-C connector, the official Uno boards use a USB-B connector.

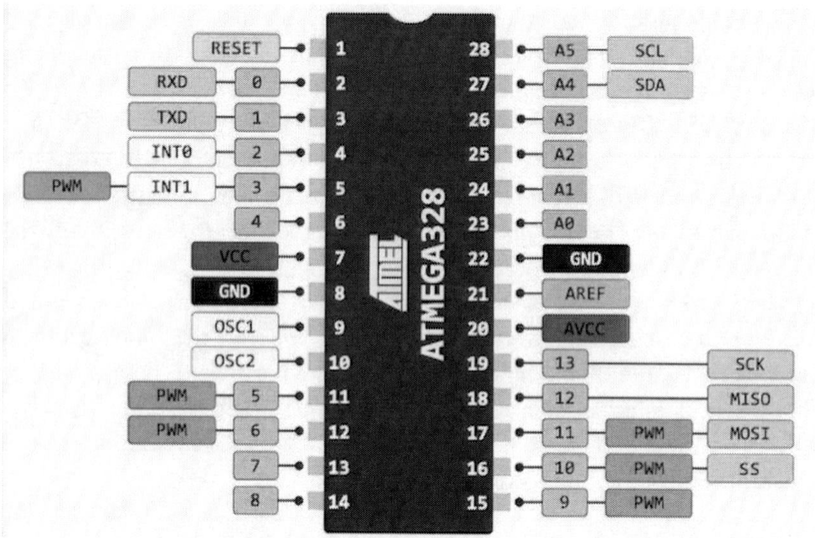

Figure 1. Microcontroller pin diagram.

Barrel jack connector, 5.5 mm or 2.1 mm. Although 6 to 20 volts are supported, it is advised to use 7 to 12 volts for official Uno boards. Because multiple voltage regulators are employed, each with varying maximum input capacities, the highest voltage permissible for Uno boards from different manufacturers may vary. To prevent inadvertent occurrences of reverse voltage, the power entering the connector is directed through a diode in series before being linked to the VIN connection.

The shield header's VIN pin. Its voltage range is comparable to that of a barrel jack. The fact that this pin lacks reverse voltage protection means that electricity can be extracted from or injected into it. If a barrel jack is used, an external series diode must be used when powering the VIN pin. This pin may lose power if the board is powered by a barrel jack.

General Pin functions

LED

The built-in LED on digital pin 13 can be controlled by setting the pin to a high or low value, which results in the LED being turned on or off, respectively.

VIN

The VIN pin allows for the connection of an external power source to the Arduino board. It accepts a variable input voltage range, typically higher than the 5V provided through USB or the regulated power source.

5V

The 5V pin provides a regulated output of 5 volts. It can be used to power external components or accessories connected to the Arduino board. Power can be supplied through the USB connector, the DC power port, or the VIN pin, but direct power supply to the 3.3V or 5V pins without going through the regulator may damage the board.

3V3

The 3V3 pin supplies a regulated power output of 3.3 volts. It has a maximum current capacity of 50 mA and can be used to power low-power components that operate at 3.3V.

GND

The GND pins are ground connections used for reference and completing electrical circuits.

IOREF

The IOREF pin serves as a voltage reference for shields connected to the Arduino board. It allows shields to identify the appropriate voltage level (5V or 3.3V) for compatibility.

Reset

The Reset pin is used for resetting the microcontroller on the Arduino board. It is commonly connected to a reset button to restart the board when needed.

Special Pin functions

Serial/UART

Pins 0 (RX) and 1 (TX) are used for serial communication, allowing the Arduino board to receive and transmit TTL serial data. These pins are connected to the USB-to-serial converter chip on the board.

External Interrupts

Pins 2 and 3 can be configured as external interrupt pins, generating interrupt signals based on specific conditions such as changes in voltage levels or transitions.

PWM (pulse width modulation)

Pins 3, 5, 6, 9, 10, and 11 are capable of generating PWM signals using the analog Write () function. This allows for controlling the intensity of output signals, which is useful for applications like controlling motor speed or LED brightness.

SPI (serial peripheral interface)

Pins 10 (SS), 11 (MOSI), 12 (MISO), and 13 (SCK) are used for SPI communication, enabling the exchange of data between the Arduino board and other SPI devices.

TWI (two-wire interface)

The A4 pin (SDA) and A5 pin (SCL) are used for TWI communication, also known as I2C. The Wire library provides functions to communicate with other I2C devices.

AREF (analog reference)

The AREF pin is used to set the reference voltage for analog inputs. It allows for the selection of an external reference voltage or the default internal reference voltage.

Communication

There are multiple methods available for establishing connections between the Arduino Uno and various devices, such as computers, other Arduino boards, and microcontrollers. The Arduino Uno utilizes UART TTL (5V) serial communication, facilitated by the ATmega328 microcontroller through digital pins 0 (RX) and 1 (TX). When connected to computer software, the ATmega16U2 chip on the board acts as a virtual COM port, enabling serial communication via USB. The 16U2 firmware utilizes standard USB COM drivers, eliminating the need for external drivers. However, on Windows, an .inf file may be required. The Arduino Software (IDE) includes a serial monitor, simplifying the exchange of textual data with the board. The RX and TX LEDs on the board indicate activity during data transmission through the

USB connection and USB-to-serial chip, but they do not illuminate when using pins 0 and 1 for serial communication. Additionally, the Software Serial library allows for serial communication on any digital pin of the Arduino Uno.

Automatic (Software) Reset

The Arduino Uno board facilitates a software-triggered reset from a connected computer, eliminating the need for manually pressing the reset button during the upload process. To achieve this, a 100 nano farad capacitor is used to establish a connection between one of the hardware flow control lines (DTR) of the ATmega8U2/16U2 and the reset line of the ATmega328. When this specific connection is activated, causing it to go low, it results in a momentary drop in the reset line, thereby initiating a reset of the chip (Galadima, 2014).

Furthermore, this setup has supplementary consequences. When the Arduino Uno is linked to a computer using USB, it experiences a reset whenever a software link is established. During a subsequent brief period of around half a second, the Uno activates its bootloader. While the bootloader is deliberated to overlook any invalid data, it does manage to capture the initial few data bytes received when the link has been initiated by the board.

ESP8266-01 Wi-Fi Module

The circuit model of the ESP8266 with pin display is shown in Figure 2. An easy-to-use and reasonably priced tool for linking your inventions to the World Wide Web is the ESP8266. The component may perform the dual roles of station (connect to wireless internet) as well as access station (make hotspots), making it easy to retrieve data and publish it to the World Wide Web, enabling connectivity to the Internet as straightforwardly as possible. Your section might access any online resource because it has the ability to obtain information from the Internet through APIs, which makes it more intelligent (Mesquita et al., 2018).

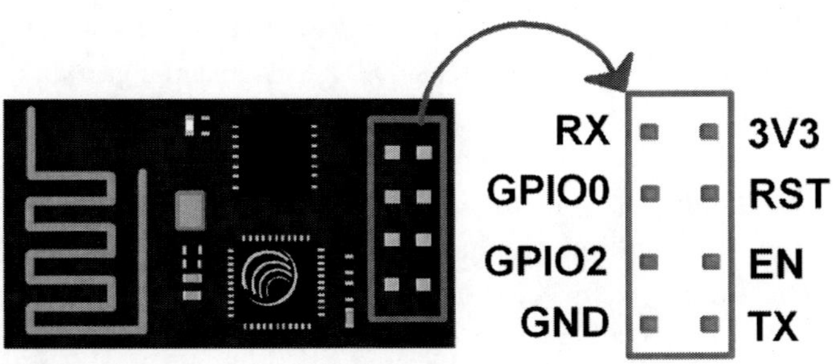

Figure 2. ESP8266-01.

Table 2. Pin Composition of the ESP8266-01

Pin No.	Pin Name	Alternate Name	General Purpose	Alternate Purpose
1	Ground	-	Connected to the circuit's ground pin	-
2	TX	GPIO–1	Attach the Rx pin of the programmer/uC to transmit the program	Serves as a general-purpose i/o pin when not being used as a TX
3	GPIO-2	-	General purpose i/o pin	-
4	CH_EN	-	Chip Enable is Highly active	-
5	GPIO-0	Flash	General purpose i/o pin	During initialization, the device enters sequential programming when the switch remains pressed down
6	Reset	-	The module is reset	-
7	RX	GPIO-3	General purpose i/o pin	Functions as a general-use i/o when not being taken as an RX
8	Vcc	-	Connect to +3.3V only	-

Another noteworthy ability of the ESP8266-01 is that it can be developed via the integrated development environment for Arduino, making the module far simpler to use (Mehta and Manan, 2015). The ESP8266 module can only be powered by 3.3 volts; anything greater than 3.7 volts would result in a fault.

The pin description for the Wi-Fi module is given in Table 2.

The ESP8266-01 Wi-Fi Module's Characteristics Are as Follows

The ESP8266-01 Wi-Fi Module is a cost-effective, robust, and portable Wi-Fi module. It operates at a supply voltage of 3.3 volts and consumes a current of up to 100 milliamperes. The module supports an I/O voltage of maximum 3.6 volts and can source a current of up to 12 milliamperes.

Equipped with a low-power 32-bit MCU running at 80MHz and 512KB of Flash Memory, it provides efficient processing capabilities. The module offers the flexibility of functioning as both a station and a gateway, making it versatile for various applications. It boasts a deep sleep mode with a power consumption of less than 10uA, enabling energy-efficient operation.

The ESP8266-01 module supports serial connections, enabling compatibility with multiple programming platforms, most notably Arduino. It can be programmed using the Arduino IDE, AT-commands, or Lua Script, providing options for different programming approaches. This module is a reliable and adaptable choice for Wi-Fi connectivity and can be seamlessly integrated into various applications. The option of BOOT for ESP8266-01 is shown in Table 3.

Table 3. Option for BOOT of ESP8266-01

GPIO–0	GPIO–2	Mode	Used For
High	High	Flash Mode	Launch the application that has previously been loaded into the component
Low	High	UART Mode	Development mode: use an Arduino or any other serial-connected device to code

The Arduino Uno finds applications in various fields and domains. Some of the applications of the Arduino Uno are:

a. IoT Initiative
b. Portals at access points
c. Electronic data logging
d. Home automation technology
e. Study networking fundamentals
f. Cellular electronics
g. Smart sockets and bulbs

Pulse Sensor

Knowing your heart rate is helpful when exercising or studying. However, figuring out the pulse of a human being is complicated. A sensor that senses pulse or heart rate is used to solve this problem. Because it is made exclusively for Arduino boards, this plug-and-play sensor is available to makers, students, developers, and artists who want to include heart rate data in their creations. The sensor's circuit is made up of an ocular pulse sensor with noise amplifiers and noise suppression capabilities. The pulse sensor is shown in Figure 3. The heart rate values provided by this circuit are prompt and accurate. It can run on a voltage of 5V and a current of 4mA, making it appropriate for mobile applications.

The Arduino board is used to connect the sensor, which allows for the simple computation of heart rate from the fingertip or human ear.

A colored wire, an ear clip, two Velcro dots, and three translucent labels are among the extras included with the pulse sensor. The pulse sensor is connected to header connections using a color-coded cable, making it simple to attach an Arduino board to a project without soldering. The ear clip is made to be the same dimension as the heart rate gauge and may be worn on the earlobe by hot gluing it to the back of the sensor. Two appropriately sized Velcro dots are provided for attaching the sensor securely with a Velcro strap, which can cover a significant portion of a fingertip. These dots are particularly useful for securing the sensor in place. Additionally, transparent stickers are included as protective layers to shield the sensor from sweat on the earlobes and fingers. The sensor features three holes along the outer edge, offering convenient attachment points for various accessories.

Figure 3. Pulse sensor pin configuration.

Pulse Sensor Specifications

This sensor is designed for detecting heartbeats and measuring biometric pulse rates. It has a 0.125 thickness and a 0.625 diameter. The sensor can operate at either +5V or +3.3V voltage levels. It is a plug-and-play sensor, making it easy to use. The current consumption is 4mA. The sensor incorporates circuits for amplification and noise cancellation. It's crucial to keep in mind that this pulse sensor is designed for academic-level research and is not intended for commercial usage in healthcare applications because it has not received FDA or medical approval.

Pin Configuration

Pin-1 (GND)

The system's ground terminal is connected to black-colored wire.

Pin-2(VCC)

The system's supply voltage is linked to the red-colored wire, which can be either +5V or +3.3V.

Pin-3 (Signal)

The pulsating output signal is connected to the purple-colored wire.

Working

A luminescent sensor and an intense red LED are included in the heart rate gauge's circuit schematic. To ensure maximum light passes through, the LED used should have a super-bright intensity. With a finger placed on the LED, the detected light spreads and passes through the finger.

The finger gradually gets opaquer as the heart pushes blood through the blood vessels, which reduces the amount of light that reaches the detector. This causes variations in the signal detected by the sensor with each heartbeat. Then, an electrical pulse is created from the fluctuating detector signal. A +5 volts logic-level output signal is created by amplifying and activating this electrical signal. Additionally, a light-emitting diode (LED) that blinks in rhythm with the heartbeat is powered by the output signal.

Potentiometer

A three-wire resistor having a contact that rotates or slides and modifies the voltage divider is called a potentiometer. It functions as an adjustable resistor or rheostat if only the two connections, a single end, and the wiper element are employed. The part implements the same concept as the potentiometer, a measurement tool that functions as a voltage divider for determining electrical potential (voltage).

Potentiometers are widely used to operate electrical gadgets, for example, the volume controls on musical instruments. Potentiometers operated by this system, for instance, can act as position transducers when used with a joystick. Potentiometers are seldom utilized for controlling significant power (greater than a watt), as the amount of energy expended through the potentiometer will be comparable to the energy generated by the controlled load.

Construction

A potentiometer is made up of an electrical terminal at each end of a resistive component, a contact that slides (the wiper) along the element and makes an electrical connection with a particular section of it, an assembly that shifts the slides from one side to another, and an enclosure that holds both the element and the wiper.

A resistive element (B) is used in the construction of many inexpensive potentiometers. When the potentiometer is cranked, a wiper (C) glides across this element, which is curved into the shape of a circle and often slightly less than a complete turn, creating electrical contact. Both angled and flat resistive elements are possible. Each of the resistive component's ends is connected to a contact (E, G) within the casing. The third connection (F), which is typically positioned in the center of the other two, is where the wiper is connected. The wiper terminal on panel potentiometers is often in the middle of three terminals. In single-turn potentiometers, this wiper normally makes a little less than one full spin around the contact. The confined area between the rotating shaft and the housing is the only site of entry for contamination.

The linear slider potentiometer is another form; instead of rotating, it includes a wiper that slides along a linear element. Anywhere along the slot the slider slides into has the potential to be contaminated, making proper sealing more challenging and jeopardizing long-term dependability. The slider position of the slider potentiometer provides a visual indicator of its setting, which is a benefit. A set of sliders can graphically represent the settings of a visual equalizer or the control knobs on a mixing console.

Graphite is frequently used as a resistive component in affordable potentiometers. Other materials utilized include carbon-filled polyethylene, resistance wire, and cermet, a ceramic/metal alloy. In addition to the carbon that gives conductive qualities, conductive polymer resistor pastes used in conductive track potentiometers also include solvents, lubricants, hard-wearing resins, and polymers.

A shaft is likewise rotated to control multiturn potentiometers, but this time, it is rotated through several turns rather than just one. Others have a spiral resistive component with a wiper that revolves over 10, 20, or more full revolutions as it passes along the helical structure. Some multiturn potentiometers contain a straight-line resistive component with a sliding interface that is manipulated by a lead screw. This type of rheostat, including user-attainable and preset ones, allows for finer modifications too.

An attenuator that is of string type is a numerous-turn attenuator that operates by twisting a connected wire reel against a spring to change linearity location into a variable resistance.

Accessible spinning potentiometers may be equipped with a switch that typically operates at the anticlockwise end of the rotation. Before the standardization of digital electronics, a component similar to it was employed for enabling television and radio sets, along with other gear, to be shifted on at a low volume with a clicking sound, after which the sound level was raised by twisting a knob. For instance, several resistance components may be ganged together in stereo audio equipment using their movable contacts on a single shaft. In other applications, such as residential light dimmers, it is recommended to leave the potentiometer in its current setting to satisfy the typical usage pattern. As a result, the switch is controlled by pushing the knob axially to turn it on and off.

Others are hidden inside the device and should only be modified to calibrate the device while it is being made or repaired. They may require a screwdriver to use rather than having a knob because they are typically physically a lot smaller than potentiometers that can be used by humans. The terms "preset potentiometers" or "trimming pots" are typically used to describe them. To enable servicing without disassembling, a small screwdriver can be used to reach several presets through a hole in the case.

Working

A potentiometer operates on the idea of moving the sliding or rotary contact or the wiper to change the resistance of a fixed resistor. By shifting the slider's position, the constantan or manganin wire's length can be adjusted. The amount of resistance provided to the circuit changes in direct proportion to the length of the wire. Even though changing a wire's cross-section is difficult, the resistance is also inversely proportional to the cross-sectional dimension of the wire. As a result, the resistive wire's length can be adjusted while the wire's cross-sectional dimension and flow of current are kept unchanged.

A potentiometer measures output between an adjustable endpoint and a fixed terminal, while intake is sent between the fixed terminals.

LM35

The analogue signal produced by a sensor that detects temperature, such as the LM35, corresponds to the actual temperature. Over a thermistor, Lm35 has the advantage of having no need for any external adjustment. It is also kept from getting too hot by the covering. Because of its inexpensiveness and improved precision, it is a favorite among hobbyists, learners, and DIY circuitry builders. Because of the LM35's inexpensive price, improved accuracy, and use in their goods, many inexpensive goods profit from it. The sensor's function has been utilized in a number of items for more than 15 years. With the rise in temperature, the resultant voltage also increases. A sensor with three terminals measures ambient temperatures in the range of negative 55 degrees Celsius and 150 degrees Celsius. The temperature sensor pin configuration is shown in Figure 4.

The LM35 sensor operates on the fundamental principle of a diode, which is that the voltage that flows across a diode increases as the temperature increases at a predetermined rate. By carefully enlarging the voltage modifications, it is easy to produce an analog output that is proportional to temperature.

Figure 4. Temperature sensor LM35.

Two transistors are located in the middle of the circuit. The size of one emitter is ten times that of the other. It possesses a current density of one tenth because identical current runs through each transistor. As a result of this, a voltage is produced over the resistance R1 that is both proportional to the temperature in absolute terms and virtually straight over the range of temperatures we are interested in.

By comparing the resultant voltages of the two transistors, the amplifier located at the top makes certain that the voltage that exists at the bottom of the left semiconductor (Q1) is proportionate to the absolute temperature. (PTAT). The amplifier converts the temperature in absolute terms (estimated in K) into either Celsius or Fahrenheit in accordance with the component's manufacturer (LM34 or LM35). An "i" inside a tiny circle represents a continuous source of current circuitry.

Both resistors are calibrated at the manufacturing facility to produce an extremely accurate temperature gauge. The Integrated Circuit contains many transistors, numerous in each amplifier, many in the permanent current source, and several in the curved correction circuitry. That's all contained in the compact, three-lead design.

Software Component

IoT: Thing Speak

IoT, also known as the Internet of Things, is a web of linked computers, including digital and mechanical machines, and people given UIDs. It is the extent of communication by sending and receiving data via a network without the requirement of communication between human beings with each other or with computers. Various methods exist as well as IDEs available along with the ESP modules, although the IDE of the Arduino is most extensively used (Gubbi et al., 2013).

The word "thing" denotes anything, living or machine, that could be assigned an IP address and can transport data over some network, including, for example, one farm animal that has an integrated biochip transponder, one car that has sensors placed in to alert the driver when there is low pressure in the tire, a patient with an implanted heart monitor, and any other living thing or machine (Swaroop et al., 2019; Tamilselvi et al., 2020).

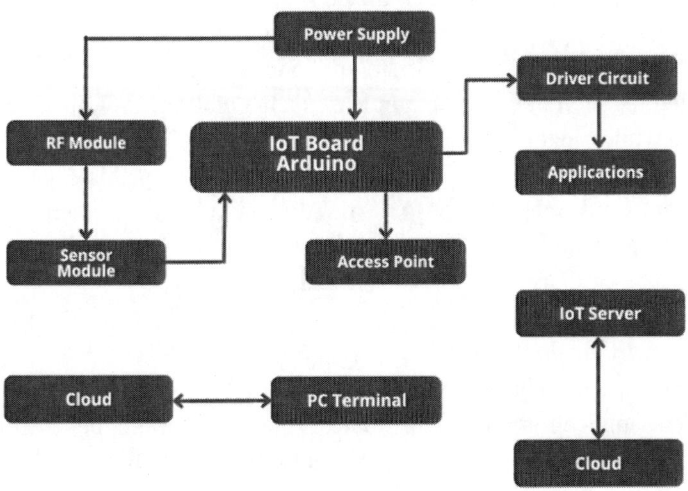

Figure 5. Block diagram of IoT.

The ecosystem that consists of the IoT is made up of smart devices with web access that use embedded systems as well as act on the information they learn about their environment. IoT devices connect to an edge device or IoT gateway, which either locally examines data or sends it to the cloud for evaluation to convey the data that they collected from the sensors. Despite the fact that clients engage with the devices in order to set them up, the gadgets themselves carry out the majority of the job without any help (Gupta and Johari, 2019; Vishwakarma et al., 2019). The protocols and technologies that enable networking, connectivity, as well as communication utilized by these devices that have the capability to connect to the internet are significantly impacted by Internet of Things applications. Machine learning and artificial intelligence (AI) may potentially be used in IoT to enable faster and more flexible data collection techniques (Madakam et al., 2015; Shafique, 2020). The block diagram of IoT is shown in Figure 5.

Applications of IoT in a Variety of Fields

In Home Appliance Automation

Home automation encompasses various aspects such as systems for heating, cooling, media, security, and cameras and is inclusive of Internet of Things (IoT) devices. Its overarching goal is to provide long-term benefits, such as energy conservation through automated shut-off of lights and electronics or by notifying occupants about their consumption patterns.

Central hubs that manage smart appliances and devices can form the basis of an intelligent home. One example of such a platform is Apple's HomeKit, which enables manufacturers to develop apps for iOS devices. The Smart Home Essentials from the Lenovo series is evidence of this capability, as it can be manipulated using the AI Siri. Alongside these commercial systems, there are also non-proprietary, open-source ecosystems available, such as Domoticz as well as Open HAB (Lee and Lee, 2015).

Taking Care of the Elderly

Assisting people who are very old and individuals with disabilities is an essential application of smart homes. These domestic devices integrate assistive technologies that cater to the specific challenges faced by the residents. By incorporating voice control, people with visual and mobility impairments can greatly benefit, while those who are hearing impaired and rely on cochlear implants can directly link alert systems to their smart devices. Moreover, the inclusion of sensors in these homes allows for the detection of medical issues such as falls or seizures. Ultimately, this utilization of smart home technology empowers individuals, granting them increased independence and an improved standard of living.

Organizations

Devices employed in professional and corporate settings are commonly known as "Enterprise IoT" devices. The projected number of devices in the EIoT by 2019 is 9.1 billion.

In the Medical sector as well as the Healthcare sector:

IoMT is an Internet of Things implementation specifically designed for the purpose of observing, collecting information, and conducting research in the domains of medicine and healthcare. It is commonly known as "Smart Healthcare" and serves as the technological foundation for establishing a digitized healthcare network that links together different medical assets and healthcare services.

IoT devices have revolutionized a wide range of tools for tracking and managing various health conditions. These monitoring devices span from basic ones like the detection of the pressure of the blood to advanced technologies capable of managing complex implants and state-of-the-art hearing aids. In certain healthcare facilities, innovative "smart beds" have been introduced, which can detect occupancy and monitor patients' attempts to get up. These beds can even autonomously adjust themselves to provide optimal pressure and support without the need for constant nurse intervention. According to a 2015 analysis by Goldman Sachs, healthcare IoT devices have the potential to save the USA over three hundred billion dollars annually by boosting sales as well as reducing costs. Furthermore, the integration of mobile technology in healthcare, known as "m-health," has been greatly influenced by the use of these devices to check health data and provide support for medical follow-ups.

Specialized sensors installed within living spaces can be utilized to observe and analyze the well-being of older individuals. These sensors are designed to ensure appropriate treatments are administered and aid patients in recovering lost mobility through therapy. To establish a connection between in-home monitoring devices and hospital systems, a network of intelligent sensors is employed. These sensors can collect, process, transmit, and analyze valuable information in various scenarios. The Internet of Things also facilitates the development of additional everyday products that are used by consumers to encourage healthy lifestyles, such as scales that are connected to a network or heart monitors that can be worn on the body. Furthermore, comprehensive IoT solutions for the monitoring of health are easily available for pregnant women as well as individuals with chronic conditions, simplifying the management of health data and ongoing medication requirements.

Recent advancements in electronics consisting of fabric and plastic manufacturing methods have enabled the production of highly affordable and disposable Internet of Medical Things (IoMT) sensors. These sensors can be conveniently created on materials like paper, allowing for sensing devices that operate without the need for wired power connections and incorporate essential RFID chips. The development of these sensors has led to the emergence of point-of-care medical diagnostic applications where the ability to carry them easily and the requirement for simple systems are of utmost importance.

Things Speak

MathWorks offers Thing Speak, an IoT analytics tool. It enables real-time data collection, analysis, and visualization from sensors or other devices. The following is a thorough explanation of how Thing Speak operates:

Overview of Thing Speak

It offers a cloud-based architecture for handling IoT data, making it simple to develop services and applications using the gathered data. Monitoring and understanding the data in real time is made much simpler by the fact that Thing Speak is equipped with built-in visualization and analytic tools. For data interchange with linked devices, it supports a number of IoT communication protocols, including HTTP, MQTT, and the Thing Speak API (Maureira, Oldenhof and Teernstra, 2011).

Key Characteristics of Thing Speak

Data Collection

Through APIs or direct integration, Thing Speak users can gather data from sensors, devices, or external sources.

Data Storage

For quick access and retrieval, Thing Speak's cloud-based database stores the gathered data.

Processing Data in Real Time

Using MATLAB, a potent programming language for scientific computing, Thing Speak offers the capacity to process and analyze data in real time.

Data visualization

Thing Speak includes integrated visualization tools that allow users to design unique dashboards, charts, and graphs to display the gathered data.

Data analysis and insights
It offers analytical tools for carrying out complex data analysis, finding anomalies, and drawing conclusions from the information gathered.

IoT Integration
Thing Speak is suitable for a variety of hardware and software ecosystems because it easily interfaces with a wide range of IoT devices, platforms, and services.

IoT Communication Protocols
The platform supports well-known IoT communication protocols like HTTP, MQTT, and CoAP, enabling simple communication between devices and the platform.

Open Source and Customizable
Because Thing Speak is open source, users have the freedom to alter and expand its functionality in accordance with their unique needs.

Working of Thing Speak
Users begin by creating a Thing Speak channel, which acts as a virtual repository for the data gathered.

Channel Fields
Users define fields inside a channel to stand in for other types of data they want to gather, such as temperature, humidity, or GPS coordinates.

Data collection
By sending HTTP or MQTT requests to Thing Speak with the required API key and field values, devices or sensors transmit data to the platform.

Data Storage
Thing Speak saves the incoming data and the timestamp of each input in the channels' predefined fields.

Data processing and analysis
Users can use MATLAB analytics to find important insights in real-time from the stored data by running computations, applying algorithms, and applying calculations.

Data visualization
Thing Speak has built-in visualization features that let users design unique dashboards, graphs, or charts that let them track and examine the gathered data graphically.

Thing Speak's integration with third-party services enables customers to link their IoT devices to external platforms or set off events in response to certain data situations.

APIs and Webhooks
Thing Speak offers APIs and webhooks for programmatic access, allowing users to communicate with the system, get information, or take actions from a distance.

Security and access control
Thing Speak offers encryption for secure communication between devices and the platform, as well as access control and authentication procedures.

Alerts and Notifications
Users can configure alerts or notifications depending on data thresholds or conditions. These alerts or notifications can be delivered via email, SMS, or customized webhooks.

Users may simply create reliable IoT applications, monitor connected devices, do real-time analytics, and receive insightful information from the gathered data by utilizing Thing Speak's capabilities. For IoT developers and academics, Thing Speak is a popular choice because of its open-source status and versatility.

Working Principle

The ESP8266 and Arduino Uno-based health monitoring system functions by gathering real-time health data and sending it to the cloud-based Thing Speak IoT platform for analysis and visualization (Valsalan et al., 2020). It also includes a pulse sensor, a temperature sensor (LM35), an LCD screen, an LED, and Thing Speak. The Arduino Uno's analogue input port can read the analogue signal from the pulse sensor, which uses the user's fingertips or earlobes to monitor variations in blood flow to calculate the user's heart rate (Mukherjee, Ghosh and Sarkar, 2019). A similar analogue voltage output proportional to the ambient temperature is provided by the LM35 temperature sensor, for which an analogue input pin on the Arduino is used to read data.

Then an Arduino Uno is used to handle the sensor information, executing the necessary filtering and calibration procedures to guarantee accurate and trustworthy readings (Soleh et al., 2018). On the LCD panel, the processed heart rate and temperature measurements are shown, giving the user real-time feedback. As Wi-Fi connectivity is enabled by the ESP8266 module, the system can connect to the Thing Speak IoT platform. The circuit diagram of the health monitoring system is shown in Figure 6.

The ESP8266 module is used to broadcast health information, including temperature and heart rate, to the Thing Speak platform via HTTP or MQTT queries. The information is structured appropriately—for example, as plain text or JSON—and sent to the relevant fields on a Thing Speak channel. The Thing Speak platform has a channel set up to accept and store the health monitoring data (Parida et al., 2019; Pasha, 2016).

To track their health data, view current and historical trends, and do data analysis, users can log into their Thing Speak accounts. For a thorough understanding of their health state, users of Thing Speak can generate charts, graphs, and other visual representations of the health data using the program's built-in visualization features. Furthermore, Thing Speak provides analytical tools that let users glean insights and patterns from the gathered data.

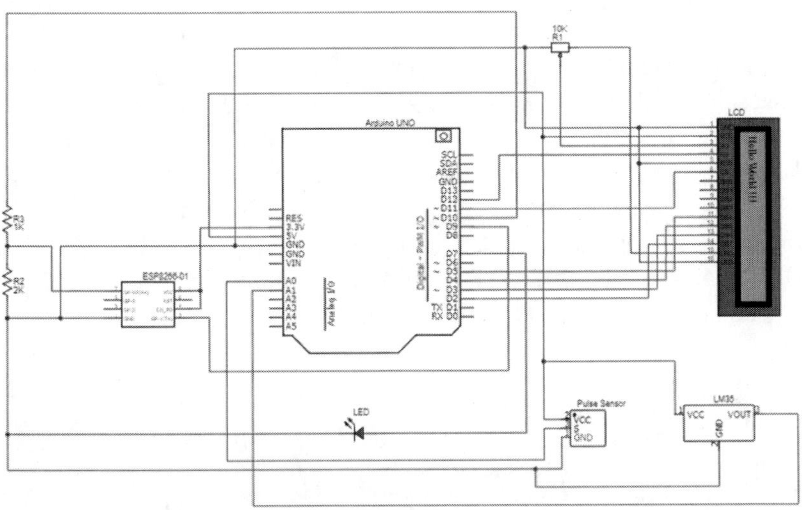

Figure 6. Circuit diagram of the health monitoring system.

Additionally, the system has an LED that is wired to an Arduino Uno and gives the user status updates or alerts. The LED, for instance, can be set to flash or show various patterns to denote certain circumstances, such as abnormal readings. Additionally, the built-in functionality of Thing Speak or third-party services can be used to construct notifications or alerts to inform the user of unusual readings or urgent situations (Brown Macheso and Meela, 2021; Deekshath et al., 2018).

In conclusion, the system that monitors health using the ESP8266-01, Arduino Uno, a sensor that detects pulses, a temperature sensor, an LCD screen, an LED, and Thing Speak allows for continuous monitoring of important health metrics, secure data storage in the cloud, data processing, and visualization (Baig et al., 2013). This fusion of physical elements with IoT technology makes it easier to administer healthcare effectively and gives people the ability to track and monitor their health in real-time.

Methodology

The hardware components required for building a system that monitors the patients' health with the use of an Arduino Uno as well as an ESP8266-01 based on the Internet of Things include an LM35 sensor (a sensor that senses and calculates temperature), an ESP8266-01, a pulse sensor, and an Arduino Uno. The sensor that detects pulse is the one that is used to determine the rate at which a patient's heart beats, and the LM35, which is a temperature sensor, is the sensor that is used to determine the patient's internal temperature. Both of these sensors are used to diagnose and treat medical conditions (Mansor et al., 2013). The ESP8266 allows the system to connect to the internet because it is a module that has Wi-Fi connectivity, while the Arduino Uno is used to control the sensors and send data to the ESP8266 (Kemis et al., 2012; khalaf, 2019; Khan et al., 2017). The detailed methodology employed in this respective project is listed below:

Setup of hardware

The UART serial communication interface is used to link the Arduino Uno and a Wi-Fi module, the ESP8266. One analog input pin among those on the Arduino is linked to the pulse sensor. The Arduino's temperature sensor, the

LM35, is attached to one of the different analog input pins. The proper interface is used to link the LCD screen to that of the Arduino Uno Board. For status indications, an LED is linked to the Arduino's digital output pin.

Sensor Readings

To determine the heart rate, the digital input pin on the Arduino is used to read the analog signal from the pulse sensor. Using the pin for the digital input on the Arduino Uno Board, the electronic voltage from the LM35 temperature sensor is read, and the transfer function of the LM35 is used to convert the analog signal to temperature.

Processing Data

To ensure accurate and trustworthy data, the heart rate and temperature measurements are processed as necessary, using any necessary filtering or calibration methods.

Setting up the LCD Screen

Initialization and configuration of the LCD screen's settings are completed. On the LCD panel, the processed heart rate and temperature information are shown.

Communication via Wi-Fi

The ESP8266 component is set up to link to the given network using Wi-Fi. Wi-Fi communication methods like HTTP or MQTT are used to create a connection to the Thing Speak IoT platform.

Transmission of Data to Thing Speak

The temperature and heart rate information are prepared in a format that is appropriate, such as plain text or JSON. The ESP8266 module is used to send the data, together with the proper API key and field values, to the Thing Speak platform via an HTTP or MQTT request.

Led Message

The LED linked to the Arduino is used to provide status signals or alerts. For example, it blinks to indicate that the system is operational or changes patterns to indicate that certain situations, such as abnormal readings, are present.

Thing Speak Integration

The data from the health monitoring system is received and stored in a channel that is set up on a Thing Speak account. The channel fields are set up to match the heart rate and temperature readings. The relevant information, accompanied by any essential additional data or relevant details, is transmitted to the appropriate fields in the channel via the Thing Speak API.

Data Analysis and Visualization

To examine the current and past data, the channel is accessible when logged into the Thing Speak account. Charts, graphs, and other visual representations of health data are made using the built-in visualization features of Thing Speak. The analytical functions of Thing Speak are used to analyze the data and derive insights from the gathered information.

Notifications and the User Interface

To monitor the health data, a user interface is developed, such as a web application, a smartphone app, or a local display coupled with the Arduino Uno. The user interface shows current statistics, past patterns, and pertinent information. To notify the user of unusual readings or urgent conditions, a notification system is established using either the built-in capabilities of Thing Speak or a third-party service.

The health monitoring system is configured and made operational by following these steps, with data being sent to Thing Speak and shown through an interface.

In conclusion, the health monitoring system uses the Arduino Uno to get information from both pulse and temperature sensors. Then the system can communicate over WLAN and deliver the information it has gathered to the Thing Speak platform thanks to the ESP8266 module. The platform saves the data, offers tools for visualization and analysis, and permits alerts and notifications. Local feedback and status indicators are provided by the LCD and LED screens. Users can view health data in real-time thanks to the user interface. The block diagram of IoT using Thing Speak, ESP8266-01, and Arduino is shown in Figure 7.

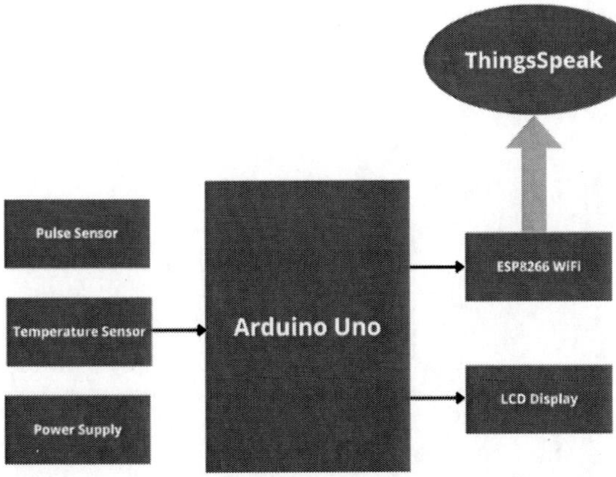

Figure 7. Block diagram of IoT using Thing Speak, ESP8266-01, and Arduino.

This simple block diagram demonstrates the ESP8266 and Arduino-based health monitoring system. The pulse sensor and LM35 temperature sensor serve the purpose of measuring the rate of heartbeat measured in beats per sixty seconds and tracking the ambient temperature correspondingly. The Arduino executes the code and carries out the specified tasks as well as sending it to a Liquid Crystal Display screen (16*2). The IoT device gets the data from the ESP8266 Wi-Fi module through Wi-Fi. Thing speak is the IoT server that has been used here. The information may also be viewed by joining the Thing speak channel from anywhere in the world.

Results and Analysis

This research work created a system that monitors the health of patients using an Arduino Uno connected to heart rate and sensors that detect body temperature. The system was powered through a USB connection and displayed the measurement data on the Arduino IDE serial monitor and an LCD display. Additionally, the data was transmitted to an IoT Platform, Thing Speak. The diagram corresponding to this whole set-up was depicted in Figure 8, while Figure 9 showed the Thing Speak data (Ahmed, 2016).

Below are the results of the test and an assessment of the patient's health parameter measurement. For the system to be tested, ten subjects, i.e., human subjects, were used for this chapter. The respective results of the measurements were gathered using the system we developed in this chapter.

The system was implemented and measured in real-world settings. The following table displays the results of sequential real-world tests conducted using the systems.

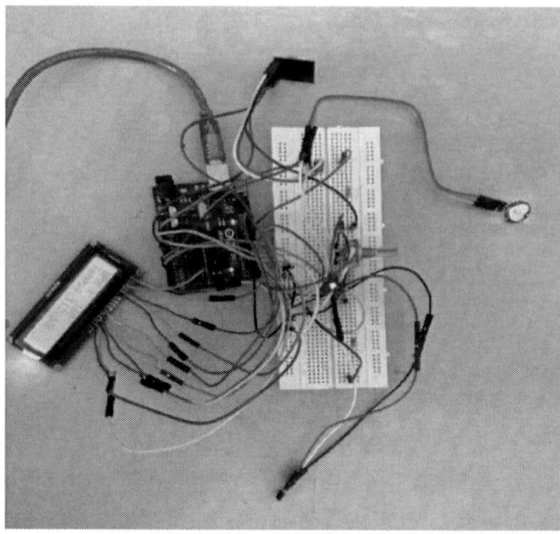

Figure 8. Full System Diagram.

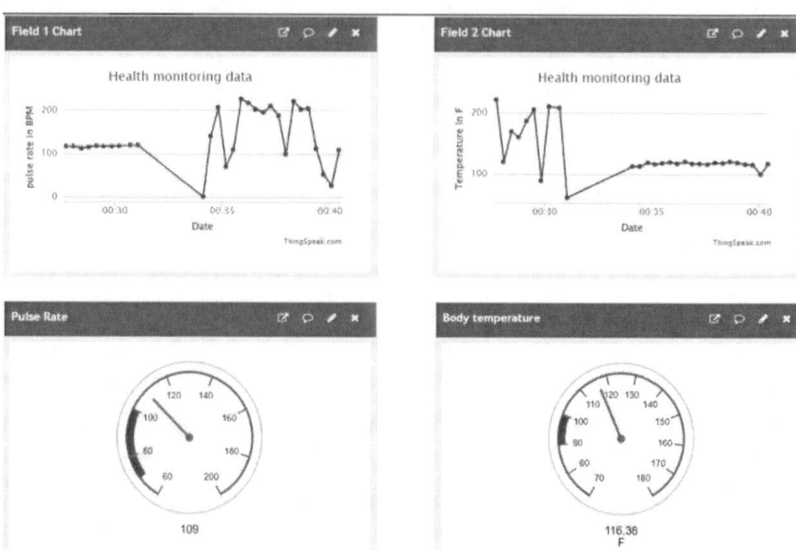

Figure 9. Things Speak Data.

Table 4. Heart rate and body temperature results of the test performed on ten people that are different from each other

	BODY TEMPERATURE (FAHRENHEIT)	HEART RATE (BPM)
User_1	117	98
User_2	120	100
User_3	103	77
User_4	105	85
User_5	110	92
User_6	108	88
User_7	121	96
User_8	115	93
User_9	100	80
User_10	113	94

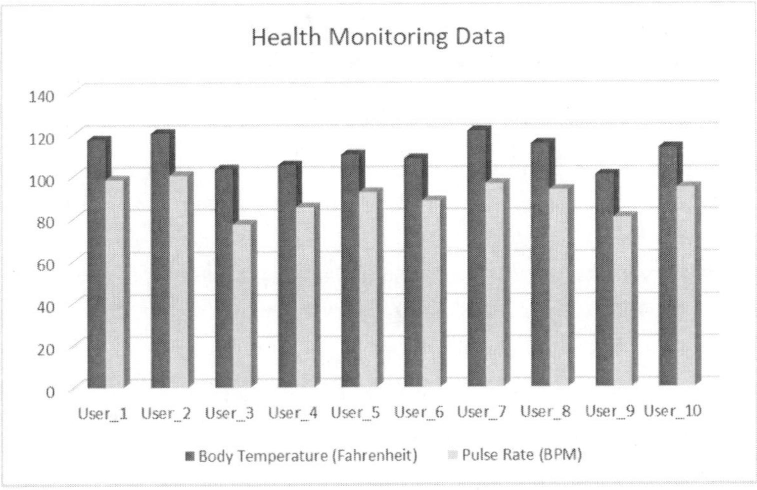

Figure 10. Health Monitoring Data.

Table 4 displays the body temperature measurement analysis and the pulse rate measurement analysis. The data showed that the temperature values varied slightly for each subject for the test due to the disparity in human bodies, but heart rates were comparable and within standard values. The temperature readings for each setting for a test subject's measurement are fairly close.

However, the data differs little for each test subject due to diverse human bodies. Table 4 shows the assessment of the measurement of the heart rate in ten people. The same individuals involved in the temperature measurement case were also involved in this case. We know the rates of the heart for the ten people may have a noticeable difference in them. However, the outcomes of the suggested system are excellent. The graph plot for the measured health monitoring data is given in Figure 10.

Discussion

Results obtained from the analysis suggest and show the importance of health monitoring devices in people's day-to-day lives. The development of a system that monitors the health of patients with the use of the ESP8266-01 and the Arduino Uno Board, integrated with heart rate and sensors that detect temperature, an LCD screen, an LED as well as Thing Speak, provides an efficient and reliable solution for continuous health monitoring. This work combines hardware integration, data processing, cloud connectivity, and a user interface to create a comprehensive health monitoring system. The system enables users to monitor their vital health parameters, store and analyze data on the Thing Speak platform, and receive real-time feedback and alerts.

The goal of a system that monitors the health of patients is to improve their outcomes by providing real-time observation and monitoring of their important health signs. This enables medical professionals to detect any abnormalities in the patient's vital signs early and take appropriate action to prevent complications. The system can also provide patients with greater independence and mobility, as they can be monitored remotely instead of requiring continuous in-person monitoring. In addition, the system can reduce healthcare costs by allowing patients to be discharged earlier and reducing the need for in-person visits to healthcare providers.

Overall, a system that monitors the health of patients with the use of the ESP8266-01 and Arduino Uno has the potential to improve patient outcomes, increase patient independence, and reduce healthcare costs by enabling the monitoring of live vital signs in a patient.

Conclusion

The development of health monitoring systems holds great promise for the future of healthcare. With advancements in technology, this system can track vital signs, detect early signs of illness, and provide real-time feedback on one's health. They are small, convenient, and non-invasive, making them a practical solution for continuous monitoring of health parameters. However, it is important to consider some of the challenges that may arise with the adoption of these systems.

Despite the challenges, the potential benefits of health monitoring systems are substantial. They have the potential to improve the quality of life for individuals by empowering them to take proactive steps towards their health and wellbeing. As technology continues to evolve, we can expect to see further advancements in this field, leading to more sophisticated and accurate health monitoring systems.

Disclaimer

None.

References

Ahmed S. Intelligent Bio-Detector. *Open Journal of Applied Sciences* (2016) 6(13), 903-937.

Baig, Mansoor M, Gholamhosseini H. Smart health monitoring systems: an overview of design and modelling. *Journal of medical systems* (2013) 37:1-14.

Brown Macheso PS, Meela AG. IoT Based Patient Health Monitoring using ESP8266 and Arduino. *International Journal of Computer Communication and Informatics* (2021) 3(2), 75-83.

Deekshath R, Dharanya P, Kabadia M K D, Dinakaran M G D, Shanthini S. IoT based environmental monitoring system using Arduino UNO and things peak. *International Journal of Science Technology & Engineering* (2018) 4(9):68-75.

Galadima AA. Arduino as a learning tool. *11th International Conference on Electronics, Computer and Computation* (2014): 1-4.

Gubbi J, Buyya R, Marusic S, Palaniswami M. Internet of Things (IoT): A vision, architectural elements, and future directions. *Future Generation Computer Systems* (2013) 29(7):1645-1660.

Gupta A. K. and Johari R. IOT based Electrical Device Surveillance and Control System. *4th International Conference on Internet of Things: Smart Innovation and Usages* (2019): 1-5.

Islam MM, Rahaman A, Islam MR. Development of smart healthcare monitoring system in IoT environment. *SN computer science* (2020) 1:1-11.

Kemis H, Bruce N, Ping W, Antonio T, Gook LB, Lee HJ. Healthcare monitoring application in ubiquitous sensor network: Design and implementation based on pulse sensor with arduino. *IEEE 6th International Conference on New Trends in Information Science, Service Science and Data Mining* (2012): 34-38.

Khalaf Abdullah S. Remote heart rate monitor system using NodeMcu microcontroller and easy pulse sensor v1. 1. In *IOP Conference Series: Materials Science and Engineering, IOP Publishing* (2019) 518(5): 052016.

Khan MM, Alanazi TM, Albraikan AA, Almalki FA. IoT-Based Health Monitoring System Development and Analysis. *Security and Communication Networks* (2022).

Lee I, Lee K. The Internet of Things (IoT): Applications, investments, and challenges for enterprises. *Business Horizons* (2015) 58(4): 431-440.

Madakam S, Lake V, Lake V, Lake V. Internet of Things (IoT): A literature review. *Journal of Computer and Communications* (2015) 3(05): 164.

Mansor H, Shukor MHA, Meskam SS, Rusli NQAM, Zamery NS. Body temperature measurement for remote health monitoring system. *2013 IEEE International conference on smart instrumentation, measurement and applications, IEEE* (2013): 1-5.

Maureira MAG, Oldenhof D, Teernstra L. Thing Speak–an API and Web Service for the Internet of Things. *World Wide Web* (2011) 25:1-4.

Mehta Manan. ESP8266: A Breakthrough in wireless sensor networks and internet of things. *International Journal of Electronics and Communication Engineering & Technology* (2015) 6(8): 7-11.

Mesquita J, Guimarães D, Pereira C, Santos F, Almeida L. Assessing the ESP8266 Wi-Fi module for the Internet of Things. *IEEE 23rd International Conference on Emerging Technologies and Factory Automation, IEEE* (2018) 1: 784-791.

Mukherjee S, Ghosh A, Sarkar SK. Arduino based Wireless Heart-rate Monitoring system with Automatic SOS Message and/or Call facility using SIM900A GSM Module. *2019 International Conference on Vision towards Emerging Trends in Communication and Networking* (2019): 1-5 Vellore, India.

Padmanaban K, Sarojini R, Ramalingam S, Sudha R. LoRA-IoT based Intelligent Healthcare Device for Physically Challenged People in Hospital Application using Artificial Intelligence. *2022 4th International Conference on Circuits, Control, Communication and Computing* (2022): 481-485.

Parida D, Behera A, Naik JK, Pattanaik S, Nanda RS. Real-time environment monitoring system using ESP8266 and Thing Speak on Internet of Things platform. *2019 International Conference on Intelligent Computing and Control Systems (ICCS), IEEE.* (2019): 225-229.

Pasha S. Thing Speak based sensing and monitoring system for IoT with MATLAB Analysis. *International Journal of New Technology and Research* (2016) 2(6):19-23.

Ru L, Zhang B, Duan J, Ru G, Sharma A, Dhiman G, Singh Gaba G, Jaha ES, Masud M. A Detailed Research on Human Health Monitoring System Based on Internet of Things. *Wireless Communications and Mobile Computing* (2021): 1-9.

Shafique K, Khawaja BA, Sabir F, Qazi S, Mustaqim M. Internet of Things (IoT) for Next-Generation Smart Systems: A Review of Current Challenges, Future Trends and Prospects for Emerging 5G-IoT Scenarios. *IEEE Access* (2020) 8: 23022-23040.

Soleh SSSM, Som MM, Abd Wahab MH, Mustapha A, Othman NA, Saringat MZ. Arduino-based wireless motion detecting system. In *2018 IEEE Conference on Open Systems (ICOS)* (2018): 71-75.

Swaroop KN, Chandu K, Gorrepotu R, Deb S. A health monitoring system for vital signs using IoT. *Internet of Things* (2019) 5:116-129.

Tamilselvi V, Sribalaji S, Vigneshwaran P, Vinu P, Geetha Ramani J. IoT based health monitoring system. *IEEE 2020 6th International conference on advanced computing and communication systems,* (2020): 386-389.

Teaw E, Hou G, Gouzman M, Tang KW, Kesluk A, Kane M, Farrell J. A wireless health monitoring system. *2005 IEEE International Conference on Information Acquisition, IEEE* (2005): 1-6.

Valsalan, Prajoona, Baomar TAB, Baabood AHO. IoT based health monitoring system. *Journal of critical reviews* (2020) (7)4: 739-743.

Vishwakarma SK, Upadhyaya P, Kumari B, Mishra AK. Smart Energy Efficient Home Automation System Using IoT. *2019 4th International Conference on Internet of Things: Smart Innovation and Usages* (IoT-SIU) (2019): 1-4.

Xu B, Xu L, Cai H, Jiang L, Luo Y, Gu Y. The design of an m-Health monitoring system based on a cloud computing platform. *Enterprise Information Systems* (2017) 11(1):17-36.

Chapter 7

Sports Training and Performance Monitoring Using IoT Technology

**V. V. Prasanth*

and G. Nallavan**

Department of Sports Technology, Tamil Nadu Physical Education and Sports University, Melakottaiyur, Chennai, Tamil Nadu, India

Abstract

Sports is one of the important areas where the IoT supports plenty of solutions utilising technological advancements. Using IoT, we can train, evaluate player strength and efficiency, guarantee safety in the surroundings, improve fan engagement, and also organise various operational activities in sports activities. This chapter aims to debate sports coaching and performance monitoring utilising IoT. Specifically, in terms of wearable gadgets in performance checking and harm avoidance, tracking the physiological and biomechanical specifications of athletes in real time, smart equipment, sensor-planted clothing, connected stadium infrastructure, tracking and positioning methods by way of GPS, video analytics and sensors, environmental monitoring, real-time observation, data analytics and insight generation, broadcast enhancement, sports analytics, dream sports, etc., Wearable science is one of the trending and progressing sciences, namely helpful to the athlete and coaches in observing the various dossiers in coaching and performance tracking, including Spo2, heart rate tracking, etc., by selecting a specific sports mode particularly applicable within the wearable instruments. Wearable instruments can work more with machine learning, artificial intelligence, and other technologies so that

* Corresponding Author's Email: prasanth199277@gmail.com.

In: The Future of IoT with Automation in Engineering and Modern Technology
Editors: Sandeep Gupta and Tarun Varshney
ISBN: 979-8-89113-655-7

injury avoidance can be further attained. Biomechanical analysis utilising IoT expanded in sports equipment or fabricated to combine athletes' physiques is used to capture dossiers. Sensors in tennis rackets and javelins can measure speed, angle, distance, and impacted forces, which provides insights to improve the players' performance by developing the perfect angle to attain speed, distance, and added forces and also prevents harm. GPS-empowered IoT devices help accompany sports coaching. The IoT-based devices play an outstanding role in gathering facts regarding environmental factors like climate, AQI (Air Quality Index), and weather prediction to optimise hydration and accommodate various climatic conditions. IoT tools also provide instant real-time feedback during instruction and coaching sessions and allow players to make necessary adaptations and improve their abilities. The data generated utilising IoT may be resolved using advanced machine learning algorithms to form conclusions based on the dossier. Through this interpretation, performance can be evaluated and patterns found. Monitoring individual physiological specifications and detecting early warning signs will help prevent injury and muscle fatigue. With this, coaches and medical crews can adjust loads and implement precautionary measures to reduce the risk of injury for athletes. These devices help identify more opportunities to execute future research in the sports industry along with IoT applications.

Keywords: IoT and sports, smart equipment in sports, Internet of Things in sports, wearables in sports

Introduction

Sports that consistently focus on championships and prove their strength in conquering the game. Even a small event and a millisecond matter in sports to determine the winner and loser accurately with the help of sensors and other advanced devices created with the integration of the Internet with those devices or systems. In these sports and games, IoT still adds extra value to the performers if they use it to improve their drills and performances. Day by day, the IoT also offers a quantity of changes that can increase the efficiency of the performer by keeping an eye on various activities that happen. Even though we have advanced techniques to measure the player's performance and train them to achieve goals in a game or match, the current methods are simply not up to the mark for more and more accurate data collection and correct training of player performance (Qiu et al., 2022). Our advanced sensor system uses advanced and trending technologies like machine learning algorithms to provide a level of accuracy never before seen in sports performance training and measure their ability to achieve the target within a stipulated period of time.

The need for accurate performance assessment goes beyond just winning or losing. It also ensures the players safety and well-being during training and keeps their performance on track with the help of wearables, which don't cause any disturbance to the player while performing an event or game on the field of sports. With the upcoming advanced system, we can identify potential areas of injury and prevent them from happening. We can also help athletes reach their full potential by identifying areas for improvement. This is why accurate performance assessment is so crucial in the world of sports. Internet of Things (IoT) utilization in sports preparation and performance auditing uses a lot of sensors and wearables to train and monitor the environmental, physical, and mental strength of the performer everywhere in the sporting surroundings. Which again supports the evaluation of actual time for action or event, and analytical advancements are further reached to achieve progress in the game of the performer.

There is research and the establishment of different appliances that are connected to sports that take place today. Wearable instruments and smart equipment are used to train players remotely when coaches are not available in person to train and monitor their performance to facilitate continued progress and support (Wang et al., 2018). Most sports addicts and sports organizations that want to show themselves in this field construct a lot of solutions, and more and more research is currently going into this field. This chapter will examine the use of IoT in sports training, coaching, and performance monitoring for athletes. This chapter is arranged into the following sections: The first portion explains the utilization of IoT in sports generally. This leads to a survey in the article of various utilizations. The next portion presents their uses and how they are expanded in sports preparation and performance monitoring. Finally, this chapter concludes with an idea of how the IoT plays a main role in enhancing performers acts. Suggestions for future research in IoT applications are also considered at the end of this chapter.

Literature Review

The smart sensors used to monitor movement pattern are also used to monitor the physical training in sports, which is achieved with the help of IoT simulation and its results (Dan et al., 2022). Effective prediction of risk can be achieved with the help of IoT devices in medicine-related diseases with the technical support of a real cloud-based fusion system (Hongmei et al., 2019). Sensors are fixed in the player's body (clothes and other wearables) to monitor the physical and psychological parameters with the help of IoT connected with ECG and EMG to know fully about the injury level (Ahmad et al., 2022; Chen et al., 2023; Nithya et al., 2022). Data that is taken with the help of smart sensors is used with intelligent data analysis algorithms/methods and smart training methods will be employed in various sports activities (Nithya et al., 2021). Heartbeat monitoring is achieved with the help of wearable sensors while athletes are involved in physical activity with the help of IoT in different positions and playing conditions in real-time (Roslan et al., 2019), which can predict the athlete's physical health through continuous monitoring (Wang et al., 2021; Huang et al., 2019; Municio et al., 2019). Intelligent management and monitoring systems for training halls through IoT are achieved with in depth analysis and research in sports training stadiums. (Qian, 2021) The education system for players and coaches is integrated with the help of the Internet of Things (IoT) and Artificial intelligence (AI) and is getting more advanced day by day (Hongtao et al., 2023; Yang, 2022). The Internet of Things employs wearable sensors to monitor rehabilitation and evaluate the physical condition and training effect in real time to develop or adjust future training in rehabilitation (Jiang, 2020; De Fazio et al., 2023).

Environmental conditions like temperature, air quality, and other climatic conditions are monitored in industries with the help of sensors that sense parameters and give this data to the cloud (Elumalai et al., 2021). This is also applied on sports fields to monitor the climatic conditions, adapt to them, and plan their training according to that data. In order to make sure that the player is in good health, wearables are used to measure and monitor the player's body temperature and reaction time to stimulus. Using that, we can also track heart rate, body temperature, muscle strength, etc. (Passos et al., 2021). The smart sports bracelet, which is an IoT device used to monitor/collect and transmit heart rate changes during sports, is listed here, along with the ZigBee wireless sensor, Bluetooth, and other communication technologies (Di Palma et al., 2019). This data will be analyzed with the help of a PC or mobile phone for real-time monitoring, storage, and analysis (Roslan et al., 2019). The detailed findings on the usage of the Internet of Things in sports are listed below.

Wearable Devices and Its Applications

Wearables are becoming increasingly popular in the field of sports as professionals and coaches demand ways to upgrade performance and prevent harm. Wearable tools can track a variety of metrics, including heart rate, distance traveled, calories burned, and even sleep quality. This dossier can then be used to design personalized coaching plans, recognize opportunities for improvement, and monitor recovery (Wang et al., 2021; Xiao et al., 2020). Here are a few of the particular uses of wearables in sports training and performance monitoring:

- *Tracking heart rate*: Heart rate is a key indicator of physical effort, and it may be used to monitor the depth of workouts and ensure that players are not overtraining as shown in Figure 1 (Wang et al., 2021; Passos et al., 2021).
- *Tracking distance traveled*: Distance well-traveled is a good measure of overall action level, and it may be used to track progress over period of time.
- *Tracking calories burned*: Calories burned are a measure of the energy used up while exercising, and they can be used to generate a calorie deficit for weight loss or to control a healthy weight.
- *Tracking sleep quality*: Sleep is essential for revival, and wearable tools can track sleep quality to recognize regions for improvement.

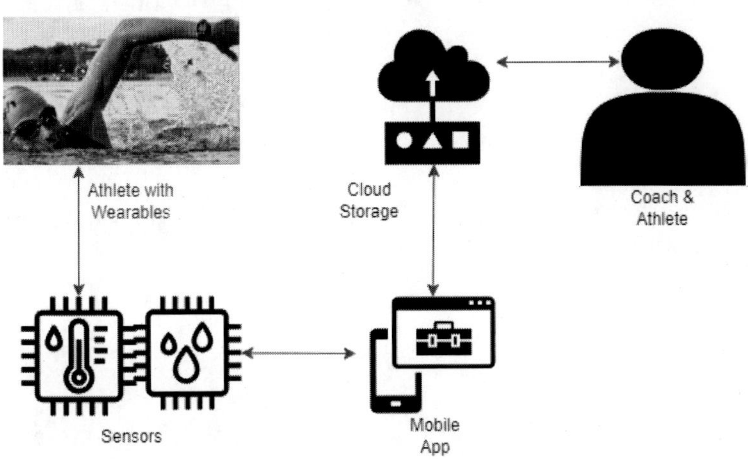

Figure 1. IoT Architecture in Sports.

Apart from these particular applications, wearable electronics can also be used to:

- *Track training load*: Training load is a measure of the overall stress placed on the body during training, and it may be used to avoid overtraining and harm.
- *Identify weaknesses*: A wearable dossier may be used to label weaknesses in an athlete's technique or health, which can then be addressed in training.
- *Monitor recovery:* Wearable dossiers may be used to monitor recovery from workouts and competitions, which can help players stay healthy and perform at their best.

On the whole, wearable electronics are a valuable tool for players and coaches who are looking to improve performance and avoid harm. By tracking a variety of metrics, wearable instruments can add valuable observations that may be used to advance training and revival. Here are a few instances of how wearables are being used in sports:

- *The NFL* is using wearable electronics to track player movement and activity levels. This data is being used to help coaches design more harmless and productive coaching programs.
- *The NBA* is utilizing wearable electronics to track athletes sleep quality. This dossier is being used to help performers advance their sleep practices and reduce the risk of harm.
- *The US Olympic Committee* is using wearable electronics to track the training of its players. This dossier is being used to help players increase training and raise their performance.

As wearable science advances further, it is likely that we will witness even more innovative uses in the realm of sports.

Smart Equipment

The Internet of Things (IoT) is revolutionizing the sports industry, accompanying smart supplies provide players and coaches with extraordinary observations into performance and training. Smart supplies can track a deep range of dossier, including heart rate, speed, distance, and location (Wang et al., 2021; Wang et al., 2018). This dossier may be used to monitor progress, identify areas for improvement, and avoid injuries. For example, smart shoes can track running gait and provide feedback on which method to use to promote efficiency. Smart bats can track swing speed and position, helping batters improve accuracy and control. Smart soccer helmets can track impact data, helping to avoid concussions. Apart from tracking dossiers, smart supplies can again be used to supply real-time observation and coaching. For example, a smart treadmill can provide feedback on running form, and a smart golf club can provide observation on swing mechanism (Roslan et al., 2019). This real-time observation can help players form adaptations to their technique and upgrade their performance.

Overall, smart supplies provide a wealth of data and observations that can help players train in a more productive manner and finish at their best. Here are a few of the benefits of utilizing smart supplies in sports training and performance monitoring:

- *Improved performance*: Smart equipment can help players track their progress, determine areas for improvement, and make changes to their preparation procedures to achieve their targets.
- *Lowered risk of injury:* The smart supplies may assist in tracking and monitoring the performance and health data of players. Additionally, anything that can assist in locating possible injuries sooner than expected and preventing their development can be of great use. (Wilkerson et al., 2018).
- *Improved decision-making*: Smart supplies can support coaches with dossiers that help them make better decisions about preparation, athlete selection, and game planning.

Smart equipment is a valuable appliance for players and coaches who are looking to improve performance, lower the risk of harm, and increase motivation. Here are a few examples of smart supplies that are being used in sports:

- *Wearable appliances*: Wearable equipment, such as smartwatches and fitness trackers, can track a variety of data points, including heart rate, steps taken, distance well-traveled, and calories burned

(Wachowicz et al., 2019). This data may be used to monitor progress, determine areas for improvement, and set targets (Wang et al., 2021).

- *Smart clothes*: Smart clothes are made with sensors that can track dossiers such as heart rate, muscle activity, and body temperature (Ahmad et al., 2022; Chen et al., 2023). This dossier can be used to monitor performance and determine feedback on preparation (Dan et al., 2022).
- *Smart equipment*: Smart supplies, like bats, balls, and rackets, may be equipped with sensors that track data, such as swing speed, position, and impact. This dossier can be used to develop methods and performance.

The use of smart supplies in sports is still in its infancy, but it has the potential to transform the way players train and perform.

Sensor Enabled Clothing in Sports

Sensor-implemented apparel is a type of wearable technology that uses sensors to accumulate dossiers about the wearer's activity, exertion, and additional physical metrics (Dan et al., 2022). This dossier can be used to track performance, recognize opportunities for development, and prevent harm. Sensor-implemented clothing has become more popular in the world of sports as players and coaches anticipate ways to improve performance and avoid injuries (Ahmad et al., 2022). There are a few diverse types of sensor-enabled attire available, each with its own specific benefits as shown in Figure 2.

Some of the most common types of sensor-implemented clothes include:

- *Heart rate monitors*: Heart rate monitors are one of the most famous types of sensor-implemented clothing. They track the wearer's heart rate, to monitor exertion levels and ensure that players are not overtraining.
- *GPS trackers*: GPS trackers monitors the wearer's movement and position, tracking distance traveled, calories burned, and additional metrics.
- *Accelerometers*: Accelerometers track the wearer's motion and can be used to track steps taken, distance traveled, and other metrics.

- *Gyroscope*: Gyroscopes track the wearer's rotation and can be used to track balance, posture, and other metrics.

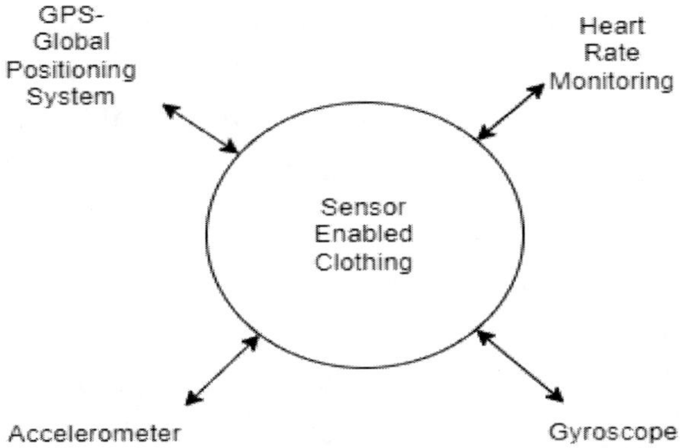

Figure 2. Athletic clothing with Sensors.

Sensor-implemented attire can be used for a variety of purposes in sports coaching and performance monitoring, including:

- *Tracking performance*: Sensor-implemented attire can be used to track performance metrics such as heart rate, distance traveled, and calories burned. This dossier can later be used to analyze areas for improving and tracking progress over a period of time.
- *Identifying weaknesses*: Sensor-implemented attire can be used to diagnose weaknesses in an athlete's approach or fitness. This dossier can then be used to point out weaknesses in training.
- *Monitoring revival*: Sensor-implemented clothing may be used to monitor revival from workouts and competitions. This dossier can help athletes stay healthy and perform at their best (Ahmad et al., 2022; Chen et al., 2023; Huang et al., 2019).
- *Avoiding injuries*: Sensor-implemented attire can be used to block harm by monitoring exertion levels and analyzing weaknesses in an athlete's technique or fitness.

Sensor-implemented clothing is a valuable accessory for players and coaches who are looking to boost performance and block injuries. By following a variety of metrics, sensor-implemented attire can specify valuable insights that may be used to enhance coaching and recovery. Here are a few examples of by virtue of what sensor-implemented attire is being used in sports:

- *The NFL* is utilizing sensor-implemented attire to track athlete evolution and exertion levels. This dossier is being used to help coaches design more harmless and productive training programs.
- *The NBA* is utilizing sensor-implemented attire to track performers sleep quality. This data is being used to help performers develop their sleep practices and reduce the risk of harm.
- *The US Olympic Committee* is utilizing sensor-enabled attire to track the training of its players.

This dossier is being used to help athletes correct their preparation and develop their performance. As sensor-implemented attire continues to evolve, it is likely that we will visualize even more creative applications in the realm of sports.

Connected Stadium Infrastructure

An amphitheater is a network of sensors, cameras, and other equipment that is used to collect data about all that occurs inside a stadium. This dossier can later be used to develop the fan experience, better operations, and track player performance. By tracking player movement, activity, and additional metrics, amphitheaters can provide valuable observations that may be used to improve preparation and avoid harm (Qian, 2021).

For example, an amphitheater can be used to track:

- *Participant movement*: This dossier may be used to determine weaknesses in an athlete's approach or fitness that can therefore be addressed in training.
- *Exertion levels*: This dossier may be used to monitor the intensity of workouts and ensure that players are not overtraining.
- *Recovery:* This dossier may be used to monitor recovery from workouts and competitions, which can help players stay healthy and perform at their best.

Apart from tracking player performance, amphitheaters can also be used to better the fan experience. For example, an amphitheater can be used to:

- *Personalize the fan experience*: By tracking fan choices, amphitheaters may be used to embody the fan experience, such as by recommending food and drinks or by providing real-time updates on the game (Roslan et al., 2019).
- *Enhance security*: Amphitheaters may be used to advance security by tracking fan activities and determining potential risks.
- *Reduce costs*: Amphitheaters may be used to lower costs by automating tasks like ticket examination and concession orders.

On the whole, amphitheaters have the potential to revolutionize the way sports are performed and observed. By collecting and evaluating dossiers, amphitheaters can gain valuable insights that may be used to advance athlete performances, the fan experience, and stadium operations.

Here are a few examples of how related stadium infrastructure is being used in sports:

- *The NFL* is utilizing amphitheaters to track player movement and exertion levels. This dossier is being used to help coaches design safer and more productive preparation programs.
- *The NBA* is utilizing amphitheaters to track athletes sleep quality. This dossier is being used to help players increase their sleep practices and reduce the risk of harm.
- *The US Olympic Committee* is using an amphitheater to track the training of its players. This data is being used to help players improve their preparation and performance.

As amphitheaters evolve, it is likely that we will see even more creative uses in the world of sports.

Smart Scoreboards and Sensors

Connected scoreboards and time lapse electronics are becoming progressively popular in running competitions. These technologies can provide a number of benefits for both runners and spectators, including:

- *Real-time updates:* Connected scoreboards can determine real-time updates on the race, including current positions, lap times, and split times. These facts may be helpful for runners to track their progress and for fans to understand the race (Roslan et al., 2019).
- *In-depth analysis*: Time lapse electronics can be used to conduct a thorough investigation of the race in terms of the runner's speed, stride length, and ground contact time. This information may be beneficial for contestants to improve their approach and for coaches to advance preparation plans.

Here are some models of in what way or manner connected scoreboards and time lapse electronics are being used in running events:

- *The Boston Marathon:* The Boston long-distance race uses connected scoreboards to provide real-time updates on the race. This information is handy for contestants, sports fans, and the media.
- *The New York City Marathon*: The New York City long-distance race uses time lapse electronics to provide an in-depth evaluation of the race. This information is available to marathoners, coaches, and publishers.
- *The London Marathon*: The London long-distance race uses connected scoreboards and time lapse electronics to develop the fan experience. This information is accessible to marathoners, spectators, and publishers.

As connected scoreboards and time lapse electronics continue to be promoted, it is likely that we will see even more creative applications in the realm of running events. Here are a few additional benefits of utilizing connected scoreboards and time lapse electronics in running events:

- *Increased protection from harm*: Connected scoreboards may be used to display useful information on hazardous conditions, such as weather conditions and road closures. This fact can help runners stay safe throughout the race.
- *Improved efficiency*: Connected scoreboards may be used to automate tasks such as timing the race and calculating results.

- *Reduced costs*: Connected scoreboards may be used to replace usual scoreboards and timekeeping methods. This can help decrease the cost of running an event.

On the whole, connected scoreboards and time lapse electronics offer a number of benefits for both marathoners and sports fans. These electronics are becoming progressively well-known in running competitions and are likely to develop even further. IoT implemented lights and other sensor instruments in amphitheaters may be used to improve the fan experience, increase operations, and track player performance. Here are a few of the ways that IoT implemented lights and other sensor instruments can be used in stadiums:

- *Improve the fan experience*: IoT implemented lights may be used to design a more immersive and engaging fan experience. The lights may be used to generate special effects similar to fireworks or laser shows. Sensors may be used to track fan movement and choices, which can personalize the fan experience; e.g., sensors can be used to determine which regions of the amphitheater are most crowded, and later fix the lighting and sound levels accordingly.
- *Optimize operations*: IoT implemented lights and other sensor devices may be used to enhance amphitheater operations. The sensors may be used to track amphitheater usage and to recognize areas where improvements could be made. For example, sensors can track the number of people using restrooms, which may help decide if more restrooms are needed.
- *Track athlete performance*: IoT implemented lights and other sensor instruments may be used to track athlete performance. The sensors may be used to track player movement, exertion levels, and revival. This data may be used to develop drill programs and avoid injuries.

The IoT technologies implemented lights and other sensor instruments offer a number of benefits for both stadiums and their consumers. These electronics are becoming progressively well-known and are likely to become even more common. Here are a few specific models of by means of what IoT implemented lights and other sensor instruments are being used in stadiums:

- *The Mercedes-Benz Amphitheater* in Atlanta, Georgia, uses IoT implemented lights to create a more immersive and intimate fan experience. When fireworks or laser displays are used to monitor fan activity and choices, which are utilized to personalize the fan experience, the lights may be used to create spectacular effects in the same way as fireworks or laser shows are used.

- *The AT&T Amphitheater* in Arlington, Texas, uses IoT enabled lights to better amphitheater movements. The lights may be automatically dimmed when there are no fans in the amphitheater, helping to sustain power costs. Sensors are used to monitor the utilization of the stadium, which enables the identification of areas that might benefit from improvement.
- *The Tottenham Hotspur Stadium* in London, England, uses IoT implemented lights and other sensor instruments to track player performance. Sensors are used to track player activity, exertion levels, and recovery. This data is used to improve training programs and avoid harm.

Tracking and Positioning Systems

The Internet of Things (IoT) is a network of physical objects that are embedded with sensors, software, and network connectivity to collect and exchange data (Li et al., 2020). This dossier may be used to track and monitor the performance of competitors in various running events. There are a number of different IoT tracking and positioning systems that can be used for this purpose. Some of the most familiar systems involve:

- *GPS trackers*: GPS trackers use satellites to determine the location of a player. This data may be used to track an athlete's distance traveled, speed, and pace.
- *Heart rate monitors*: Heart rate monitors use sensors to measure an athlete's heart rate. These facts may be used to track an athlete's exertion level and fitness (Wang et al., 2021).
- *In-footwear sensors*: In-footwear sensors measure an athlete's foot strike, stride length, and ground contact period. This data can be used to enhance a player's running form.

IoT tracking and positioning systems may be used to train and monitor the conduct of players in a number of different ways. Coaches can use this dossier to:

- *Track an athlete's progress over time*: By tracking a player's distance traveled, speed, and pace, coaches can see by what method a player is progressing over period. This information may be used to regulate a player's training program to help them reach their targets.
- *Identify areas where an athlete needs development*: By tracking a player's heart rate, foot strike, and stride length, coaches can recognize areas where a player needs bettering. This information can be used to supply the player with distinguishing training exercises to help them develop their performance.
- *Avoid injuries*: By tracking an athlete's exertion level, coaches can avert injuries by ensuring that an athlete does not over train. IoT tracking and positioning systems are valuable gadgets for coaches and players. By utilizing this technology, coaches can track a player's progress over period, describe areas where an athlete needs bettering, and block harm (Di Palma et al., 2019). Here are some supplementary benefits of utilizing IoT tracking and positioning methods in running competitions:
- *Improved safety*: IoT tracking systems can help develop safety by providing real-time location data for players. This information can be used to track contestants all the while races and training runs and to help locate athletes who are lost or injured.
- *Increased efficiency*: IoT tracking methods can help increase adeptness by providing real-time dossier on player performance. This data may be used to develop training programs and race game plans, and to help athletes reach their full potential.
- *Enhanced fan experience*: IoT tracking systems can improve the fan experience by providing real-time data on player performance and race statistics.

These facts can be used to create more engaging and interactive experiences for fans and to help them better understand the sport of running. On the whole, IoT following and locating structures offer a number of benefits for professionals, coaches, and fans. By utilizing these electronics, players in running events can boost their efficiency, security, and effectiveness.

Sensors in Sports Video Analysis

Sensors are progressively being used in Video analysis to provide coaches and players with more detailed insights into their performance. Sensors can track a variety of metrics, including movement, speed, acceleration, and heart rate, which may be used to recognize areas for improvement and avoid harm. Some of the most accepted sensors used in video analysis as shown in Figure 3, include:

- *Accelerometers:* Accelerometers measure acceleration and may be used to track motion, speed, and impact.
- *Gyroscopes:* Gyroscopes measure rotation and may be used to track balance, movement, and orientation.
- *GPS*: GPS devices track location and can be used to track distance traveled, speed, and pace.
- *Heart rate monitors*: Heart rate monitors measure heart rate and may be used to track exertion, improvement, and fitness level.
- *EMG:* EMG devices measure muscle activity and may be used to track exertion, fatigue, and method (Nithya et al., 2022).

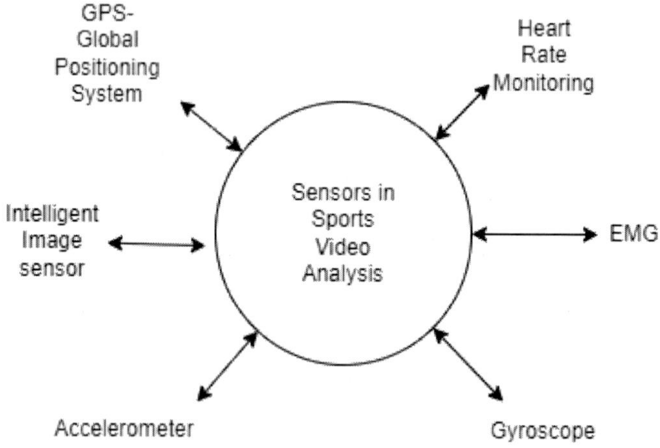

Figure 3. Sensors in Sports Video Analysis.

Sensor dossiers may be used to create detailed heat maps that show where players are mobile on the field or court. These facts can be used to recognize areas where players are investing too much or too little time, which can help coaches evolve plans to improve team performance. Sensor dossiers can likewise be used to track player movement and speed over period. This information may be used to recognize trends in player performance that can help coaches label fields where players need to develop. Sensory dossiers can be used to track heart rate and exertion levels. Listed below are a few particular examples of how sensors are being used in the process of video analysis:

- *MLB*: Major League Baseball (MLB) is utilizing sensors to track the movement of performers and the speed of pitches. This dossier is being used to enhance the accuracy of umpire calls and to evolve new game plans for pitchers and hitters.
- *NFL*: The National Football League (NFL) is utilizing sensors to track the movement of performers and the impact of hits. This data is being used to enhance performer safety and develop new rules for the game.
- *NBA*: The National Basketball Association (NBA) is utilizing sensors to track the movement of athletes and the speed of passes. This dossier is being used to improve athlete performance and evolve new game plans for coaches.

Sensors are being used more in video analysis to provide coaches, players, and fans with a deeper understanding of the game. By combining sensor data with video footage, analysts can track athlete movements, measure performance, and recognize trends. Here are some of the ways that sensors are being used in video analysis:

- *Tracking player movement*: Sensors may be used to track player movement on the field or court. This data may be used to measure distance traveled, speed, and acceleration. It can also be used to identify patterns in player movement, in as how frequently an athlete changes direction or how much time they spend in each area of the field.
- *Measuring performance*: Sensors may be used to measure athlete performance in terms of speed, strength, and endurance. This dossier may be used to track progress over period, identify areas for bettering, and make sure that players are training safely.
- *Identifying trends*: Sensors may be used to recognize trends in player performance. This dossier may be used to predict future performance, identify areas of weakness, and develop new training programs.

Sensors are a powerful tool that may be used to improve athlete performance, avoid injuries, and analyze games in sports. As technology continues to develop, we can anticipate even more creative uses for sensors in Video analysis. Here are a few distinguishing examples of how sensors are being used in sports program analytics:

- *In baseball*, sensors are being used to track the movement of the ball and the bat. This data may be used to identify best choice pitches for each batter and to improve the accuracy of the strike zone.
- *In football*, sensors are being used to track the movement of players and the ball. This data may be used to identify the best plays for each situation and to develop the accuracy of the down and distance.
- *In basketball*, sensors are being used to track the movement of athletes and the ball. This dossier may be used to identify the best shots for each player and to raise the accuracy of the shot clock.

Environmental Monitoring

Environmental impact analysis is the process of gathering and analyzing information about the surrounding environment. In sports training and performance monitoring, environmental monitoring can be used to track a variety of factors, including:

- *Weather conditions*: Temperature, humidity, wind speed and direction, and air quality can all influence an athlete's performance. By tracking weather conditions, coaches and players can draw informed conclusions about training and competition.
- *Air quality*: Air quality may be affected by pollution, smoke, and other circumstances. Poor air quality can irritate body parts and make it difficult for players to breathe. By tracking air quality, coaches and players can avoid preparing for or competing in regions with poor air quality.
- *Altitude*: Altitude can affect an athlete's performance by lowering the amount of oxygen available in the air. This can bring about fatigue, shortness of breath, and other difficulties. By tracking altitude, coaches and athletes can regulate their training and contests accordingly.

- *Noise levels*: Noise levels may be a distraction for players and can also damage hearing. By tracking noise levels, coaches and players can find quiet places to train and compete (Elumalai et al., 2021).

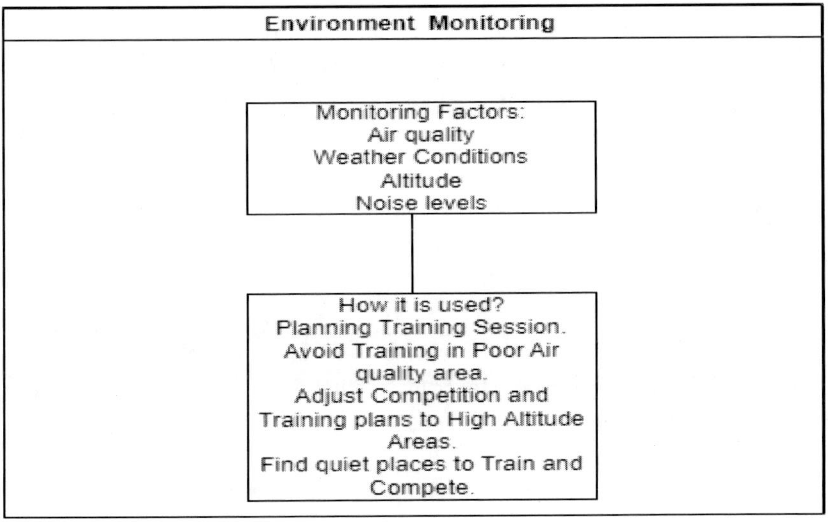

Figure 4. Benefits of Environment Monitoring in Sports using IoT.

Environmental monitoring can be used to advance player performance in a number of ways as shown in Figure 4. By tracking environmental factors, coaches and players can:

- Plan training sessions that are appropriate for the weather conditions. For example, on hot days, coaches may choose to train inside or focus on activities that do not require enough running.
- Avoid training or competing in areas with poor air quality. This can help prevent respiratory difficulties and enhance performance.
- Adjust training and competition plans for high-altitude surroundings. This can help prevent altitude sickness and advance performance.
- Find quiet places to train and compete. This can help improve focus and concentration.

Environmental monitoring is a valuable tool for coaches and athletes who are looking to upgrade performance. By tracking environmental factors, coaches and athletes can make informed decisions about training and contests and create a more optimal environment for peak performance (Elumalai et al., 2021). Here are a few supplementary benefits of environmental monitoring in sports preparation and performance monitoring:

- *Improved safety*: Environmental monitoring can help label and mitigate environmental hazards that pose a risk to players. For example, monitoring air quality can help identify areas with extreme levels of contamination, which can bring about respiratory problems.
- *Increased efficiency*: Environmental monitoring can help coaches and players be more adept at managing their time and resources; e.g., by tracking weather conditions, coaches can plan training sessions that are seemingly productive.
- *Enhanced decision-making*: Environmental monitoring can help coaches and athletes make better decisions about training and competition; e.g., by tracking altitude, coaches can make sure that players are adequately acclimatized before contesting at high altitudes.

On the whole, environmental monitoring is a valuable tool that may be used to improve safety, efficiency, and decision-making in sports training and performance monitoring. Internet of Things (IoT) devices are becoming increasingly well-known in sports training and performance monitoring.

Real-Time Feedback with IoT

The provision of real-time feedback to the athletes is a very crucial element that will assist them in acquiring training in a more effective manner. Here are a few of the devices that may be used to support real-time feedback on coaching and the actions of athletes using IoT as shown in Figure 5:

- *Smartwatches*: Smartwatches can track heart rate, steps taken, distance traveled, and calories burned. They can also be used to receive notifications, make phone calls, and send text messages. Some smartwatches have built-in GPS, which can be used to track speed and distance traveled.
- *Fitness trackers:* Fitness trackers can track steps taken, distance traveled, calories burned, and sleep quality (Wachowicz et al., 2019).

They can still be used to set goals and track progress. Some fitness trackers also include GPS, which may be used to track speed and distance traveled.

- *Headbands:* Headbands can track heart rate, brain activity, and muscle activity. They can also be used to provide feedback on actions and find areas for bettering. Some headbands also have built-in EEG sensors that may be used to track brain activity.
- *Goggles*: Goggles can track speed, distance traveled, altitude, and heart rate. They can also be used to provide feedback on form and method. Some goggles also have built-in cameras that may be used to record video of coaching sessions.
- *Sensors:* Sensors can be attached to various parts of the body to track a variety of things, such as heart rate, muscle activity, and body temperature. This data can therefore be used to determine feedback on actions and recognize areas for bettering.
- *Virtual reality headsets:* Virtual reality headsets can be used to create immersive coaching environments. This can help players practice skills in a reliable and reserved environment. Some virtual reality headsets also have built-in sensors that may be used to track dossiers in the same way that heart rate and muscle activity are tracked.
- *Wearable technology*: wearable electronics refers to any device that may be worn on the body. This includes smartwatches, fitness trackers, headbands, and goggles. Wearable technology may be used to accumulate a variety of dossiers, in the way that heart rate, steps taken, distance traveled, and calories burned (Passos et al., 2021). This dossier can then be used to provide evaluation of the act and recognize areas for bettering.

These devices can be used to accumulate dossiers about athletes' coaching and actions. This data can therefore be used to determine real-time feedback for players and coaches. This feedback may be used to improve coaching, identify areas for improvement, and avoid harm. Here are some of the benefits of utilizing IoT devices to support real-time feedback on coaching and acting:

- *Improved act:* Players can use real-time feedback to make adaptations to their coaching and competition. This can help them advance their act and reach their goals.

- *Reduced risk of injury*: Real-time feedback can help athletes recognize and correct some potential problems associated with their form or method. This can help reduce the risk of harm.
- *Personalized coaching*: Real-time feedback can be used to create personalized coaching plans for each player. This can help athletes reach their goals more quickly and efficiently.

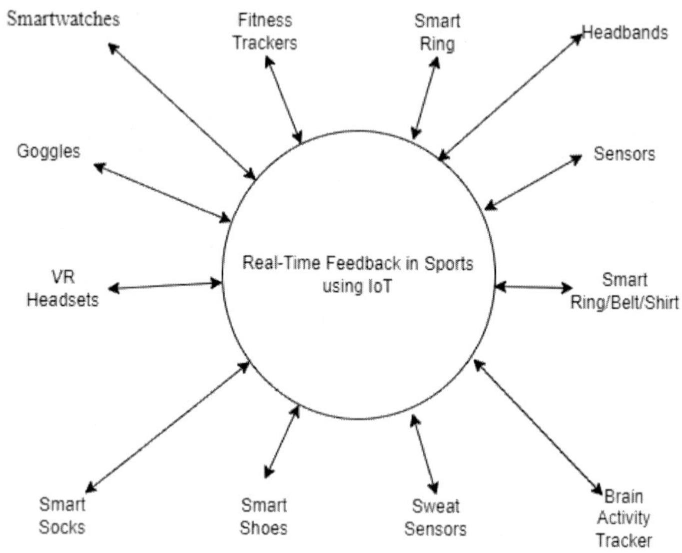

Figure 5. Real-Time Feedback in Sports using IoT.

- *Improved safety:* Real-time feedback may be used to track players' location and activity. This can help improve safety and prevent accidents.

On the whole, IoT tools may be used to provide real-time feedback on coaching and acting. This feedback can be used to advance actions, reduce the risk of harm, personalize coaching, and upgrade safety.

Data Analytics and Insight Generation

IoT based data analytics and insight creation in sports preparation and accomplishment monitoring are rapidly increasing fields. IoT instruments such as sensors, wearables, and cameras can track an expansive range of data points, including player movement, heart rate, and fatigue levels (Zhou et al., 2021). This data may be used to:

- *Improve training*: Crews can use IoT dossier to identify areas where players need to develop, create personalized preparation plans, and track progress over time.
- *Optimize performance*: Players can use IoT dossier to monitor their own performance and make adjustments to their method or game plan.
- *Prevent injuries*: IoT dossier can be used to recognize athletes who are in danger of injury and do something to prevent them from getting hurt (Wilkerson et al., 2018).
- *Improve fan experience*: Sports crews can use IoT dossiers to create customized and engaging experiences for fans, such as providing real-time stats and insights on their favorite performers.

Here are some examples of how IoT data analytics are being used in sports preparation and performance monitoring:

- *The NFL* is utilizing IoT data to track player movement and analyze potential harm. The NFL is utilizing sensors in player helmets and shoulder pads to track their movement and identify potential harm. This dossier is being used to expand new rules and training protocols to help avoid harm.
- *The NBA* is utilizing IoT dossier to track player fatigue. The NBA is utilizing dossier from wearable gadgets to track performer fatigue. This dossier is being used to help coaches make decisions about performer rotations and substitutions.
- *The MLB* is utilizing IoT dossier to improve fan experience. The MLB is utilizing dossier from sensors in baseballs and bats to track the speed and location of pitches and swings. This dossier is being used to create a more immersive experience for fans at the local area and at home.

IoT data analytics is a powerful tool, particularly for revamping the sports industry. By providing teams and players accompanying unprecedented amounts of dossier, IoT is helping them to train, compete, and recover better than ever before. Here are some additional benefits of utilizing IoT data analytics in sports training and performance monitoring:

- *Improved decision-making*: IoT dossiers can help coaches and players make better decisions about training, strategy, and tactics. Increased safety: IoT data may be used to identify and avoid harm.
- *Improved fan engagement*: IoT data may be used to devise personalized and engaging experiences for fans.

On the whole, IoT data analytics is a powerful tool that may be used to advance sports in a variety of ways. By using IoT data analytics, teams and players can upgrade their performance, lower harm, and engage fans in new and exciting ways. Here are some specific examples of by what method IoT data analytics are being used in sports training and performance monitoring:

- *The NBA* is utilizing IoT dossier to track player fatigue. The NBA is using dossier from wearable devices to track player fatigue. This dossier is being used to help coaches make decisions about athlete rotations and substitutions. E.g., the NBA's San Antonio Spurs use dossiers from Catapult wearables to track player evolution and fatigue. This dossier helps the Spurs coaches recognize when athletes are getting exhausted and need to be substituted out of the game. This helps prevent harm and keeps athletes fresh for the playoffs.
- *The NFL* is using IoT dossier to track player movement and recognize potential harm. The NFL is using sensors in athletes' helmets and shoulder pads to track their movement and recognize potential injuries. This dossier is being used to expand new rules and training protocols to help avoid harm. For example, the NFL's New England Patriots use dossiers from Zebra Technologies' Smart Sensors to track player movement and recognize potential harm. This dossier helps the Patriots coaches recognize when players are in danger of harm and create adaptations to their training regimen. This helps to prevent harm and keep performers healthy for the season.
- *The MLB* is utilizing IoT to improve fan experience. The MLB is utilizing data from sensors in baseballs and bats to track the speed and area of pitches and swings. This data is being used to generate a more immersive experience for fans at the ballpark and at home. For instance, the MLB's New York Yankees use data from Track-Man to

track the speed and location of pitches and swings. This dossier is being used to forge a more immersive experience for fans at Yankee Amphitheater. Fans can visualize the speed and location of each pitch in real time, and they can also visualize how each pitch compares to the pitcher's average. This dossier helps fans understand the game better and appreciate the skill of the players.

These are just a few examples of how IoT data analytics are being used in sports training and performance monitoring. As the technology continues to expand, we can expect to visualize even more creative and imaginative ways to use IoT to improve sports.

Broadcast Enhancement Using IoT

The Internet of Things (IoT) is revolutionizing the sports industry, and broadcast improvement is one of the most exhilarating areas of innovation. IoT devices are being used to accumulate data on everything from player performance to fan engagement, and this dossier is being used to build new and immersive experiences for spectators. Here are some distinguishing instances of how IoT is being used to reinforce sports preparation and performance:

- *Sensor Integration*: IoT implements the integration of various sensors into sports equipment, playing fields, and athletes' gear. For instance, sensors may be embedded in balls, goalposts, or player dresses to collect data on metrics like speed, trajectory, distance, heart rate, and even biometrics. This dossier can be communicated in real-time to broadcasters, who can therefore provide spectators accompanying supplementary insights and analysis all along the broadcast.
- *Wearable Devices*: Athletes can wear IoT-implemented wearable designs, such as smart jerseys or sensors installed in their equipment, to capture data all throughout a game or competition. This data may be communicated wirelessly to broadcasters, admitting them to provide real-time statistics, performance analysis, and even live player tracking on-screen. Spectators can get a deeper understanding of the game and observe their favorite players more closely.

- *Connected Cameras with Microphone*: IoT allows cameras used in sports broadcasting to be connected to the network and equipped with accompanying additional capabilities. Microphones are used to collect crowd response and noise, which is being utilized to bettering fan engagement. For example, cameras may be unified with motion sensors or GPS to track performers movements and determine dynamic, immersive viewing experiences. This can include overlaying virtual computer graphics on the screen, featuring player stats, or offering unique camera angles based on the flow of the game and the noise from the crowd.
- *Fan Interaction*: IoT technology allows broadcasters to engage fans in new ways throughout sports broadcasts. For instance, fans can use their mobile devices to participate in live polls, trivia, or virtual gambling. IoT-implemented devices can again provide synchronized real-time dossiers to fans, such as personalized stats, highlights, or interactive replays, enhancing their overall viewing experience.
- *Smart Stadiums*: IoT is utilized to form smart stadiums that improve the spectator experience. Sensors and beacons fixed throughout the venue can provide real-time facts about parking availability, concession stand wait times, washroom occupancy, and even seat upgrades. This data may be shared with accompanying broadcasters to provide appropriate updates to viewers and advance the overall amphitheater experience for fans.
- *Real-time data analytics*: IoT gadgets can accumulate data on player movements, ball location, and other factors in real time (Zhou et al., 2021). This dossier may be used to support coaches and players by providing feedback on their performance. E.g., coaches could use data from IoT tools to track the speed and accuracy of a player's throws in baseball or the distance traveled by a performer in football.
- *Virtual reality (VR) training*: VR headsets may be used to create immersive training environments that allow performers to practice in safe and regulated surroundings. For instance, a baseball player could use VR to practice striking pitches from different angles.
- *Augmented reality (AR) training*: AR overlays can be used to provide performers with real-time feedback on their performance. For instance, a soccer player could use AR to visualize their running path highlighted on the field.

- *Remote coaching*: IoT devices may be used to link coaches and players remotely, allowing coaches to provide feedback and education to performers even when they are not physically present. Self-monitoring: IoT tools can be used to track athlete performance data, such as heart rate, sleep quality, and nutrition consumption. This dossier can be used by performers to monitor their own progress and make adaptations to their preparation regimen (Hongtao et al., 2023; Yang, 2022).
- *Data collection:* IoT designs can be used to accumulate dossiers about athletes' movements, heart rate, and other physiological calculations (Qiu et al., 2022). This dossier can then be used to track progress, identify areas for improvement, and hinder harm. For example, the NBA is utilizing IoT designs to collect data about performers' movements during games. This dossier is being used to improve player performance and decrease the risk of injuries.
- *Broadcasting*: IoT instruments can be used to form new and engaging ways to broadcast sports. For example, broadcasters can use IoT instruments to determine real-time dossiers about player movements, stats, and additional information. This dossier may be used to create more immersive and informative broadcasts. For instance, the BBC is using IoT instruments to determine real-time data about player movements all along its coverage of the Premier League. This dossier is being used to create more immersive and informative broadcasts.

On the whole, IoT has the potential to considerably enhance sports preparation and performance. By collecting dossiers, providing feedback, and creating new ways to broadcast sports, IoT instruments can help players improve their act, coaches improve their decisions, and broadcasters devise more engaging content.

Player Health Monitoring and Injury Prevention

Performer well-being monitoring and harm avoidance in sports have been considerably enhanced with the integration of IoT (Internet of Things) science (Huifeng et al., 2020; Li et al., 2020; Samsuddin et al., 2021). By leveraging IoT tools and data, teams and medical personnel can monitor players' well-being, track their performance, and recognize potential injury risks (Hongmei et al., 2019; Mora et al., 2017; Wilkerson et al., 2018). Here's how IoT is used for player well-being monitoring and harm avoidance in sports:

- *Wearable Sensors*: IoT-enabled wearable sensors, like smart vests, patches, or devices attached to athletes' equipment, can accumulate real-time dossiers on various physiological parameters, including heart rate, body temperature, breathing rate, hydration levels, and movement patterns (Passos et al., 2021). This data helps monitor athletes' overall well-being, detect fatigue, and identify abnormal patterns that may indicate health risks.
- *Biomechanical Tracking*: IoT devices can track and analyze athletes' biomechanics throughout training or competitions. Wearable sensors can capture data on joint movements, forces used, impact levels, and body positioning. By evaluating this information, coaches and medical staff can determine biomechanical imbalances, improper methods, or overuse patterns that may cause harm. Athletes can receive real-time feedback on their form and make adjustments to prevent injuries.
- *GPS and Movement Tracking*: GPS-enabled devices are used to track players' movements, speed, acceleration, and distance covered throughout preparation and games. This information helps evaluate workload, monitor fatigue levels, and analyze changes in movement patterns that could display potential harm. Coaches and medical staff can adjust preparation programs based on these insights to improve performance and weaken the risk of harm.
- *Real-Time Monitoring and Alerts*: IoT devices allow for real-time monitoring of players' vital signs and performance metrics. Medical staff can endure alerts and notifications if certain parameters, such as heart rate or hydration levels, go beyond predetermined thresholds. This enables quick intervention and prompt medical support, preventing potential health issues or harm from increasing.
- *Data Analytics and Machine Learning*: IoT-generated dossiers may be processed and resolved utilizing advanced analytics and machine learning algorithms (Nithya et al., 2021). By joining player-specific dossiers with historical harm data, preparation records, and extrinsic factors like weather conditions, models may be developed to predict harm risks. This enables proactive measures to be taken, such as

adjusting preparation loads, modifying recovery plans, or providing targeted interventions for individual performers.

- *Remote Monitoring and Telemedicine*: IoT tools allow remote auditing of athletes' health and performance. Medical staff can access real-time data and support virtual consultations with athletes, allowing for unending monitoring and prompt medical guidance, particularly (Hongmei et al., 2019; Samsuddin et al., 2021) when performers are traveling or participating in events remotely.
- *Rehabilitation and Recovery Monitoring*: IoT devices may be employed to monitor players' rehabilitation progress and track their recovery from harm. Wearable sensors can measure range of motion, muscle activation, and rehabilitation exercises performed. This information helps determine the influence of rehabilitation programs and ensures players advance safely before returning to play (Jiang, 2020; De Fazio et al., 2023).
- *Environmental Monitoring*: IoT gadgets can monitor environmental factors to a degree, such as temperature, humidity, and air quality. Extreme weather conditions or poor air quality can impact player performance and increase the risk of harm. By keeping an eye on these aspects in real-time, teams can make informed decisions regarding preparation schedules, game postponements, or implementing preventive measures to diminish potential risks (Elumalai et al., 2021).
- *Load Management*: IoT devices assist in load management, whatever involves tracking and managing the workload imposed on players all along training and contest. By monitoring parameters like heart rate, GPS data, and training intensity, teams can ensure players are not overexerted, which can bring about fatigue and raise susceptibility to harm. Load management helps enhance training programs, hamper overtraining, and lower the risk of injuries induced by excessive stress on the body.
- *Data Integration and Collaboration*: IoT designs create vast amounts of data, and accommodating this data with additional methods, such as electronic medical records or sports performance software, reinforces the overall health monitoring and harm prevention process (Huifeng et al., 2020). This integration allows a comprehensive view of a player's health profile, facilitating better cooperation between

coaches, medical staff, and additional stakeholders involved in player care.

- *Injury Rehabilitation Optimization*: IoT devices stretch to play a crucial role during the rehabilitation process (De Fazio et al., 2023). They can track an athlete's progress, ensure adherence to prescribed exercises, and provide feedback on movement quality. By monitoring and analyzing rehabilitation dossiers, medical staff can change medicine plans, determine the effectiveness of interventions, and create evidence-based decisions to better the recovery process (Hongmei et al., 2019; Jiang, 2020).
- *Long-Term Athlete Monitoring*: IoT technology grants long-term monitoring of players' health and acting styles. By accumulating and analyzing dossiers over an extended period, teams can label patterns, detect potential risk factors for harm, and develop personalized strategies for injury prevention and long-term athlete development.
- *Injury Risk Mitigation*: Through the use of IoT devices, teams can gain insights into specific harm risks associated with different sports, positions, or playing styles. This information helps in designing targeted preventive measures, such as personalized preparation protocols, conditioning programs, or rule changes, to minimize the occurrence of specific harms.
- *Performance Optimization*: While the primary focus of player health monitoring and injury prevention is to ensure players' well-being, IoT technology provides more opportunities for accomplishment optimization (Mora et al., 2017). By pursuing various performance metrics and physiological parameters, teams can label areas for bettering, tailor preparation programs, and make data-driven decisions to increase an athlete's potential while minimizing injury risks.
- *Education and Awareness*: IoT devices not only provide real-time dossiers but further facilitate educational opportunities for athletes and coaches. Players can gain a better understanding of their bodies, injury risks, and the significance of harm avoidance strategies. Coaches can approach valuable observations to enhance their knowledge of preparation methodologies, load management, and harm prevention methods (Hongtao et al., 2023; Yang, 2022).
- Video analysis can also be used to monitor player well-being. This can be done by tracking things like player movement patterns, impact

forces, and collision dossiers. This data may be used to label potential injuries and expand preparation programs that can help prevent them.

- Medical tests can still be used to monitor performers well-being. This can involve things like blood tests, urine tests, and imaging tests. This dossier can be used to diagnose latent well-being conditions that could put a player in danger of harm (Hongmei et al., 2019).

Player well-being Monitoring is a fundamental part of keeping athletes harmless and well-being. By collecting and analyzing dossiers about an athlete's physical and mental well-being, it is possible to identify potential risks and prevent harm before they occur. Here are a few of the benefits of player well-being monitoring:

- *Reduced risk of harm*: Player well-being monitoring can help identify players who are in danger of injury and provide them with accompanying preventive care. This can help reduce the number of injuries that occur during preparation and event.
- *Improved performance*: By monitoring player well-being, coaches can ensure that their players are properly rested and recovered. This can help to upgrade their performance and decrease the risk of harm.
- *Increased player satisfaction*: Athletes who feel that their well-being is being observed are more likely to be satisfied with their preparation and contest. This can lead to improved performance and increased enjoyment of the sport.

Here are a few of the challenges of player well-being monitoring:

- *Cost:* Athlete well-being monitoring may be high-priced, especially if it includes the use of wearable devices and medical tests.
- *Data privacy*: Players may worry about the secrecy of their well-being data. It is important to guarantee that this dossier is collected and stocked securely.
- *Acceptance*: Few players may be willing to wear wearable instruments or have medical tests. It is important to educate players about the benefits of player well-being monitoring and to get their consent before collecting some dossiers.

Regardless of the challenges, player well-being monitoring is a valuable tool that can help maintain athletes safety and well-being. As the technology continues to evolve, we can expect to see even more creative ways to use athlete well-being monitoring to improve athletic accomplishment and hinder injuries. IoT science advances to evolve and play an important role in developing player well-being monitoring and harm prevention in sports. By leveraging real-time data, analytics, and connectivity, teams can proactively protect players' well-being, advance performance, and guarantee sustainable athletic careers.

Artificial Intelligence and IoT in Sports

AI is expeditiously transforming the sports industry, with the IoT playing a key role in enabling these technologies. Here are a few of the ways that AI and IoT are being used in sports:

- *Athlete performance and injury prevention:* Sensors installed in sports equipment and wearable instruments can accumulate data on player performance, such as heart rate, speed, and distance traveled. This data may be used to track player progress over time, identify areas where they need to raise their game, and hinder injuries. For instance, the NBA's Next Gen Stats program uses sensors in basketballs and performer jerseys to track performers movement and performance. This dossier has assisted teams to improve their player development programs and decrease harm (Nithya et al., 2021).
- *Game analysis and strategy*: AI may be used to analyze game footage and determine trends and patterns that would be difficult for human beings to spot. These facts can be used to improve the team's game plan and strategies. For example, the NFL's Next Gen Stats program uses AI to evaluate game footage and recognize factors that contribute to successful plays. This fact has helped teams boost their play calling and execution.
- *Fan engagement*: IoT designs may be used to accumulate data on fan behavior, such as which performers they cheer for, what food and drinks they purchase, and where they sit in the amphitheater. This dossier can be used to improve the fan experience by personalizing in-stadium experiences, such as providing targeted advertising and

offering discounts on merchandise. E.g., the NBA's MyStake program uses sensors in basketballs to track fan participation in real time. This dossier is used to award prizes to fans who make successful guesses about game outcomes.

These are just a few of the ways that AI and IoT are being used in sports. As these technologies continue to evolve, we can expect to visualize even more creative uses in the years to come. Here are a few supplementary instances of by what method AI and IoT are being used in sports:

- *Virtual referees:* AI-powered video assistant referees (VARs) are being used in few sports, such as soccer, to review close calls and make sure that the correct calls are made.
- *Player tracking*: Sensors fixed in player uniforms can track athlete movement and performance data, such as speed, distance traveled, and heart rate. This dossier can be used to resolve performer acts, identify areas where they need to correct them, and block harm.
- *Fan experience:* IoT tools may be used to accumulate dossiers on fan behavior, in the way that which players they cheer for, what food and drinks they purchase, and where they sit in the amphitheater. This dossier may be used to increase the fan experience by personalizing in-amphitheater experiences, providing targeted advertising, and offering discounts on merchandise.

These are just any instances of what AI and IoT are doing secondhand in sports. As these electronics mature, we can expect to visualize even more creative applications in the years to come.

Biomechanical Analysis

This analysis is the study of the movement of the human body. It may be used to better sports performance by identifying and fixing inabilities in movement. IoT (Internet of Things) ploys may be used to collect dossiers on competitor movement, which can then be evaluated by coaches and competitors to improve performance. There are a number of different IoT tools that may be used for this analysis in sports. Some ordinary designs include:

- *GPS trackers:* GPS trackers can be used to track an athlete's speed, distance, and location. This information may be used to analyze areas where a player is expending excessive energy or not covering enough ground.
- *Accelerometers*: Accelerometers may be used to measure the force and direction of a player's movement. This information may be used to determine to what extent a player is not utilizing their body weight efficiently or if they are in danger of injury.
- *Gyroscopes:* Gyroscopes may be used to measure the rotation of an athlete's body. These facts may be used to analyze areas where a player is not utilizing their balance effectively or is in danger of harm.

The data collected from IoT tools may be used to create biomechanical models of an athlete's movement (Qiu et al., 2022). These models can later be used to identify areas where a player can improve their accomplishments. For instance, if an athlete is not using their body load effectively, the model may be used to analyze particular exercises that will help them develop their strength and power.

IoT devices can also be used to provide real-time feedback to players throughout training. This feedback can help players make adjustments to their movements and increase their agility immediately. This analysis utilizing IoT is an effective tool that may be used to advance sports performance. By collecting dossiers on player movement and using them to generate biomechanical models, coaches and players can analyze and correct inefficiencies in movement. This can produce enhanced speed, power, and lastingness, further lowering the risk of injury.

Here are a few of the benefits of utilizing biomechanical analysis and IoT in sports preparation and performance:

- *Improved efficiency*: Biomechanical evaluation can help players identify and correct inabilities in their movement, which can lead to upgraded speed, power, and lastingness.
- *Reduced risk of harm*: Biomechanical reasoning can help athletes label and correct movement patterns that are in danger of causing harm.
- *Personalized training*: This analysis may be used to generate embodied training programs for players that can help them reach their full potential.

- *Improved decision-making*: Biomechanical findings can help coaches make better verdicts about preparation and contest.

On the whole, biomechanical analysis utilizing IoT is a valuable gadget that may be used to improve sports performance, lower the risk of harm, and improve decision-making.

Remote Training in Sports with IoT

Remote training and performance monitoring utilizing IoT in sports is a rapidly developing field that has the potential to transform the way players train and compete. IoT tools, such as wearable sensors and smart equipment, can accumulate an extensive amount of data about players' movements, heart rate, sleep patterns, and additional metrics (Ikram et al., 2015; Wang et al., 2021). This dossier can then be used to design personalized preparation programs, track progress, and identify areas for bettering. There are a number of benefits to using IoT for remote preparation.

First, it grants athletes the ability to train from anywhere in the realm, without having to travel to a training facility. This may be especially advantageous for athletes who live in detached fields or who have active schedules.

Second, IoT can help players track their progress over time and identify areas where they need to increase. These facts can then be used to design personalized preparation programs that are tailored to the player's individual needs.

Third, IoT can help players stay safe and prevent harm. By tracking dossiers such as heart rate and sleep patterns, coaches can recognize athletes who are in danger of harm and do something to prevent it.

On the whole, remote preparation using IoT is an effective tool that can help players reach their full potential. By collecting dossiers about players' movements, heart rate, sleep patterns, and other metrics (Wang et al., 2021), IoT tools can generate personalized preparation programs, track progress, and recognize opportunities for improvement. These facts can then be used to help players train in a more excellent manner, stay safe, and prevent injuries.

Here are a few models of by means of what IoT is being used for this activity in sports:

- Nike+ is a fitness tracking platform that uses GPS, accelerometers, and additional sensors to track players' movements. Nike+ may be used to track distance, speed, calories burned, and other metrics. It can also be used to generate personalized training plans and track progress.
- Catapult is a sports technology company that develops wearable sensors that track players' movements. The catapult's sensors may be used to track speed, acceleration, distance, and other metrics. It can further be used to recognize areas where athletes need to increase.
- Stryd is a running power meter that uses GPS, accelerometers, and other sensors to track players' running abilities. Stryd's running power meter can be used to track distance, speed, calories burned, and additional metrics. It can also be used to generate personalized preparation plans and track progress.

These are just a few examples of how the IoT is being used for remote training and performance monitoring in sports. As the technology continues to develop, we can anticipate even more creative habits to use IoT to help athletes train in an excellent manner and reach their full potential.

Future Research Suggestions

Here are a few future research suggestions in sports training and performance adopting IoT:

- *Develop more accurate and reliable IoT devices*: IoT devices are becoming more accurate and reliable, but there is still room for improvement. Researchers can continue to develop new and enhanced IoT devices that can accumulate more exact and trustworthy data about player movement, heart rate, sleep patterns, and other metrics.
- *Create personalized training programs*: IoT tools may be used to construct personalized preparation programs for players. However, there is still space for bettering. Researchers can continue to expand new and revised algorithms that can use IoT data to create more personalized preparation programs that are tailored to the player's individual needs.

- *Develop new ways to use IoT data in order to avoid harms*: IoT tools can be used to track dossier such as heart rate and sleep patterns. This dossier may be used to recognize athletes who are in danger of harm and take steps to avoid it. Researchers can develop new and upgraded ways to use the IoT dossier to prevent harm.
- *Develop new ways to use IoT data to advance decision-making*: IoT tools can be used to accumulate an endless amount of dossier about athlete movement, heart rate, sleep patterns, and additional metrics. This dossier may be used to better decision-making by coaches and players. Researchers can continue to develop new and enhanced ways to use the IoT dossier to improve decision-making.

These are just some suggestions for future research in sports training and performance utilizing IoT. As the technology continues to advance, we can anticipate seeing even more creative ways to use IoT to help players train more effectively, reach their full potential, and avoid harm.

Conclusion

This chapter has introduced the concept of sports training and performance monitoring with the association of Internet of Things (IoT) devices and their uses in collecting data from the player and examining the data for further use by the coach and the athlete for the betterment of performance. The data is collected from all around the player's environment and the player's physical and mental abilities before and during the performance, which can be kept on record and can also be used for prediction purposes. We can then come up with a solution to overcome the on-field stress, anxiety, and other factors that are influencing the athletes, which mainly occur due to the external and internal disturbances of the players physically, mentally, and in the surroundings of the arena.

However, we are also lagging in getting more accurate data and prediction models in the implementation part, which is to be streamlined and effective use of the system should be made in maintaining the players comfort all the way they are involved in sports activity. To avoid this kind of lagging in the advancement of technology related to IoT and other advancements and to improve sporting activity with efficient data monitoring solutions, sports boards and sports enthusiasts should join hands together, and even more research should be done around the world. Also, the governing bodies of each and every country should allocate a lot of funding for making the game more interesting in terms of maintaining our health, training effectively, and making fair judgements in real matches. By providing a fair decision to the players who have been making more effort for years and some have spent their entire lives for the sporting activity, they will be rewarded without any misjudgments by the organizers of the sports events. Also, they can avoid injury by predicting it before it occurs, which saves time and helps them take the necessary action to overcome it. This chapter gives a detailed explanation of the data that is collected with the help of IoT devices from various angles for the benefit of adding more value to enhance player performance and also provides future research suggestions to evolve further in this field for better IoT implementation in this sports field.

References

Ahmad, Wan Nurlisa Wan, Mohd Azrul Hisham Mohd Adib, and Mon Redee Sut Txi. Enhanced the anxiety monitoring system among athletes with IoT for sports performance: a review. *Journal of Physical Education and Sport* (2022) 22(11): 2700-2707.

Chen Meng, Hui Fang Szu, Hsin Yen Lin, Yifan Liu, Ho yin Chan, Yufan Wang, Yuliang Zhao, Guanglie Zhang, Jeffrey Da Jeng Yao, Wen Jung Li. Phase-based Quantification of Sports Performance Metrics Using a Smart IoT Sensor. *IEEE Internet of Things Journal* (2023) 10(18): 15900–15911.

Dan Juan, Yanjun Zheng, Jianping Hu. Research on sports training model based on intelligent data aggregation processing in internet of things. *Cluster Computing* (2022) 25(1): 1-8.

De Fazio Roberto, Vincenzo Mariano Mastronardi, Massimo De Vittorio, Paolo Visconti. Wearable Sensors and Smart Devices to Monitor Rehabilitation Parameters and Sports Performance: An Overview. *Sensors* (2023) 23(4): 1856.

Elumalai Ga, Nallavan Gb, Ramakrishnan Rc. Smart industry monitoring and controlling system using IoT. *Smart Intell Comput Commun Technol* (2021)38: 449.

Hongmei Ma, Xiaofeng Pang. Research and analysis of sport medical data processing algorithms based on deep learning and Internet of Things. *IEEE Access* (2019) 7: 118839-118849.

Hongtao Yu, Yang Mi. Application Model for Innovative Sports Practice Teaching in Colleges Using Internet of Things and Artificial Intelligence. *Electronics* (2023) 12(4): 874.

Huang Zejiang, Qingguo Chen, Lifeng Zhang, Xiaohai Hu. Research on intelligent monitoring and analysis of physical fitness based on the internet of things. *IEEE Access* (2019) 7: 177297-177308.

Huifeng Wang, Seifedine Nimer Kadry, Ebin Deni Raj. Continuous health monitoring of sportsperson using IoT devices based wearable technology. *Computer Communications* 160 (2020): 588-595.

Ikram Mohammed Abdulaziz, Mohammad Dahman Alshehri, Farookh Khadeer Hussain. Architecture of an IoT-based system for football supervision (IoT Football). *IEEE 2nd World Forum on Internet of Things (WF-IoT)* (2015): 69-74.

Jiang Yanping. Combination of wearable sensors and internet of things and its application in sports rehabilitation. *Computer Communications* (2020)150: 167-176.

Mora Higinio, David Gil, Rafael Munoz Terol, Jorge Azorín, Julian Szymanski. An IoT-based computational framework for healthcare monitoring in mobile environments. *Sensors* (2017) 17(10): 2302.

Municio, Esteban, Glenn Daneels, Mathias De Brouwer, Femke Ongenae, Filip De Turck, Bart Braem, Jeroen Famaey, Steven Latré. Continuous athlete monitoring in challenging cycling environments using IoT technologies. *IEEE Internet of Things Journal* (2019) 6(6): 10875-10887.

Nithya N, Nallavan G. Study on Intelligent Data Algorithms Implemented in Wearable for Sports Applications. *Smart Intelligent Computing and Communication Technology* (2021) 38: 123.

Nithya N, Nallavan G, Sriabirami V. A study on surface electromyography in sports applications using IoT. *Intelligent Data Communication Technologies and Internet of Things: Proceedings of Springer Nature Singapore* (2021): 855-867.

Palma Di, Davide, Pompilio Cusano, Carmine Russo, and Antonio Ascione. New technologies in sport through the internet of things systems. *Research Journal of Humanities and Cultural Studies* (2019) 5(1): 16-22.

Passos João, Sérgio Ivan Lopes, Filipe Manuel Clemente, Pedro Miguel Moreira, Markel Rico González, Pedro Bezerra, Luís Paulo Rodrigues. Wearables and Internet of Things (IoT) technologies for fitness assessment: a systematic review. *Sensors* (2021) 21(16): 5418.

Qian Hui. Optimization of intelligent management and monitoring system of sports training hall based on internet of things. *Wireless Communications and Mobile Computing* (2021) 2021: 1-11.

Qiu Yonghong, Gaicheng Liu, Bala Anand Muthu, Sivaparthipan CB. Design of an energy efficient IoT device with optimized data management in sports person health monitoring application. *Transactions on Emerging Telecommunications Technologies* (2022) 33(10): e4258.

Roslan, Muhammad Faris. Internet of Things (IoT)-based solution for real-time monitoring system in high jump sport. *International Journal of Integrated Engineering* (2019) 11(8): 197-205.

Samsuddin, Muhammad Naim Mohd, Anis Farihan Mat Raffei, Nur Shamsiah Abdul Rahman. IoT based sport healthcare monitoring system. *IEEE 2021 International Conference on Software Engineering & Computer Systems and 4th International Conference on Computational Science and Information Management (ICSECS-ICOCSIM)* (2021): 316-319.

Shuisheng Li, Baoxin Zhang, Panfeng Fei P, Mohamed Shakeel, Dinesh Jackson Samuel R. Computational efficient wearable sensor network health monitoring system for sports athletics using IoT. *Aggression and Violent Behavior* (2020): 101541.

Wachowicz Anna, Bożena Małysiak Mrozek, Dariusz Mrozek. Combining data from fitness trackers with meteorological sensor measurements for enhanced monitoring of sports performance. *Computational Science–ICCS 2019: 19th International Conference, Faro, Portugal, Part III Springer International Publishing* (2019) 19: 692-705.

Wang Shuaishuai. Sports training monitoring of energy-saving IoT wearable devices based on energy harvesting. *Sustainable Energy Technologies and Assessments* (2021) 45: 101168.

Wang Yufan, Meng Chen, Xinyu Wang, Rosa HM Chan, Wen J Li. IoT for next-generation racket sports training. *IEEE Internet of Things Journal* (2018) 5(6): 4558-4566.

Wang Zhonghua, Zhonghe Gao. Analysis of real-time heartbeat monitoring using wearable device Internet of Things system in sports environment. *Computational Intelligence* (2021) 37(3): 1080-1097.

Wilkerson, Gary B, Gupta Ashish, Marisa A Colston. Mitigating sports injury risks using internet of things and analytics approaches. *Risk analysis* (2018) 38(7): 1348-1360.

Xiao, Ningning, Wei Yu, and Xu Han. Wearable heart rate monitoring intelligent sports bracelet based on Internet of Things. *Measurement* (2020) 164: 108102.

Yang Li. Data Collection and Analysis in Sports Practice Teaching Based on Internet of Things Technology. *Journal of Sensors* (2022) 2022.

Zhou Yuanling, Xin Chen. Simulation of sports big data system based on Markov model and IoT system. *Microprocessors and Microsystems* (2021) 80: 103525.

Chapter 8

Investigating the Use of IoT for Smart Waste Management

J. Sridevi[1,*], PhD
M. S. R. Mariyappan[2], MA
and C. Vijai[1], PhD
[1]Department of Commerce and Business Administration,
Vel Tech Rangarajan Dr. Sagunthala R&D Institute of Science and Technology, India
[2]School of Management, Vel Tech Rangarajan Dr. Sagunthala R&D Institute of Science and Technology, India

Abstract

Investigating the use of IoT for smart waste management is a significant step towards building sustainable and efficient waste management systems. The Internet of Things (IoT) technology allows for the interconnectivity of various devices and sensors, enabling real-time data collection and analysis. When applied to waste management, IoT can revolutionize the way waste is handled, monitored, and optimized. By deploying IoT sensors in waste bins, containers, and recycling centers, it becomes possible to track the fill level, temperature, and even detect hazardous materials or leaks. This data can be transmitted to a centralized platform, providing waste management authorities with valuable insights to streamline collection routes, optimize resource allocation, and reduce environmental impact. The implications of this study could have the potential to create cleaner and healthier environments, reduce waste generation, and contribute to the overall sustainability goals of cities and communities.

---

* Corresponding Author's Email: sridevij@veltech.edu.in.

In: The Future of IoT with Automation in Engineering and Modern Technology
Editors: Sandeep Gupta and Tarun Varshney
ISBN: 979-8-89113-655-7

Keywords: mobile technologies, smart phones, IoT, waste management, resource allocation, sustainability

Introduction

Waste control is a crucial part of a sustainable and healthy community. However, it is often not noted, specifically in growing international locations. Accumulation of solid waste can cause soil pollution, landscape degradation, soil contamination, pollution of air and water, health issues, and even the devastation of land and water animals (Singh R, 2019). Solid waste can also pollute water bodies and the environment. Urban India generates solid waste of about 42.0 million TPD (heaps per day). Out of which, 83.378 TPD are generated in 423 Class I cities. Continuing with the Annual Report on Solid Waste Management (2020-21), CPCB, Delhi, the overall amount of Solid waste generated inside the country is 160038.9 TPD, of which 152749.5 TPD of waste is gathered at a set efficiency of 99.54%. 79956.3 TPD (50%) of waste is handled, and 29427.2 (18.4%) TPD is landfilled. 50655. (Sosunova et al., 2022). However, with nearly two-thirds of the world's population projected to live in cities by 2030, waste disposal is one of the most significant challenges that cities will face. One solution for smart waste management is the Internet of Things (IoT) (Kumar et al., 2022). The Internet of Things (IoT) technology allows for the interconnectivity of various devices and sensors, enabling real-time data collection and analysis (Paturi et al., 2021) When applied to waste management, IoT can revolutionize the way waste is handled, monitored, and optimized. By deploying IoT sensors in waste bins, containers, and recycling centers, it becomes possible to track the fill level, temperature, and even detect hazardous materials or leaks. This data can be transmitted to a centralized platform, providing waste management authorities with valuable insights to streamline collection routes, optimize resource allocation, and reduce environmental impact.

Different Aspects with IoT Technology

IoT and Sensor Technologies

IoT involves connecting various devices and sensors to the Internet to gather and share data. In the context of smart waste management, sensors can be placed in waste bins to monitor their fill levels in real-time. These sensors can use various technologies, such as ultrasonic, infrared, or weight-based measurements, to accurately determine how full a bin is. This data can then be used to optimize waste collection routes and schedules, reducing fuel consumption and operational costs.

Data Analytics and Predictive Maintenance

The data collected from IoT sensors can be analyzed to identify patterns and trends. Predictive analytics can help municipalities and waste management companies anticipate when bins will reach their capacity, allowing them to plan collection routes more efficiently. Additionally, IoT data can be used for predictive maintenance of waste collection vehicles, ensuring they are in good working condition and minimizing downtime.

Environmental Impact and Sustainability

Implementing IoT-based smart waste management solutions can lead to a reduction in fuel consumption and greenhouse gas emissions. By optimizing collection routes, vehicles spend less time on the road and consume less fuel. Additionally, smart waste management encourages recycling and proper waste separation, contributing to overall environmental sustainability.

Cost Efficiency and Resource Allocation

IoT-enabled waste management can optimize resource allocation by deploying collection trucks only when bins are close to being full. This reduces unnecessary trips and lowers labor and fuel costs. Moreover, the collected data can help decision-makers allocate resources more effectively based on actual waste generation patterns.

Public Participation and Engagement

Smart waste management systems can engage the public by providing real-time data on waste collection schedules and encouraging participation in recycling programs. Mobile apps or websites can offer users information about the nearest recycling centers, guidelines for waste separation, and updates on their community's waste management efforts.

Challenges and Considerations

While the potential benefits are significant, there are challenges to consider, including data security and privacy concerns (since IoT involves data collection), initial implementation costs, and ensuring that the technology is accessible to all segments of the population. Furthermore, integration with existing waste management systems and regulations may require careful planning and coordination.

Case Studies and Best Practices

Research existing case studies and successful implementations of IoT-based smart waste management solutions in different regions. These real-world examples can provide valuable insights into the benefits, challenges, and strategies for effective deployment.

Future Directions

Investigate emerging technologies such as AI and machine learning, which can enhance the capabilities of IoT in waste management. For instance, AI algorithms can analyze data from sensors to predict waste generation patterns, enabling even more efficient collection and disposal processes.

Provide the Meaning, Components, and Critical Areas of IoT

The principal motive of smart waste control is to limit the adverse consequences on the environment. The steps concerned are the collection of solid wastes, disposal of strong wastes, and utilization of solid wastes (Pal et al., 2022). The important processing technologies are compaction, incineration, and manual separation. The primary demanding situations confronted with the aid of India in stable waste management are:

The disposal of solid waste material is overcome by using IoT in smart waste management (Salehi et al., 2022). IoT enables the collection and exchange of data across a large network of devices, which opens new possibilities for more intelligent and automated systems. Utilizing the Internet of Things (IoT) in waste management can help cut down on waste costs caused by operational waste collection inefficiencies. Thus, the use of the Internet of Things (IoT) is essential for improving smart city applications by monitoring and managing city processes in real-time.

Meaning with Components of IoT

The Internet of Things refers to the network of physical devices, motors, home appliances, and different objects embedded with electronics, software, sensors, and community connectivity, allowing them to accumulate and exchange information. The IoT allows those gadgets to interact with every different and with the surroundings and allows the creation of smart structures and services (Ali et al., 2020) A tool linked to every other tool at one time may not be connected at all over again. IoT devices are not always related to store bandwidth and battery, gadgets must be powered off periodically otherwise, connections may also become unreliable and consequently inefficient (Aloui et al., 2023).

IoT systems are usually composed of several components, including IoT devices, verbal exchange networks, gateways, and cloud-primarily based data processing and storage structures (Hasan et al., 2022). IoT devices use sensors and different technologies to gather records and then ship those records to the cloud for evaluation and storage. The cloud additionally presents a centralized platform for coping with and controlling IoT devices and networks (Baldo et al., 2021).

Areas Where IoT Enables Waste Management

There are three critical areas where IoT enables waste management processes: route optimization, smart recycling, and data analysis.

Route Optimization

Waste management systems have traditionally relied on predetermined routes based on historical trends to schedule the collection and emptiness of recycling point receptacles, regardless of their capacity. IoT devices, however, turn this model upside down by detecting the location, temperature, and fill level of smart trash bins in real time. This data is used to plan optimized collection routes, which leads to an optimized pickup process, saving fuel and human resources. The data also helps with long-term planning, helping to determine where more bins need to be placed or where fewer can be placed. In addition, the data collected from smart bins helps reduce the number of "pissed" pickups or the number of overflowing bins. An automatic alert is triggered when a sensor detects a full bin, allowing waste managers to schedule an additional pickup.

Smart Recycling

With an ever-increasing number of electronic devices going to landfills, the importance of e-waste in solid waste management has been recognized. E-waste often contains harmful chemicals, such as lithium from a smartphone battery, which can seep into groundwater. It also provides an opportunity to reclaim valuable base metals, like gold and copper. IoT management systems create a digital record of devices and batteries. When the battery dies, IoT sensors can be activated to locate the location of phones and other electronic devices. Manufacturers or waste managers can schedule a pickup and sometimes even bring a replacement long before they ever go to a landfill (Antora et al., 2022). By embedding IoT technologies into the receptacles, machine learning, AI, and computer vision can be used to process the type of materials in the container, resulting in better sorting and reducing human error, as well as easier downstream work at recycling centers. In addition, new smart bins can classify, sort, and compress waste, alerting sanitation workers to fill levels for each waste category, including glass, paper, plastic, and metal, making society more sustainable (Acharya et al., 2022).

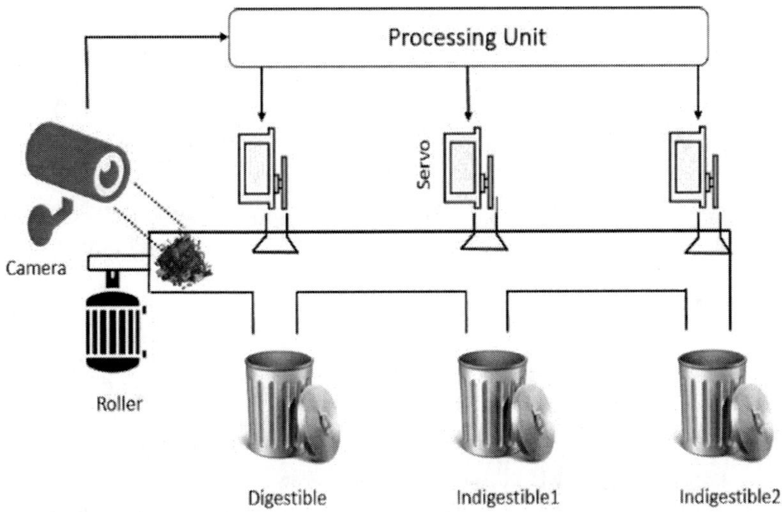

Figure 1. The process of Data colletion.

Data Analysis

Connected devices record how quickly bins fill up, as well as how often they are emptied and what is in them. Data unlocks endless opportunities, from planning better bin distribution to eliminating improper disposal practices and even reducing landfilling. Data analytics can help analyze trends to plan better waste management processes, resulting in better resource allocation and a happier population. A smart city application can give citizens the power to input on-site information. This can be used in real time, for example, to report a smashed bin, which can then be fed into data collected from other data sources to further optimize processes, as shown in Figure 1 (Malche et al., 2021).

The Role of IoT in Smart Waste Management

Internet of Things (IoT) technology plays a pivotal role in revolutionizing the field of waste management. By incorporating IoT devices, sensors, and data analytics, waste management systems can become more efficient, sustainable, and responsive. Here is a closer look at the key roles IoT plays in smart waste management:

Real-Time Monitoring

IoT-enabled sensors placed in waste bins and containers continuously monitor fill levels. This real-time data is transmitted to a central management system as shown in Figure 2. With this information, waste collection teams can optimize their routes, ensuring that bins are collected when they are nearing full capacity, minimizing unnecessary trips, and reducing fuel consumption.

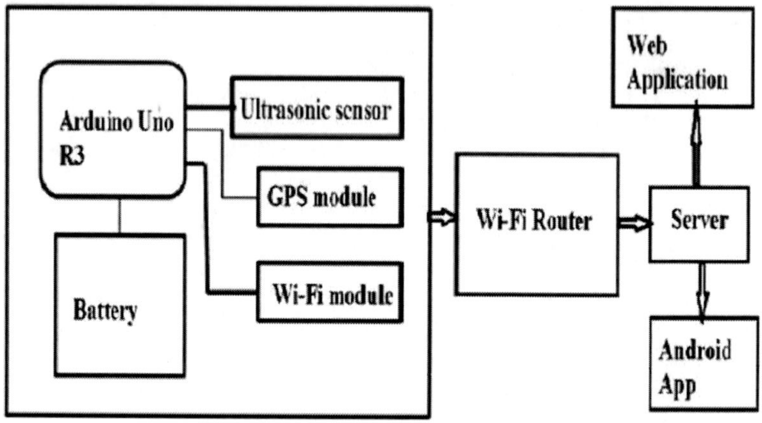

Figure 2. Real time monitoring process.

Data Analytics and Insights

The data collected from IoT devices offers valuable insights into waste generation patterns, collection frequency, and seasonal variations. These insights enable waste management agencies to make informed decisions, adjust collection schedules, and allocate resources effectively.

Route Optimization

IoT-driven data analytics allow for dynamic route optimization. Algorithms process real-time data to identify the most efficient collection routes, minimizing travel time and reducing carbon emissions. This contributes to cost savings and a smaller environmental footprint.

Predictive Maintenance

IoT sensors can monitor the health and performance of waste collection vehicles and processing equipment. By analyzing data on factors like engine performance and wear-and-tear, maintenance needs can be predicted, preventing breakdowns, and improving operational efficiency.

Environmental Monitoring

IoT devices can track environmental conditions such as air quality, temperature, and humidity in waste processing facilities and landfills. This enables the early detection of issues like gas leaks or temperature variations, facilitating prompt intervention and minimizing environmental hazards.

Resource Optimization

Smart waste management systems help optimize resource utilization. By collecting and analyzing data, waste management agencies can determine the optimal number of bins needed in specific areas, reducing waste overflow and litter.

Citizen Engagement

IoT-enabled waste management systems can engage citizens through mobile apps and online platforms. These platforms provide real-time information about waste collection schedules, recycling guidelines, and environmental impact. This increases public awareness and encourages responsible waste disposal practices.

Recycling Enhancement

IoT technology can enhance recycling processes by sorting and segregating recyclable materials more effectively. Sensors and robotics can identify and separate different types of materials, improving the quality and efficiency of recycling operations.

Cost Savings

By optimizing routes, minimizing fuel consumption, and reducing unnecessary collection trips, IoT-driven smart waste management systems lead to significant cost savings for waste management organizations.

Sustainability and Green Initiatives

Smart waste management aligns with sustainability goals by minimizing waste overflow, reducing emissions from collection vehicles, and encouraging recycling. This contributes to greener, more eco-friendly waste management practices.

Approach to Using IoT for Smart Waste Management

The following approach can be examined to use IoT for smart management:

Technical Feasibility

By following these steps, one should systematically assess the technical feasibility and efficacy of IoT devices; it will be helpful to make informed decisions about their adoption and integration in the organization's infrastructure as shown in Figure 3.

1. Define the Objectives
2. Research and Selection
3. Prototype Testing:
4. Data Collection and Analysis
5. Comparisons and Benchmarking
6. Consider Scalability and Integration:
7. User Feedback and Validation

8. Cost Analysis
9. Documentation and Reporting

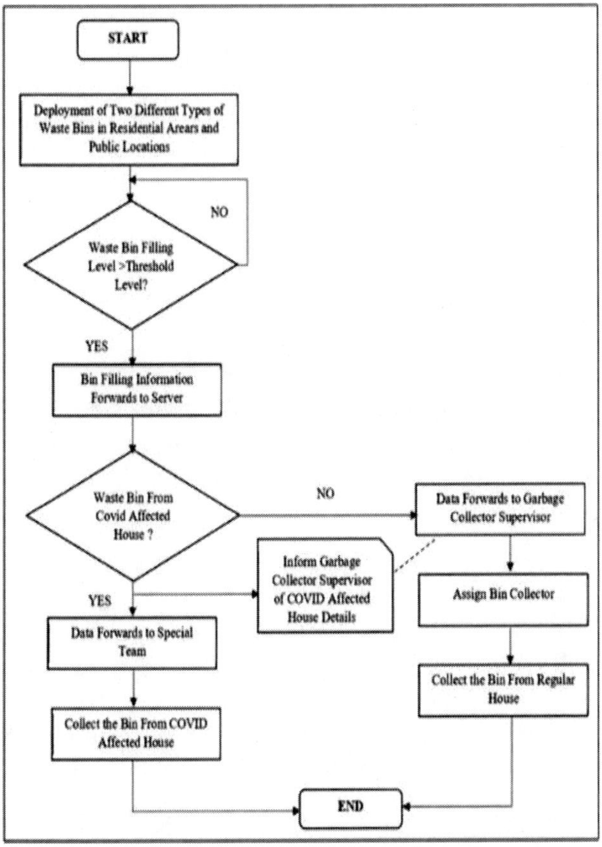

Figure 3. Flow chart for the IoT based Smart Waste Management.

Reliability

The reliability of IoT in waste management depends on various factors, including the quality of IoT devices, the robustness of the underlying network infrastructure, and the effectiveness of data management and analysis. When implemented correctly, IoT can significantly enhance the reliability of waste management systems.

Level of Precision

While IoT technology can provide a high level of precision in waste management, it is important to note that there may still be some inherent limitations or sources of uncertainty. Factors such as environmental conditions, variability in waste composition, and sensor limitations can introduce a degree of variability or measurement errors. Regular calibration, maintenance, and continuous improvement efforts are essential to maximize the precision of IoT in waste management operations.

Durability

IoT devices can offer durability in waste management. It is important to consider the specific requirements and challenges of the waste management environment. Adhering to best practices, implementing proper maintenance protocols, and choosing reliable and durable IoT devices can help ensure their long-term effectiveness in waste management operations.

Interoperability

Studying the interoperability of IoT devices in waste management involves assessing how well different devices, systems, and protocols can work together to exchange data and communicate seamlessly. This understanding will help in making informed decisions, selecting compatible devices and systems, and promoting seamless integration for efficient waste management operations.

Challenge Analysis

- *Security and Privacy:* Evaluate potential security risks and privacy concerns associated with IoT implementation. Consider data breaches, unauthorized access, and the collection of personal information. Identify strategies to mitigate these risks, such as encryption, access controls, and compliance with data protection regulations.

- *Interoperability and Compatibility:* Analyze the interoperability challenges that may arise when integrating various IoT devices, platforms, or legacy systems. Assess the compatibility of devices, communication protocols, and data formats to ensure seamless integration.
- *Scalability and Complexity:* Consider the scalability of IoT systems and the complexity of managing many connected devices. Assess the ability to scale the infrastructure, handle increasing data volumes, and maintain system performance and reliability as the deployment expands.
- *Skill and Knowledge Gap:* Evaluate the existing skill sets within the organization and the potential need for additional training or hiring to effectively manage and utilize IoT technologies. Identify any knowledge gaps that need to be addressed.
- *Risk Assessment:* Conduct a risk assesment to identify and analyze potential risks associated with IoT implementation. Consider factors such as system failures, technical glitches, data loss, and the impact on business continuity. Develop strategies to mitigate these risks and ensure business resilience.
- *Cost-Benefit Analysis:* Perform a cost-benefit analysis to weigh the potential benefits against the challenges and associated costs. Consider upfront investment costs, ongoing maintenance expenses, and potential returns on investment. Evaluate the feasibility and viability of IoT implementation based on the analysis.
- *Stakeholder Engagement and Communication:* Engage with relevant stakeholders to gather their input, address concerns, and foster support for IoT implementation. Communicate the potential benefits and address the challenges transparently to gain buy-in and ensure a smooth implementation process.
- *Documentation and Reporting:* Document the findings of the analysis, including the potential benefits and challenges of IoT implementation. The analysis should be in a comprehensive report that outlines the key findings, recommendations, and a roadmap for successful implementation.

Cost Effective Is Deploying IoT

The cost-effectiveness of deploying IoT (Internet of Things) can vary depending on several factors, including the specific use case, the scale of deployment, the complexity of the IoT solution, and the return on investment (ROI) achieved. While there are costs associated with implementing IoT, it can lead to long-term cost savings and efficiency improvements. It is important to note that the cost-effectiveness of deploying IoT can vary depending on the specific case and the successful implementation of the solution. Thorough cost-benefit analysis, careful planning, and a focus on long-term outcomes are crucial in ensuring the cost-effectiveness of IoT deployments (Malche et al., 2021).

Maintenance Factors

1. *Maintenance Factors:* Such as sensors, gateways, and communication modules, is crucial. This includes inspecting devices for physical damage, cleaning them to prevent debris or dirt buildup, and ensuring they are securely mounted. Regular battery checks or replacements, firmware updates, and calibration of sensors should also be performed as part of device maintenance. (Bakar et al., 2023)
2. *Connectivity and Network Maintenance:* Monitoring and maintaining the connectivity infrastructure is essential to ensure continuous data transmission and communication between IoT devices and the central management system. This includes monitoring network connectivity, addressing any connectivity issues or outages promptly, and ensuring proper network security measures are in place.
3. *Data Management and Storage:* Maintenance of data management systems and storage infrastructure is important for maintaining data integrity and accessibility. Regular data backups, system updates, and security patches should be performed. Monitoring data storage capacity and optimizing data retention policies can help ensure efficient data management.
4. *Analytics and Insights Maintenance:* If analytics and insights are derived from IoT data, maintenance of the analytics platform is necessary. This involves monitoring the performance of the analytics system, verifying data accuracy, updating algorithms or models as needed, and refining data visualization and reporting mechanisms.

5. *Security and Privacy Maintenance:* Maintaining the security and privacy of IoT systems is crucial to protect against cyber threats and unauthorized access. Regular security audits, vulnerability assessments, and updates to security protocols should be conducted. This includes ensuring secure communication channels, implementing access controls, and applying encryption mechanisms.
6. *Training and Skill Development:* Providing ongoing training and skill development programs to waste management personnel is essential. This helps them understand the operation and maintenance of IoT devices, interpret data insights, and effectively utilize the IoT system. Training programs should cover device troubleshooting, data analysis techniques, and best practices for IoT maintenance.
7. *Performance Monitoring and Optimization:* Regular monitoring and performance analysis of the IoT system can help identify potential issues, bottlenecks, or inefficiencies. This includes monitoring device performance, data transmission rates, response times, and overall system reliability. Optimization measures can be implemented based on performance insights to enhance the system's efficiency and effectiveness.
8. *Vendor and Supplier Relationships:* Maintaining relationships with IoT device vendors and suppliers is important. Regular communication with vendors ensures access to technical support, firmware updates, and any necessary hardware replacements. Staying updated with the latest product releases, security patches, and industry advancements is crucial for effective maintenance.

Recent Development on IoT for Smart Waste Management

Advanced Sensing Technologies

Advancements in sensor technologies enable more accurate and versatile data collection from waste bins. This includes sensors capable of measuring not only fill levels but also factors like temperature, humidity, and even types of waste materials, which can aid in better waste sorting and management.

Real-time Data Analytics

The integration of real-time data analytics is gaining traction, allowing waste management systems to process and analyze data as it is collected. This enabled more responsive decision-making, route optimization, and predictive maintenance of waste collection vehicles.

Edge Computing

Edge computing, which involves processing data closer to the source (such as on the IoT devices themselves), is being explored to reduce latency and improve the speed of decision-making in waste management systems.

Artificial Intelligence (AI) Integration

AI technologies, including machine learning algorithms, are being integrated with IoT systems to provide more accurate predictions of waste generation patterns and optimize waste collection schedules based on historical data and real-time inputs.

Waste Sorting and Recycling Optimization

IoT is being used to optimize waste sorting and recycling processes in recycling facilities. Smart waste bins with sensors could help identify and separate different types of waste, improving recycling efficiency.

Cloud Integration

Cloud platforms are being used to centralize data from various IoT devices across different locations. This allowed waste management companies to manage and analyze data on a larger scale, supporting decision-making across wider areas.

Smart City Integration

Smart waste management is becoming an integral part of broader smart city initiatives. Integration with other city systems, such as traffic management and energy optimization, is being explored to create more holistic urban solutions.

Citizen Engagement Apps

Mobile apps and web platforms are being developed to engage citizens in waste management efforts. These apps provided real-time information on collection schedules, recycling guidelines, and nearby recycling points, fostering better waste disposal habits.

Pilot Projects and Collaborations

Many municipalities and waste management companies are launching pilot projects and collaborating with technology providers to test and refine IoT-based waste management solutions in real-world settings.

Focus on Sustainability

There is an increased emphasis on the sustainability aspects of IoT for waste management. This included exploring ways to make IoT devices energy-efficient, using recyclable materials in their production, and considering the overall environmental impact of these technologies.

IoT Based Waste Management and Smart Cities

IoT (Internet of Things) based waste management is a significant component of the broader concept of creating smart cities. Smart cities leverage technology and data to enhance the quality of life for residents, improve efficiency, and promote sustainability. IoT technology plays a crucial role in achieving these goals in waste management by enabling real-time monitoring, data-driven decision-making, and resource optimization.

Real-Time Monitoring

IoT devices, such as sensors and cameras, can be deployed in waste bins and containers to monitor their fill levels in real-time. This data can help optimize collection routes, ensuring that garbage trucks only visit containers that are nearing capacity. This reduces unnecessary trips, fuel consumption, and traffic congestion.

Optimized Collection Routes

With data from sensors, waste management companies can create optimized collection routes based on real-time data, traffic conditions, and fill levels. This results in reduced operational costs and carbon emissions.

Efficient Resource Allocation

By analyzing historical data, city officials can better allocate resources like labor, vehicles, and equipment. This prevents overstaffing during low-demand periods and ensures efficient waste collection during peak times.

- *Reduced Costs:* IoT-based waste management systems can lead to significant cost savings due to optimized collection routes, reduced labor requirements, and better management of resources.
- *Environmental Impact:* Reducing unnecessary waste collection trips and optimizing routes reduces carbon emissions and traffic congestion. This contributes to the overall sustainability of the city.
- *Alerts and Notifications:* IoT devices can send alerts when waste containers are almost full, preventing overflow and maintaining cleanliness. This ensures a better living environment for residents.
- *Data-Driven Decision Making:* The data collected from IoT devices can be analyzed to identify trends, patterns, and areas that require attention. City officials can make informed decisions about waste management strategies based on this data.
- *Behavioral Insights:* IoT data can provide insights into resident behaviors related to waste disposal. This information can be used to

design effective awareness campaigns and initiatives to encourage proper waste disposal practices.

- *Recycling and Waste Segregation:* IoT devices can be used to monitor recycling and waste segregation practices. This can help encourage residents to separate their waste correctly and increase recycling rates.
- *Remote Management:* IoT technology allows for remote monitoring and management of waste systems. This can lead to quicker response times for addressing issues such as blocked containers or equipment malfunctions.

Potential and Limitations of IoT in Waste Management

IoT technology offers several ways to improve waste management processes, leading to more efficient and sustainable practices (Singh et al., 2022). Here are some key areas where IoT holds potential in waste management:

Smart Waste Collection

IoT enables real-time monitoring of waste bins and containers, providing accurate information on fill levels. This data allows waste management authorities to optimize collection routes, reduce unnecessary pickups, and improve operational efficiency. By implementing IoT sensors, waste collection can be made more efficient and cost-effective.

Smart Bin Monitoring

IoT sensors can be installed in waste bins and containers to monitor their fill levels in real-time. This data helps waste management authorities optimize collection routes, schedule pickups based on actual needs, and avoid unnecessary trips, resulting in reduced fuel consumption and lower carbon emissions. It also helps prevent overflowing bins, keeping the environment clean and reducing the risk of vermin or health hazards

Predictive Maintenance

IoT devices can monitor the performance and condition of waste management equipment, such as compactors, waste sorting machines, or recycling systems. By leveraging data collected from these devices, predictive maintenance models can be developed to identify maintenance needs proactively, reducing downtime and maximizing equipment lifespan.

Waste Sorting and Recycling

IoT can enhance waste sorting and recycling processes. By using sensors and AI-powered image recognition technologies, waste sorting systems can efficiently identify and categorize different types of waste materials, improving recycling accuracy. IoT can also enable the tracking of recycled materials, providing transparency and traceability in the recycling supply chain.

Energy Management

IoT can optimize energy consumption in waste management facilities. By integrating IoT with energy management systems, energy usage can be monitored and controlled in real-time, allowing for better energy efficiency, load balancing, and demand response strategies.

Environmental Monitoring

IoT devices can be deployed to monitor environmental conditions related to waste management, such as air quality, temperature, and humidity. This data can help assess the impact of waste management activities on the environment and enable timely interventions to mitigate potential issues.

Data-Driven Decision Making

IoT generates a vast amount of data that can be analyzed to derive valuable insights. Waste management authorities can leverage this data to make informed decisions, optimize operations, and identify areas for improvement. Data analytics and machine learning algorithms can provide valuable information on waste generation patterns, waste composition, and operational efficiency.

Public Engagement and Education

IoT can facilitate public engagement and education initiatives related to waste management. Smart waste bins equipped with IoT devices can provide real-time feedback to users, incentivize proper waste disposal, and encourage responsible waste management practices. IoT-powered platforms can also facilitate communication and information sharing between waste management authorities and the public.

Environmental Monitoring

IoT sensors can be deployed to monitor environmental factors related to waste management, such as air quality, temperature, and noise levels. This information helps in assessing the environmental impact of waste management activities and implementing measures to mitigate any adverse effects (Kumar et al., 2021). By harnessing the potential of IoT in waste management, municipalities, waste management companies, and environmental organizations can improve operational efficiency, reduce costs, promote recycling, and enhance sustainability efforts. However, successful implementation requires careful planning, stakeholder engagement, and a comprehensive understanding of the specific waste management challenges and needs of the community or organization. While IoT (Internet of Things) offers significant potential in waste management, it also has certain limitations. Here are some key limitations to consider: (Kabir et al., 2020)

- *Initial Investment and Infrastructure Requirements:* Implementing IoT in waste management often requires significant upfront investment in IoT devices, connectivity infrastructure, and data management systems. The cost of deployment and infrastructure setup can be a barrier, particularly for small-scale waste management operations or resource-constrained environments.

- *Connectivity and Network Reliability:* IoT devices rely on stable and reliable network connectivity for seamless data transmission. However, network outages, coverage limitations in certain areas, or connectivity issues can disrupt the functioning of IoT systems. The reliance on connectivity introduces a potential point of failure and may impact the real-time monitoring and data collection aspects of waste management.
- *Data Security and Privacy Concerns:* The vast amount of data generated by IoT devices raises security and privacy concerns. Protecting sensitive data, ensuring secure communication channels, and addressing cybersecurity threats are crucial. The collection and sharing of personal or sensitive information requires robust security measures and compliance with data protection regulations.
- *Interoperability Challenges:* The diversity of IoT devices, protocols, and platforms can pose interoperability challenges. Integrating different IoT devices and systems, ensuring data incompatibility and seamless communication can be complex. Lack of standardization and compatibility issues between different vendors' products can hinder the scalability and interoperability of IoT solutions in waste management.
- *Data Management and Analysis:* Handling and analyzing the vast amount of data generated by IoT devices can be challenging. Proper data management systems, storage capacity, and data analytics capabilities are required to process and derive meaningful insights from the data. Inadequate data management practices or the inability to extract valuable insights can lead to inefficiencies and missed opportunities.
- *Maintenance and Updates:* IoT devices and systems require regular maintenance, firmware updates, and software patches to ensure optimal performance and security. Failure to perform timely maintenance and updates may lead to device malfunctions, security vulnerabilities, or obsolescence. Ongoing maintenance efforts can add to the operational costs and resource requirements of IoT in waste management.

- *Ethical and Social Implications:* The adoption of IoT in waste management raises ethical considerations, such as data ownership, privacy concerns, and potential job displacement due to automation. Ensuring responsible and ethical implementation requires addressing these concerns and considering the broader social and economic implications.
- *Environmental Impact:* While IoT can contribute to improved waste management practices, the manufacturing and disposal of IoT devices themselves can have environmental consequences. Proper disposal and recycling of IoT devices at their end-of-life stage are important to minimize their environmental impact. (Mohanram et al., 2021)

Addressing these limitations requires careful planning, risk mitigation strategies, and continuous monitoring and improvement of IoT systems. It is important to evaluate these limitations in the context of specific waste management needs, resources, and goals to determine the feasibility and suitability of IoT implementation.

Opportunities of IoT for Smart Waste Management

The integration of IoT (Internet of Things) technologies into smart waste management presents numerous opportunities that can revolutionize how waste is collected, managed, and disposed of. Here are some key opportunities that IoT offers in the context of smart waste management:

Real-Time Monitoring and Data Collection

IoT-enabled sensors placed in waste bins can provide real-time data on fill levels. This data allows waste management companies to optimize collection routes and schedules, ensuring that bins are emptied only when necessary. This reduces unnecessary trips and conserves resources.

Efficient Resource Allocation

With accurate data on fill levels and waste generation patterns, waste management companies can allocate their resources more efficiently. This includes deploying collection trucks to areas with high waste accumulation and adjusting schedules based on demand.

Cost Savings

By reducing fuel consumption, optimizing collection routes, and minimizing unnecessary trips, IoT-based smart waste management systems can lead to significant cost savings for waste management companies and municipalities.

Environmental Impact

Smart waste management can contribute to environmental sustainability by minimizing the carbon footprint of waste collection. Reduced fuel consumption and optimized routes lead to lower greenhouse gas emissions, aligning with broader environmental goals.

Improved Public Health and Aesthetics

Smart waste management helps prevent overflowing bins and litter accumulation, which can attract pests and pose health risks. Maintaining cleaner streets and public spaces enhances the overall aesthetic appeal of a city or community.

Data-Driven Decision Making

IoT generates a wealth of data that can be analyzed to identify waste generation patterns, trends, and areas with higher waste volumes. This information allows waste management authorities to make informed decisions and adjust their strategies accordingly.

Predictive Analytics

Using historical data and machine learning algorithms, predictive analytics can forecast waste generation patterns. This enables waste management companies to proactively plan collection schedules and allocate resources, reducing the chances of overflowing bins.

Public Engagement

Smart waste management can engage citizens by providing real-time information on collection schedules, nearby recycling points, and waste reduction tips. This fosters a sense of community involvement and encourages responsible waste disposal practices.

Remote Monitoring and Maintenance

IoT allows for remote monitoring of waste bins and collection vehicles. Maintenance issues can be detected early, minimizing downtime, and reducing the likelihood of service disruptions.

Integration with Smart Cities

IoT-based waste management is a component of the larger smart city ecosystem. Integrating waste management data with other city infrastructure data can lead to more comprehensive urban planning and resource allocation.

Innovation and Technological Growth

The development and implementation of IoT solutions for waste management drive innovation in technology and software development. This growth can lead to the creation of new jobs and economic opportunities.

Compliance with Regulations

IoT systems can provide accurate data on waste collection and disposal, aiding in compliance with environmental regulations and reporting requirements.

Challenges for IoT Smart Waste Management

While IoT offers promising opportunities for smart waste management, there are also several challenges that need to be addressed to effectively implement and maintain these systems. Some of the key challenges include:

Data Security and Privacy

IoT systems involve the collection, transmission, and storage of sensitive data about waste generation, collection schedules, and user behavior. Ensuring the security and privacy of this data is crucial to prevent unauthorized access, breaches, and potential misuse.

Connectivity and Infrastructure

Reliable connectivity is essential for IoT devices to transmit data in real-time. In areas with poor network coverage, connectivity issues may arise, leading to delays or incomplete data transmission. Developing robust and resilient network infrastructure is essential for consistent data flow.

Initial Implementation Costs

Deploying IoT sensors, setting up data collection infrastructure, and integrating the technology into existing waste management systems can be expensive. Municipalities and waste management companies need to carefully assess the return on investment and long-term benefits.

Maintenance and Upkeep

IoT devices require regular maintenance, including software updates, battery replacements, and hardware repairs. Ensuring the continuous functionality of sensors and devices is essential to avoid disruptions in data collection and system performance.

Compatibility and Interoperability

Incorporating IoT solutions into existing waste management systems may require compatibility and interoperability between different devices, sensors, and software platforms. Ensuring seamless integration can be challenging, particularly when dealing with legacy systems.

Data Management and Analysis

Collecting a large volume of data from IoT sensors requires efficient data management and analysis. Developing algorithms and analytics tools to process and extract meaningful insights from this data can be complex.

Stakeholder Collaboration

Implementing IoT-based smart waste management systems often requires collaboration among various stakeholders, including municipalities, waste management companies, technology providers, and regulatory bodies. Effective communication and coordination are essential to ensure a successful rollout.

Power Consumption and Sustainability

IoT devices often rely on batteries or power sources. Ensuring that these devices are energy-efficient and sustainable is important to minimize environmental impact and reduce the frequency of battery replacements.

Public Awareness and Acceptance

Citizens need to be educated about the benefits of IoT-based waste management and how it contributes to a cleaner environment. Public acceptance and cooperation are critical for the success of such initiatives.

Regulation and Compliance

IoT systems for waste management may need to adhere to local regulations, privacy laws, and environmental standards. Ensuring compliance can be complex, especially when operating in different jurisdictions.

Scaling and Adaptability

As waste management needs evolve and grow, IoT systems must be scalable and adaptable to accommodate changing requirements, new waste streams, and shifts in waste generation patterns.

Environmental Impact

The production, deployment, and disposal of IoT devices can contribute to electronic waste and environmental concerns. Designing devices with eco-friendly materials and considering end-of-life disposal is crucial.

Visual Modeling for Performance Just in Time

Visual modeling for performance just in time is another central instructional approach for effective mobile learning. This instructional strategy often involves reducing extraneous cognitive load on the spot, providing worked examples right before performing a critical task, and visualizing learning object in three dimensional presentations as shown in Figure 4.

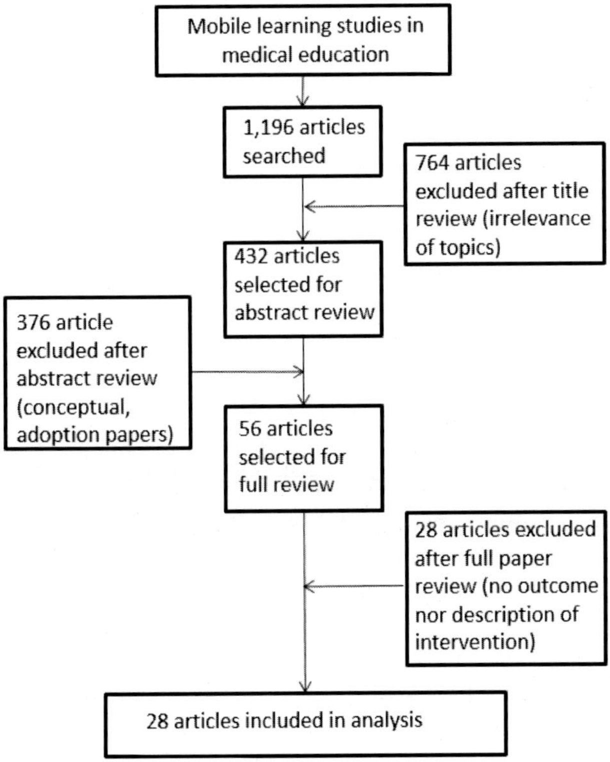

Figure 4. Inclusion and exclusion process.

Table 1. Summary of included articles

Population	Specialty domain	Intervention (Mobile Technology)	Conceptual framework/ Instructional design features
Undergraduate medical education (UME)	Emergency medicine	Videos delivered on a mobile device	Just-in-time (JIT) learning Watching the instructional video before entering a patient room
Physician Assistant (PA)/Nursing/ Medic/Tech	Military trauma	Learning modules delivered on a mobile device	JIT learning
Nursing	Pharmacology	Short message service (SMS)	Information processing theory Providing reminders to review the content

There are several limitations in this study. The selection of the database, key words, and years may not include studies available in other databases and journals. Additionally, there may be a selection bias from unpublished studies showing no effects or benefits to mobile learning. Findings in this study may not represent all possible instructional strategies exhaustively but provided some of the potentials of mobile learning processes. Simply adopting traditional e-learning approaches may not necessarily lead to positive mobile learning experiences as mobile learning leans more toward informal, personal, context-oriented, instant, and opportunistic experiences rather than formal, structured, and media-rich traditional e-learning experiences. More insightful, thoughtful, and innovative design approaches aligned with the mobile learning characteristics should be investigated and studied.

Hawkes et al., (2013) investigated the effect of short visual instruction right before performing newborn intubation and found that this approach is effective for improving both knowledge and procedural skills for novice learners. Medical students performed better with patient encounters in an emergency department setting when they had immediate access to an instructional video right before seeing a patient in the emergency room (Tews et al., 2011). A similar effect is found in another study. According to Noguera et al. (2013), when second year students in physical therapy had access to two- or three-dimensional images of anatomy on their mobile devices during a practice session, their knowledge gain is higher than those who did not have such learning environments. With resources on their mobile devices, the students are able to visualize specific anatomy of the knee, ankle, and pelvic zone as they practiced physical therapy as per Table 1. This allowed the participants to deeply engage in learning how physical therapy works in relation to a specific anatomy structure.

Conclusion

In conclusion, the adoption of IoT (Internet of Things) in waste management offers significant potential to revolutionize the industry. By leveraging IoT devices, connectivity, and data analytics, waste management operations can become more efficient, sustainable, and data driven. IoT enables real-time monitoring of waste bins, predictive maintenance of equipment, optimized waste collection routes, and improved resource management. It also facilitates better waste sorting and recycling, enhances environmental monitoring, and empowers data-driven decision-making.

However, it is important to consider the limitations of IoT in waste management, such as initial investment costs, connectivity challenges, data security and privacy concerns, interoperability issues, and ongoing maintenance requirements. These limitations highlight the need for careful planning, investment analysis, proper infrastructure setup, and robust data management and security protocols.

Despite the challenges, when implemented effectively, IoT in waste management can result in cost savings, operational efficiencies, reduced environmental impact, and an enhanced customer experience. It has the potential to transform waste management practices by optimizing waste collection, improving recycling rates, minimizing equipment downtime, and promoting sustainable resource management. To fully harness the benefits of IoT in waste management, collaboration among waste management authorities, technology providers, and stakeholders is crucial. Proper training and skill development for personnel, adherence to data protection regulations, and addressing ethical implications are essential considerations. Overall, IoT has the potential to drive innovation, efficiency, and sustainability in waste management, paving the way for smarter and more effective waste management systems that contribute to a cleaner and more sustainable future.

Disclaimer

None.

References

Acharya B, Dey S, and Zidan M. IoT-Based smart Waste Management for environmental sustainability. *CRC Press eBooks* (2022). https://doi.org/10.1201/9781003184096.

Ali T, Irfan M, Alwadie A, and Głowacz A. IOT-Based smart waste bin monitoring and municipal solid waste Management system for smart cities. *Arabian Journal for Science and Engineering* (2020) 45(12): 10185–10198. https://doi.org/10.1007/s13369-020-04637-w.

Aloui N, Almukadi W, Belghith A. Towards an IOT Approach for Smart Waste Management based on Context ntology: A Case Study. *Engineering, Technology & Applied Science Research* (2023) 13(1), 10186–10191. https://doi.org/10.48084/etasr.5530.

Antora NA, Rahman MA, Mosharraf AA, Ibn Ehsan M, Alve M, Elahi MM. Design and Implementation of a Smart Bin using IOT for an Efficient Waste Management System. *25th International Conference on Computer and Information Technology (ICCIT)* (2022): 774-779.

Bakar M A, Yusof YM, Sam SM, Azizan A, Ahmad NA, Abas H, Shafie N. Garbage Segregation and Monitoring Using Low-Cost IoT System for Smart Waste Management. *Open International Journal of Informatics* (2023) 11(1): 23-40.

Baldo D, Mecocci A, Parrino S, Peruzzi G, Pozzebon A. A Multi-Layer LORAWAN infrastructure for smart waste management. *Sensors* (2021) 21(8): 2600. https://doi.org/10.3390/s21082600.

Hasan MK, Khan MA, Issa GF, Atta A, Akram AS, and Hassan M. Smart Waste Management and Classification System for Smart Cities using Deep Learning. *International Conference on Business Analytics for Technology and Security (ICBATS)* (2022). https://doi.org/10.1109/icbats54253.2022.9759087.

Kabir MH, Roy S, Ahmed MT, and Alam M. IoT Based Solar Powered Smart Waste Management System with Real Time Monitoring- An Advancement for Smart City Planning. *Global Journal of Computer Science and Technology* (2020): 11–20. https://doi.org/10.34257/gjcstgvol20is5pg11.

Kumar A, Kumar S, Arya R, Goyal, R. A Novel Approach of Using IoT Methodology for Smart Waste Management System-SIM900. *2022 International Conference on Advances in Computing, Communication and Materials (ICACCM)* (2022): 1-7.

Kumar S, Kaur M, Rakesh N. IOT Based Smart Waste Management System. *Advances in science, technology & innovation* (2021): 133–139. https://doi.org/10.1007/978-3-030-66218-9_15.

Malche T, Tiwari PK, Tharewal S, Tiwari R. Smart Waste Management System for Smart City based on Internet of Things (IoT). *Turkish Journal of Computer and Mathematics Education (TURCOMAT)* (2021) 12(10): 4491-4499.

Mohanram P, Viswanath S, Musaraf PM, Karthikeyan R, Chandran K, and Deborah SA. IoT Based Smart Waste Management Reporting and Monitoring System. *5th International Conference on Computer, Communication and Signal Processing (ICCCSP)* (2021): 208–215. https://doi.org/10.1109/icccsp52374.2021.9465507.

Pal MS, Bhatia M. Lifetime maximization of BiN level IoT sensor and route optimization for smart waste management in Hilly City Shimla, India: a comparative analysis. 2nd *International Conference on Advances in Electrical, Computing, Communication and Sustainable Technologies (ICAECT)* (2022). https://doi.org/10.1109/icaect54875.2022.9807864.

Paturi M, Puvvada S, Ponnuru BS, Simhadri M, Egala BS, and Pradhan AK. Smart Solid Waste Management system using blockchain and IoT for smart cities. *IEEE International Symposium on Smart Electronic Systems (iSES)* (2021). https://doi.org/10.1109/ises52644.2021.00107.

Salehi Amiri A, Akbapour N, Hajiaghaei Keshteli M, Gajpal Y, and Jabbarzadeh A. Designing an effective two-stage, sustainable, and IoT based waste management system. *Renewable & Sustainable Energy Reviews* (2022) 157, 112031. https://doi.org/10.1016/j.rser.2021.112031.

Singh P, Bajpai A. Smart Trucks: An IoT-based Novel Approach for Smart and Effective Waste Management System. *IEEE Conference on Interdisciplinary Approaches in Technology and Management for Social Innovation (IATMSI)* (2022): 1–6. https://doi.org/10.1109/iatmsi56455.2022.10119341.

Singh R. Internet of things (IOT) for smart waste management in Himachal Pradesh, Western Himalaya, India. *International Journal of Recent Trends in Engineering & Research* (2019) 05(12): 21–28. https://doi.org/10.23883/ijrter.2019.5103.tqnq8.

Sosunova I, Porras J. IoT-Enabled Smart Waste Management Systems for Smart Cities: A Systematic review. *IEEE Access* (2022) 10: 73326–73363. https://doi.org/10.1109/access.2022.3188308.

Chapter 9

IoT-based Solar Tracking and Monitoring System

Sandeep Kanaujia[1,*], MTech
Satya Prakash Singh[2], MTech
and Sandeep Gupta[3], PhD

[1]Electronics and Communication Department, United University Jhalwa, Prayagraj, U.P, India
[2]Electronics and Communication Department, UCER Naini Prayagraj, U.P, India
[3]Department of Electrical Engineering, Graphic Era (Deemed to be University), Dehradun, India

Abstract

Modern day living requires having access to energy. How well a country is doing has some correlation with energy availability. Therefore, using renewable energy is the only way to satisfy public demand. Solar energy is the most famous, sustainable, and environmentally friendly type of energy. It is readily gathered with the aid of solar photovoltaic (PV) panels. Most solar panels, however, are positioned at predetermined angles. The implementation of a solar tracking system using IoT can lead to several positive outcomes and results. Solar tracking systems optimize the alignment of solar panels with the sun's position, resulting in increased energy generation. By utilizing IOT technology, the solar tracking system can continuously monitor environmental conditions, such as sunlight intensity and cloud cover, and adjust the panels' orientation in real-time. This ensures that maximum solar energy is captured throughout the day, leading to higher energy production compared to fixed solar panels.

---

[*] Corresponding Author's Email: sandeepkanaujiamnnit@gmail.com.

In: The Future of IoT with Automation in Engineering and Modern Technology
Editors: Sandeep Gupta and Tarun Varshney
ISBN: 979-8-89113-655-7

Keywords: solar tracking system, Internet of Things, Interfacing

Introduction

Using a solar tracking device to follow the sun orthogonally throughout the day is an effective way to optimize solar energy capture and increase the overall efficiency of a solar power system, particularly in areas with substantial daily and seasonal changes in the sun's position (Bensaid et al., 2019). A light-dependent resistor (LDR) is required for the tracking mechanism of the sun to sense the maximum amount of light availability and two DC servo motors for two axis movement (i.e., vertical and horizontal) to control the position of the solar panel. IoT technology, and solar tracking systems are connected to a network of devices and systems, enabling real-time monitoring, control, and optimization of solar panels' orientation and performance. This connectivity opens a range of opportunities and benefits for solar tracking systems.

The future of solar tracking systems is quite promising, as they play a crucial role in maximizing the efficiency and output of solar energy systems. Solar tracking technology allows solar panels or solar concentrators to follow the movement of the sun throughout the day, ensuring that they are always facing the sun at the optimal angle.

Solar Tracking System

A solar tracking system is a piece of equipment used to line solar panels or solar collectors with the sun's position throughout the day to maximize the efficiency of collecting solar energy (Mani et al., 2022). To maximize the solar panels' exposure to sunlight and boost overall energy output, the system automatically adjusts the orientation of the solar panels using a variety of mechanisms and sensors. Traditional fixed solar panel installations are positioned at a fixed angle relative to the ground, typically based on the latitude of the installation site. While this setup allows for basic solar energy capture, it does not fully exploit the potential of the sun's movement across the sky. Solar tracking systems aim to overcome this limitation by actively tracking and following the sun's path, enabling solar panels to maintain an optimal perpendicular angle to the sun's rays.

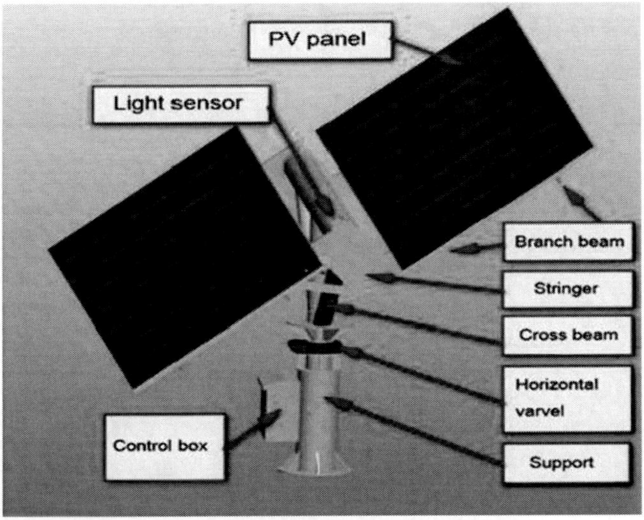

Figure 1. Solar tracking system.

Solar Tracker

A solar tracker is a tool or system that automatically changes the placement of solar collectors or panels to maximize their exposure to sunlight, as shown in Fig. 1. Solar trackers make sure that the solar panels are positioned so that they are perpendicular to the sun's rays, maximizing energy absorption and raising the overall efficiency of the solar installation (Li et al., 2018). Solar trackers utilize various mechanisms and technologies to achieve accurate tracking. Here are the main components and types of solar trackers:

- *Sensors:* Solar trackers use light sensors or photodiodes to detect the intensity and direction of sunlight. These sensors provide feedback to the control system, enabling it to determine the sun's position.
- *Control System:* The control system processes the information from the sensors and calculates the sun's position. It sends commands to the actuator or motor to adjust the position of the solar panels accordingly.
- *Actuator or Motor:* The actuator or motor is responsible for physically moving the solar panels or collectors. It can be driven by electric power, hydraulic systems, or pneumatic systems, depending on the specific design of the solar tracker.

- *Single-Axis Trackers:* Single-axis trackers move the solar panels along one axis, typically from east to west, to track the sun's movement from sunrise to sunset. They can be either horizontal-axis trackers (azimuth) or tilted-axis trackers (elevation).
- To follow the path of the sun from sunrise to sunset, single-axis trackers move the solar panels along one axis, often from east to west. They can be either tilted-axis trackers for elevation or horizontal-axis trackers for azimuth.
- *Dual-Axis Trackers:* Dual-axis trackers can track the sun's azimuth and altitude since they have two moving axes (Jana et al., 2017). As a result, the solar panels can track the sun more precisely throughout the day and year, maximizing energy absorption. Although dual-axis trackers are more complicated and pricier than single-axis trackers, they often give larger energy yields.

Solar trackers offer several advantages over fixed solar installations. They can increase energy generation by 20% to 40% or more, depending on the location and tracking system. By maximizing energy production, solar trackers improve the return on investment and shorten the payback period for solar projects. Additionally, solar trackers can be integrated into various types of solar installations, including utility-scale power plants, commercial buildings, and residential rooftops (Prakash et al., 2018).

Solar trackers also have some considerations. They require additional components and maintenance compared to fixed installations, adding to the initial cost and complexity. Mechanical wear and tear associated with moving parts may require periodic maintenance and repair. Moreover, trackers consume some energy for their operation, which reduces the net energy gain compared to fixed installations. Despite these considerations, solar trackers continue to gain popularity as technology advances and costs decrease. Ongoing research and innovation (Bharti et al., 2019) aim to improve the reliability, durability, and cost-effectiveness of solar tracking systems, further driving their adoption in the renewable energy industry.

Internet of Things

The Internet of Things refers to a vast network of interconnected physical devices, objects, or "things" that are embedded with sensors, software, and communication capabilities, allowing them to collect and exchange data over the internet without requiring human-to-human or human-to-computer interaction. These devices can be everyday objects, appliances, industrial machines, vehicles, and more. IoT has applications across multiple industries, including smart homes, healthcare, agriculture, transportation, manufacturing, and more. As technology continues to evolve, the IoT ecosystem is expected to grow, leading to even more interconnected and intelligent devices.

There is immense potential for IoT technology to revolutionize various aspects of our lives. There are key areas where IoT is already making a significant impact and has the potential to bring further transformation. One of the key advantages of IoT is its ability to enhance efficiency and automation (Singh et al., 2018; Saini et al., 2019). Through IoT, devices can be remotely monitored and controlled, allowing for streamlined processes and optimized operations. For example, in smart homes, IoT-enabled devices such as thermostats, lighting systems, and appliances can be connected and controlled through a central hub or mobile app, offering convenience and energy savings.

The Implementation of a Solar Tracking System Using IoT

It can lead to several positive outcomes and results. Here are some key results that can be achieved:

- *Improved Efficiency and Performance:* The dynamic adjustment of solar panels based on real-time data enables optimal positioning for maximum energy output (Chen, 2020). By integrating IoT sensors, weather forecasts, and historical data, the solar tracking system can make intelligent decisions on panel positioning, considering factors such as sunlight intensity, shading, and temperature. This enhances the efficiency and performance of the solar energy system.
- *Cost Savings and Return on Investment:* The increased energy generation and improved efficiency of the solar tracking system can result in cost savings and a higher return on investment. By generating more energy, the system can reduce or even eliminate the need for additional energy sources, leading to reduced utility bills. Additionally, the improved performance and longevity of the solar panels can contribute to long-term cost savings.

- *Real-time Monitoring and Maintenance:* IoT connectivity allows for real-time monitoring of the solar tracking system's performance and operational parameters. By integrating sensors and data analytics, the system can detect any anomalies or deviations from expected behavior. This makes proactive maintenance possible since any problems may be quickly identified and fixed, minimizing downtime and improving system efficiency.
- *Remote Control and Management:* With IoT connectivity, the paper (Kalyani et al., 2019) systems can be remotely controlled and managed. Operators can access the system's data and performance metrics from anywhere, allowing for centralized monitoring and control. Remote management capabilities enable quick adjustments, troubleshooting, and system optimization without the need for on-site visits, saving time and resources.
- *Integration with Energy Management Systems:* The IoT-enabled solar tracking system can integrate seamlessly with energy management systems and smart grids. This integration enables demand response mechanisms, load balancing, and efficient energy distribution. The solar tracking system can align its operation with the energy demand patterns and grid conditions, contributing to overall grid stability and optimized energy utilization.
- *Environmental Benefits:* The increased energy generation from the solar tracking system reduces reliance on fossil fuel-based energy sources, leading to a reduction in greenhouse gas emissions. By maximizing the utilization of renewable solar energy, the IoT-enabled solar tracking system contributes to a cleaner and more sustainable energy mix.

It is important to note that the specific results may vary depending on factors such as system design, geographical location, weather conditions, and the scale of the installation. However, the integration of IoT technology in solar tracking systems offers significant potential for improved energy generation, efficiency, cost savings, remote monitoring and control, and environmental benefits. The integration of solar tracking systems with the Internet of Things (IoT) holds great promise for the advancement and optimization of solar energy generation.

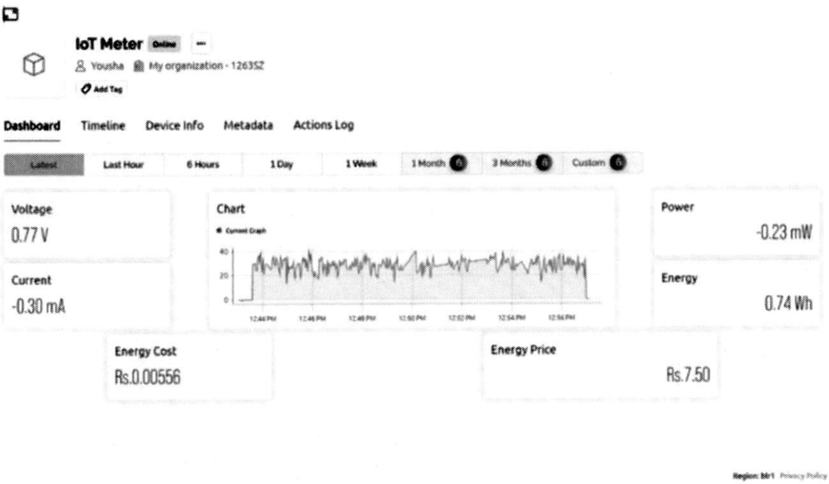

Figure 2. IoT meter display.

IoT-enabled solar tracking systems can continuously receive and analyze data from various sources, such as weather stations, sensors, and energy demand patterns (Yadav et al., 2020). This data-driven approach allows for dynamic adjustments in solar panel positioning, optimizing their angle and alignment with the sun. As a result, the efficiency and energy output of the solar system can be maximized. IoT-based solar tracking systems can integrate seamlessly with smart grid infrastructure and energy management systems. This integration enables intelligent energy distribution, demand response mechanisms, and load balancing. Solar tracking systems can adjust their orientation based on real-time energy demand and grid conditions, contributing to grid stability and efficient energy utilization. By leveraging IoT and data analytics capabilities, solar tracking systems can gather and analyze a wealth of operational data. This data can be used to identify patterns, optimize performance, and predict maintenance needs as shown in Figure 2. Predictive maintenance algorithms can detect potential failures or degradation in the system, allowing for timely intervention and reducing maintenance costs.

In summary, the integration of solar tracking systems with IoT offers numerous benefits, including enhanced efficiency, real-time monitoring and maintenance, integration with smart grids, data analytics and predictive maintenance, energy optimization, cost savings, and scalability. By leveraging the power of IoT, solar tracking systems can unlock their full potential, contributing to the growth and adoption of renewable energy and paving the way for a more sustainable future.

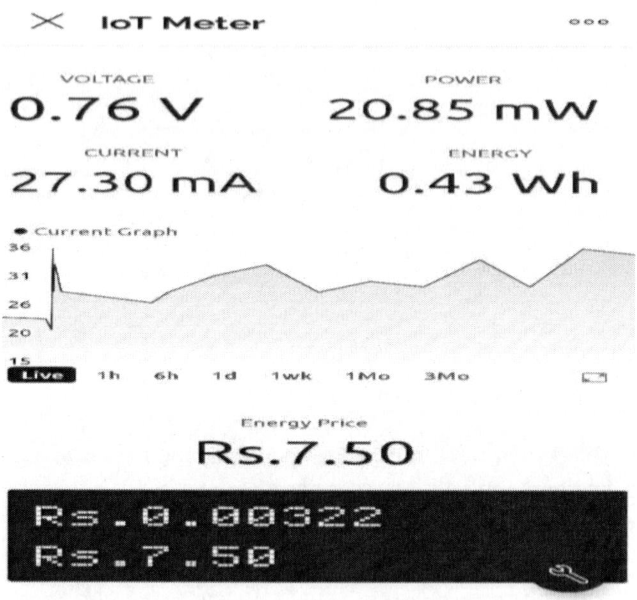

Figure 3. Data fetched from cloud (IoT).

Literature Review

The concept is described in (Srinivasan et al., 2018) uses an ARM7TDMI CPU to collect data from sensors and direct a motor to follow the sun as shown in Figure 3. The LPC2148 controller, which is based on an ARM7 TDMI processor, is used to design and implement the monitoring controller, which uses a closed loop algorithm. As a result, the solar panel's maximum current is acquired to maximize energy output.

The paper (Turjman et al., 2018) describes a system that uses a programmable system on chip device to control a scale replica of a solar tracker. The PSoC (Programmable System on Chip) is supplied with input voltage between the solar panel and a photo resistor to be processed, and then the geared DC motor receives the output. Many solar panels can be controlled by a single microprocessor; only accurate data needs to be transmitted. Efficiency is nearly two times more efficient.

A realistic, intelligent sun tracking system to maximize solar energy was designed, developed, and tested, according to (Turjman et al., 2018). It will be run by a Microchip PIC 18F452 microcontroller. The system's foundation consists of two mechanisms. The first one finds the location of the sun using a search engine (PILOT). The second mechanism (intelligent PANELS) doesn't align with the PILOT until most of the energy has been able to be retrieved.

The paper (Chen et al., 2019) unveiled a photovoltaic panel-based intelligent IoT-based solar tracking system. They used IoT components in their system, such as sensors, actuators, and a centralized control system. The best location for the solar panels was chosen using data collected, analyzed, and utilized in real-time on sunshine intensity and panel orientation. In comparison to a static solar panel, the results indicated higher energy output and improved performance. The paper (Mahmoud et al., 2018) centered on the development and deployment of an Internet of Things-based solar tracking system. To monitor and manage the orientation of solar panels, they used IoT devices and wireless connectivity. To dynamically alter the panel location, the system collected data on ambient factors, such as temperature and sunshine intensity. The study showed enhanced energy production and cost reductions in comparison to fixed solar panels.

The paper (Ankit et al., 2021) created a Raspberry Pi-based Internet of Things-based real-time solar tracking system. To gather information about the environment and modify the direction of the solar panel, the system combined IoT devices, sensors, and actuators. The study illustrated improved energy production and illustrated the viability of IoT-based real-time monitoring and control.

The literature review highlights the growing interest in IoT-based solar tracking systems and their potential to enhance energy generation and efficiency. These studies demonstrate the use of IoT technologies, such as wireless sensor networks, data transmission protocols, and cloud platforms, to enable real-time monitoring, control, and optimization of solar panel positioning. By integrating IoT with solar tracking systems, researchers have achieved improved energy output, remote monitoring capabilities, and cost-effective maintenance.

It is evident from the reviewed literature that IoT-based solar tracking systems offer numerous advantages, including increased energy generation, improved efficiency, remote control and monitoring, and cost savings. These results offer a solid basis for the creation and application of a solar tracking system based on the Internet of Things.

Working Methodology

Internet of Things (IoT) (Kumar et al., 2021) technology is integrated with the conventional solar tracking system as part of the operation of an IoT-based solar tracking system. The system can monitor and manage the tracking mechanism, gather and communicate data, and optimize energy production thanks to IoT technology. Here is a general description of the process:

- *Sensor Data Acquisition:* IoT-based solar tracking systems employ various sensors to gather relevant data. These sensors include light intensity sensors, temperature sensors, and GPS modules. Light intensity sensors detect the intensity of sunlight, while temperature sensors monitor the ambient temperature. GPS modules provide location information for accurate tracking.
- *Data Transmission:* The acquired data from the sensors is transmitted to a central control unit using wireless communication protocols such as Wireless, Bluetooth, or mobile networks. The data can be sent in real-time or periodically, depending on the system requirements.
- *Data Processing and Analysis:* The central control unit processes and analyzes the received data. It determines the optimal position and orientation of the solar panels depending on the solar azimuth and elevation angles. Algorithms and mathematical models are used to calculate the sun's posture and predict its trajectory.
- *Actuation and Control:* Once the optimal position is determined, the control unit sends commands to actuators, which adjust the solar panels' orientation and tilt angles. The actuators can be mechanical systems, motors, or servo mechanisms, depending on the design of the solar tracking system. These actuators ensure that the solar panels are aligned to receive maximum solar radiation throughout the day.
- *Monitoring and Feedback:* The IoT-based solar tracking system continuously monitors the performance of the solar panels, tracking accuracy, and environmental conditions. It collects data on energy generation, tracking errors, and other relevant parameters. This

information is transmitted back to the central control unit for analysis and feedback.

- *Remote Monitoring and Control:* The solar tracking system may be remotely monitored and managed thanks to IoT technology. Data and performance metrics for the system are accessible to users via online interfaces or mobile applications. They can also remotely adjust the tracking parameters or receive alerts and notifications regarding system status and maintenance requirements.
- *Optimization and Energy Management:* The collected data and analytics can be used for optimization purposes. Machine learning algorithms or optimization techniques can be applied to fine-tune the tracking algorithm, improve energy generation efficiency, and minimize tracking errors. The integration with energy management systems allows for coordinated energy generation and consumption, maximizing the overall efficiency of the solar energy system.

By leveraging IoT technology, solar tracking systems can enhance their functionality, flexibility, and monitoring capabilities. The integration of real-time data acquisition, analysis, and remote control enables efficient solar tracking and optimization, resulting in increased energy harvesting efficiency and improved performance of the solar energy system.

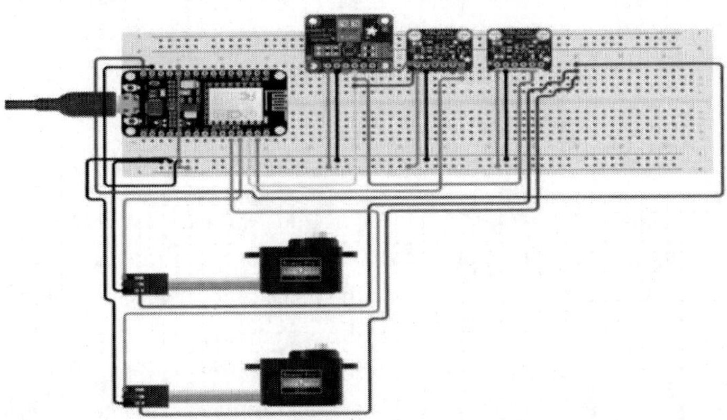

Figure 4. Circuit diagram of solar tracking system.

Implementation of Solar Tracking System

The implementation of an IoT-based solar tracking system (Sheikh, 2020) involves the integration of IoT technology with the traditional solar tracking system as shown in Figure 4. Here is a general outline of the implementation process:

Hardware Setup

Install the solar panels and the mechanical tracking system as per the design requirements. Choose and install appropriate sensors such as light intensity sensors, temperature sensors, and GPS modules to collect relevant data. Install the actuators that control the movement of the solar panels based on the tracking algorithm.

IoT Device Integration

Select IoT devices or microcontrollers capable of collecting and processing sensor data and communicating with the central control unit. Connect the sensors and actuators to the IoT devices, ensuring proper wiring and compatibility. Configure the IoT devices to collect data from the sensors and transmit it to the central control unit using wireless communication protocols such as Wi-Fi, Bluetooth, or cellular networks.

Central Control Unit

Set up a central control unit that acts as the brain of the IoT-based solar tracking system. This control unit can be a computer, a microcontroller, or a dedicated IoT gateway. Develop or install software to receive and process data from the IoT devices. Implement algorithms to analyze the data, calculate the sun's position, and determine the optimal orientation and tilt angles for the solar panels. Use the control unit to send commands to the actuators for adjusting the position of the solar panels.

Connectivity and Communication

Establish a reliable network connection between the central control unit and the IoT devices. Ensure proper network configuration and security measures to protect the system from unauthorized access. Set up a data transmission protocol to facilitate real-time or periodic data exchange between the IoT devices and the central control unit.

Monitoring and Control

Develop a user interface or a mobile application to enable remote monitoring and control of the solar tracking system. Implement features such as real-time tracking status, energy generation monitoring, and system alerts or notifications. Enable users to remotely adjust tracking parameters, monitor system performance, and receive insights and recommendations for optimization.

Testing and Calibration

Conduct thorough testing and calibration of the IoT-based solar tracking system to ensure accurate tracking and optimal energy generation. Validate the system's performance under different environmental conditions and tracking scenarios. Fine-tune the tracking algorithm and control parameters based on the collected data and feedback.

Maintenance and Upgrades

Regularly maintain and inspect the IoT-based solar tracking system to ensure its proper functioning. Monitor and address any hardware or software issues that may arise. Consider upgrades or enhancements to improve the system's efficiency, security, and integration with other energy management systems. Implementing an IoT-based solar tracking system requires a combination of mechanical, electrical, and software integration. It is essential to follow industry best practices, safety guidelines, and local regulations while implementing the system.

Flowchart of Solar Tracking System

- *Initialize IoT Device:* The system initializes and sets up the IoT device, which includes any necessary hardware components and software configurations.
- *Connect to Wi-Fi Network:* The IoT device establishes a connection to a Wi-Fi network to enable communication with other devices and the internet.
- *Retrieve Current Time and Date:* The system retrieves the current time and date information, which is important for determining the position of the sun at any given moment.
- *Calculate Solar Position:* Using the current time and date, the system calculates the position of the sun relative to the location of the solar tracking system. This information helps determine the ideal position for the solar panel.
- *Measure Solar Intensity:* The system measures the intensity of the sunlight falling on the solar panel. This measurement is used to assess whether solar tracking is necessary and how much adjustment is needed.
- *Compare Current Position with Ideal Position:* The system compares the current position of the solar panel with the ideal position based on the calculated solar position. This step determines whether the solar panel needs adjustment as shown in Figure 5.
- *Is Solar Tracking Necessary?* The system checks whether solar tracking is necessary by comparing the current position with the ideal position. If no adjustment is needed, the system maintains its current position; otherwise, it proceeds to the next step.
- *Adjust Solar Panel Position:* If solar tracking is necessary, the system calculates the required adjustment for the solar panel to align it with the ideal position. This adjustment may involve tilting or rotating the panel.
- *Send Adjustment Commands to Actuators:* The system sends the necessary commands to the actuators (e.g., motors) responsible for adjusting the solar panel's position. These commands initiate the physical movement of the panel.
- *Monitor Solar Tracking:* The system continuously monitors the solar tracking process to ensure the solar panel is moving towards the ideal position.

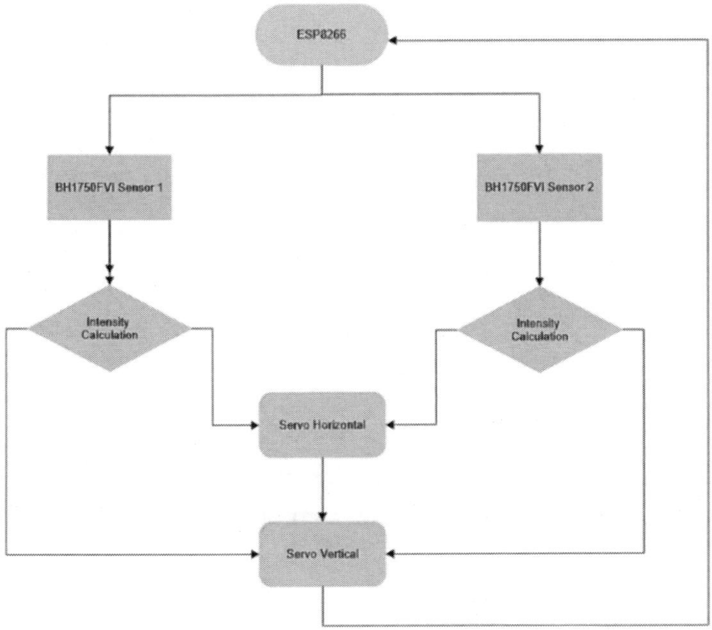

Figure 5. Flowchart of Solar Tracking System.

- *Is Tracking Successful?* The system checks whether the solar panel has successfully aligned with the ideal position. If successful, the system continues tracking the sun; otherwise, it proceeds to the next step.
- *No - Generate Error Alert:* In the case of tracking failure or any other error, the system generates an error alert. This alert can be sent to the user or a maintenance team for troubleshooting.
- *End:* The system reaches the end of the flowchart and stops.

This flowchart provides an overview of the key steps involved in an IoT-based solar tracking system, which helps optimize the solar panel's position to maximize its exposure to sunlight throughout the day.

Result of Proposed System

From the result obtained in Figure 6, we can see that power obtained by a tracker connected with IoT in comparison to a fixed one has greater value. The integration of solar tracking systems with IoT offers numerous benefits, including enhanced efficiency, real-time monitoring and maintenance, integration with smart grids, data analytics and predictive maintenance, energy optimization, cost savings, and scalability.

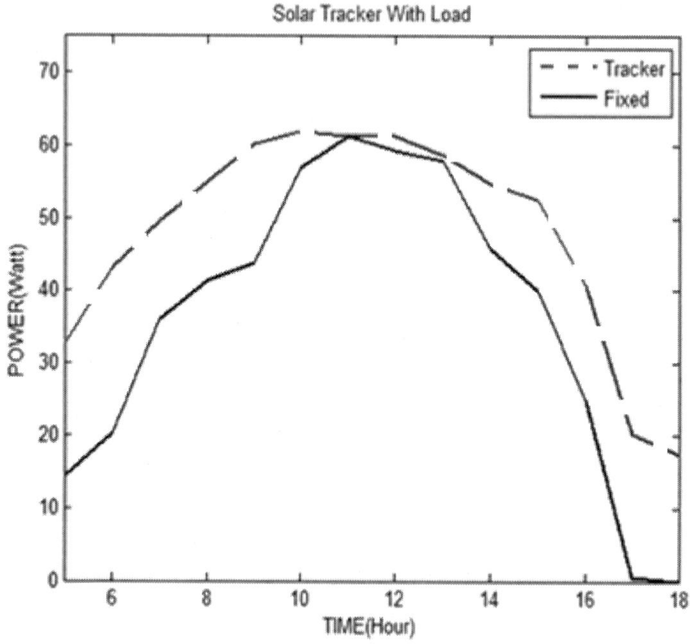

Figure 6. Comparison of output between fixed and moving tracker.

Conclusion and Future Scope

Solar tracking systems can be integrated with smart grid infrastructure and Internet of Things (IoT) technology to enable real-time monitoring, control, and optimization. Through connectivity, solar trackers can communicate with the grid, weather stations, and other devices, allowing for dynamic adjustments based on energy demand, weather conditions, and energy pricing. This integration helps maximize energy production and grid stability. Overall, the future scope of solar tracking systems encompasses increased efficiency, improved energy output, integration with energy storage, advancements in tracking technologies, integration with smart grids and IoT, adaptation to various applications, and cost reduction. These factors contribute to the continued growth and development of solar tracking systems, making them an essential component of the future renewable energy landscape.

Appendix

```
#define BLANK_PRNT Serial
#include <ESP8266WiFi.h>
#include <BlankSimpleEsp8266.h>
#include <Wire.h>
#include <BH1750.h>
#include <Adafrut_INA219.h>
#include <Servo.h>
/*************************************************************************/
// #define BLANK_TEMPLATE_ID “TMPL3ql6FQsRJ”
// #define BLANK_TEMPLATE_NAME “IoT Meter”
#define INA219_ADDRESS (0x40)
#define BLANK_AUTH_TOKEN
“FggmscRgwHuhhCorYonxPjTl3Qj8HPvf” //Enter your blynkauth token
charauth[] = BLANK_AUTH_TOKEN;
charssid[] = “HUSSAIN”; //Enter your WIFI name
char pass[] = “1234567890”; //Enter your WIFI password
/*************************************************************************/
// INA219 Configurations
Adafruit_INA219 ina219(INA219_ADDRESS);
unsigned long previousMillis = 0;
unsigned long interval = 2000;
float energy = 0.00, energyCost, energyPrevious, energyDifference;
floatenergyPrice = 7.50;
/*************************************************************************/
// Servos Configurations
Servo servohorizontal;
intservoh = 0;
intservohLimitHigh = 160;
intservohLimitLow = 20;
Servo servovertical;
```

```
intservov = 0;
intservovLimitHigh = 160;
intservovLimitLow = 20;
/****************************************************
*******************/
// BH1750 Configurations
BH1750 lightSensor1; //<<<<<<<<<<<<<<<<<<<<<<<<<<
BH1750 lightSensor2; //<<<<<<<<<<<<<<<<<<<<<<<<<<
/****************************************************
*******************/
void setup(void) {
Serial.begin(115200);
delay(10);
Blynk.begin(auth, ssid, pass);
Wire.begin(); //(sda, scl) //<<<<<<<<<<<<<<<<<<<<<<<<<<<<<<<<<<
ina219.begin();
lightSensor1.begin(BH1750::CONTINUOUS_HIGH_RES_MODE,
0x23);
lightSensor2.begin(BH1750::CONTINUOUS_HIGH_RES_MODE,
0x5C);
servohorizontal.attach(D3); //<<<<<<<<<<<<<<<<<<<<<<<<<<
servohorizontal.write(0);
servovertical.attach(D4); //<<<<<<<<<<<<<<<<<<<<<<<<<<<<
servovertical.write(0);
delay(1000);
}
/****************************************************
*******************/
void loop(void) {
Blynk.run();
ina219.begin();
unsigned long currentMillis = millis();
if (currentMillis - previousMillis>= interval) {
previousMillis = currentMillis;
ina219values();
}
/****************************************************
*******************/
// Read light levels from the Sensors
```

```
int lux1 = lightSensor1.readLightLevel();
int lux2 = lightSensor2.readLightLevel();
intavgleft = (lux1 - lux2) / 2; //average of left LDRs
intavgright = (lux2 - lux1) / 2; //average of right LDRs
/************************************************************
*****************/
// Read data from the Servos
servoh = servohorizontal.read();
servov = servovertical.read();
/************************************************************
*****************/
// Calcutaing angles
if (lux2 > lux1) {
servovertical.write(servov + 5);
if (servov>servovLimitHigh) {
servov = servovLimitHigh;
}
delay(10);
} else if (lux1 > lux2) {
servovertical.write(servov - 2);
if (servov<servovLimitLow) {
servov = servovLimitLow;
}
delay(10);
} else {
servovertical.write(servov);
}
//<<<<<<<<<<<<<<<<<<<<<<<<<<>>>>>>>>>>>>>>>>>>>>>>>>>>
>>>>
if (avgleft>avgright) {
servohorizontal.write(servoh + 1);
if (servoh>servohLimitHigh) {
servoh = servohLimitHigh;
}
delay(10);
} else if (avgright>avgleft) {
servohorizontal.write(servoh - 1);
if (servoh<servohLimitLow) {
servoh = servohLimitLow;
```

```
}
delay(10);
} else {
servohorizontal.write(servoh);
}
delay(50);
Serial.print("Sensor 1: ");
Serial.print(lux1);
Serial.println(" lux");
Serial.print("Sensor 2: ");
Serial.print(lux2);
Serial.println(" lux");
Serial.print("Servo Horizontal: ");
Serial.print(servoh);
Serial.println(" Degrees");
Serial.print("Servo Vertical: ");
Serial.print(servov);
Serial.println(" Degrees");
Serial.println("""");
delay(1000);

}

/****************************************************************
*******************/

// Read data from the INA219
void ina219values() {
floatshuntvoltage = ina219.getShuntVoltage_mV();
floatbusvoltage = ina219.getBusVoltage_V();
float current = ina219.getCurrent_mA();
floatloadvoltage = busvoltage + (shuntvoltage / 1000);
float power = loadvoltage * current;
energy = energy + power / 3600; //Wh
float capacity = capacity + current / 1000;
energyDifference = energy - energyPrevious;
energyPrevious = energy;
energyCost = energyCost + (energyPrice / 1000 * energyDifference);
```

```
/************************************************************
******************/

// Sending data to blynk....
// VOLTAGE
Blynk.virtualWrite(V0, String(loadvoltage, 2) + String(" V"));
// CURRENT
if (current > 1000) {
Blynk.virtualWrite(V1, String((current / 1000), 2) + String(" A"));
} else {
Blynk.virtualWrite(V1, String(current, 2) + String(" mA"));
}
// POWER
if (power > 1000) {
Blynk.virtualWrite(V2, String((power / 1000), 2) + String(" W"));
} else {
Blynk.virtualWrite(V2, String(power, 2) + String(" mW"));
}
//Energy Consumption

if (energy > 1000) {
Blynk.virtualWrite(V3, String((energy / 1000), 2) + String(" kWh"));
} else {
Blynk.virtualWrite(V3, String(energy, 2) + String(" Wh"));
}
// ENERGY PRICE
Blynk.virtualWrite(V4, String("Rs.") + String(energyPrice));
// ENERGY COST
Blynk.virtualWrite(V5, String("Rs.") + String(energyCost, 5));
// Current Graph
Blynk.virtualWrite(V6, current);
delay(1000);
/************************************************************
*****************/

// Print the data to the serial monitor
Serial.print("Load Voltage: ");
Serial.print(loadvoltage);
Serial.println(" V");
```

```
Serial.print("Current: ");
Serial.print(current);
Serial.println(" mA");
Serial.print("Power: ");
Serial.print(power);
Serial.println(" mW");
}
/******************************** END OF CODE*******************************/
```

References

Bensaid R, Iddaoudi O. IoT-based Smart Solar Tracker for Optimizing Energy Generation. *IEEE International Conference on Wireless Technologies, Embedded and Intelligent Systems (WITS)* 2019:1-6.

Chandra A, Misra S, Obaidat M S. *Internet of Things: Novel Advances and Envisioned Applications*. John Wiley & Sons (2016).

Chen W. Design of IoT-Based Sun Tracking System for Solar Energy. *IEEE International Conference on Industrial Electronics for Sustainable Energy Systems (IESES)* (2020): 1-5.

Chen W, Wang H, Zhang X, Cai L, Zhang M, Huang Z. IoT-Based Real-Time Monitoring and Control System for Solar Energy Tracking. *IEEE 3rd Information Technology, Networking, Electronic and Automation Control Conference (ITNEC)* (2019): 1310-1315.

Kalyani GB, Laxmi V. IoT-Based Smart Solar Power Monitoring and Management System. *Advances in Communication, Devices and Networking Springer* (2019): 367-377.

Mani PK, Sunagar Prashant, Madhuri NS, Joseph Lourdu Rajah A, Ramya D, Kathir I. IoT-based Solar Panel Tracking System to Enhance the Output Power. *IEEE 3rd International Conference on Smart Electronics and Communication (ICOSEC)* (2022): 488-493.

Li Z, Li D, Wu S, Chen S, Hu L. Design and implementation of IoT-based solar tracking system. *IEEE International Conference on Mechatronics and Automation (ICMA)* (2018): 1-6.

Ankit NS, Bharti PP, Sinha SK. IoT Based Dual Axis Solar Tracker Using Light Intensity and Temperature Sensors. *International Conference on Intelligent Sustainable Systems (ICISS)* (2021): 1-8.

Prakash R, Arumugam T, Srinivasan V. IoT-Based Solar Energy Monitoring and Tracking System. *IEEE International Conference on Inventive Communication and Computational Technologies (ICICCT)* (2018): 1830-1834.

Bharti RS, Tiwari AN, Kumar S, Singh AK. Design and Implementation of IoT Based Solar Tracking System. *IEEE 5th International Conference on Computing, Communication, Control and Automation (ICCUBEA)* (2019): 1-6.

Jana S, Bhowmik B, Bandyopadhyay SK. IoT-Based Dual Axis Solar Tracking System for Efficient Energy Harvesting. *IOP Publishing International Conference on Intelligent Sustainable Systems (ICISS)* (2017): 032024.

Singh S, Gupta AK, Singhal P. Design and Implementation of IoT based Solar Tracking System. *IEEE International Conference on Computing, Power and Communication Technologies (GUCON)* (2018): 1-6.

Saini S, Anand RS. Design and Development of IoT based Solar Tracking System. *IEEE International Conference on Computational Intelligence and Computing Research (ICCIC)* (2019): 11-17.

Kumar Kanhaiya, Lokesh Varshney, Ambikapathy A, Inayat Ali, Ashish Rajput, Anant Bhatnagar, Sajal Omar. Vision based solar tracking system for efficient energy harvesting. *International Journal of Power Electronics and Drive Systems* (2021) 12(3): 1431.

Sheikh MH. IoT-Based Sun Tracking System Using Raspberry Pi for Solar Energy Harvesting. *Journal of Electrical Engineering and Automation* (2020) 2(1): 15-22.

Singh S, Singh A, Kumar N. Design and Development of IoT-Based Solar Tracking System. *IEEE International Conference on Smart City and Emerging Technologies (ICSCET)* (2018): 1-6.

Srinivasan S, Lai LL, Sivanandam SN, Thambidurai. IoT based solar tracking system using Arduino. *International Conference on Recent Trends in Advanced Computing (ICRTAC)* (2018): 35-43.

Turjman Al F, Abdulkadir A. Smart-Grid and Solar Energy Harvesting in IoT-based Cities. *Intelligence in IoT enabled Smart Cities CRC Press* (2018): 45-62.

Yadav D, Ramesh V, Panda SK. IoT-based solar tracking system using Raspberry Pi. *7th International Conference on Internet of Things: Systems, Management and Security (IOTSMS)* (2020): 112-120.

Chapter 10

Development of a Three-Tier Home Entrance Security System Using IoT and Image Processing

Deepti Mittal*, **PhD**
Kalash Pandey, BE
Sparsh Gupta, BE
Dev Vijh, BE
and Mandeep Singh, PhD
Electrical and Instrumentation Engineering Department,
Thapar Institute of Engineering and Technology, Patiala, Punjab, India

Abstract

A three-tier home entrance security system using IoT, and image processing is presented in this chapter. In our proposed system, we develop a method for face detection using the haar cascade frontal face feature detection and recognition using the KNN algorithm. We obtained some simulation results using PyCharm. In this research work, we can achieve Tier 1. To accomplish Tier 2, we also designed a remotely accessible door lock system using IoT, which can be controlled using the Blynk app, and a surveillance device using a PIR sensor for intruder detection, which is Tier 3 of this project. Our proposed system consists of a Raspberry Pi 4 B+, a Raspberry Pi camera, a node MCU, a solenoid lock, and a PIR sensor. The Node MCU is a microcontroller used to control the relay remotely, the relay switches for the solenoid lock, and

* Corresponding Author's Email: deepti.mittal@thapar.edu.

In: The Future of IoT with Automation in Engineering and Modern Technology
Editors: Sandeep Gupta and Tarun Varshney
ISBN: 979-8-89113-655-7

the PIR sensor. The PIR senses any human activity that occurs inside the house. In cases of connectivity issues, a tactile switch is also used inside the house to open the door lock manually. If the person wants to exit the house, they can press the switch to unlock the door. The Node MCU is also connected to the Blynk cloud platform to control the door lock and PIR sensor remotely.

Keywords: IoT, home automation, home security, PIR sensor

Introduction

The primary line of defence against unlawful entry is the front door. An entrance door must ensure that no unauthorized entrant can enter private homes or an apartment complex. According to a recent survey conducted in the US, 90% of people prefer security systems. For residential purposes, locks and security systems must offer protection against theft and be user-friendly. A home entrance security system, as the name suggests, is something that protects you and your home from theft and intruders. To secure a home, there are many security systems available, and these are utilized in various fields, such as automotive and other businesses (Hasan et al., 2020; Taiwo et al., 2022; Pandey et al., 2023). The traditional door locking system is made up of mechanical locks that are operated using keys. The major drawback of traditional door-looking systems is that they are vulnerable to (i) duplication of keys and (ii) intrusion in several ways and hence lack security. Wired home networks are well-known in the early development of home security systems. These wired systems are very messy and difficult to set up, and now, wireless communication is being used instead (Park et al., 2009). Therefore, wired systems are outdated and need to be upgraded. The many advancements in home security systems have been brought together as a result of the convergence of trending technology and design advancements.

A security system is a network of hardware modules that work together to secure your home. Security alarm systems with various sensors are becoming very popular in residential communities. A classic system consists of a control panel, door sensors, a high decibel security alarm, motion detectors, and signs for your yard and windows. Each module plays an important role in keeping your home secure from theft, with the control panel acting as the primary control center.

There are a lot of valuable goods that people want to retain in their houses, particularly expensive jewelry, expensive electrical equipment, and other expensive stuff. The majority of individuals spend a considerable amount of time away from their houses on a daily basis. It is common for individuals to forget to lock the rear door of their houses. Therefore, security must be a priority. As technology advances, there is an increase in demand for security systems. There is a requirement for intelligent or AI-based systems that can ensure safety without any human effort for modern residents. The advantage of using face recognition instead of another identification process, like iris or fingerprint identification, is that it is more secure and less intrusive (Hassan et al., 2012). Face recognition is frequently used for biometric authentication. During this era of trending digital and wireless technologies, automated security systems are becoming increasingly intelligent. Wi-Fi plays an important role for security systems to enable reliable data transmission and enable the owner to monitor the systems remotely. So, a security system helps in eliminating thefts and creates a safer neighborhood for everyone.

Literature Survey

A door lock system is developed consisting of a Zigbee module for communication purposes and attached to the door lock (Park et al., 2009). The primary control of the whole automation system is the door lock itself. For user authentication, there is a provision for the RFID reader in the door lock system, an LCD, and a servo motor for the opening and closing of the door.

The RFID technology-based system is designed to be digitally controlled. This system is passive-type and can activate and authenticate the user (Verma et al., 2010). Upon authentication, access is allowed. The RFID reader reads the RFID tag automatically every millisecond, and the RFID reader sends the data contained by the tag to the main control circuitry through the serial port. This system functions in real-time and allows access to the door when the authenticated user puts their tag in contact with the RFID reader. Materials, like metal and liquid, limit this technology because they can impact signals. Therefore, systems based on this technology may not be as accurate or reliable as barcode scanners.

A facial recognition-based GUI system is developed (Hassan et al., 2012). In Matlab r2009a, there is a provision for interfacing the GUI, and this can be used to auto-switch the door lock with a microcontroller for a security system. The USB serial communication is used to establish an interface between the

PIC microcontroller and the GUI to allow data transmission to the microcontroller through the GUI. A major limitation of this security system is that once a face is recognized, the door automatically unlocks without alerting the owner, which can create safety concerns. A system is implemented and deployed that can provide access using the web, and the system is based on face recognition (Sahani et al., 2015). It is based on the wireless technique Zigbee, and for face recognition purposes, a PCA algorithm is used. Using a web page equipped with JavaScript and HTML, an owner can monitor entrants and control the system by providing signals to the system. The limitations of this system are that it has a low transmission rate, a short coverage limit, and is not as secure as a Wi-Fi-based security system.

A door lock system is proposed based on a 'Remote Embedded Control System' (Subudhi et al., 2016). This system works on the GSM platform and the web for authentication. An interface has been developed for communication purposes through Zigbee module in the embedded security system. Electromagnetic door lock technology has implemented automated control of door movement. This system used the PCA algorithm for face recognition, which can lead to information loss in the data set if precision is not maintained and the system has a short coverage range up to only 100 meters. A GSM-based digital door lock system is designed by using the PIC (Adnan et al., 2016). In this system, you can set a password for your door lock to secure your house. The door lock is connected to a gear motor that helps lock/unlock the door. They used a PIC microcontroller, geared motor, LCD, GSM module, motor control IC, and a buzzer. In this arrangement, if a person enters the wrong password three times, the owner receives a text message alert on his/her phone.

A system is designed that can be controlled using voice, and it makes use of the voice recognition module and uses an RF module to establish communication between the Raspberry Pi MCU and the Arduino Uno (Vineeth et al., 2017). The password for this security system is the user's voice. This kind of system is very useful for handicapped individuals. The major drawback of this system is that it doesn't allow an owner to control the system remotely. Also, errors can occur during the authentication process due to background noises.

A password-protected door lock system is designed (Goswami et al., 2017). This automatic door lock system uses an electronic control assembly to control the output via a password. This system's flaw is that passwords are simple targets for theft and cannot grant the owner remote access. Thus, the door lock system is not reliable for home security. A Wi-Fi-based smart door lock system is introduced that can be unlocked remotely with the availability of an internet connection (Tilala et al., 2017). This system used the Firebase cloud messaging service to notify the user about activity near the door. It also consists of an accelerometer to calculate the swing rate of the door and a magnetometer to check the door's status (open or closed). Along with this, they also include an OTP-based system, which acts as a 2-step verification service. The hardware they use is an ESP8266 WeMos, an accelerometer, and a magnetometer.

It is focused on the user's convenience to use door locks (Vongchumyen et al., 2017). So, they designed a web application and passcode-based door lock, which can be unlocked using a key. They introduce sensors that constantly check the door's status, whether open or close. When someone knocks on the door, the user receives a notification on their phone, after which the user can generate a temporary passcode that is valid for the set time interval. They used Raspberry pi, Attiny2313, stepper motor, and sensors. On the software side, they designed the web application.

It is known about the level of security that door locks provide in the current market (Mathew et al., 2017). Most of the door locks only have a single level of security; therefore, in this lock system, they introduced multiple encryptions using RFID and two-factor authentication. They worked on a door lock that can work in confidential areas where only authentic people can enter. They have used a PIC microcontroller, LCD, Zigbee module, RFID module, and keypad matrix. The work of this project is based on an OTP generation method. When a person scans their RFID card, the system will authenticate the user, generate an OTP, and send it to the user. After entering the OTP with the help of the keypad matrix, the door will be unlocked. A work talked about an intelligent security lock prototype digital door lock system (Pandit et al., 2018). It is an app-based door lock that works on a Bluetooth connection. This research paper includes a face recognition algorithm for an application. They include real-time surveillance on the app itself. The hardware they used comprises a Raspberry Pi, a solenoid-based mechanical lock, a motor driver IC, a magnetic sensor, and a PIR sensor.

A system is designed that can be controlled globally based on remote sensing technology (Komol et al., 2019). This system alerts the owner if any person passes the door by providing a notification to the owner. One of the limitations of GSM is that multiple users use the same bandwidth, and this can cause interference in transmission. Therefore, trending technologies such as 3G have an added advantage over other modes of networks, such as CDMA; although it is the latest one, it is not up to par due to GSM limitations.

A door lock system based on IoT is implemented (Adiono et al., 2019). This system remains secure even though it does not need any input from the user. The system consists of an STM32L100 microcontroller and a Zigbee module for communication purposes with the host of the smart home and to receive status regarding the GPS position of the user. This research's limitations are that Zigbee is a low-data-speed, low complexity and short-range module. Low transmission makes it unfit for security purposes. In addition, it is not remotely accessible by the user.

The prototype for a smart lock based on IoT is developed (Asman et al., 2020). This security system can be controlled with any Android smartphone, but it must have a Blynk application. A solenoid lock is used as an output for the door lock system. This system does not require any authentication, such as face recognition or barcode scanning; therefore, it is not secure.

Design Methodology

The proposed system consists of a Raspberry Pi sensor with an image processing concept. The PIR sensor is used for detecting motion. The fixed sensors on the door invoke digital cameras in the rooms to capture images or motion. The captured image is sent to the server to be stored in the database. The Raspberry Pi camera is used to capture the image. Once the image is captured, it will be sent to the server to detect the face and recognize the person. If the image is recognized, the message is sent to the owner's device. If the face does not get recognized, it sends an alert message to the owner. Here, image processing techniques analyses and interpret the captured image, as shown in Figure 1.

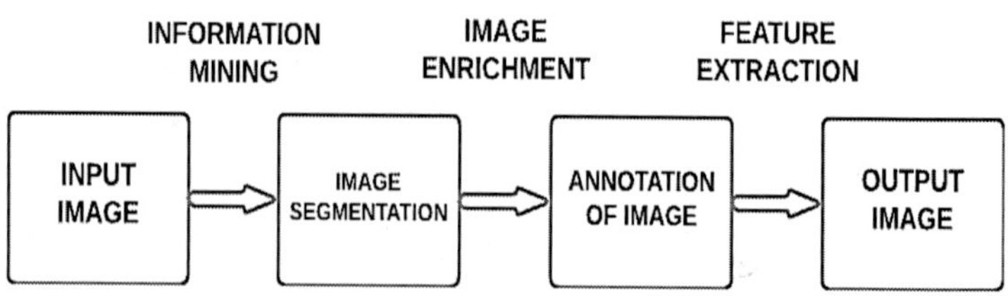

Figure 1. Mechanism of image processing.

Concept Map and Flow Chart

The overall methodology of the system is explained after splitting the system's work into two parts, as shown in Figure 2, i.e., the inside and outside of the door. The system consists of a Raspberry Pi 4 B+, a solenoid lock, PIR sensors, a Pi camera, and other basic components.

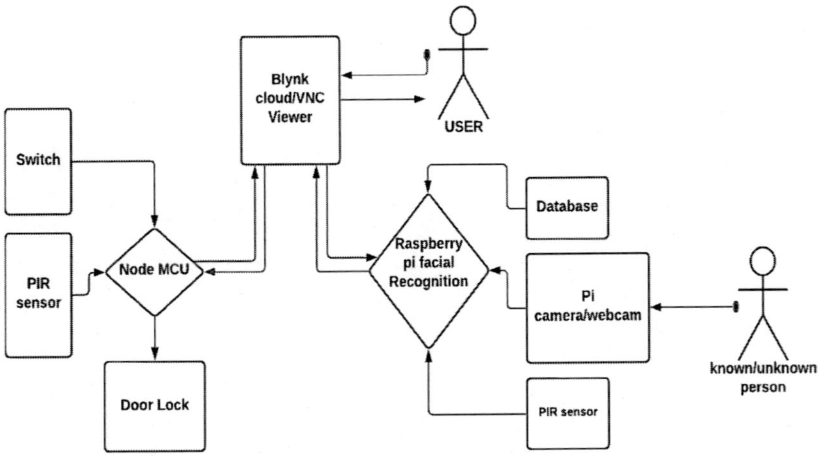

Figure 2. Overall flow of the system.

Outside the Door

A PIR sensor is placed in the door frame. When someone approaches the door, the PIR sensor detects the motion and alerts the camera to take a picture of the person. The image is then sent to a Raspberry Pi, which compares it to a database of images that have been stored in the cloud. If the image matches a face in the database, the Raspberry Pi will unlock the door. If the image does not match any of the faces in the database, the Raspberry Pi will not unlock the door. Here are the steps in more detail:

1. The PIR sensor detects motion and alerts the camera.
2. The camera takes a picture of the person.
3. The image is sent to the Raspberry Pi.
4. The Raspberry Pi compares the image to the database of images.

5. If the image matches a face in the database, the Raspberry Pi unlocks the door.
6. If the image does not match any of the faces in the database, the Raspberry Pi does not unlock the door.

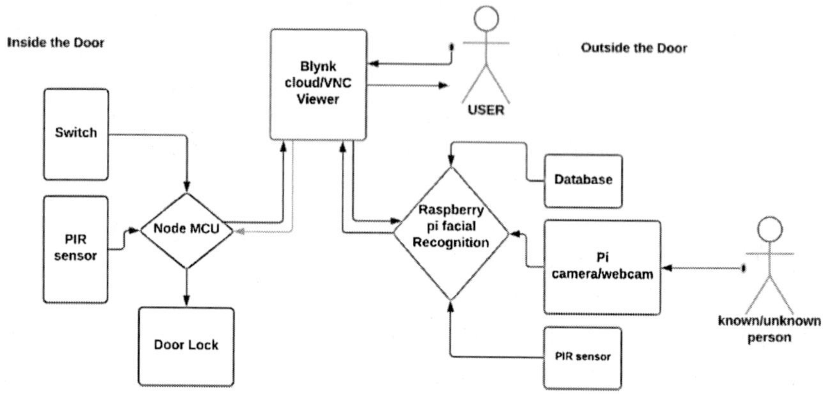

Figure 3. Flow diagram – outside the door.

This system uses image processing algorithms to compare the captured image to the images in the database, as shown in Figure 3. The image processing algorithms are able to identify features in the images, such as facial features, that can be used to match the images. This system can be used to secure a home or office by only allowing people who are authorized to enter. The system can also be used to track the comings and goings of people in a building.

Inside the Door

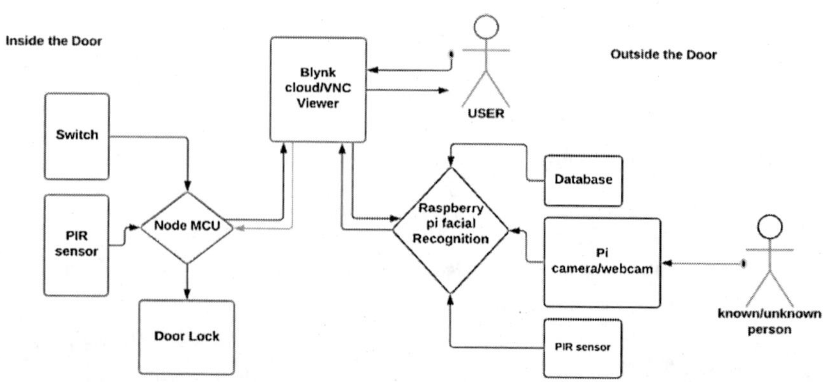

Figure 4. Flow diagram – inside the door.

The system consists of a switch and a PIR sensor on the other side of the door. The work of the switch is that if a person wants to exit the house, he or she can simply press the switch, which opens the door lock for five seconds. Simultaneously, the owner can monitor the live-time status of the door lock, as shown in Figure 4.

Face Detection: Haar Cascade Algorithm

The face is required to be isolated from the background. But the major problem with previous face detection algorithms is that they are computationally expensive. Pixel-by-pixel analysis in face detection is a tedious, time-consuming task that is tough to achieve. The reason behind this is the wide variation of attributes and shapes within a human face. For scaling and precision, pixels are required. The Haar Classifiers algorithm rapidly detects human faces using AdaBoost classifier cascades based on Haar-like features.

Haar Cascade Classifiers

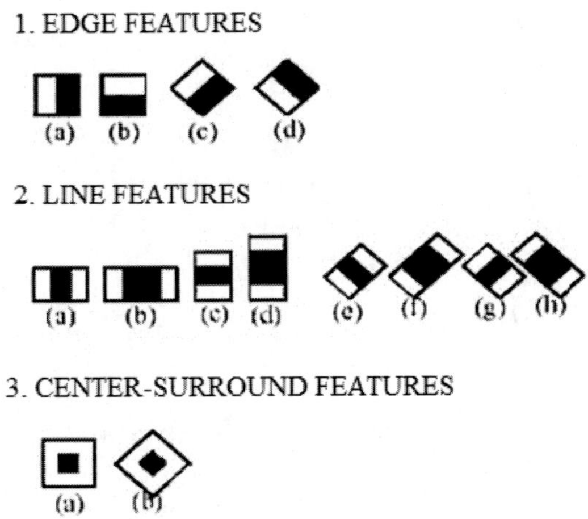

Figure 5. Common haar features.

Haar-like features are the basis for face detection using a Haar classifier. The advantage of these features is that they use the change in contrast rather than the intensity of a pixel. Darker and lighter areas are determined by contrast variances among the groups of pixels. Scaling of HAW features can be done by increasing or decreasing the size of a pixel. The formation of Haar-like features is done by using two or three adjacent groups. Haar-like features, used to detect a facial image, are shown in Figure 5.

The Haar Cascade Classifiers first need to be trained to perform face detection using human facial features like eyes, mouth, and nose. In order to train classifiers, gentle Haar feature algorithms and the AdaBoost algorithm must be implemented. To ease the implementation of computer vision, Intel developed an open-source library called the Open Computer Vision Library (OpenCV). This library is developed to be used in collaboration with applications that can be used where there is a need for visualization, such as in the field of image processing, biometrics, etc.

Feature Extraction

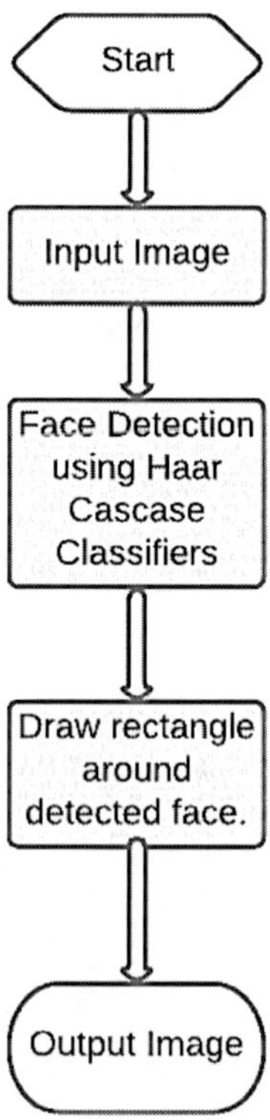

Figure 6. Flowchart of the face detection process.

The main advantage of using features rather than pixels is that features can encode ad hoc domain knowledge, which is impossible to learn by using training data. This is because features are typically handcrafted to represent specific aspects of an image, such as the shape of a nose or the location of an eye. This allows the facial feature extraction algorithm to be more accurate and robust to changes in lighting, pose, and expression. The process of facial feature extraction typically involves two steps: facial feature detection and feature extraction. Facial feature detection is the process of identifying the location of the face in an image. Once the face has been detected, the feature extraction step can be used to identify the location of the facial features, such as the eyes, nose, and mouth, as shown in Figure 6.

Dataset Generation

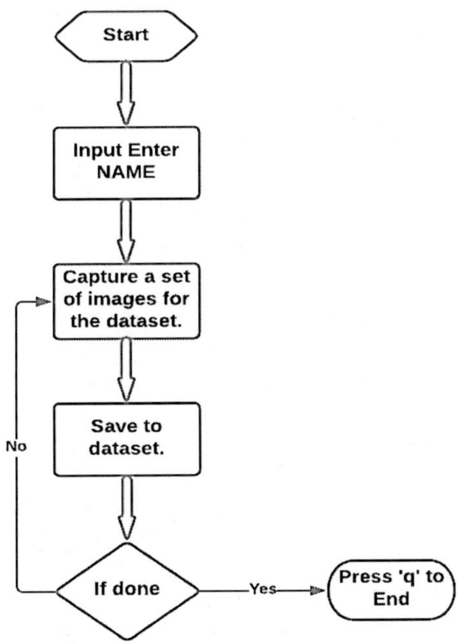

Figure 7. Flowchart of dataset generation

RGB images are three-dimensional arrays where each element of an array is a pixel, and the colour of each pixel is a combination of RGB values. In contrast, 0 is taken as a black pixel value and 255 as a white pixel value for a grayscale image. Python uses captured image data in the form of a NumPy array. In the face dataset collection programme, images are converted into NumPy arrays and stored in a folder as shown in Figure 7, where the folder name is the same as the name of a person, so that while recognizing, it can fetch the name to display on the output.

Face Recognition

In order to perform face recognition, it is required to detect faces and then compare them with the images stored in the dataset folder, as shown in Figure 8. For this purpose, we will use the KNN algorithm. It stores the dataset and then performs operations on it; therefore, it is also known as a lazy learner algorithm as it does not learn from the training set immediately.

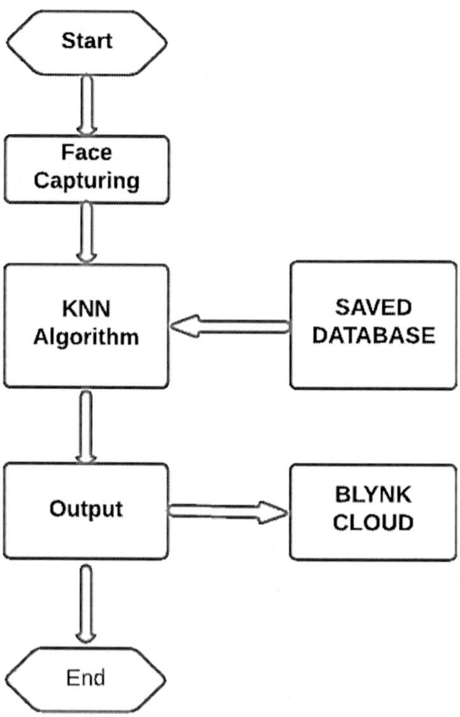

Figure 8. Flowchart of the face recognition process.

Working

1. Select value of K.
2. Calculation of the Euclidean Distance of K Neighbors.
3. After calculating Euclidean Distance, pick the nearest distance to K.
4. Suppose if we have two categories, then count the number of nearest data points.
5. New data points will be allocated to the category having the maximum number of data points, as shown in Figure 9.

If we choose the value of K = 5, then for:

- Category A there are 3 data points which are near to K and
- Category B there are 2 data points which are near to K

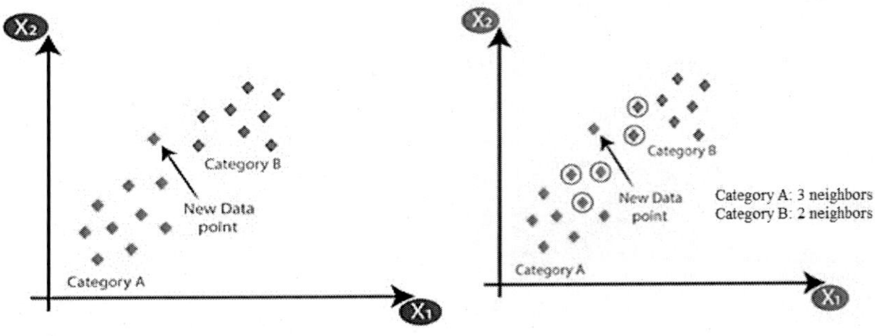

Figure 9. Datapoint mapping.

So, a maximum number of data points are in category A, so new data points will belong to Category A.

KNN Algorithm Working

- First, we need to load the data.
- Then we choose any number to initialize the K value.
- For each dataset that is stored in the dataset:
- Calculate the Euclidean distance from the data stored in the dataset.
- Create an ordered collection and add the distance and the index.

- Using the lambda function, sort the ordered collection consisting of distances and indices from smallest to largest (in ascending order) according to the distances.
- From the sorted collection, choose the first K entries.
- Get the labels for the selected K entries.
- Return the mean of the K labels if regression.
- Else return the mode of the K labels, if classification.

Live Streaming

The live streaming feature provides the owner with an inside view of the house remotely in case any intruder is detected. As the intruder comes in front of the door, the infrared radiation of the intruder generates the differential output, which triggers the PIR sensor, and this triggering of the PIR sensor signals the microcontroller to send the notification to the Blynk application installed on the owner's device. On getting such a notification, the owner can switch on the live streaming feature to check on the intruder. In the Blynk app, there is a dedicated video streaming widget to access the live stream, which supports RTSP, HTTPS/S progressive streaming, and HTTP/S live streaming. Blynk doesn't have its own streaming servers. Therefore, it is required to use third-party services to stream the video. To access the live stream of the remote location, we just need to enter the IP address at which streaming is active inside the video streaming widget.

Mathematical Analysis and Calculations

Euclidean Distance Calculation

$$\sqrt{(y2 - y1)^2 + (x2 - x1)^2} \quad (1)$$

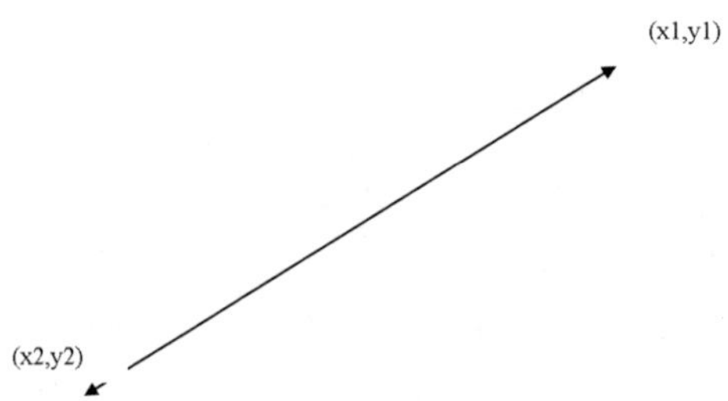

Figure 10. Euclidean distance calculation.

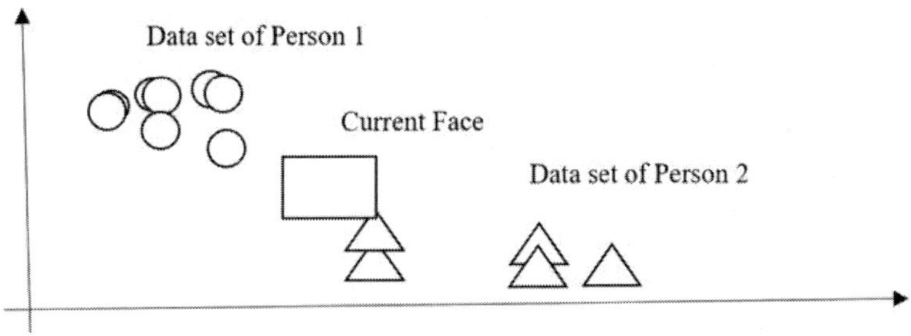

Figure 11. Face mapping with a dataset.

In order to perform face recognition using the KNN algorithm, it is required to calculate the Euclidean distance between data points of the stored dataset and data points of the current face. Recognition of face is done by the calculation of the shortest Euclidean distance, as shown in Figures 10 & 11.

$$\sqrt{(y2 - y1)^2 + (x2 - x1)^2} \qquad (1)$$

Hardware Design

Several standards and research papers are referred to before arriving at the final design of the hardware model. Major components that are directly involved in achieving the objectives of the project are the PIR sensor, Raspberry Pi camera, Raspberry Pi 4B+, node MCU, and solenoid lock. Here is a detailed overview of each component and their contribution to achieving the objectives as stated earlier:

Door Lock System

The door lock system comprises components such as the node MCU, relay module, PIR sensor, solenoid lock, and power supply. The Node MCU is a microcontroller that controls the relay. Here, the relay acts as a switch for the solenoid lock and PIR sensor. The PIR sensor relates to the MCU, which senses any human activity that occurs inside the house. The PIR sensor can be switched on or off automatically by the user. There is also a tactile switch present that is placed inside the house to open the door lock manually.

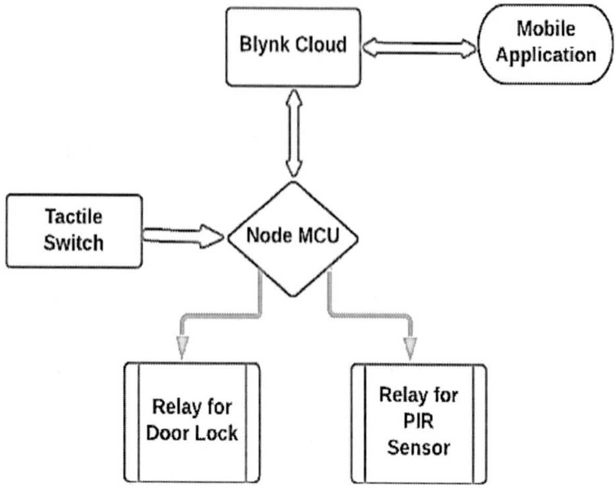

Figure 12. Block diagram of door lock system.

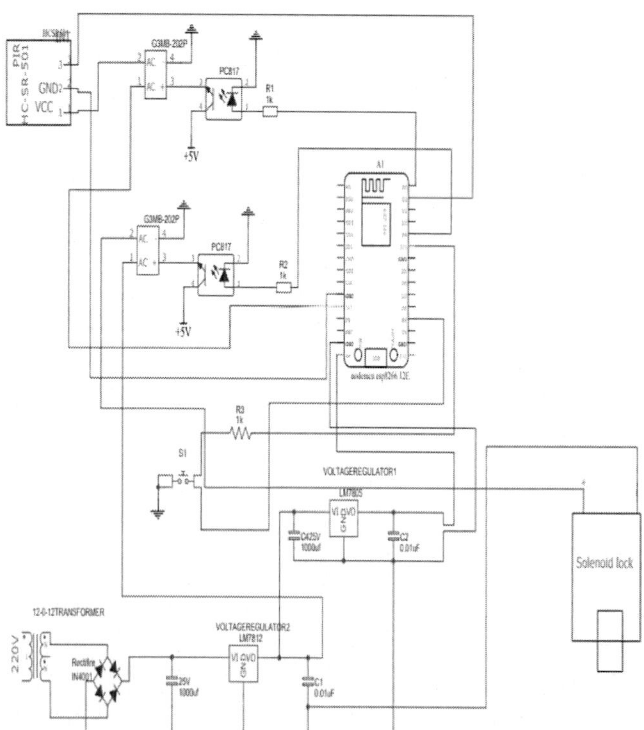

Figure 13. Schematic diagram of door lock system.

If the person wants to exit the house, they can press the switch to unlock the door, as shown in Figure 12. This switch will be beneficial if there is a connectivity issue. The dual-channel relay is connected to pins d0 and d4 of the node MCU. The pin of the PIR sensor is connected to the d1 pin, as shown in Figure 13. The Node MCU is also connected to the Blynk cloud platform so that we can control the door lock and PIR sensor remotely.

Conclusion

Tier 1

To achieve the first tier of security, we have placed a PIR sensor in the front portion of the model. It is a device that is sensitive to infrared radiation. Whenever any warm body or human passes by it, it generates a signal that detects the motion whenever there is any change in the inputs of two slots. When the sensor is idle, it means that both slots receive the same amount of infrared radiation, and the differential output generated will be zero in this case, but when any warm body passes by, it provides the input to one half of the PIR sensor, thus generating differential output, and the same process occurs whenever a warm body leaves the area again, generating differential output in the opposite direction. We have used this function of the PIR sensor to trigger the Raspberry Pi camera to switch on, which is placed at the front of the door. Once the camera is triggered, it starts detecting and recognizing the faces present in the span of the Pi camera. If a face is detected, then the Raspberry Pi will send the signal to the Blynk cloud, which will notify the owner through the Blynk app that "someone is waiting at the door." If the face is recognized using the Face recognition algorithm, then it will also output the name of the entrant by comparing it to the dataset previously stored in the database; in this case, the person will be notified with a message like "Sparsh is waiting at the door."

Tier 2

Once the owner gets the notification on their device, the owner can remotely, with a click of a button, send a signal through the server to the Node MCU to unlock the door and let the person in. In cases of low network connectivity, the owner can also manually unlock the door using a switch, which further eliminates the use of keys and provides a more secure entrance to the house.

Tier 3

To provide the third tier of security, we have used another PIR sensor that is placed on the backside of the door in order to capture the inside of the house. To minimize thefts and increase security, we provide intruder detection and live streaming features. So, when the owner is not at home, our system using the PIR sensor will detect any false activity inside the house in his absence. If any such activity or movement is found, it will directly send a notification to the owner using the same Blynk cloud: “Intruder detected.” On getting this notification, the owner can immediately open his mobile device and switch on the live streaming feature present on the home page of the Blynk application. If an intruder is seen on the stream, the owner can play a loud alarm on the system to inform the neighbours and further inform the police.

In this way, our hardware model will be able to provide the stated three tiers of security to the home of the owner.

Disclaimer

None.

References

Adiono T, Fuada S, Anindya SF, Purwanda IG, Fathany MY. IoT-enabled door lock system. *Int J Adv Comput Sci App* (2019) 10(5): 445–449.

Asman FF, Permata E, Fatkhurrokhman M. Prototype of smart lock based on internet of things (IOT) with ESP8266. *J Ilm. Tek. Elektro Komput. dan Inform* (2020) 5(2): 101-111.

Goswami S, Choudhury A, Das S, Banerjee T. Automated password protected door lock system. *Advances in Industrial Engineering and Management* (2017) 6(1): 48–52.

Hassan H, Bakar RA, Mokhtar ATF. Face recognition based on auto-switching magnetic door lock system using microcontroller. *Proc 2012 Int Conf Syst Eng Technol ICSET* (2012): 1-6.

Hasan Y, Abdurrahman, Wijanarko Y, Muslimin S, Maulidda R. The automatic door lock to enhance security in RFID system. *J Phys Conf Ser 1500 012132* (2020):1-8.

Ibrahim A, Paravath A, Aswin PK, Iqbal SM, Abdulla SU. GSM based digital door lock security system. *Proc 2015 IEEE Int Conf Power Instrumentation Control Comput PICC* (2015):1-6.

Komol MMR, Podder AK, Arafat A, Nabeed T. Remote sensing global ranged door lock security system via mobile communication. *Int. J. Wirel. Microw. Technol.* (2019) 9(5): 25–37.

Mathew M, Divya RS. Super secure door lock system for critical zones. *2017 Int Conf Networks Adv Comput Technol NetACT* (2017): 242–245.

Pandey N K, Kumar K, Saini G, Mishra AK. Security issues and challenges in cloud of things-based applications for industrial automation. *Annals of Operations Research* (2023): 1-20.

Pandit V, Majgaonkar P, Meher P, Sapaliga S, Bojewar S. Intelligent security lock. *Proc Int Conf Trends Electron Informatics ICEI* (2018): 713–714.

Park YT, Sthapit P, Pyun JY. Smart digital door lock for the home automation. *IEEE Reg 10 Annu Int Conf Proceedings/TENCON* (2009): 1–6.

Sahani M, Nanda C, Sahu AK, Pattnaik B. Home security system based on face recognition. *2015 Int Conf Circuits, Power Comput Techno*l (2015): 1–6.

Sahani M, Subudhi S, Mohanty MN. Design of face recognition based embedded home security system. *KSII Trans Internet Inf Syst* (2016) 10(4):1751–1767.

Saivineeth KV, Vamshi B, Mittal VK. Wireless voice-controlled multi-functional secure eHome. *2017 Int Conf Adv Comput Commun Informatics ICACCI* (2017): 2235–2240.

Taiwo O, Ezugwu AE, Oyelade ON, Almutairi MS. Enhanced intelligent smart home control and security system based on deep learning model. *Wireless Communications and Mobile Computing Article ID 9307961* (2022): 1-22.

Tilala P, Roy AK, Das ML. Home access control through a smart digital locking-unlocking system. *IEEE Reg 10 Annu Int Conf Proceedings TENCON* (2017): 1409–1414.

Verma GK, Tripathi P. A digital security system with door lock system using RFID technology. *Int J Comput Appl* (2010) 5(11): 6–8.

Vongchumyen C, Watanachaturaporn P, Jinjakam C, Watcharapupong A, Kasemsiri W, Tongprasert K, Walairacht A, Penpokai T, Jenweerawat T, Hami A. Door lock system via web application. *IEEE 2017 International Electrical Engineering Congress (iEECON)* (2017): 1-4.

Chapter 11

IoT-based Edge and Fog Computing for Smart Grids: Revolutionizing Power Distribution

L. N. Sastry Varanasi*

Department of Electrical Engineering, National Institute of Technology Andhra Pradesh (NIT AP), Tadepalligudem, W. G. District, India

Abstract

The exponential progress of the Internet of Things (IoT) has presented novel opportunities for transforming electricity distribution systems. Smart grids have become a crucial solution due to the rising integration of renewable energy sources, the increasing demand for electric vehicles, and the necessity for effective energy management. Nevertheless, the traditional centralized structure of smart grids encounters certain obstacles in relation to scalability, latency, and privacy. This study investigates the potential of edge and fog computing based on the Internet of Things (IoT) in revolutionizing smart grids by effectively tackling the aforementioned difficulties. Edge computing involves localization of computational capabilities close to edge devices, but fog computing expands upon this concept by extending the computational capabilities to intermediate fog nodes. The integration of edge and fog computing facilitates decentralized processing, instantaneous data analysis, and localized decision-making within the framework of intelligent power grids. The work provides a comprehensive overview of smart grids and their key components, highlighting the limitations of the centralized architecture. It then delves into the fundamentals of IoT, edge computing, and fog computing, emphasizing their relevance and benefits in the context of smart grids. The work is also given state-of-the-art in the case

* Corresponding Author's Email: sastry.sclr@nitandhra.ac.in.

In: The Future of IoT with Automation in Engineering and Modern Technology
Editors: Sandeep Gupta and Tarun Varshney
ISBN: 979-8-89113-655-7

of IoT based edge and fog computing by identifying gaps and research opportunities. The proposed methodology involves developing a conceptual framework for integrating IoT, edge computing, and fog computing into smart grids. Machine learning and data analytics techniques will be employed to enable real-time monitoring, predictive maintenance, load balancing, and demand response in the smart grid system. Performance metrics such as latency, scalability, energy efficiency, and privacy will be assessed to quantify the benefits of the proposed IoT-based edge and fog computing approach. Comparative analysis will be conducted against traditional centralized smart grid architectures to highlight the advantages and improvements achieved.

Keywords: edge computing, fog computing, smart grid, power distribution, real-time data analysis, energy management, grid reliability, sustainability.

Introduction

The power distribution landscape is undergoing a significant transformation with the advent of smart grids, driven by the increasing integration of renewable energy sources, the proliferation of electric vehicles, and the need for efficient energy management. Smart grids offer promising solutions for optimizing power generation, distribution, and consumption through advanced monitoring, control, and automation. However, the conventional centralized architecture of smart grids faces challenges in terms of scalability, latency, and privacy, calling for innovative approaches to revolutionize power distribution.

The advent of the Internet of Things (IoT) in recent years has resulted in the proliferation of interconnected devices and sensors, presenting extensive prospects for augmenting the functionalities of smart grids. Edge and fog computing technologies are at the forefront of this transformative process. Edge computing facilitates the dispersion of processing capacities in proximity to edge devices, whereas fog computing expands this capability to intermediary fog nodes. Collectively, these technologies facilitate the implementation of distributed processing, real-time analytics, and localized decision-making, hence enhancing the performance and efficiency of smart grid systems to a considerable extent. This book chapter aims to explore the transformative potential of IoT-based edge and fog computing in smart grids, with a specific focus on revolutionizing power distribution. It investigates how these emerging technologies can address the limitations of traditional centralized architectures and unlock new possibilities for scalable, efficient, and privacy-preserving power distribution networks.

Background

Traditional power distribution systems have relied on centralized architectures, where power generation and control were primarily managed from a central location (Smith, 2018). However, these centralized systems face challenges in meeting the evolving needs of modern power grids. The increasing need for renewable energy sources, electric vehicles, and distributed energy generation necessitates the development of a power distribution infrastructure that is more adaptable, expandable, and effective (Li et al., 2019). The emergence of the Internet of Things (IoT) has opened new possibilities for transforming smart grids (Gungor et al., 2011). The Internet of Things (IoT) refers to a network of many networked devices, sensors, and actuators capable of gathering and exchanging data through the Internet. In the context of smart grids, IoT devices can provide real-time data on energy consumption, power quality, and equipment performance, enabling better monitoring and control of the distribution network (Liu et al., 2019). Edge and fog computing have emerged as key technologies that complement the capabilities of IoT in smart grid applications (Mao et al., 2017). Edge computing reduces latency, improves responsiveness, and enables localized decision-making, making it ideal for time-sensitive applications in smart grids (Shi et al., 2016). Fog computing extends the capabilities of edge computing by introducing intermediate fog nodes, which provide additional computational resources and storage capacity (Bonomi et al., 2012). These fog nodes can perform more complex analytics and collaborate with other nodes and provide a distributed computing infrastructure. Fog computing enables scalable and fault-tolerant processing, enhancing the efficiency and reliability of smart grid operations (Yi et al., 2015).

The integration of IoT, edge computing, and fog computing in smart grids offers several benefits (Ahmed et al., 2019). It enables real-time monitoring of power consumption, equipment status, and grid performance. It facilitates predictive maintenance, where advanced analytics techniques can detect equipment failures or anomalies and schedule maintenance proactively. It supports load balancing and demand response, allowing for optimized energy distribution and better management of peak loads. Additionally, it enhances privacy and security by minimizing the need to transmit sensitive data to centralized locations (Chiang et al., 2016).

By leveraging IoT-based edge and fog computing, smart grids can overcome the limitations of traditional centralized architectures. They enable scalable, efficient, and privacy-preserving power distribution networks, paving the way for a more sustainable and intelligent energy infrastructure (Jin et al., 2020). Given the potential of IoT-based edge and fog computing in revolutionizing power distribution in smart grids, this book chapter aims to explore these technologies in detail. It will delve into the concepts, design principles, applications, and performance evaluation of IoT-based edge and fog computing in the context of smart grid systems. The chapter will provide insights and guidance for researchers, practitioners, and policymakers interested in harnessing the transformative capabilities of these technologies to revolutionize power distribution.

Objectives

- *Explore the potential of IoT-based edge and fog computing*: The chapter seeks to provide an in-depth understanding of the capabilities and benefits of IoT-based edge and fog computing in the context of smart grids. It aims to highlight how these technologies can revolutionize power distribution by addressing the limitations of traditional centralized architectures.
- *Investigate the challenges faced by centralized architectures:* The chapter aims to analyze the challenges and limitations associated with traditional centralized architectures in smart grids. It will explore issues such as scalability, latency, privacy, and security, emphasizing the need for innovative approaches to overcome these challenges.
- *Develop a conceptual framework for integrating IoT, edge computing, and fog computing*: The chapter aims to present a comprehensive conceptual framework that outlines the integration of IoT, edge computing, and fog computing into smart grids. It will discuss the design principles, architecture, and deployment considerations for creating a cohesive and efficient power distribution infrastructure.
- *Examine real-time monitoring and predictive maintenance techniques:* The chapter aims to explore how IoT-based edge and fog

computing can enable real-time monitoring of power consumption, equipment performance, and grid conditions. It will investigate the application of machine learning and data analytics techniques for predictive maintenance, allowing for proactive identification of equipment failures or anomalies.

- *Investigate load balancing and demand response strategies:* The chapter aims to explore how edge and fog computing can facilitate load balancing and demand response in smart grids. It will examine strategies for optimizing energy distribution, managing peak loads, and enabling demand response programs to ensure efficient and reliable power distribution.
- *Identify future research directions and implications:* The chapter aims to provide insights into future research directions and implications of IoT-based edge and fog computing in smart grids. It will identify potential areas for further exploration, highlight challenges that need to be addressed, and discuss the broader implications and impact of these technologies on power distribution networks.

Organization of the Chapter

The organization of the book chapter is structured as follows:

- *Introduction:* The chapter commences with an introductory section that offers a comprehensive review of smart grids. It emphasizes the limitations associated with conventional centralized designs and presents the fundamental concepts of Internet of Things (IoT), edge computing, and fog computing. This paper delineates the research aims and elucidates the rationale for investigating the integration of Internet of Things (IoT)-based edge and fog computing within the context of smart grids.
- *Background:* The chapter provides a background section that sets the context for the exploration of IoT-based edge and fog computing. It discusses the evolution of power distribution systems, the emergence of smart grids, and the role of IoT in transforming power distribution. It also introduces the concepts of edge computing and fog computing and their relevance to smart grids.

- *IoT-Based Edge Computing in Smart Grids:* This section delves into the utilization of edge computing within the context of smart grids. This paper examines the various benefits and advantages associated with edge computing, including the reduction of latency, enhancement of responsiveness, and facilitation of localized decision-making. This study investigates several use scenarios and provides illustrative examples to demonstrate the potential of edge computing in augmenting power distribution within smart grid systems.
- *Fog Computing in Smart Grids:* This section extends the discussion to fog computing and its application in smart grids. It explains how fog computing complements edge computing by providing additional computational resources and storage capacity. It explores the benefits of fog computing, including enhanced scalability, fault tolerance, and collaborative decision-making. Use cases and examples of fog computing in power distribution are also discussed.
- *Integration of IoT, Edge Computing, and Fog Computing:* This section presents a conceptual framework for integrating IoT, edge computing, and fog computing into smart grids. It discusses the design principles, architecture, and deployment considerations for creating a cohesive and efficient power distribution infrastructure. It explores the interactions between edge devices, fog nodes, and the central smart grid infrastructure.
- *Real-Time Monitoring and Predictive Maintenance:* This section focuses on real-time monitoring and predictive maintenance techniques enabled by IoT-based edge and fog computing. It discusses the use of machine learning and data analytics for real-time monitoring of power consumption, equipment performance, and grid conditions. It explores how these technologies facilitate predictive maintenance, allowing for proactive equipment failure detection and maintenance scheduling.
- *Load Balancing and Demand Response*: This section examines the application of edge and fog computing in load balancing and demand response strategies. It explores how these technologies optimize energy distribution, manage peak loads, and enable demand response programs to ensure efficient and reliable power distribution. It discusses the benefits and challenges associated with load balancing and demand response in smart grids.

- *Future Research Directions and Implications*: The chapter concludes with a discussion on future research directions and implications of IoT-based edge and fog computing in smart grids. It identifies potential areas for further exploration, discusses challenges to be addressed, and explores the broader implications and impact of these technologies on power distribution networks.

Smart Grids: An Overview

Definition and Key Components

The provided diagram, depicted as Figure 1, presents a comprehensive representation of the structural framework of a smart grid. The term "smart grid" pertains to a sophisticated and updated infrastructure for electrical grids that utilizes digital communication, automation, and advanced technologies to facilitate the efficient, dependable, and sustainable distribution of energy (Farhangi, 2010). The integration of a bidirectional exchange of electricity and information between utility providers and consumers represents a notable advancement beyond conventional power grids. Key features and components of smart grids include the use of Advanced Metering Infrastructure (AMI) (Arghandeh et al., 2017). Smart grids employ smart meters to monitor and record energy consumption at a granular level. These meters enable real-time data collection, accurate billing, and support for demand response programs. Grid automation is another important aspect of smart grids (Li et al., 2011). Smart grids utilize automation technologies to enhance grid operations and control. This includes automated fault detection, isolation, and restoration (FDIR), remote monitoring and control, and self-healing capabilities. Smart grids also facilitate the integration of renewable energy sources into the grid (Momoh et al., 2013). This allows for the efficient utilization of distributed energy resources, such as solar panels and wind turbines, and better management of variable generation. Demand response and load management programs are enabled by smart grids (Boud et al., 2015). These programs involve adjusting energy consumption based on grid conditions or price signals, helping balance electricity demand and supply, manage peak loads, and improve grid stability. Through real-time monitoring and analytics, smart grids optimize power distribution (Poudineh et al., 2016). By analyzing consumption patterns, identifying areas of congestion or inefficiency, and implementing strategies for load balancing and voltage regulation, smart grids enhance distribution system optimization. The importance of strengthening grid security is emphasized as a critical component of smart grid systems (Zhang et al., 2011). Smart grids are equipped with sophisticated cybersecurity protocols to safeguard against cyber threats and uphold the integrity and confidentiality of grid data and communication. Finally, smart grids enable users to receive real-time energy data, as stated by Chen et al., (2014). This empowers consumers to make well-informed decisions regarding their energy usage, effectively decrease their consumption, and actively engage in energy efficiency initiatives.

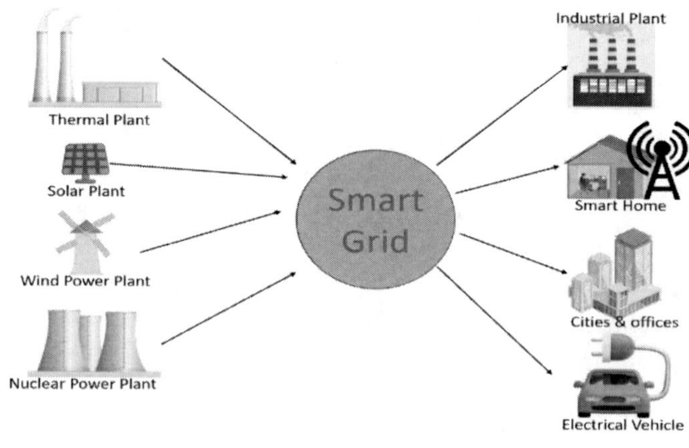

Figure 1. Overview of Smart Grid.

Challenges in Existing Architectures

a. *Aging Infrastructure:* Many existing power grids have outdated infrastructure that was not designed to accommodate the evolving needs of a smart grid. Upgrading or replacing the existing infrastructure to support advanced communication, automation, and monitoring systems can be a costly and time-consuming process.
b. *Lack of Standardization:* There is a lack of standardization in smart grid technologies, protocols, and communication interfaces. This makes it challenging to integrate diverse components and systems from different vendors, leading to compatibility issues and interoperability challenges.

c. *Cybersecurity Risks:* Smart grids are vulnerable to cybersecurity threats and attacks. As the grid becomes increasingly interconnected and reliant on digital communication, it becomes a potential target for hackers and cybercriminals. Ensuring robust cybersecurity measures and protocols is crucial to safeguard the integrity, privacy, and reliability of the grid.
d. *Privacy Concerns:* Smart grids are capable of gathering extensive quantities of data pertaining to patterns of energy usage, user behavioral patterns, and the overall performance of the grid. Privacy concerns are raised in relation to the collecting, storage, and utilization of this data. The implementation of comprehensive data privacy protections and the maintenance of transparency with consumers are crucial.
e. *Scalability and Flexibility:* Traditional grid architectures may lack the scalability and flexibility required to accommodate the increasing integration of renewable energy sources, distributed generation, and electric vehicles. Upgrading the infrastructure to handle variable and decentralized power generation poses challenges in terms of grid stability, load balancing, and voltage regulation.
f. *Communication Infrastructure:* Smart grids heavily rely on a robust communication infrastructure to facilitate real-time data exchange and control. The availability, reliability, and coverage of communication networks in certain areas may pose challenges in implementing and operating smart grid systems effectively.
g. *Data Management and Analytics:* Smart grids generate massive amounts of data from various sensors, meters, and devices. Managing and analyzing this data in real-time to derive actionable insights can be challenging. Advanced data management techniques and analytics tools are required to process and interpret the data effectively.
h. *Regulatory and Policy Framework:* The regulatory and policy frameworks governing the energy sector may not be aligned with the requirements and capabilities of smart grid technologies. Updating regulations, standards, and policies to support the deployment and operation of smart grid infrastructure can be complex and time-consuming.
i. *Cost and Return on Investment:* Implementing smart grid technologies involves significant upfront costs, including infrastructure upgrades, deployment of advanced sensors and devices, and implementation of communication networks. Ensuring a

favorable return on investment and cost-effectiveness of smart grid deployments is crucial for widespread adoption.

Need for Innovation and Transformation

The need for innovation and transformation of smart grids arises from several key factors. Firstly, the increasing global energy demand requires more efficient and optimized energy generation, distribution, and consumption. The integration of renewable energy sources is another critical driver, as smart grids enable the efficient integration and management of renewables, reducing reliance on fossil fuels and addressing climate change. Additionally, the resilience and reliability of power grids need to be enhanced due to ageing infrastructure and the growing threat of extreme weather events and cyberattacks. Energy efficiency and demand-side management play a crucial role in addressing energy challenges, and smart grids provide real-time data and tools for consumers to make informed decisions and participate in demand response programs. The shift towards decentralized and distributed energy generation, along with the integration of electric vehicles, requires the flexibility and adaptability that smart grids offer. The advanced monitoring, analytics, and customer engagement capabilities of smart grids empower consumers and utilities to optimize grid operations and asset utilization. Finally, supportive policies and regulations are essential to incentivize innovation, promote grid modernization, and create an enabling environment for smart grid transformation.

IoT, Edge Computing, and Fog Computing

IoT Fundamentals and Applications in Smart Grids

The Internet of Things (IoT) has significantly impacted the smart grid sector by enabling advanced and interconnected systems for efficient, reliable, and sustainable energy distribution. Smart grids leverage IoT technology, incorporating devices, sensors, and systems that facilitate seamless data collection and exchange (Atzori et al., 2010). This chapter explores the fundamentals of IoT, including its architecture and communication technologies, and delves into its applications in smart grids. Key applications include advanced metering infrastructure (AMI) for real-time data collection and demand response programs (Ke et al., 2018), grid monitoring and control, integration of renewable energy sources, demand response and load management (Zhou et al., 2016), and predictive maintenance and fault detection. However, the implementation of IoT in smart grids also presents challenges such as data privacy and security (Abomhara et al., 2014), interoperability, scalability, and communication infrastructure. Addressing these challenges is crucial to fully realize the potential of IoT in transforming smart grids. Overall, the integration of IoT in smart grids offers numerous benefits, including enhanced grid monitoring and control, efficient utilization of renewable energy, demand response capabilities, and improved operational efficiency. The chapter provides valuable insights into the application of IoT in smart grids and emphasizes the need to overcome challenges to harness its transformative potential.

Edge Computing: Bringing Computation to the Edge

Edge computing is an emerging paradigm that aims to relocate computational tasks and data storage in close proximity to the network's periphery, thereby reducing latency and enhancing efficiency by minimizing the distance between the data source and processing resources. The aforementioned study by Satyanarayanan (2017) highlights how this approach effectively mitigates the constraints associated with conventional cloud computing frameworks. It achieves this by facilitating instantaneous data processing, minimizing latency, and enhancing scalability. By distributing computational tasks to edge devices and servers, edge computing creates a decentralized computing infrastructure that complements cloud computing. This paradigm shift offers new opportunities for applications that require low latency, high bandwidth, and localized decision-making, such as autonomous vehicles, industrial automation, smart cities, and healthcare systems (Shi et al., 2016).

The key components of edge computing include edge devices, which encompass sensors, actuators, and gateways, responsible for collecting and preprocessing data locally. These edge devices are connected to edge servers, deployed in close proximity, that provide additional computational power and storage capacity. Edge analytics plays a crucial role in processing and analyzing data at the edge, enabling real-time insights and autonomous decision-making (Mao et al., 2017). The convergence of the Internet of Things (IoT), edge computing, and advanced analytics has paved the way for efficient resource management, predictive maintenance, and improved operational efficiency.

While edge computing offers numerous benefits, it also presents challenges. These challenges include managing the heterogeneous and distributed nature of edge devices, ensuring data privacy and security at the edge, and addressing the resource constraints of edge devices. Additionally, interoperability and standardization are vital for seamless integration of edge computing solutions across different domains. Despite these challenges, the potential of edge computing to revolutionize data processing and analysis at the edge of the network is driving significant research and development efforts.

Fog Computing: Extending Computation to Intermediate Nodes

Fog computing is an emerging paradigm that augments the functionalities of edge computing by the integration of intermediary nodes, known as fog nodes, positioned between edge devices and the cloud. The major goal of fog computing is to address the limitations encountered by edge computing in domains such as compute capabilities, storage capacity, and network connectivity. The introduction of fog nodes in this paradigm aims to establish a computing environment that is more resilient and effective, effectively bridging the divide between edge devices and cloud-based resources. Fog nodes are strategically positioned inside the network infrastructure, in close proximity to edge devices, with the purpose of offering supplementary processing capabilities and storage space. According to (Bonomi et al., 2012), the utilization of these nodes facilitates advanced data processing, analytics, and collaboration among many edge devices, resulting in improved efficiency and reliability in the operations of smart grids.

Fog computing plays a vital role in enabling scalable and fault-tolerant processing in smart grids. By distributing computational tasks across fog nodes, it alleviates the burden on edge devices and reduces the reliance on centralized cloud servers. Fog nodes can perform more complex analytics, such as real-time data aggregation, pattern recognition, and anomaly detection, enabling faster and more accurate decision-making in smart grid applications (Yi et al., 2015). The collaboration among fog nodes also allows for distributed computing, where computational tasks can be offloaded and shared among multiple nodes, further enhancing the efficiency of data processing and analysis in smart grid systems (Yannuzzi et al., 2018).

The integration of fog computing in smart grids offers several advantages. It enables real-time monitoring of power consumption, equipment status, and grid performance, facilitating proactive maintenance and optimizing power distribution. Fog computing also supports load balancing and demand response, allowing for optimized energy distribution and better management of peak loads. Additionally, it enhances privacy and security by minimizing the need to transmit sensitive data to centralized locations, reducing the risk of data breaches (Shi et al., 2019).

Benefits and Advantages of IoT-Based Edge and Fog Computing

Incorporating IoT-based edge and fog computing into smart grids brings forth a host of benefits and improvements that elevate the effectiveness, dependability, and security of power distribution systems. A pivotal advantage lies in the real-time monitoring and management of power usage, equipment status, and overall grid performance. By deploying IoT devices at the network's edge, operators can access instantaneous data on energy consumption, power quality, and equipment functionality, granting them a detailed and precise perspective of the distribution network. (Hosseini et al., 2018). This real-time monitoring enables proactive maintenance, where advanced analytics techniques can detect equipment failures or anomalies, allowing for timely repairs and minimizing downtime.

Another advantage is the support for predictive maintenance. By leveraging advanced analytics and machine learning algorithms, IoT-based edge and fog computing can analyze historical data, detect patterns, and predict equipment failures. This enables utilities to schedule maintenance proactively, avoiding costly breakdowns and optimizing the lifespan of assets (Biswas et al., 2019). Additionally, the integration of edge and fog computing allows for localized decision-making, reducing the dependence on centralized control systems. By processing data and making decisions at the network edge, latency is reduced, and real-time actions can be taken to address grid events or fluctuations in energy demand (Yi et al., 2015).

Conceptual Framework for IoT-Based Edge and Fog Computing in Smart Grids

Design Principles and Architecture

The design principles and architecture of IoT-based edge and fog computing in smart grids play a crucial role in optimizing the performance and efficiency of power distribution systems. One of the key design principles is the decentralized and distributed nature of edge and fog computing. Instead of relying on a centralized architecture, edge and fog computing leverage a network of interconnected edge devices and fog nodes to perform data processing and analysis at the network edge (Yi et al., 2015). This decentralized approach reduces latency, improves responsiveness, and enables localized decision-making, making it ideal for time-sensitive applications in smart grids.

Another important design principle is scalability and flexibility. Smart grid systems are continuously evolving, and the architecture of edge and fog computing should be able to adapt to changing requirements and accommodate the growing number of connected devices and data streams. Scalability is achieved by leveraging the distributed nature of fog computing, where additional fog nodes can be deployed as needed to handle increased computational loads and storage demands (Bonomi et al., 2012). Furthermore, the architecture should be flexible enough to support various applications and use cases in smart grids, such as real-time monitoring, predictive maintenance, demand response, and load balancing.

When considering the field of architecture, the implementation of Internet of Things (IoT)-based edge and fog computing within smart grids generally encompasses three primary layers: the edge layer, the fog layer, and the cloud layer. The edge layer encompasses a variety of components, including sensors, smart meters, and other edge devices, which are responsible for gathering data pertaining to energy consumption, power quality, and the operational state of equipment. The fog layer consists of intermediate fog nodes that engage in data processing, analytics, and collaboration among several edge devices. According to (Yi et al., 2015), the fog nodes possess computing powers and storage capacity that enable them to effectively manage and process more intricate activities. The cloud layer, which serves as a centralized cloud infrastructure, offers supplementary storage and processing resources for the purpose of long-term data analysis, machine learning, and decision-making.

Edge Device Deployment and Infrastructure

The deployment of edge devices and the establishment of robust infrastructure are critical aspects of implementing smart grids. Edge devices, such as smart meters, sensors, and actuators, play a pivotal role in collecting real-time data on energy consumption, power quality, and equipment performance at the edge of the network. These devices are typically deployed at various points in the power distribution system, including homes, businesses, substations, and distribution transformers (Li et al., 2017). The widespread deployment of edge devices enables granular monitoring and control of power distribution, facilitating efficient energy management and grid optimization.

To support the deployment of edge devices, a robust infrastructure is necessary. This infrastructure includes communication networks, data storage systems, and computational resources. Communication networks enable seamless data transmission between edge devices, fog nodes, and cloud infrastructure, ensuring timely exchange of information for real-time monitoring and control (Khan et al., 2019). Data storage systems store the vast amount of data generated by edge devices, allowing for historical analysis, predictive maintenance, and long-term planning. Computational resources, both at the edge and in the fog layer, are essential for data processing, analytics, and localized decision-making. These resources enable real-time processing of data, reducing latency and enabling quick responses to grid events and fluctuations in energy demand (Zhang et al., 2019).

The deployment of edge devices and the establishment of infrastructure in smart grids require careful planning and coordination. Factors such as device connectivity, power supply, network coverage, and cybersecurity measures need to be considered. Connectivity options, including wired and wireless technologies, should be evaluated based on their reliability, bandwidth, and scalability. Power supply solutions, such as batteries, solar panels, or grid connections, should be designed to ensure continuous operation of edge devices. Network coverage should be evaluated to ensure seamless communication between devices, and adequate cybersecurity measures must be in place to protect against unauthorized access and data breaches (Khan et al., 2019).

Fog Node Placement and Communication

Fog node placement and communication strategies are crucial aspects of designing efficient and reliable smart grid systems. Fog nodes, which serve as intermediate computing and storage resources in fog computing architectures, need to be strategically placed to optimize their performance and coverage. The placement of fog nodes should consider factors such as network topology, proximity to edge devices, computational capacity, and energy efficiency. Placing fog nodes close to edge devices reduces data transmission latency and enhances real-time monitoring and control capabilities (Simmhan et al., 2018). Moreover, the distribution of fog nodes across the smart grid network should ensure adequate coverage and computational resources to handle the data processing requirements of various applications, such as load balancing, demand response, and fault detection.

Effective communication between fog nodes is essential for coordinated decision-making and collaborative data processing in smart grids. Communication protocols and networking technologies need to be selected to facilitate seamless and reliable data exchange between fog nodes. These protocols should support low latency, high bandwidth, and efficient utilization of network resources. Additionally, fault-tolerant communication mechanisms should be implemented to ensure the continuous operation of fog nodes even in the presence of network failures or disruptions. Technologies such as wireless communication, including Wi-Fi, cellular networks, or dedicated communication networks like power line communication (PLC), can be utilized to establish connectivity between fog nodes and enable efficient data sharing and synchronization (Chen et al., 2020).

Strategic placement of fog nodes and robust communication infrastructure contribute to the overall performance and reliability of smart grid systems. Well-planned fog node placement ensures optimal resource utilization, reduces communication overhead, and improves response times for critical grid operations. Additionally, efficient communication between fog nodes enables collaborative processing, allowing for distributed analytics, load balancing, and real-time decision-making. These factors collectively enhance the scalability, fault tolerance, and responsiveness of smart grids, enabling efficient power distribution, load management, and grid optimization.

Interactions with Central Smart Grid Infrastructure

The interactions among edge devices, fog nodes, and the core smart grid infrastructure are of paramount importance in facilitating effective and uninterrupted communication and control inside the system. Edge devices, including smart meters, sensors, and actuators, function as both the data origins and termination points within the smart grid network. Real-time data pertaining to energy usage, power quality, and grid conditions is collected and subsequently transmitted to the fog nodes for the purpose of processing and analysis. The edge devices act as the frontline data collectors and provide essential information for monitoring and controlling the power distribution network (Ou et al., 2019). They also receive commands and instructions from the central infrastructure or fog nodes to perform specific actions, such as load shedding or demand response.

Fog nodes, on the other hand, serve as intermediate computing and storage resources that bridge the gap between edge devices and the central smart grid infrastructure. They receive data from multiple edge devices, perform local processing and analysis, and provide aggregated information to the central infrastructure for higher-level decision-making. Fog nodes also play a critical role in enabling localized decision-making by executing certain control functions at the network edge. This reduces the latency in data transmission and allows for timely responses to critical events or grid conditions (Zhang et al., 2020). The interactions between fog nodes and edge devices involve data exchange, command delivery, and synchronization mechanisms to ensure the seamless flow of information within the smart grid system.

The central smart grid infrastructure serves as the control and coordination center of the entire system. It receives data from fog nodes, performs advanced analytics, and generates actionable insights for grid management. The central infrastructure also sends control commands and instructions to fog nodes and edge devices for load balancing, demand response, or other grid optimization tasks. This two-way communication between the central infrastructure, fog nodes, and edge devices enables real-time monitoring, control, and coordination of the smart grid operations (Hassan et al., 2017). It facilitates the integration of various applications, such as fault detection and isolation, renewable energy integration, and demand-side management, to ensure efficient and reliable power distribution.

Real-Time Monitoring and Predictive Maintenance

Edge Computing for Real-Time Monitoring

Edge computing plays a crucial role in facilitating real-time monitoring within smart grid systems. The proliferation of sensors and intelligent devices inside the grid infrastructure necessitates the implementation of effective data processing and analysis at the edge. This is crucial in facilitating prompt decision-making and response. Edge computing is a paradigm that involves the localization of computational capabilities in close proximity to the data sources, hence enabling accelerated processing and diminished latency. In the realm of real-time monitoring within smart grids, the utilization of edge computing facilitates the acquisition, examination, and comprehension of data produced by a multitude of devices including smart meters, sensors, and actuators.

By leveraging edge computing, real-time monitoring in smart grids becomes more efficient and effective. The edge devices, equipped with computational power and analytics capabilities, can process the incoming data locally and extract valuable insights without relying on centralized systems. This not only reduces the burden on the central infrastructure but also enables faster response times for critical events and abnormalities in the grid. For example, real-time monitoring at the edge can detect power fluctuations, abnormal energy consumption patterns, or equipment failures, allowing for immediate action to mitigate potential risks and ensure grid stability.

Furthermore, edge computing for real-time monitoring enhances the reliability and resiliency of smart grids as shown in Figure 2. By distributing the monitoring and analytics tasks to the edge devices, the system becomes less dependent on a single point of failure. Even in the event of network disruptions or communication failures, the edge devices can continue to monitor and analyze data, ensuring continuous monitoring capabilities. This decentralized approach improves the overall reliability and fault tolerance of the monitoring system, making it more robust in the face of unforeseen circumstances.

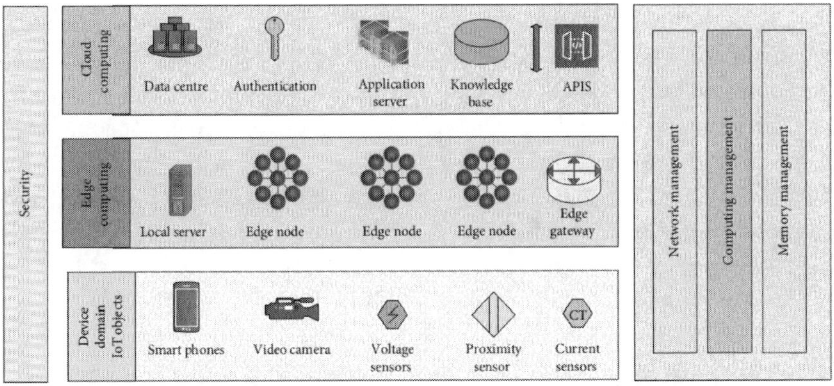

Figure 2. Structural framework for IoT based Edge Computing for Smart Grid (Mehmood et al., 2021).

Fog Computing for Predictive Maintenance

Fog computing plays a crucial role in enabling predictive maintenance in smart grid systems. With the increasing complexity and scale of the grid infrastructure, there is a growing need to proactively identify and address potential equipment failures or anomalies. Fog computing, which extends the capabilities of edge computing, provides an ideal platform for performing advanced analytics and predictive maintenance tasks in the smart grid context.

By leveraging fog computing, smart grids can collect and analyze a vast amount of data from various sources, including sensors, meters, and equipment monitoring systems. This data can be processed and analyzed in real-time at the fog nodes, which are strategically placed in the network to provide computational resources and storage capacity. Advanced analytics techniques, such as machine learning and artificial intelligence algorithms, can be applied to the collected data to detect patterns, anomalies, or early signs of equipment failures. This enables predictive maintenance, where potential issues can be identified and addressed proactively before they cause significant disruptions or failures in the grid.

The use of fog computing for predictive maintenance in smart grids brings several benefits. First, it improves the reliability and uptime of the grid by minimizing unplanned outages and reducing equipment downtime. By detecting and resolving potential issues before they escalate, the grid can maintain optimal performance and avoid costly disruptions. Second, it enhances the operational efficiency of the grid by optimizing maintenance schedules and resource allocation. By prioritizing maintenance tasks based on predictive insights, resources can be allocated more effectively, leading to cost savings and improved resource utilization. Additionally, fog computing enables intelligent decision-making by providing actionable insights derived from real-time data, facilitating more informed and timely maintenance decisions.

Machine Learning Techniques for Anomaly Detection

Machine learning techniques have emerged as powerful tools for anomaly detection in various domains, including smart grid systems. Anomaly detection plays a critical role in identifying abnormal behavior or patterns that deviate from the expected norm, allowing for timely intervention and mitigation of potential risks. In the context of smart grids, where large volumes of data are generated from diverse sources, machine learning techniques offer the capability to detect anomalies in real-time and enable proactive measures to ensure grid stability and reliability.

One commonly used machine learning technique for anomaly detection is the Support Vector Machines (SVM) algorithm. SVM is a supervised learning method that can effectively classify data into different classes, including normal and abnormal instances. It works by finding an optimal hyperplane that separates the data points in a high-dimensional space. SVM has been successfully applied in anomaly detection tasks in smart grids, such as detecting abnormal power consumption patterns or identifying equipment failures. For instance, in a study by Li et al., (2016), SVM was utilized to detect power theft in smart grids by analyzing electricity consumption data.

Another popular machine learning approach for anomaly detection is the Random Forest algorithm. Random Forest is an ensemble learning method that combines multiple decision trees to make predictions. It can be employed for anomaly detection by training the model on a dataset with known normal behavior and then identifying instances that significantly deviate from the learned patterns. Random Forest has been applied in various smart grid anomaly detection scenarios, such as identifying cyber-attacks on the grid infrastructure or detecting abnormal power quality events. For example, a study by Thakur et al., (2020) used Random Forest to detect power quality anomalies by analyzing voltage and current waveforms in smart grid systems.

Load Balancing and Demand Response

Edge-Assisted Load Balancing Strategies

Edge-assisted load balancing strategies have gained significant attention in the context of modern smart grids, where the distribution of power consumption is becoming increasingly dynamic and unpredictable. Load balancing aims to distribute the workload across the grid infrastructure efficiently, ensuring optimal utilization of resources and preventing overload conditions. By leveraging edge computing capabilities, load balancing strategies can be enhanced to achieve better performance and responsiveness in managing the power distribution network.

One approach to edge-assisted load balancing is through the utilization of edge servers or gateways strategically placed within the grid infrastructure. These edge devices can collect and process real-time data on power consumption, grid conditions, and network traffic at the edge of the network. By analyzing this data locally, edge servers can make informed decisions about load balancing, such as redirecting power to less congested areas or dynamically adjusting voltage levels to optimize energy distribution. This distributed decision-making reduces the reliance on centralized control and improves the overall efficiency and responsiveness of load balancing operations.

Furthermore, edge-assisted load balancing strategies can also leverage machine learning algorithms to predict power consumption patterns and anticipate future load demands. By training models on historical data and considering real-time inputs, these algorithms can forecast power consumption trends and identify potential imbalances in the grid. This proactive approach allows for preemptive load balancing actions, such as redistributing power or initiating demand response programs to manage peak loads. A study by Samet et al., (2019) explored the application of machine learning techniques for load forecasting in smart grids, demonstrating the effectiveness of these methods in improving load balancing efficiency.

Fog Computing for Demand Response

Fog computing has emerged as a promising technology in the context of demand response (DR) programs within smart grids. Demand response aims to manage electricity consumption by adjusting it based on grid conditions, pricing signals, and user preferences. Fog computing provides a distributed computing infrastructure by introducing intermediate fog nodes that can process and analyze data closer to the end-users and devices. This proximity enables faster response times and localized decision-making, making it well-suited for real-time DR applications.

One of the primary benefits of fog computing in the context of demand response lies in its capacity to effectively manage the substantial amount of data produced by smart meters and Internet of Things (IoT) devices. These gadgets offer instantaneous data on energy usage, grid conditions, and user preferences. By utilizing fog computing, the aforementioned data may be efficiently processed and analyzed in close to real-time at the periphery of the network, hence facilitating prompt decision-making and response to grid-related occurrences. The utilization of fog computing for demand response in a smart grid setting was examined in a study conducted by (Wang et al., 2018). The study emphasized the efficacy of fog computing in diminishing response durations and improving the overall efficiency of demand response initiatives.

Fog computing also enables improved coordination and collaboration among various entities involved in demand response, including users, utility providers, and grid operators. Fog nodes can act as intermediaries, aggregating and integrating data from multiple sources to enable efficient communication and decision-making. This facilitates the implementation of advanced DR strategies such as dynamic pricing, load shifting, and demand forecasting. Additionally, fog computing enhances the privacy and security of demand response operations by minimizing the need to transmit sensitive data to centralized servers, as most processing and analysis occur locally at the edge. A study by Liu et al., (2020) explored the application of fog computing in demand response and emphasized its potential in enabling secure and privacy-preserving DR programs.

Advanced Analytics and Decision-Making at the Edge

The progressions in edge computing have facilitated the development of sophisticated analytics and decision-making abilities at the periphery of the network, thereby bringing intelligence in closer proximity to the data source within the framework of smart grids. Real-time analytics can be conducted on streaming data provided by IoT devices, sensors, and smart meters by utilizing robust computational resources and machine learning algorithms deployed on edge devices. This capability facilitates prompt analysis and well-informed decision-making in order to optimize the functioning of the grid, promote energy efficiency, and improve the overall performance of the smart grid system.

Edge analytics in smart grids offer several benefits, including reduced latency, improved responsiveness, and efficient resource utilization. By analyzing data at the edge, critical decisions can be made locally, minimizing the need for data transmission to centralized servers and reducing network congestion. Furthermore, edge analytics enable real-time monitoring and anomaly detection, allowing for the early identification of equipment failures, grid disturbances, or abnormal energy consumption patterns. This proactive approach enhances the reliability and resilience of the grid and enables predictive maintenance strategies. A study by Li et al., (2019) explored the application of edge analytics for real-time anomaly detection in smart grid systems, demonstrating its effectiveness in detecting abnormal behaviors and improving the system's overall performance.

The integration of machine learning algorithms at the edge devices also enables intelligent decision-making based on local data. By training models at the edge using historical data and deploying them for real-time analysis, edge devices can make autonomous decisions, such as load balancing, fault detection, and optimal energy distribution. This decentralized decision-making reduces reliance on centralized control systems and improves the scalability and flexibility of the smart grid. Research by Pan et al., (2020) investigated the use of machine learning algorithms at the edge for load forecasting and balancing, highlighting its potential in optimizing energy distribution and mitigating peak demand.

Conclusion

IoT-based edge and fog computing present significant opportunities for revolutionizing power distribution in smart grids. These technologies, coupled with the Internet of Things, enable real-time monitoring, localized decision-making, and distributed processing, offering a more efficient, scalable, and intelligent power distribution infrastructure. By bringing computational capabilities closer to the edge devices and introducing intermediate fog nodes, smart grids can overcome the limitations of traditional centralized architectures and address the evolving needs of modern power grids.

The integration of IoT devices, edge computing, and fog computing brings several advantages to smart grids. It allows for real-time monitoring of energy consumption, equipment performance, and grid conditions, enabling proactive maintenance, optimized energy distribution, and improved grid stability. It supports load balancing and demand response programs, enabling efficient management of peak loads and better utilization of renewable energy sources. Moreover, the deployment of edge devices and fog nodes enhances privacy and security by minimizing the transmission of sensitive data to centralized locations.

However, the adoption of IoT-based edge and fog computing in smart grids also presents challenges. It requires careful consideration of infrastructure requirements, connectivity, and power supply for edge device deployment and fog node placement. The design of efficient communication protocols and data transmission strategies is crucial to ensure reliable and timely data exchange. Furthermore, advanced analytics algorithms and decision-making models tailored for edge and fog computing need to be developed to extract valuable insights from the vast amount of data generated in smart grids.

Future Scope

In the future, the application of IoT-based edge and fog computing in smart grids is expected to witness further advancements and opportunities for revolutionizing power distribution. Here are some potential future scopes:

The incorporation of Artificial Intelligence (AI) methodologies, including machine learning and deep learning, within the framework of Internet of Things (IoT)-based edge and fog computing has the potential to augment the cognitive powers and decision-making capacities of intelligent grids. Artificial intelligence (AI) algorithms possess the capability to analyze and acquire knowledge from the large volume of data produced by Internet of Things (IoT) devices. This ability facilitates the implementation of predictive maintenance, anomaly detection, and optimum energy management strategies. The integration of several components might potentially enhance the operational efficiency, dependability, and environmental sustainability of power distribution systems.

Edge Intelligence and Autonomy: The advancement of edge computing capabilities can enable edge devices to become more intelligent and autonomous. Edge devices can not only collect and process data but also make localized decisions and take actions in real-time. This empowers edge devices to actively participate in load balancing, demand response, fault detection and isolation, reducing the dependency on centralized control and improving the overall efficiency of the grid.

Cybersecurity and Privacy Enhancements: As the deployment of IoT devices and the exchange of sensitive data increase in smart grids, ensuring cybersecurity and privacy becomes crucial. Future research can focus on developing robust security mechanisms, encryption techniques, and privacy-preserving algorithms specifically tailored for IoT-based edge and fog computing in smart grids. This will enable secure communication, data integrity, and confidentiality, mitigating potential cyber threats and protecting the critical infrastructure.

Standardization and Interoperability: To fully harness the benefits of IoT-based edge and fog computing in smart grids, standardized protocols, and interoperable systems are essential. Future efforts can concentrate on developing industry-wide standards and frameworks that facilitate seamless integration and communication between different edge devices, fog nodes, and central smart grid infrastructure. This will promote interoperability, scalability, and easy deployment of IoT-based solutions in diverse smart grid environments.

Disclaimer

None.

References

Abomhara M, Koien GM, Skomedal A. Securing the Internet of Things: A systematic review. *Journal of Computer and System Sciences* (2014) 80(5): 967-983.

Ahmed MU, Pohjolainen S, Tenhunen H. A survey on edge computing and fog computing for the Internet of Things. *Journal of Ambient Intelligence and Humanized Computing* (2019) 10(9): 4005-4039.

Arghandeh R, Scaglione A, Thomas RJ. Smart grid data analytics for advanced metering infrastructure and beyond. *Proceedings of the IEEE* (2017) 105(7): 1331-1352.

Atzori L, Iera A, Morabito G. The Internet of Things: A survey. *Computer Networks* (2010) 54(15): 2787-2805.

Bonomi F, Milito R, Natarajan P, Zhu J. Fog computing: A platform for internet of things and analytics. *Springer Big data and internet of things: A roadmap for smart environments* (2012): 169-186.

Bonomi F, Milito R, Zhu J, Addepalli S. Fog computing and its role in the Internet of Things. *ACM Proceedings of the First Edition of the MCC Workshop on Mobile Cloud Computing* (2012):13-16.

Boud R, Gungor VC, Sen S. Demand response in smart grid: Key players, technologies, and strategies. *IEEE Transactions on Industrial Informatics* (2015) 11(3): 570-582.

Biswas S, Misra S, Chattopadhyay S. Smart grid: A survey on data analytics and machine learning approaches. *ACM Computing Surveys (CSUR)* (2019) 52(1): 11:39.

Chen M, Mao S, Liu Y. Big data: *A survey. Mobile Networks and Applications* (2014) 19(2): 171-209.

Chiang M, Zhang T, Hsieh H. Fog and IoT: An overview of research opportunities. *IEEE Internet of Things Journal* (2016) 3(6): 854-864.

Chen W, Guo S, Zhang Y, Zhang Y. A Survey of Communication Technologies for Internet of Things: Applications, Challenges, and Opportunities for Smart Grids. *IEEE Communications Surveys & Tutorials* (2020) 22(1): 522-550.

Farhangi H. The path of the smart grid. *IEEE Power and Energy Magazine* (2010) 8(1): 18-28.

Gungor VC, Sahin D, Kocak T, Ergut, S, Buccella C, Cecati C, Hancke GP. Smart grid technologies: Communication technologies and standards. *IEEE Transactions on Industrial Informatics* (2011) 7(4): 529-539.

Hosseini SM, Yazdi S, Ishizu K. IoT-based edge computing architecture for smart grids: A review of emerging concepts and research challenges. *Energies* (2018) 11(10): 2732.

Hassan R, Rehman MH, Hossain MS, Abdelgawad A. Fog Computing in Smart Grids: A Review, Taxonomy, and Future Research Directions. *IEEE Access* (2017) 5: 9206-9230.

Jin L, Liu L, Wang H, Chen X, Zhang H. A survey on the architecture, applications, and security of fog computing. *IEEE Access* (2020) 8: 85026-85042.

Ke S, Tsai CW, Liao WC, Chiang MF. An IoT architecture with energy harvesting for renewable energy monitoring and smart grid. *IEEE Internet of Things Journal* (2018) 5(2), 744-753.

Khan NH, Lee GM, Son J, Kim K. A review of IoT-based edge computing for smart grids: Fundamentals, applications, and research challenges. *Energies* (2019) 12(9): 1645

Li Y, Chen Y, Zhang L, Zhou Y. Internet of things in smart grid: Architecture, applications, challenges, and security. *IEEE Internet of Things Journal* (2019) 6(1): 148-157.

Li J, Qian Y, Sharif H, Tipper D. A survey on smart grid communication infrastructures: Motivations, requirements and challenges. *IEEE Communications Surveys & Tutorials* (2011) 14(4): 944-980.

Li P, Hong Y, Zhang Y, Xu Z, Huang G. IoT Based Smart Grid Communication Infrastructure: A Comprehensive Survey. *IEEE Communications Surveys & Tutorials* (2017) 19(1): 475-494.

Li Y, Xu W, Hu X. Power Theft Detection in Smart Grids: A Support Vector Machines Approach. *IEEE Transactions on Industrial Informatics* (2016) 12(2): 656-665.

Li X, Yang Z, Zhao Y, Wu J. Edge Analytics for Real-Time Anomaly Detection in Smart Grid Systems. *IEEE Transactions on Industrial Informatics* (2019) 15(6): 3317-3326.

Liu Y, Xiong N, Wu J, Sun Y, Yin J. Fog Computing for Demand Response in Smart Grids: A Review, Taxonomy, and Future Directions. *IEEE Transactions on Industrial Informatics* (2020) 17(1): 423-432.

Liu X, Wang N, Yang Y. A survey on communication technologies of smart grid: Applications, architectures, requirements and standardizations. *Future Generation Computer Systems* (2019) 96: 668-679.

Mehmood MY, Oad A, Abrar M, Munir HM, Hasan SF, Muqeet HAU, Golilarz NA. Edge computing for IoT-enabled smart grid. *Security and Communication Networks* (2021) 2021: 1-16.

Mao Y, You C, Zhang J, Huang K, Letaief KB. A survey on mobile edge computing: The communication perspective. *IEEE Communications Surveys & Tutorials* (2017) 19(4): 2322-2358.

Momoh JA, Fadugba SE. Smart grid and its relevance to developing economies. *Electric Power Systems Research* (2013) 96: 17-22.

Ou C, Han Z, Wu J, Zhang L. Fog Computing in Smart Grid Communications: Challenges and Solutions. *IEEE Network* (2019) 33(2): 78-84.

Pan J, Wang H, Zhang X, Huang Y, Li X, Lin X. Load Forecasting and Balancing in the Edge Computing-Aided Smart Grid. *IEEE Transactions on Industrial Informatics* (2020) 16(2): 992-1001.

Poudineh R, Jamasb T. Distributed generation, storage, demand response and energy efficiency as alternatives to grid capacity enhancement. *Applied Energy* (2016) 179: 1321-1335.

Satyanarayanan, Mahadev. The emergence of edge computing. *Computer* (2017) 50(1): 30-39.

Satyanarayanan M, Bahl P, Caceres R, Davies N. The case for VM-based cloudlets in mobile computing. *IEEE Pervasive Computing* (2017) 8(4): 14-23.

Sadeghi Yazdankhah A, Kazempour S J, Moghaddam M P. Distributed energy resources management for microgrids: A new approach. *IEEE Transactions on Smart Grid* (2015) 6(3): 1262-1275.

Samet R, Zekri L, Djeddi C. Machine Learning Based Techniques for Short Term Load Forecasting in Smart Grids. *Energies* (2019) 12(7): 1303.

Shi W, Cao J, Zhang Q, Li Y, Xu L. Edge computing: Vision and challenges. *IEEE Internet of Things Journal* (2016) 3(5): 637-646.

Shi W, Cao J, Zhang Q, Li Y, Xu L. Edge computing: Opportunities and challenges. *Information Sciences* (2019) 485: 1-17.

Simmhan Y, Wang C, Krishnamurthy A, Prasanna V. Fog Computing and its Role in the Internet of Things. *Springer Handbook of Big Data Technologies* (2018): 409-430.

Smith C. The evolution of power distribution: What's next for the grid? *GE Power* (2018). Retrieved from https://www.ge.com/power/transform/article.transform/articles/2018/the-evolution-of-power-istribution-whats-next-for-the-grid

Thakur A, Chaudhuri S, Ghosh S. Anomaly detection and classification in power quality using Random Forests. *IET Generation, Transmission & Distribution* (2020) 14(10): 2044-2052.

Wang H, Zhang C, Guo X. Fog Computing Based Demand Response Strategy for Smart Grids. *IEEE International Conference on Smart Internet of Things (Smart IoT)* (2018): 127-132.

Yi S, Li C, Li Q, Qian Y. A survey of fog computing: Concepts, applications and issues. *ACM Proceedings of the 2015 workshop on mobile big data* (2015): 37-42.

Yannuzzi M, Domingo Pascual J, Lefevre L. A survey of fog computing: Concepts, applications, and issues. *ACM Computing Surveys* (CSUR) (2018) 51(5): 1-39.

Zhang C, Zhao H, Chen Y. A survey of communication/networking in smart grids. *Future Generation Computer Systems* (2011) 28(2): 391-404.

Zhang H, Tang S, Qin Y, Huang G. Edge Computing for Smart Grid: A Comprehensive Survey. *IEEE Access* (2019) 7: 64716-64732.

Zhang Y, He R, Wang S. Edge Computing and Data Analytics for Smart Grid: A Comprehensive Review. *IEEE Transactions on Industrial Informatics* (2020) 16(6): 4022-4033.

Zhou S, Wang L, Wang Q, Wang Y. A comprehensive survey on demand response in smart grids. *Sensors*, (2016) 16(5): 668.

Chapter 12

Performance Enhancement in a Smart Grid Using the Internet of Things (IoT)

Dheeraj Nagar[1,*], MTech
Anand Vardhan Bhalla[1], MTech
and Rajiv Dey[2], PhD
[1]Department of Electronics and Communication Engineering, Eklavya University, School of Engineering, Damoh, Madhya Pradesh, India
[2]Department of Electronics and Computer Engineering, BML Munjal University, School of Engineering and Technology, Gurugram, Haryana, India

Abstract

The generation, transmission, and consumption of electricity have been completely transformed by the incorporation of Internet of Things (IoT) technologies into smart grids. An overview of the main components of performance improvement made possible by IoT implementation in smart grid systems is given in this chapter. This starts by outlining the difficulties that traditional power networks encounter, including poor visibility, ineffective load balancing, and susceptibility to failure. The idea of IoT-enabled smart grids is then introduced. These grids use real-time data collection, sophisticated analytics, and intelligent decision-making algorithms to enhance the performance and dependability of the grid. This research work lists five crucial areas where IoT improves the efficiency of the smart grid. The first topic covered is better monitoring and control capabilities made possible by IoT devices. These capabilities allow for precise assessment of energy production, consumption, and distribution. Utilities can see inefficiencies, find errors, and optimize

* Corresponding Author's Email: dheeraj.nagar1@gmail.com.

In: The Future of IoT with Automation in Engineering and Modern Technology
Editors: Sandeep Gupta and Tarun Varshney
ISBN: 979-8-89113-655-7

resource allocation in real-time because of this improved visibility. Secondly, the abstract highlights how IoT helps smart grids implement demand response and load management. To actively control energy demand during peak hours and lessen the load on the grid and the need for expensive infrastructure upgrades, utilities can communicate and work with consumers by exploiting IoT devices installed in homes, companies, and industrial sites. In addition, the chapter illustrates how IoT might improve grid resilience and fault management. IoT-enabled sensors and monitoring tools can locate faults quickly and perform preventative maintenance by detecting and communicating interruptions. This feature decreases downtime, accelerates the time it takes to fix faults, and increases grid reliability overall. This chapter also discusses the advantages of data-driven analytics for enhancing smart grid performance. Numerous data points are produced by IoT devices, which can be analyzed to learn more about patterns in energy usage, anticipate changes in demand, and improve energy production and distribution methods. Utility companies can make wise decisions, increase grid efficiency, and save operating costs thanks to these data-driven insights. Finally, this chapter highlights the importance of IoT-enabled smart grids in addressing the changing energy requirements of the future while encouraging sustainability and dependability.

Keywords: Internet of Things (IoT), smart grid, data analytic, energy demand, load management

Introduction

The integration of Internet of Things (IoT) technologies into smart grids has revolutionized the generation, transmission, and consumption of electricity (Ullah et al., 2021). By leveraging real-time data collection, advanced analytics, and intelligent decision-making algorithms, IoT-enabled smart grids have significantly enhanced the performance and dependability of power systems (Minoli, 2020). This abstract provides an overview of the key areas where IoT implementation has led to performance improvements in smart grids. Traditional power networks often face challenges such as poor visibility, inefficient load balancing, and vulnerability to failures (De Carvalho et al., 2017). However, the advent of IoT-enabled smart grids has paved the way for substantial improvements in these areas. This abstract introduces the concept of IoT-enabled smart grids, which utilize IoT devices to collect data, apply sophisticated analytics, and make intelligent decisions to optimize the grid's operations.

This chapter focuses on five crucial areas where IoT contributes to the efficiency of smart grids. Firstly, it emphasizes the enhanced monitoring and control capabilities facilitated by IoT devices. With improved visibility into energy production, consumption, and distribution, utilities can identify inefficiencies, detect errors, and optimize resource allocation in real-time. By leveraging IoT devices installed in homes, businesses, and industrial sites, utilities can actively communicate and collaborate with consumers to control energy demand during peak hours, reducing the strain on the grid and minimizing the need for costly infrastructure upgrades. Furthermore, the research work discusses how IoT enhances grid resilience and fault management. IoT-enabled sensors and monitoring tools can rapidly locate faults, enabling timely preventive maintenance and efficient fault resolution. This capability reduces downtime, accelerates fault resolution, and enhances the overall reliability of the grid.

The integration of IoT technologies into smart grids transforms conventional power grids into intelligent, effective, and resilient systems (Meloni et al., 2018). The chapter emphasizes the importance of IoT-enabled smart grids in addressing the changing energy requirements of the future while promoting sustainability and dependability. However, it also acknowledges that there are challenges to overcome, such as ensuring data security and privacy, managing the vast amount of data generated by IoT devices, and integrating IoT technologies seamlessly into existing infrastructure (Mocrii et al., 2018).

Looking ahead, the prospects for IoT-based performance enhancement in smart grids are promising. Advancements in IoT technologies, data analytics, and communication networks will further optimize grid performance and enable more efficient energy management (Bejoy et al., 2017). However, addressing the challenges and ensuring robust cyber security measures will be crucial for the successful implementation of IoT-enabled smart grids (Mocrii et al., 2018).

In summary, this research work highlights the significant contributions of IoT technology to performance enhancement in smart grids. IoT-enabled smart grids transform conventional power systems into intelligent, efficient, and resilient networks through improved monitoring, demand response, fault management, and data-driven analytics (De Carvalho et al., 2017). These advancements are crucial to meeting the evolving energy requirements of the future while promoting sustainability and reliability.

Background

Traditional power grids have been the backbone of energy distribution for many years. However, they face several challenges that limit their efficiency and effectiveness in meeting the demands of a rapidly evolving energy landscape. These challenges include limited visibility into grid operations, ineffective load balancing, and vulnerability to failures (Mulla et al., 2014).

One of the primary limitations of traditional power grids is the lack of visibility into grid operations. Conventional grids often rely on manual monitoring and periodic inspections, which provide limited real-time data on energy production, consumption, and distribution. This lack of visibility makes it difficult for utilities to identify inefficiencies, detect errors, and optimize resource allocation in a timely manner.

In addition, ineffective load balancing is another significant challenge faced by traditional power grids. As energy demands fluctuate throughout the day, grids must efficiently manage and distribute power to meet the varying needs of consumers. However, without accurate and real-time data on energy consumption and demand patterns, utilities struggle to balance loads effectively, leading to overloads or underutilization of resources. Inefficient load balancing can result in power outages, increased costs, and reduced customer satisfaction (Kayes et al., 2019).

Furthermore, traditional power grids are vulnerable to failures, including equipment malfunctions, natural disasters, and cyberattacks. The lack of real-time monitoring and fault detection mechanisms makes it challenging for utilities to promptly identify and respond to these failures. As a result, downtime and disruptions occur, impacting the reliability and resilience of the grid.

As energy demands continue to rise and the integration of renewable energy sources becomes more prevalent, there is an urgent need to address these limitations and enhance the performance of power grids (Doan et al., 2020). This is where the incorporation of Internet of Things (IoT) technologies comes into play. IoT offers the potential to transform traditional power grids into smart grids, enabling more efficient energy distribution and management (Minoli, 2020). By integrating IoT devices and technologies into smart grids, utilities can collect real-time data from various sources, such as power plants, substations, and smart meters. These IoT devices, equipped with sensors and connectivity, enable continuous monitoring of energy production, consumption, and distribution. The real-time data collected by IoT devices provides utilities with enhanced visibility and insights into grid operations.

allowing them to identify inefficiencies, detect errors, and optimize resource allocation in a more proactive and efficient manner.

Moreover, IoT facilitates demand response and load management in smart grids. Through IoT-enabled devices installed in homes, businesses, and industrial sites, utilities can establish a seamless communication infrastructure (Al Turjman et al., 2019). This enables utilities to interact with consumers, provide real-time energy usage information, and incentivize load management during peak hours. By leveraging IoT for demand response, utilities can balance loads effectively, reduce strain on the grid, and promote energy efficiency without the need for costly infrastructure upgrades.

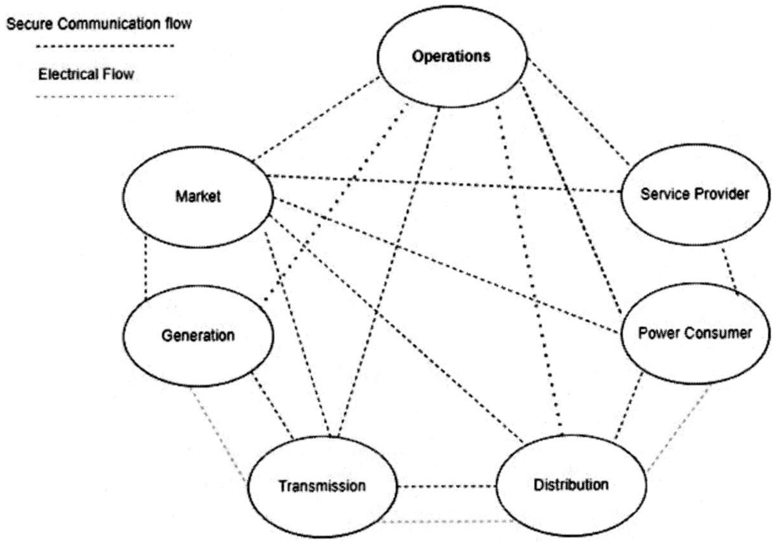

Figure 1. IoT in Smart Grid.

Furthermore, IoT plays a crucial role in enhancing grid resilience and fault management. IoT devices equipped with sensors and monitoring tools continuously monitor the grid's components and infrastructure, enabling quick detection and localization of faults. The real-time data provided by IoT devices facilitates prompt communication of interruptions and faults, enabling utilities to perform preventative maintenance, minimize downtime, and enhance the overall reliability and resilience of the grid.

In conclusion, traditional power grids face limitations that hinder efficient energy distribution and management. The integration of IoT technologies into smart grids offers a promising solution to address these challenges (Doan et al., 2020). By leveraging real-time data collection, demand response capabilities, enhanced monitoring, and fault management, IoT-enabled smart grids can enhance the performance, reliability, and resilience of power grids as shown in Figure 1, meeting the evolving energy requirements of the future while promoting sustainability and dependability (Al Turjman et al., 2019).

Motivation

The integration of Internet of Things (IoT) technologies in smart grids holds tremendous potential for overcoming the limitations and challenges faced by traditional power grids (Doan et al., 2020). IoT offers a range of benefits, including real-time data collection, advanced analytics, and intelligent decision-making algorithms, which can revolutionize the way electricity is generated, transmitted, and consumed. The motivation behind this chapter is to explore the various ways in which IoT can enhance the performance of smart grids.

One of the key motivations for incorporating IoT in smart grids is the need for real-time data collection. Traditional power grids rely on manual inspections and periodic readings, which provide limited and often outdated information about energy consumption, production, and distribution. In contrast, IoT devices, such as smart meters, sensors, and monitoring tools, enable continuous and real-time data collection. This real-time data allows utilities to have a comprehensive and up-to-date understanding of the grid's behavior, enabling them to make informed decisions and take proactive measures to optimize grid performance.

Another motivation for utilizing IoT in smart grids is the advanced analytics capabilities it brings. The vast amount of data collected by IoT devices can be analyzed using sophisticated algorithms and techniques to uncover valuable insights (Minoli, 2020). These insights can help utilities understand energy usage patterns, identify trends, and anticipate changes in demand. By leveraging data-driven analytics, utilities can optimize energy production and distribution, improve load balancing, and implement demand response strategies effectively. This ultimately leads to enhanced grid performance, increased efficiency, and cost savings.

Intelligent decision-making is another significant motivation for incorporating IoT in smart grids. With real-time data collection and advanced analytics, utilities can deploy intelligent algorithms and systems that automate decision-making processes. These algorithms can analyze the collected data.

detect anomalies, and trigger actions to address potential issues or optimize grid operations. For example, in the event of a fault or disruption, IoT-enabled sensors can quickly identify the location and severity of the problem, allowing utilities to respond promptly and minimize downtime. Intelligent decision-making algorithms enable utilities to enhance the reliability, resilience, and overall performance of the smart grid (Al Turjman et al., 2019).

Furthermore, the increasing complexity of energy systems and the integration of renewable energy sources necessitate the adoption of IoT in smart grids. Renewable energy sources, such as solar and wind, are inherently intermittent and fluctuate based on weather conditions. IoT technologies enable real-time monitoring of these renewable energy sources, allowing utilities to adjust energy generation and distribution accordingly. By optimizing the integration of renewable energy sources, smart grids can maximize their utilization, reduce reliance on fossil fuels, and promote sustainable energy practices.

Overall, the motivation behind exploring the incorporation of IoT technologies in smart grids is driven by the desire to overcome the limitations of traditional power grids and leverage the potential benefits offered by IoT. Real-time data collection, advanced analytics, intelligent decision-making, and the integration of renewable energy sources are key factors that drive the adoption of IoT in smart grids. By enhancing grid visibility, optimizing energy distribution, and improving operational efficiency, IoT-enabled smart grids have the potential to revolutionize the way electricity is generated, transmitted, and consumed, paving the way for a more sustainable and efficient energy future.

IoT-Enabled Smart Grids: An Overview

Definition and Components of IoT

The Internet of Things (IoT) refers to a network of interconnected devices that have the capability to collect, exchange, and analyze data. These devices, often embedded with sensors, connectivity technologies, and data analytics capabilities, enable seamless communication and interaction between physical objects and the digital world. In the context of smart grids, IoT plays a crucial role in enhancing the performance and efficiency of the power distribution system (Adi et al., 2020).

The components of IoT can be categorized into several key elements:

- *Sensors:* Sensors are fundamental components of IoT devices. They capture real-world data such as temperature, humidity, energy consumption, and other relevant parameters. In the context of smart grids, sensors can be deployed at various points within the grid infrastructure, including power plants, substations, transformers, and smart meters. These sensors continuously collect data, providing valuable insights into grid operations, energy consumption patterns, and equipment performance.
- *Actuators:* Actuators are devices that enable physical action based on the data received from sensors. In the context of smart grids, actuators can be used to control and manage grid operations. For example, based on data collected by sensors, actuators can adjust the flow of electricity, control power distribution, and manage demand response initiatives. Actuators enable utilities to respond dynamically to changing energy demands and optimize grid performance.
- *Communication Protocols:* Communication protocols are the set of rules and standards that enable devices to exchange data and communicate with each other (Islam et al., 2017). In IoT, communication protocols facilitate the seamless transfer of data between sensors, actuators, and other devices. Common protocols used in IoT include Wi-Fi, Bluetooth, Zigbee, and cellular networks. These protocols ensure reliable and secure communication within the IoT ecosystem, enabling real-time data exchange and decision-making (Tomar, 2011).
- *Data Storage:* Data storage refers to the infrastructure and technologies used to store and manage the vast amount of data generated by IoT devices. In the context of smart grids, IoT-generated data includes real-time energy consumption data, grid performance metrics, and historical trends. Robust data storage systems, such as cloud storage or on-premises servers, are employed to store, process, and analyze this data. Efficient data storage enables utilities to access historical data for trend analysis, predictive modelling, and optimization of grid operations.
- *Analytics Platforms:* Analytics platforms are essential components of IoT ecosystems. These platforms leverage advanced algorithms and techniques to process and analyze the collected data. In the context of

smart grids, analytics platforms can extract meaningful insights from IoT-generated data. By analyzing patterns, trends, and anomalies in energy consumption, grid performance, and equipment health, utilities can optimize energy distribution, predict demand fluctuations, and improve overall grid efficiency.

In the context of smart grids, IoT integrates these components to create an intelligent network of interconnected elements. By leveraging sensors, actuators, communication protocols, data storage, and analytics platforms, IoT enables seamless communication and collaboration between various devices and systems within the grid infrastructure. This integration empowers utilities to make data-driven decisions, optimize grid operations, enhance energy efficiency, and improve overall performance and reliability of the smart grid system.

Key Objectives of IoT-Enabled Smart Grids

Iot-Enabled Smart Grids Are Designed to Achieve Several Key Objectives

Improved Monitoring and Control

One of the significant benefits of incorporating IoT devices in smart grids is the ability to improve monitoring and control capabilities. Traditional power grids often rely on manual readings and periodic inspections, which provide limited visibility into energy production, consumption, and distribution. However, with the integration of IoT devices, utilities can collect real-time data from various points within the grid infrastructure, enabling precise monitoring and control.

IoT devices, such as smart meters, sensors, and monitoring tools, continuously collect and transmit data on energy production, consumption, and distribution. This real-time data allows utilities to have a comprehensive and accurate understanding of the grid's behavior and performance. By accessing real-time information, utilities can monitor energy flows, identify any inefficiencies or anomalies, and promptly respond to changes in demand or grid conditions.

With improved monitoring and control capabilities, utilities can identify and address inefficiencies in energy production, consumption, and distribution. By analyzing the collected data, utilities can detect errors or deviations from optimal performance, such as equipment malfunctions, voltage fluctuations, or imbalances in load distribution. This enables utilities to take immediate corrective actions, optimizing resource allocation and improving grid efficiency.

For example, if sensors detect an unusually high energy consumption pattern in a particular area, utilities can investigate the cause and take measures to rectify it. This may involve identifying and repairing faulty equipment, optimizing energy distribution routes, or implementing demand response strategies. By promptly addressing inefficiencies, utilities can minimize energy wastage, reduce costs, and enhance overall grid performance.

Moreover, IoT devices enable utilities to have better control over grid operations. Through real-time data collection and analysis, utilities can dynamically adjust energy generation and distribution based on demand patterns. For instance, during peak hours, when energy demand is high, utilities can use the data collected by IoT devices to implement load balancing strategies. This may involve shifting energy consumption to alternative sources, redirecting energy flows, or incentivizing consumers to reduce their demand. By actively managing energy consumption, utilities can optimize grid operations, reduce strain on the grid, and avoid overloading or blackouts.

Furthermore, the integration of IoT devices allows for remote monitoring and control of grid infrastructure. Utilities can access real-time data and make informed decisions from anywhere, without the need for physical inspections or manual interventions. This remote monitoring capability improves operational efficiency, reduces response time to grid issues, and enables utilities to proactively address potential problems before they escalate.

Overall, the integration of IoT devices in smart grids enhances monitoring and control capabilities by providing real-time data on energy production, consumption, and distribution. This improved visibility enables utilities to identify inefficiencies, errors, and imbalances, leading to optimized resource allocation, enhanced grid efficiency, and improved overall performance. By leveraging the power of IoT, utilities can transform traditional power grids into intelligent and proactive systems, ensuring reliable and efficient energy delivery.

Demand Response and Load Management

IoT technologies play a pivotal role in enabling demand response and load management strategies in smart grids. By leveraging IoT devices installed in homes, businesses, and industrial sites, smart grids can establish effective communication channels with consumers, facilitating active collaboration to manage energy demand during peak hours (Islam et al., 2017).

Demand response programs aim to optimize energy consumption by incentivizing consumers to adjust their energy usage patterns based on grid conditions. With the integration of IoT devices, utilities can remotely monitor and control energy consumption in real-time, allowing for dynamic management of demand. IoT-enabled devices, such as smart thermostats, smart appliances, and energy management systems, provide consumers with the ability to monitor and control their energy usage. These devices can receive signals or notifications from utilities indicating periods of high demand or grid stress. Through these IoT devices, utilities can communicate pricing signals, incentive programs, or requests for load reduction to consumers (Islam et al., 2017).

For instance, during periods of peak demand, utilities can send signals to IoT-enable smart thermostats, requesting consumers to adjust their temperature settings or reduce energy-intensive activities (Al Turjman et al., 2019). Consumers can then respond by remotely adjusting their thermostats, reducing energy consumption, or shifting non-essential activities to off-peak hours. By actively managing energy demand during peak hours, smart grids can alleviate strain on the grid and minimize the need for costly infrastructure upgrades. Instead of relying solely on increasing energy generation capacity or building additional power plants, utilities can leverage IoT devices and demand response programs to optimize energy utilization. Implementing demand response and load management strategies can lead to several benefits. First, it helps to balance energy supply and demand, ensuring a stable and reliable grid operation. By reducing peak demand through load management, utilities can avoid overloading the grid and mitigate the risk of power outages or voltage fluctuations.

Second, demand response programs promote energy efficiency and conservation. By encouraging consumers to reduce their energy consumption during peak periods, utilities can optimize the utilization of existing resources and minimize energy waste. This not only benefits the environment by reducing greenhouse gas emissions but also helps to achieve sustainability goals.

Furthermore, demand response programs can result in cost savings for both utilities and consumers. By effectively managing peak demand, utilities can avoid costly investments in infrastructure upgrades and grid expansion. Additionally, consumers who actively participate in demand response programs can benefit from lower energy bills or incentives provided by utilities.

Several real-world examples and case studies demonstrate the successful implementation of demand response and load management using IoT technologies. For instance, in the United States, the Pacific Gas and Electric Company (PG&E) implemented a demand response program called Smart AC. This program utilized IoT-enabled smart thermostats to remotely adjust air conditioning settings during periods of high demand, resulting in reduced strain on the grid and improved grid reliability.

In another example, the Netherlands implemented a demand response program called Power Matching City. This project used IoT devices and advanced algorithms to enable real-time matching of energy supply and demand at the neighborhood level. By leveraging IoT technologies, the program achieved efficient load balancing, reduced peak demand, and optimized energy utilization.

Overall, the integration of IoT devices in smart grids enables effective demand response and load management. By leveraging IoT-enabled devices installed in homes, businesses, and industrial sites, utilities can actively communicate with consumers, encourage load reduction during peak hours, and optimize energy utilization. These strategies alleviate strain on the grid, reduce the need for infrastructure upgrades, promote energy efficiency, and lead to cost savings for both utilities and consumers.

Grid Resilience and Fault Managemen

Grid resilience and fault management are critical aspects of maintaining a reliable and robust power grid. IoT-enabled sensors and monitoring tools play a crucial role in enhancing grid resilience by quickly detecting and locating faults within the grid infrastructure. This enables utilities to promptly communicate interruptions, perform preventative maintenance, and accelerate fault resolution, minimizing downtime and improving overall grid reliability (Islam et al., 2017).

IoT devices, such as fault sensors, power quality monitors, and intelligent monitoring systems, are deployed at various points within the grid infrastructure. These devices continuously collect and analyze data related to grid operations, equipment performance, and power quality. By monitoring parameters such as voltage levels, frequency, and current flow, IoT sensors can detect anomalies or deviations from normal operating conditions, indicating the presence of faults or potential disruptions.

When a fault occurs within the grid, IoT sensors can quickly identify the location of the fault, enabling utilities to take immediate action. By transmitting real-time data on fault occurrence and location, these sensors provide utilities with valuable information to initiate a rapid response. This allows utilities to dispatch maintenance crews to the precise location of the fault, minimizing the time it takes to identify and resolve the issue.

Furthermore, IoT sensors can aid in the implementation of preventative maintenance strategies. By continuously monitoring equipment health and performance, these sensors can detect signs of potential failures or deteriorating conditions (Ullah et al., 2021). This proactive approach enables utilities to schedule maintenance activities before faults occur, reducing the risk of unexpected failures and minimizing downtime.

By leveraging IoT-enabled fault detection and communication, utilities can significantly improve fault resolution time. Rapid identification and communication of faults allow maintenance crews to promptly address the issues, reducing the duration of outages and disruptions to energy supply. This enhanced fault management capability translates into increased grid reliability and customer satisfaction.

Real-time fault detection and communication also contribute to grid resilience during extreme weather events or natural disasters. IoT sensors can detect power outages, infrastructure damage, or other grid disturbances caused by such events. By promptly communicating these disruptions to utilities, emergency response teams can be deployed, and necessary repairs can be initiated swiftly, restoring power to affected areas in a timely manner.

For example, in the aftermath of Hurricane Sandy in 2012, Con Edison, a utility company in New York City, deployed IoT-enabled sensors to detect power outages and monitor grid conditions. These sensors provided real-time data on the extent of the damage, allowing crews to prioritize restoration efforts and minimize the duration of outages.

In another case, the integration of IoT sensors and monitoring tools in the Scottish and Southern Electricity Networks (SSEN) helped improve fault management and grid resilience. IoT devices enabled rapid fault detection and location identification, allowing SSEN to dispatch maintenance crews efficiently and reduce outage durations.

Overall, the incorporation of IoT-enabled sensors and monitoring tools in smart grids enhances grid resilience and fault management. By quickly detecting and locating faults within the grid infrastructure, utilities can initiate timely responses, perform preventative maintenance, and accelerate fault resolution. This results in minimized downtime, improved grid reliability, and enhanced overall resilience, ensuring a more robust and dependable power supply for consumers.

Data-driven Analytics for Decision-Making

One of the significant advantages of incorporating IoT devices in smart grids is the generation of vast amounts of data points related to energy consumption, weather conditions, grid operations, and other relevant parameters. Through data analytics, utilities can unlock valuable insights from this data, enabling informed decision-making and optimization of grid operations (Adi et al., 2020).

IoT devices continuously collect and transmit real-time data on energy consumption, grid performance, and environmental factors. This data, when analyzed using advanced analytics techniques, allows utilities to identify patterns, correlations, and trends in energy usage and grid behavior. By leveraging data-driven insights, utilities can make informed decisions to improve grid efficiency and reduce operating costs. One key application of data-driven analytics in smart grids is the identification of energy usage patterns. By analyzing the collected data, utilities can gain a comprehensive understanding of how energy is consumed at different times of the day, days of the week, or seasons of the year. This knowledge helps utilities anticipate changes in energy demand and plan for effective energy production and distribution strategies.

For example, data analysis may reveal that energy demand spikes occur during specific times, such as weekday evenings. Armed with this insight, utilities can adjust energy generation schedules, optimize load balancing, and implement demand response strategies to meet peak demand efficiently. This not only ensures reliable energy supply but also helps utilities avoid unnecessary energy generation and reduce costs.

Data-driven analytics also enables utilities to optimize energy production and distribution methods. By analyzing the data collected from IoT devices, utilities can gain insights into the performance of various energy sources, identify inefficiencies, and optimize energy generation techniques. For instance, analytics may reveal that renewable energy sources, such as solar or wind, are most effective during certain weather conditions or times of the day. Utilities can leverage this information to adjust energy generation strategies, maximize the use of renewable sources, and minimize reliance on non-renewable and costly energy generation methods.

Moreover, data-driven insights can assist utilities in identifying opportunities for energy conservation and efficiency improvements. By analyzing energy consumption patterns, utilities can identify areas or sectors with high energy usage and implement targeted energy efficiency programs. For example, data analysis may reveal that a specific industrial sector consumes a significant amount of energy during non-productive periods. Utilities can collaborate with these industries to implement energy management strategies, such as load shifting or equipment optimization, to reduce energy waste and increase overall efficiency.

Data analytics in smart grids can also contribute to predictive maintenance strategies. By analyzing data from IoT devices, utilities can detect patterns or anomalies that indicate potential equipment failures or maintenance requirements (Adi et al., 2020). This enables utilities to schedule maintenance activities proactively, reducing the risk of unexpected breakdowns and optimizing the lifespan of grid infrastructure. Predictive maintenance can minimize downtime, improve reliability, and lower maintenance costs.

Several real-world examples highlight the benefits of data-driven analytics in smart grid decision-making. For instance, in the city of Austin, Texas, the utility company Austin Energy implemented an advanced data analytics platform that leveraged IoT data to optimize energy efficiency. By analyzing energy consumption patterns, the company identified opportunities for energy savings and implemented targeted energy efficiency programs, resulting in reduced costs and improved grid performance.

In another example, the Italian utility company Enel utilized data analytics to optimize renewable energy generation (Adi et al., 2020). By analyzing weather data and energy generation patterns, Enel adjusted its renewable energy production strategies, maximizing energy output and reducing reliance on fossil fuels.

In summary, the integration of IoT devices and data-driven analytics enables utilities to uncover valuable insights from the vast amount of data generated by the smart grid as shown in Figure 2. By analyzing this data, utilities can identify energy usage patterns, anticipate changes in demand, optimize energy production and distribution methods, and implement targeted energy efficiency programs. These data-driven insights empower utilities to make informed decisions, improve grid efficiency, reduce operating costs, and ultimately provide reliable and sustainable energy to consumers.

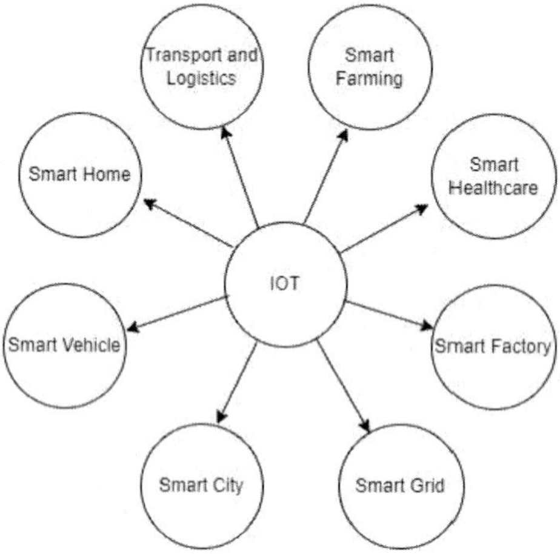

Figure 2. IoT Enabled Smart Grid.

Improved Monitoring and Control

Real-Time Data Collection

Real-time data collection is a fundamental aspect of smart grids enabled by the integration of IoT devices. These devices are strategically deployed throughout the grid infrastructure, including power plants, substations, and smart meters, to collect and transmit data in real-time (Pau et al., 2018). This continuous monitoring and data collection process provides utilities with accurate and up-to-date information about energy production, consumption, and distribution within the grid.

One of the key benefits of real-time data collection is the improved visibility it offers to utilities. Traditional power grids often suffer from limited visibility, where utilities have limited insights into the actual state of the grid at any given moment. However, with IoT devices, utilities can gather data in real-time, allowing them to have a comprehensive and detailed understanding of grid operations.

By collecting data on energy production, utilities can monitor the performance of power plants, including the output of different energy sources, such as renewable energy installations or conventional power generation units. This real-time monitoring enables utilities to assess the efficiency and reliability of their energy production systems and identify any anomalies or deviations from expected performance. By promptly identifying inefficiencies or errors, utilities can take corrective measures to optimize energy production and reduce waste (Anwar et al., 2016).

Real-time data collection also extends to monitoring energy consumption within the grid. IoT devices, such as smart meters installed at consumer premises, provide utilities with real-time information about energy usage patterns, load profiles, and demand fluctuations (Pau et al., 2018). This information helps utilities understand consumer behavior, identify peak demand periods, and anticipate changes in energy consumption. Armed with this knowledge, utilities can implement demand response programs, incentivize energy conservation, and effectively manage energy supply during peak hours.

Furthermore, real-time data collection facilitates accurate monitoring of energy distribution throughout the grid. By monitoring parameters such as voltage levels, current flow, and power quality, IoT devices can detect irregularities or deviations from normal operating conditions. Utilities can promptly identify issues such as voltage fluctuations, overloads, or faulty equipment that may impact the stability and reliability of the grid. This early detection allows utilities to take immediate action, minimizing the risk of failures or disruptions in energy distribution.

The availability of real-time data also enables utilities to identify inefficiencies and optimize resource allocation. By analyzing the data collected from IoT devices, utilities can identify areas where energy is being underutilized or wasted. For example, they can identify substations or distribution lines with high losses or areas with excessive energy consumption. With this information, utilities can implement corrective measures such as infrastructure upgrades, load balancing, or equipment optimization to improve overall grid efficiency.

Real-time data collection in smart grids has tangible benefits for utilities and consumers alike. By providing utilities with accurate and up-to-date information, real-time data collection improves decision-making processes, enables proactive management of the grid, and enhances overall operational efficiency. Utilities can identify and address issues promptly, leading to reduced downtime, improved reliability, and cost savings. Consumers also benefit from a more reliable and efficient energy supply, as utilities can optimize energy distribution and implement demand response programs based on real-time data.

A real-world example of real-time data collection in smart grids is the Pacific Gas and Electric (PG&E) Company in California. PG&E implemented an advanced metering infrastructure (AMI) system that integrated smart meters with IoT capabilities. The real-time data collected from these smart meters provided PG & E with insights into energy consumption patterns, load profiles, and demand fluctuations. This allowed the company to optimize energy distribution, implement demand response programs, and improve overall grid efficiency.

In conclusion, real-time data collection enabled by IoT devices in smart grids enhances the visibility and performance of the grid. By continuously monitoring energy production, consumption, and distribution, utilities can make informed decisions, identify inefficiencies, and optimize resource allocation. Real-time data collection leads to improved grid performance, reduced downtime, and enhanced reliability, ultimately benefiting both utilities and consumers.

Intelligent Decision-Making Algorithms

Intelligent decision-making algorithms play a crucial role in maximizing the potential of IoT-enabled smart grids. These algorithms leverage the vast amount of data collected from IoT devices and apply advanced analytics techniques to extract meaningful insights. By analyzing this data, utilities can make informed decisions and implement proactive measures to enhance the performance and efficiency of the grid.

One of the primary advantages of intelligent decision-making algorithms is their ability to uncover energy usage patterns and trends. By analyzing the data collected from IoT devices, these algorithms can identify regular consumption patterns, peak demand periods, and fluctuations in energy usage. This knowledge allows utilities to optimize resource allocation and plan energy production and distribution strategies more effectively. For example, during periods of low demand, intelligent algorithms can adjust the energy generation schedule to minimize waste and reduce costs.

Moreover, intelligent algorithms can detect anomalies or deviations from normal operating conditions within the grid. By continuously monitoring the collected data, these algorithms can identify potential issues such as equipment malfunctions, voltage fluctuations, or distribution line overloads. When anomalies are detected, the algorithms can automatically trigger actions such as alerting maintenance teams, rerouting energy flows, or adjusting grid parameters to address the issue promptly. This proactive approach helps utilities minimize downtime, prevent failures, and improve the overall reliability of the grid.

Intelligent decision-making algorithms also enable predictive analytics, allowing utilities to anticipate and mitigate potential problems before they occur. By analyzing historical data and combining it with real-time data, these algorithms can identify patterns and trends that may indicate future issues. For example, they can identify patterns of increased energy demand during specific weather conditions or forecasted events. Utilities can then take pre-emptive actions, such as implementing load shedding measures or allocating additional resources, to ensure a smooth and uninterrupted energy supply.

Furthermore, intelligent algorithms facilitate demand response programs in smart grids. By analyzing real-time data on energy consumption and demand, these algorithms can identify opportunities to engage consumers in load management strategies. For instance, during peak demand periods, the algorithms can communicate with IoT-enabled devices in homes, businesses, and industrial sites to adjust energy consumption patterns. This can include actions such as optimizing HVAC systems, adjusting lighting levels, or temporarily reducing non-essential energy-consuming activities. By actively managing energy demand, utilities can reduce strain on the grid, avoid costly infrastructure upgrades, and promote more efficient energy utilization.

Case studies and real-world examples showcase the benefits of intelligent decision-making algorithms in smart grid applications. For instance, in the city of Lyon, France, an IoT-based smart grid project implemented intelligent algorithms to optimize energy distribution and reduce energy waste (Hossein et al., 2020). By analyzing real-time data, the algorithms identified areas of high energy consumption and implemented load balancing strategies to optimize energy distribution, resulting in improved grid efficiency and reduced costs.

In another example, the UK Power Networks utilized intelligent decision-making algorithms to manage peak demand during a major sporting event. By analyzing real-time data on energy consumption patterns, the algorithms predicted spikes in demand and proactively communicated with consumers to encourage energy conservation. This demand response strategy helped the utility manage the increased demand without overloading the grid or resorting to expensive infrastructure upgrades.

In summary, intelligent decision-making algorithms in IoT-enabled smart grids provide utilities with valuable insights and the ability to make informed decisions. By analyzing data, detecting anomalies, enabling predictive analytics, and facilitating demand response programs, these algorithms enhance grid performance, improve reliability, and optimize resource allocation. The integration of intelligent algorithms with IoT technologies is a key driver in transforming traditional power grids into intelligent and efficient systems that can meet the evolving energy demands of the future.

Demand Response and Load Management

IoT-Enabled Communication Infrastructure

The IoT-enabled communication infrastructure in smart grids plays a vital role in establishing a seamless and efficient connection between utilities and consumers. This infrastructure relies on IoT devices, such as smart meters, sensors, and actuators, installed in homes, businesses, and industrial sites (Pau et al., 2018). These devices serve as the interface for communication and data exchange between the grid and the end-users.

One of the key benefits of the IoT-enabled communication infrastructure is the real-time exchange of energy usage information between utilities and consumers. Smart meters, for example, collect detailed data on energy consumption at regular intervals and transmit this information to the utility company (Islam et al., 2016). This real-time data allows consumers to have a better understanding of their energy usage patterns, enabling them to make informed decisions about their energy consumption and potentially reduce their energy costs. Utilities, on the other hand, gain valuable insights into consumer behavior and can implement demand response programs or provide personalized energy efficiency recommendations to consumers.

The IoT-enabled communication infrastructure also enables utilities to deliver real-time information and notifications to consumers. Through IoT devices, utilities can send alerts, updates, and critical information related to energy supply, grid maintenance, or any other relevant announcements. This enables consumers to stay informed about energy-related matters and take necessary actions if needed (Hossein et al., 2020).

Furthermore, the IoT-enabled communication infrastructure facilitates efficient energy management through bidirectional communication between utilities and consumers. This two-way communication allows utilities to remotely monitor and control energy consumption, adjust energy supply, and implement load management strategies. For instance, during peak demand periods, utilities can send signals to IoT-enabled devices to reduce energy usage temporarily or shift certain energy-intensive processes to off-peak hours. This demand response capability helps utilities balance energy demand, avoid grid overloads, and promote more sustainable energy consumption practices.

Moreover, the IoT-enabled communication infrastructure enables utilities to detect and respond to grid faults and outages more effectively. IoT devices deployed throughout the grid can detect anomalies, such as voltage fluctuations or equipment malfunctions, and communicate this information to the utility company in real-time. This allows utilities to promptly identify and address issues, dispatch maintenance crews to the affected areas, and minimize the duration of outages. By improving fault detection and response, the IoT-enabled communication infrastructure enhances the overall reliability and resilience of the grid.

To illustrate the impact of the IoT-enabled communication infrastructure, we can look at the case study of Austin Energy's smart grid deployment in Texas, USA (Hossein et al., 2020). The utility implemented a comprehensive communication infrastructure utilizing IoT devices, including smart meters, in homes and businesses (Pau et al., 2018). This infrastructure allowed Austin Energy to communicate real-time energy usage information to consumers, enabling them to monitor and manage their energy consumption more efficiently. Additionally, Austin Energy utilized the bidirectional communication capabilities to implement demand response programs, resulting in reduced peak demand and optimized grid performance.

In summary, the IoT-enabled communication infrastructure in smart grids enables seamless and efficient communication between utilities and consumers. It facilitates real-time exchange of energy usage information, empowers consumers to make informed decisions, enables utilities to implement demand response programs, and improves fault detection and response. By leveraging this infrastructure, utilities can enhance customer engagement, optimize energy management, and create a more resilient and reliable smart grid system (Bejoy et al., 2017).

Peak Hour Load Balancing

Peak hour load balancing is a critical aspect of smart grid management, and IoT technology offers valuable solutions to effectively address this challenge. With the integration of IoT-enabled devices and systems, utilities can implement demand response programs that actively manage energy demand during peak hours. This proactive approach helps utilities balance the load on the grid, enhance grid stability, and optimize energy utilization (Kayes et al., 2019).

IoT-enabled devices, such as smart meters, thermostats, and appliances, serve as the communication channels between utilities and consumers during peak hour load balancing. These devices are equipped with sensors, connectivity capabilities, and data analytics functionalities that enable real-time monitoring and control of energy consumption (Adi et al., 2020).

During peak hours when energy demand is at its highest, utilities can utilize the IoT infrastructure to send signals or pricing information to consumers, encouraging them to reduce their energy usage temporarily. For example, utilities can send notifications to consumers' smart devices, indicating high-demand periods and requesting them to adjust their energy consumption accordingly. This can include actions such as reducing heating or cooling levels, optimizing lighting usage, or deferring non-essential energy-consuming activities.

By actively managing energy demand during peak hours, utilities can alleviate strain on the grid and prevent potential blackouts or overloads. This approach avoids the need for expensive infrastructure upgrades, such as constructing additional power plants or transmission lines, to meet the peak demand. Instead, load balancing through IoT-based demand response programs optimizes the existing resources and infrastructure, ensuring efficient energy distribution (Ullah et al., 2021).

Furthermore, peak hour load balancing with IoT technology promotes energy efficiency and cost savings. By reducing energy consumption during high-demand periods, consumers can lower their electricity bills and contribute to overall energy conservation efforts. Moreover, the optimization of energy utilization through load balancing helps utilities minimize the reliance on expensive and less environmentally friendly energy sources (Kayes et al., 2019). This aligns with the goals of sustainability and reduces the carbon footprint of the energy sector (Hossein et al., 2020).

To illustrate the effectiveness of IoT-enabled peak hour load balancing, we can look at the case study of the Pacific Gas and Electric Company (PG&E) in California, USA. PG&E implemented an IoT-based demand response program called Smart AC, which utilized IoT devices to remotely control and manage air conditioning units during peak demand periods. Through the program, PG&E was able to reduce peak demand and avoid the need for building additional power plants, resulting in cost savings and improved grid reliability (Rahimiet al., 2020).

In summary, IoT technology enables utilities to actively manage energy demand during peak hours through demand response programs. By leveraging IoT-enabled devices and communication infrastructure, utilities can communicate with consumers, encourage load reduction, and optimize energy distribution. This approach helps balance the load on the grid, prevent blackouts, minimize infrastructure costs, promote energy efficiency, and contribute to sustainable energy management (Bejoy et al., 2017).

Grid Resilience and Fault Management

IoT-Enabled Fault Detection and Localization

Fault detection and localization are crucial aspects of maintaining a reliable and resilient smart grid infrastructure. IoT technology plays a vital role in enabling quick and efficient fault detection and localization by utilizing sensors and monitoring tools.

IoT-enabled devices installed throughout the smart grid continuously monitor various components and infrastructure, including power lines, transformers, substations, and distribution equipment. These devices are equipped with sensors that can detect anomalies, such as voltage fluctuations, abnormal temperatures, or equipment malfunctions. The sensors collect data in real-time, providing valuable insights into the health and performance of the grid (Shen et al., 2020). By continuously monitoring the grid, IoT devices can promptly identify any abnormalities or disruptions that may indicate the presence of a fault. For example, if a transformer overheats or a power line experiences a sudden voltage drop, the IoT devices can detect these deviations from normal operating conditions and trigger an alert.

The collected data from IoT devices is analyzed in real-time, leveraging advanced analytics and machine learning algorithms. These algorithms can detect patterns, trends, and abnormalities in the data, enabling the identification of potential faults or areas of concern. By analyzing the data, utilities can gain insights into the root causes of faults and make informed decisions regarding maintenance and repairs (Shen et al., 2020). One of the significant advantages of IoT-enabled fault detection is the ability to precisely localize the fault within the smart grid (Kumariet al., 2019). IoT devices deployed at different locations can provide valuable information about the specific area or component experiencing the fault. For instance, sensors installed along power lines can help identify the exact segment of the line affected by a fault, facilitating faster response times for repairs.

The timely detection and localization of faults through IoT technology enable utilities to respond quickly and effectively. The information provided by IoT devices allows utilities to dispatch maintenance crews to the precise location of the fault, minimizing downtime and reducing the impact on the overall grid operation. This leads to improved grid reliability and customer satisfaction.

To illustrate the effectiveness of IoT-enabled fault detection and localization, we can consider the case study of the Spanish utility company, Endesa. Endesa implemented an IoT-based fault detection system called Self-healing Grid in their smart grid infrastructure. The system utilized IoT devices and sensors to monitor the grid's components and detect faults. Through real-time data analysis and precise fault localization, Endesa was able to significantly reduce fault detection and resolution times, leading to improved grid reliability and reduced outage durations.

In summary, IoT-enabled fault detection and localization enhance the resilience and reliability of smart grids (Kumariet al., 2019). By utilizing sensors and monitoring tools, IoT devices continuously monitor the grid, detect anomalies, and provide real-time data for analysis. The ability to localize faults precisely enables utilities to respond quickly and minimize the impact on the grid's overall operation. With IoT technology, utilities can enhance grid reliability, reduce downtime, and improve customer satisfaction.

Preventative Maintenance

Preventative maintenance is a crucial aspect of ensuring the reliability and longevity of smart grid infrastructure. IoT devices equipped with sensors and monitoring capabilities enable utilities to adopt proactive maintenance strategies by continuously monitoring grid components and detecting early signs of potential faults or failures.

IoT-enabled sensors are deployed throughout the smart grid, including substations, transformers, distribution lines, and other critical infrastructure. These sensors collect data in real-time, monitoring various parameters such as temperature, voltage levels, current flow, and equipment performance. By continuously analyzing the collected data, IoT devices can identify anomalies or deviations from normal operating conditions.

The early detection of anomalies through IoT sensors allows utilities to take preventive action before an actual failure occurs. When a sensor detects a potential issue or abnormality, it immediately sends an alert or notification to the utility's monitoring system. This real-time communication enables utilities to promptly respond and initiate appropriate maintenance actions.

By proactively addressing potential faults or failures, utilities can perform maintenance activities before the situation worsens. For example, if a sensor detects an abnormal temperature rise in a transformer, it can indicate an impending failure. The utility can then dispatch maintenance crews to inspect and repair the transformer, preventing a complete failure and subsequent power outage.

The benefits of IoT-enabled preventative maintenance are significant. Firstly, it reduces downtime by addressing potential issues before they escalate into major failures. By detecting and addressing problems at an early stage, utilities can minimize service interruptions and maintain a more reliable power supply for customers.

Secondly, IoT-enabled preventative maintenance accelerates fault resolution. Since potential faults are detected early, utilities can allocate resources and schedule repairs more efficiently. Maintenance crews can be deployed to the specific location of the detected issue, reducing the time required to identify and fix the problem. This leads to faster fault resolution and faster restoration of power in the event of an outage.

Additionally, proactive maintenance through IoT devices enhances the overall reliability and resilience of the smart grid. By continuously monitoring the grid and performing preventative maintenance, utilities can identify and address potential vulnerabilities or weak points in the system. This helps prevent cascading failures and improves the overall stability of the grid.

To illustrate the effectiveness of IoT-enabled preventative maintenance, we can consider the case study of the utility company Consolidated Edison (Con Edison) in New York. Con Edison implemented an IoT-based monitoring and maintenance system called Smart Grid Investment Model (SGIM). Through the use of IoT devices and advanced analytics, Con Edison was able to detect early signs of equipment degradation, such as worn-out cables or failing transformers. By performing proactive maintenance based on the data collected, Con Edison significantly reduced equipment failures, improved system reliability, and achieved cost savings.

In conclusion, IoT-enabled preventative maintenance is a valuable approach to enhance the reliability and resilience of smart grids. By continuously monitoring grid components and detecting potential faults or failures, utilities can take proactive measures to address issues before they escalate. This reduces downtime, accelerates fault resolution, and improves overall grid performance. With IoT technology, utilities can optimize maintenance practices, provide more reliable power supply to customers, and ensure the long-term sustainability of the smart grid infrastructure.

Data-Driven Analytics for Performance Optimization

Iot-Generated Data Points

IoT devices in smart grids generate a wealth of data points that offer valuable insights into various aspects of energy consumption, grid operations, and consumer behavior. These data points are collected through sensors, meters, and other IoT devices deployed throughout the grid infrastructure.

One of the primary sources of IoT-generated data points is smart meters installed in homes, businesses, and industrial sites (Pau et al., 2018). These meters measure and record energy consumption data in real-time, providing utilities with detailed information about how and when energy is being used. By analyzing this data, utilities can identify usage patterns, peak demand periods, and potential opportunities for energy optimization.

In addition to energy consumption data, IoT devices also gather data on weather conditions. Weather sensors deployed in strategic locations can collect data on temperature, humidity, wind speed, and solar radiation. This weather data is crucial for understanding how external factors influence energy demand and generation. For example, utilities can analyze the correlation between temperature and air conditioning usage to optimize energy distribution during hot summer days.

Furthermore, IoT devices capture data on grid operations and performance. Sensors installed in substations, transformers, and other grid components monitor parameters such as voltage levels, current flow, and equipment health. These data points provide insights into the operational status of the grid, enabling utilities to detect abnormalities, anticipate potential failures, and optimize grid performance.

IoT-generated data points also offer insights into consumer behavior and preferences. Smart grid applications and connected devices can collect data on energy usage habits, peak demand periods, and response to demand management programs. This information helps utilities understand consumer needs, tailor energy efficiency programs, and optimize load management strategies.

The real-time nature of IoT-generated data points is a key advantage. The data is collected and processed instantaneously, allowing utilities to have a comprehensive and up-to-date understanding of the grid's behavior. Real-time data analysis enables utilities to respond quickly to changes in demand, detect anomalies or faults promptly, and make informed decisions for grid optimization.

To leverage the potential of IoT-generated data points, utilities employ advanced data analytics techniques. Big data analytics, machine learning, and artificial intelligence algorithms are applied to uncover patterns, trends, and correlations within the data (Bibri, 2018). By analyzing the vast amount of data, utilities can gain valuable insights into energy consumption patterns, forecast future demand, optimize energy production and distribution, and improve overall grid efficiency.

To illustrate the significance of IoT-generated data points, we can consider the case of Pacific Gas and Electric (PG&E) in California. PG&E utilizes IoT devices and data analytics to analyze energy consumption patterns and identify energy-saving opportunities. By analyzing the data generated by smart meters and other IoT devices, PG&E was able to identify energy-intensive periods and implement demand response programs to reduce peak demand, leading to more efficient grid operations and cost savings for consumers (Islam et al. 2016).

In conclusion, IoT-generated data points are a valuable asset for smart grids. The vast amount of data collected from IoT devices provides utilities with insights into energy consumption patterns, grid operations, consumer behavior, and external factors. Real-time data analysis allows utilities to optimize grid performance, improve energy efficiency, and make informed decisions for grid management and planning. By leveraging IoT-generated data, utilities can enhance the reliability, efficiency, and sustainability of smart grid systems (Kumariet al.,2019).

Data Analysis and Insights

Data analysis plays a critical role in unlocking the value of the vast amount of data generated by IoT devices in smart grids. By applying data analytics techniques and utilizing advanced tools and algorithms, utilities can extract meaningful insights from the data, enabling them to make informed decisions and optimize grid operations (Trappey et al., 2017).

One of the primary objectives of data analysis is to uncover hidden patterns, correlations, and trends in energy usage. By analyzing historical energy consumption data, utilities can identify regular patterns and seasonal variations in demand (Mulla et al., 2014). This information helps in forecasting future energy demand and planning resources accordingly. For example, utilities can anticipate higher energy usage during certain times of the year, such as winter or summer, and adjust energy production and distribution accordingly to ensure a reliable supply.

Data analysis also allows utilities to identify energy inefficiencies and areas for improvement. By examining the data, utilities can pinpoint specific locations or systems where energy is being wasted or consumed inefficiently. For instance, analytics may reveal that certain buildings or industrial sites have consistently higher energy usage compared to similar facilities. Utilities can then work with these consumers to identify energy-saving opportunities and implement targeted efficiency measures.

Furthermore, data analysis provides insights into the effectiveness of demand response programs and load management strategies. By analyzing the response of consumers to demand signals or pricing incentives, utilities can assess the impact of these programs on reducing peak demand and balancing the grid. This information helps utilities refine and optimize their demand response strategies, ensuring maximum participation and efficiency.

Another area where data analysis proves valuable is in optimizing energy production and distribution. By analyzing data on energy generation, transmission, and distribution, utilities can identify bottlenecks, inefficiencies, and opportunities for optimization. For example, analytics may reveal that certain transmission lines experience higher losses or that specific areas have higher voltage fluctuations. Armed with this knowledge, utilities can take corrective actions to improve grid stability, reduce losses, and enhance overall energy delivery.

Data-driven insights also enable utilities to implement predictive maintenance strategies. By analyzing data on equipment performance, sensor readings, and historical failure patterns, utilities can identify early warning signs of potential equipment failures. This proactive approach allows utilities to schedule maintenance activities before failures occur, minimizing downtime and optimizing maintenance resource allocation.

To illustrate the significance of data analysis and insights, we can look at the case of the Amsterdam Smart City project in the Netherlands. This initiative utilizes data analytics to optimize energy consumption and promote sustainability. By analyzing data from various sources, including smart meters, weather sensors, and energy usage patterns, the project was able to identify opportunities for energy savings and develop targeted energy efficiency measures (Islam et al., 2016). The data-driven insights enabled the project to achieve significant reductions in energy consumption and carbon emissions (Mulla et al., 2014).

In conclusion, data analysis is a powerful tool for unlocking the potential of IoT-generated data in smart grids. By leveraging data analytics techniques, utilities can uncover patterns, correlations, and trends in energy usage, identify areas for improvement, optimize energy production and distribution, and implement predictive maintenance strategies. Data-driven insights empower utilities to make informed decisions, enhance grid efficiency, and promote sustainability in the ever-evolving energy landscape.

Decision-Making and Grid Efficiency

Data-driven decision-making is a crucial aspect of leveraging IoT-generated data to optimize grid performance and enhance overall efficiency. By utilizing advanced analytics tools and algorithms, utilities can extract valuable insights from the vast amount of data collected from IoT devices. These insights empower utilities to make informed decisions that improve grid efficiency, reduce operating costs, and promote sustainable energy practices.

One area where data-driven decision-making proves beneficial is energy conservation. By analyzing energy consumption patterns and identifying areas of high energy usage, utilities can develop targeted energy conservation strategies. For example, analytics may reveal that certain buildings or industrial sites consume a significant amount of energy during non-peak hours. By implementing measures such as adjusting energy usage schedules or implementing energy-efficient technologies, utilities can reduce overall energy consumption and optimize resource allocation.

Load balancing is another critical aspect of grid efficiency that can be optimized through data-driven decision-making. By analyzing real-time data on energy demand and grid capacity, utilities can identify periods of peak demand and potential strain on the grid. With this information, utilities can implement load balancing strategies such as demand response programs, incentivizing consumers to reduce their energy consumption during peak hours. This helps in distributing the energy load evenly throughout the grid, minimizing the risk of blackouts, and avoiding the need for costly infrastructure upgrades.

Furthermore, data-driven decision-making facilitates the integration of renewable energy sources into the grid. By analyzing data on renewable energy generation, weather conditions, and demand patterns, utilities can optimize the utilization of renewable resources (Kayes et al., 2019). For instance, analytics may reveal that solar energy generation peaks during certain hours of the day. By aligning energy demand with renewable energy availability, utilities can maximize the use of clean energy sources, reduce reliance on fossil fuels, and promote sustainable energy practices.

In addition to energy-related decisions, data-driven insights also support grid optimization and maintenance. By analyzing data on grid operations, equipment performance, and fault detection, utilities can make informed decisions regarding grid maintenance and upgrades. For example, analytics may indicate that a particular section of the grid experiences frequent faults or has outdated equipment. Armed with this information, utilities can prioritize maintenance efforts, upgrade infrastructure, and optimize grid reliability and performance.

To illustrate the impact of data-driven decision-making on grid efficiency, we can consider the case of the UK's National Grid. By analyzing data on energy consumption, generation, and weather conditions, the National Grid was able to optimize the dispatch of power and balance supply and demand effectively. This data-driven decision-making enabled National Grid to minimize energy wastage, reduce carbon emissions, and ensure a reliable and efficient energy supply.

In conclusion, data-driven decision-making based on insights derived from IoT-generated data is essential for optimizing grid performance and enhancing overall efficiency. By leveraging advanced analytics tools, utilities can make informed decisions regarding energy conservation, load balancing, renewable energy integration, and grid optimization. These data-driven decisions contribute to reduced operating costs, improved grid reliability, and the promotion of sustainable energy practices. By embracing data-driven decision-making, utilities can navigate the complexities of the modern energy landscape and achieve an efficient and sustainable smart grid.

Discussion

The chapter on "Performance Enhancement in a Smart Grid Using the Internet of Things (IoT)" provides a comprehensive overview of how IoT implementation in smart grid systems can improve their efficiency and performance. The abstract effectively highlights the main components and areas where IoT brings significant enhancements to traditional power networks.

The chapter begins by addressing the limitations of traditional power grids, such as poor visibility, ineffective load balancing, and vulnerability to failure. This sets the stage for introducing IoT-enabled smart grids as a solution to overcome these challenges (Ferrag et al., 2020). By incorporating real-time data collection, sophisticated analytics, and intelligent decision-making algorithms, smart grids can be transformed into more efficient and dependable systems (Meloni et al., 2018).

One of the key areas where IoT devices contribute to performance improvement is better monitoring and control capabilities. The abstract emphasizes that IoT enables precise assessment of energy production, consumption, and distribution. This enhanced visibility allows utilities to identify inefficiencies, detect errors, and optimize resource allocation in real-time. By having a clear understanding of the grid's performance, utilities can take proactive measures to improve efficiency and address issues promptly (Anwar et al., 2016).

The abstract also highlights the role of IoT in demand response and load management. IoT devices installed in homes, companies, and industrial sites enable effective communication and collaboration between utilities and consumers. This facilitates the implementation of demand response programs, where consumers can actively control their energy consumption during peak hours. By balancing the load on the grid and reducing the need for costly infrastructure upgrades, utilities can optimize energy utilization and enhance overall grid efficiency (Kayes et al., 2019).

Another significant contribution of IoT to smart grid performance is in the area of grid resilience and fault management (Trappey et al., 2017). IoT-enabled sensors and monitoring tools play a crucial role in quickly detecting and locating faults within the grid. By promptly communicating interruptions, utilities can perform preventative maintenance, minimizing downtime and accelerating fault resolution. This improves the reliability and resilience of the grid, ensuring an uninterrupted energy supply.

Data-driven analytics is another key aspect discussed in the abstract. IoT devices generate a vast amount of data points that can be analyzed to gain insights into energy usage patterns, anticipate changes in demand, and optimize energy production and distribution methods. By leveraging these data-driven insights, utilities can make informed decisions, increase grid efficiency, and reduce operating costs. This highlights the power of data analytics in improving the performance of smart grids.

In conclusion, the abstract summarizes the main points discussed in the chapter and emphasizes the transformative impact of IoT on smart grid performance enhancement. By incorporating IoT technologies, smart grids can become more intelligent, effective, and resilient. The abstract highlights the importance of IoT-enabled smart grids in addressing the evolving energy requirements of the future while promoting sustainability and dependability.

Overall, the abstract provides a clear and concise overview of the chapter's main points, setting the stage for a comprehensive discussion on the performance enhancement in smart grids using IoT. The abstract effectively highlights the significance of IoT in improving monitoring and control, demand response, grid resilience, fault management, and data-driven analytics. It creates a strong foundation for further exploration of these topics in the chapter, addressing the challenges, future prospects, and the importance of continued research and development in this field.

Conclusion

In conclusion, this chapter has explored the various ways in which the Internet of Things (IoT) can enhance the performance of smart grids. By incorporating IoT technologies into smart grid systems, several key areas of improvement have been identified.

Firstly, the IoT enables improved monitoring and control capabilities. Real-time data collection from IoT devices allows utilities to have precise visibility into energy production, consumption, and distribution. This enhanced visibility enables the identification of inefficiencies and errors, leading to optimized resource allocation and improved grid performance.

Secondly, the IoT facilitates demand response and load management. Through IoT-enabled devices installed in homes, businesses, and industrial sites, utilities can actively communicate and collaborate with consumers. This enables utilities to manage energy demand during peak hours, reducing strain on the grid and minimizing the need for costly infrastructure upgrades. This approach promotes energy efficiency and cost savings.

Additionally, IoT plays a crucial role in grid resilience and fault management. IoT devices equipped with sensors and monitoring tools continuously monitor the grid, promptly detecting and locating faults. By quickly communicating interruptions, utilities can perform preventative maintenance, minimizing downtime and accelerating fault resolution. This enhances the overall resilience and reliability of the grid.

The chapter highlights the advantages of data-driven analytics in enhancing smart grid performance. IoT-generated data provides valuable insights into energy usage patterns, demand fluctuations, and grid operations. By applying data analytics techniques, utilities can uncover hidden patterns, anticipate changes in demand, and optimize energy production and distribution methods. These data-driven insights enable utilities to make informed decisions, improving grid efficiency and reducing operating costs.

The chapter concludes the transformative potential of IoT in revolutionizing smart grids and addresses the importance of continued research and development in this field. By harnessing the power of IoT, smart grids can become more efficient, reliable, and sustainable, paving the way for a smarter and greener energy future.

References

Adi E, Anwar A, Baig ZA, and Zeadally S. Machine learning and data analytics for the IoT. *Neural Computing and Applications* (2020) 32(20):16205–16233.

Al Turjman F, Abujubbeh M. IoT-enabled smart grid via SM: An overview. *Future Generation Computer Systems* (2019) 96: 579–590.

Anwar A, Mahmood AN. Stealthy and blind false injection attacks on SCADA EMS in the presence of gross errors. *Proc. IEEE Power Energy Soc. Gen. Meeting (PESGM) Boston* (2016): 1–5.

Bibri SE. The IoT for smart sustainable cities of the future: An analytical framework for sensor-based big data applications for environmental sustainability. *Sustainable Cities and Society* (2018) 38: 230–253.

Bejoy E, Islam SN, and Oo AMT. Optimal scheduling of appliances through residential energy management. *Proc. AAustralas. Universities Power Eng. Conf. (AUPEC)* Melbourne, VIC, Australia (2017): 1–6.

De Carvalho Silva J, Rodrigues JJPC, Alberti AM, Šolić P, Aquino ALL LoRa. WAN-A low power WAN protocol for Internet of Things: A review and opportunities. *Proc. 2nd Int. Multidisciplinary Conf. Comput. Energy Sci. (SpliTech)* (2017): 1-6.

Doan Q, Kayes ASM, Rahayu W, Nguyen KPP. Integration of IoT streaming data with efficient indexing and storage optimization. *IEEE Access* (2020) 8: 47456-47467.

Ferrag MA, Babaghayou M, Yazici M A. Cyber security for fog based smart grid SCADA systems: Solutions and challenges. *J. Inf. Secur. Appl.* (2020) 52: 102500.

Islam SN, Mahmud MA, Oo AMT. Secured Communication among IoT Devices in the Presence of Cellular Interference. *IEEE 85th Veh. Technol. Conf. (VTC Spring) Sydney, Australia* (2017): 1-6.

Islam SN, Mahmud MA, Oo AMT. Relay aided smart meter to smart meter communication in a microgrid. *Proc. IEEE Int. Conf. Smart Grid Commun. (Smart Grid Comm) Sydney, Australia* (2016): 128-133.

Kayes ASM, Rahayu W, Dillon TS. Critical situation management utilizing IoT-based data resources through dynamic contextual role modeling and activation. *Computing* (2018) 101(7):743–772.

Kumari A, Tanwar S, Tyagi S, Kumar N, Obaidat MS, and Rodrigues JJPC. FOG computing for smart grid systems in the 5G environment: Challenges and solutions. *IEEE Wireless Communications* (2019) 26(3):47–53.

Meloni A, Pegorar PA, Atzori L, Benigni A, Sulis S. Cloud-based IoT solution for state estimation in smart grids: Exploiting virtualization and edge-intelligence technologies. *Computer Networks* (2018) 130: 156–165.

Minoli D. Positioning of blockchain mechanisms in IOT-powered smart home systems: A gateway-based approach. *Internet of Things* (2020) 10: 100147.

Mocrii D, Chen Y, and Musilek P. IoT-based smart homes: A review of system architecture, software, communications, privacy and security. *Internet of Things* (2018) 1(2):81–98.

Motlagh NH, Mohammadrezaei M, Hunt JD, and Zakeri B. Internet of things (IoT) and the energy sector. *Energies* (2020) 13(2): 494.

Mukherjee M, Matam R, Shu L, Μαγλαράς Λ, Ferrag MA, Choudhury N, and Kumar V. Security and privacy in fog computing: challenges. *IEEE Access* (2017) 5: 19293-19304.

Mulla A, Baviskar J, Kazi F, and Wag S. Implementation of ZigBee/802.15.4 in Smart Grid communication and analysis of power consumption: A case study. *Proc. Annu. IEEE India Conf. (INDICON)* (2014): 1–7.

Pau M, Patti E, Barbierato L, Estebsari A, Pons E, Ponci F, and Monti A. A cloud-based smart metering infrastructure for distribution grid services and automation. *Sustainable Energy, Grids and Networks* (2018) 15: 14–25.

Rahimi M, Songhorabadi M, Kashani MH. Fog based smart homes: A systematic review. *Journal of Network and Computer Applications* (2020) 153, 102531.

Shen X, Zhu L, Xu C, Sharif K, Lu R. A privacy-preserving data aggregation scheme for dynamic groups in fog computing. *Information Sciences* (2020) 514: 118-130.

Tomar A. Introduction to ZigBee technology. *Global Technology Centre* (2011) 1: 1-24.

Trappey AJ, Trappey CV, Chuang A C, and Sun JJ. A review of essential standards and patent landscapes for the Internet of Things: A key enabler for Industry 4.0. *Advanced Engineering Informatics* (2017) 33: 208–229.

Ullah A, Azeem M, Ashraf H, Alaboudi AA, Humayun M, Jhanjhi N Z. Secure healthcare Data Aggregation and Transmission in IoT-A survey. *IEEE Access* (2021) 9: 16849–16865.

List of Contributors

Rajiv Dey
Department of Electronics and Computer Engineering,
BML Munjal University, School of Engineering and Technology,
Gurugram, Haryana, India.

Anand Vardhan Bhalla
Department of Electronics and Communication Engineering,
Eklavya University, School of Engineering, Damoh, Madhya Pradesh, India.

Dheeraj Nagar
Department of Electronics and Communication Engineering,
Eklavya University, School of Engineering, Damoh, Madhya Pradesh, India.

Ramsagar Yadav
Department of Mathematics and Computing,
L. S. Raheja College, University of Mumbai, Maharashtra, India

Seema Ukidve
Department of Mathematics and Computing,
L. S. Raheja College, University of Mumbai, Maharashtra, India

Jasleen Randhawa
Department of Education,
Panjab University Chandigarh, India

Doopinder Kaur
Department of English,
Government Mohindra College Patiala, India

Bhawana Mathur
Department of Master of Computer Application,
Sri Balaji College of Engg and Technology, Jaipur, India.

Suman Lata
Department of Electrical Electronics and Communication Engineering,
School of Engineering and Technology, Sharda University, India.

Tarun Varshney
Department of Electrical Electronics and Communication Engineering,
School of Engineering and Technology, Sharda University, India.

Soma Deb
Department of Electrical Electronics and Communication Engineering,
School of Engineering and Technology, Sharda University, India.

Burhan U Din Abdullah
Department of Electrical Electronics and Communication Engineering,
School of Engineering and Technology, Sharda University, India.

Lenience Saha
Department of Electrical Engineering,
Tezpur University, Napaam, Tezpur, India

Shneha Prasad
Department of Electrical Engineering,
Tezpur University, Napaam, Tezpur, India

Himangshu Chetia
Department of Electrical Engineering,
Tezpur University, Napaam, Tezpur, India

Sanjay Chural
Department of Electrical Engineering,
Tezpur University, Napaam, Tezpur, India

Anish Ahmad
Department of Electrical Engineering,
Tezpur University, Napaam, Tezpur, India

Prasanth V V
Department of Sports Technology,
Tamil Nadu Physical Education and Sports University,
Melakottaiyur, Chennai, Tamil Nadu, India

Nallavan G
Department of Sports Technology,
Tamil Nadu Physical Education and Sports University,
Melakottaiyur, Chennai, Tamil Nadu, India

Sridevi
Department of Commerce and Business Administration,
Vel Tech Rangarajan Dr. Sagunthala R&D Institute of Science and Technology, India.

Larry Hurtubise
School of Management,
Vel Tech Rangarajan Dr. Sagunthala R&D Institute of Science and Technology, India.

Mariyappan
Department of Commerce and Business Administration,
Vel Tech Rangarajan Dr. Sagunthala R&D Institute of Science and Technology, India.

Sandeep Kanaujia
Electronics and communication department,
United university Jhalwa, Prayagraj, U.P, India.

Satya Prakash Singh
Electronics and communication department,
UCER Naini Prayagraj, U.P, India.

Sandeep Gupta
Electrical Engineering Department,
Graphic Era (Deemed to be University), Dehradun (Uttarakhand), India

Deepti Mittal
Electrical and Instrumentation Engineering Department,
Thapar Institute of Engineering and Technology, Patiala, Punjab, India.

Kalash Pandey
Electrical and Instrumentation Engineering Department,
Thapar Institute of Engineering and Technology, Patiala, Punjab, India.

Sparsh Gupta
Electrical and Instrumentation Engineering Department,
Thapar Institute of Engineering and Technology, Patiala, Punjab, India.

Dev Vijh
Electrical and Instrumentation Engineering Department,
Thapar Institute of Engineering and Technology, Patiala, Punjab, India.

Mandeep Singh
Electrical and Instrumentation Engineering Department,
Thapar Institute of Engineering and Technology, Patiala, Punjab, India.

L N Sastry Varanasi
Department of Electrical Engineering,
National Institute of Technology Andhra Pradesh (NIT AP),
Tadepalligudem, W. G. Dist., India

Index

A

B

C

D

E

F

G

H

I

L

M

N

O

P

R

S

T

U

W